A fan sent me handmade
rubber stamps of Asta and Nero.
Stamp! *Stamp stamp stamp*!
Seriously cute!
Thank you so much!!

—*Yūki Tabata, 2016*

YŪKI TABATA

was born in Fukuoka Prefecture
and got his big break in the 2011
Shonen Jump Golden Future Cup
with his winning entry, *Hungry
Joker*. He started the magical fantasy
series *Black Clover* in 2015.

BLACK CLOVER
VOLUME 5
SHONEN JUMP Manga Edition

Story and Art by YŪKI TABATA

Translation ✤ TAYLOR ENGEL, HC LANGUAGE SOLUTIONS, INC.

Touch-Up Art & Lettering ✤ ANNALIESE CHRISTMAN

Design ✤ FAWN LAU

Editor ✤ ALEXIS KIRSCH

Printed in the U.S.A.

Published by VIZ Media, LLC
P.O. Box 77010
San Francisco, CA 94107

10 9 8 7 6 5
First printing, February 2017
Fifth printing, April 2022

ratings.viz.com RATED T TEEN

PARENTAL ADVISORY
BLACK CLOVER is rated T for Teen and is recommended for ages 13 and up. This volume contains fantasy violence.

VIZ MEDIA
viz.com

SHONEN JUMP

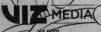

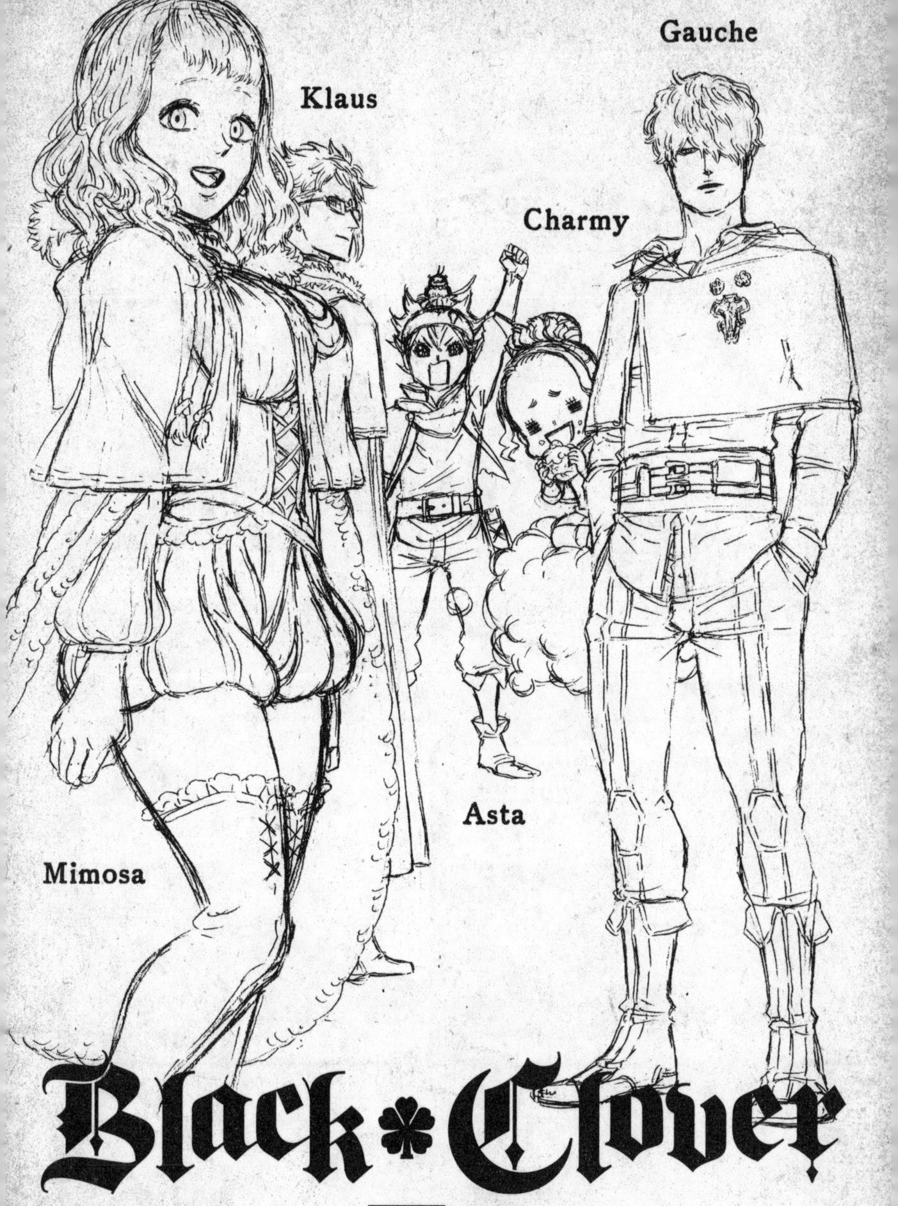
Gauche
Klaus
Charmy
Asta
Mimosa

Black Clover

5

YŪKI TABATA

LIGHT

Yuno

Squad: The Golden Dawn
Magic: Wind

Asta's best friend, and a good rival who's been working to become the Wizard King right alongside him since they were little.

Asta

Squad: The Black Bulls
Magic: None (Anti-Magic)

He has no magic, but he's working to become the Wizard King through sheer guts and his well-trained body.

Charmy Pappitson

Squad:
The Black Bulls
Magic: Cotton

She's small, but she eats like a maniac.

Noelle Silva

Squad:
The Black Bulls
Magic: Water

A royal. She's really impudent, but can be kind too.

Finral Roulacase

Squad:
The Black Bulls
Magic: Spatial

A flirt who likes girls so much it gets in the way of his missions.

Luck Voltia

Squad:
The Black Bulls
Magic: Lightning

A battle maniac who smiles constantly and has a problematic personality.

Nero

A mysterious bird that always follows Asta around for some reason.

Gauche Adlai

 Squad:
The Black Bulls
Magic: Mirror

A former convict with a blind, pathological love for his little sister.

Fuegoleon Vermillion

Squad: The Crimson Lion Kings
Magic: Flame

A captain with a strong sense of justice. He's Mimosa's cousin and Leopold's older brother.

Julius Novachrono

Wizard King

The strongest mage in the Clover Kingdom. Also a peerless magic fanatic.

Rades

Squad: The Eye of the Midnight Sun
Magic: Wraith

He once belonged to a Magic Knights brigade, but was exiled.

Mimosa Vermillion

Squad:
The Golden Dawn
Magic: Plant

Noelle's cousin. She's calm, gentle, and a bit of an airhead.

❀ ❀ ❀

STORY

In a world where magic is everything, Asta and Yuno are both found abandoned on the same day at a church in the remote village of Hage. Both dream of becoming the Wizard King, the highest of all mages, and they spend their days working toward that dream.

The year they turn 15, both receive grimoires, magic books that amplify their bearer's magic. They take the entrance exam for the Magic Knights, nine groups of mages under the direct control of the Wizard King. Yuno, whose magic is strong, joins the Golden Dawn, an elite group, while Asta, who has no magic at all, joins the Black Bulls, a group of misfits. With this, the two finally take their first step toward becoming the Wizard King…

The Magic Knights engage in a fierce battle against the terrorist group that launched a surprise attack on the royal capital. However, the results are brutal: Fuegoleon sustains massive injuries that leave him near death, and Asta is abducted. Calling themselves The Eye of the Midnight Sun, the enemies claim they will destroy the kingdom, then they vanish…

CONTENTS

BLACK ✣ CLOVER

5

Page 35: The Strongest Guy

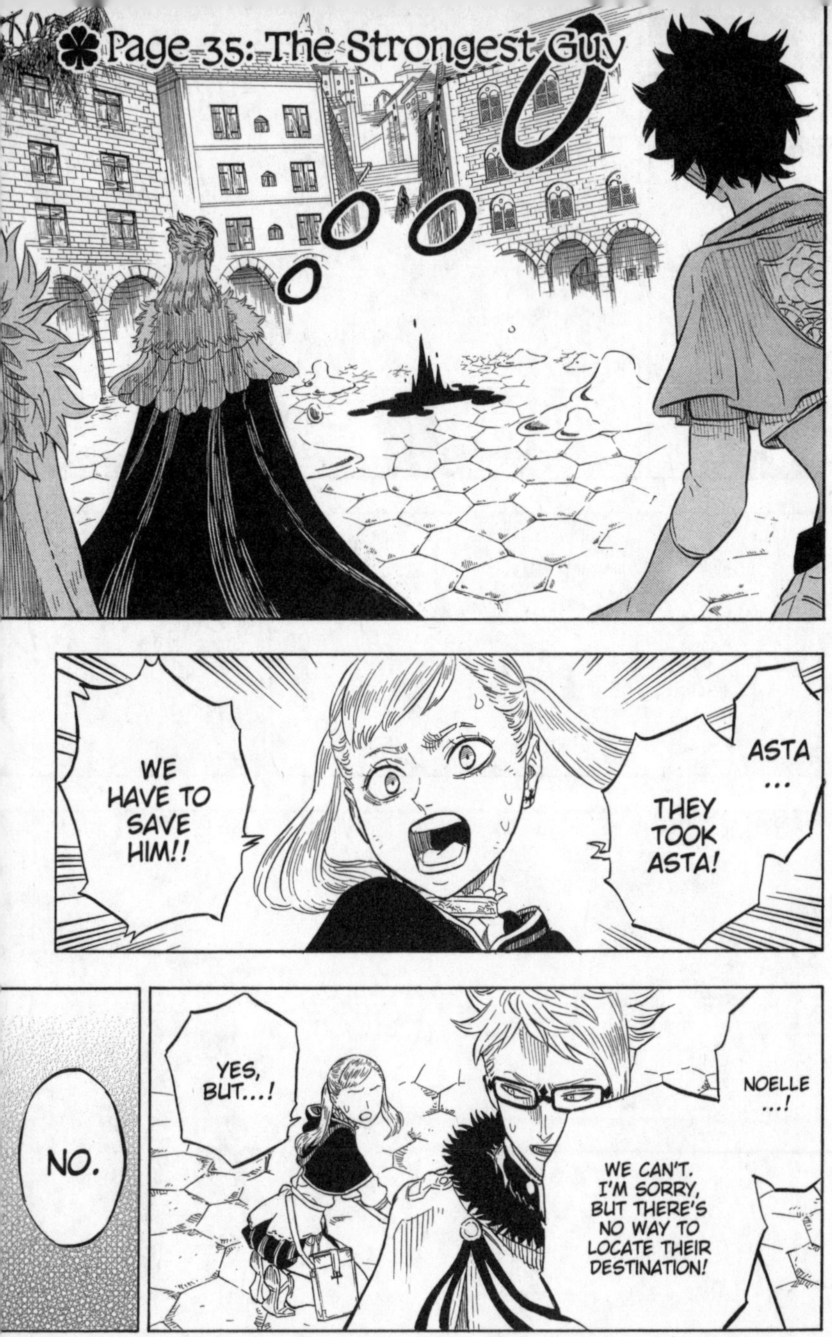
ASTA ...
THEY TOOK ASTA!
WE HAVE TO SAVE HIM!!
NOELLE ...!
WE CAN'T. I'M SORRY, BUT THERE'S NO WAY TO LOCATE THEIR DESTINATION!
YES, BUT...!
NO.

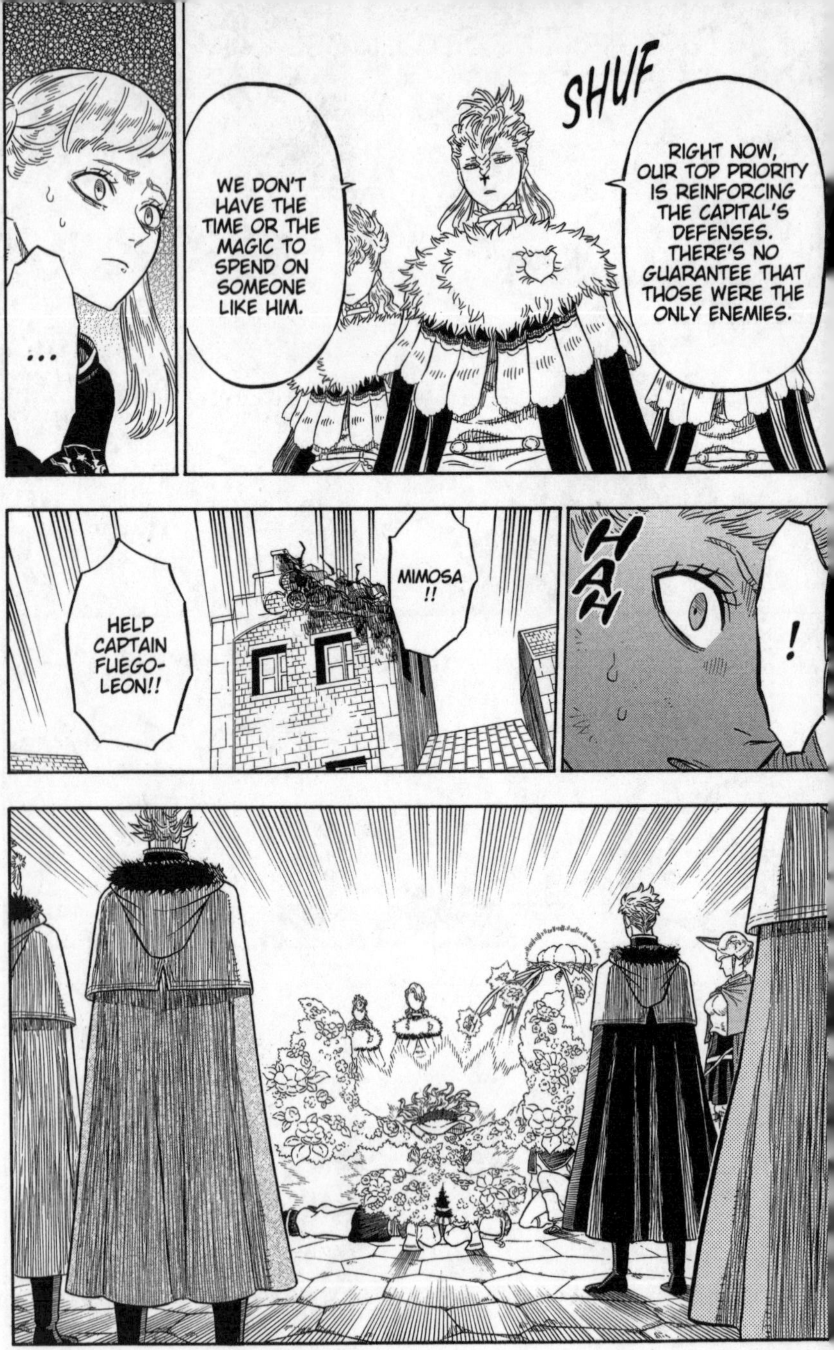
SHUF
RIGHT NOW, OUR TOP PRIORITY IS REINFORCING THE CAPITAL'S DEFENSES. THERE'S NO GUARANTEE THAT THOSE WERE THE ONLY ENEMIES.
WE DON'T HAVE THE TIME OR THE MAGIC TO SPEND ON SOMEONE LIKE HIM.
...
HAH
!
MIMOSA!!
HELP CAPTAIN FUEGO-LEON!!

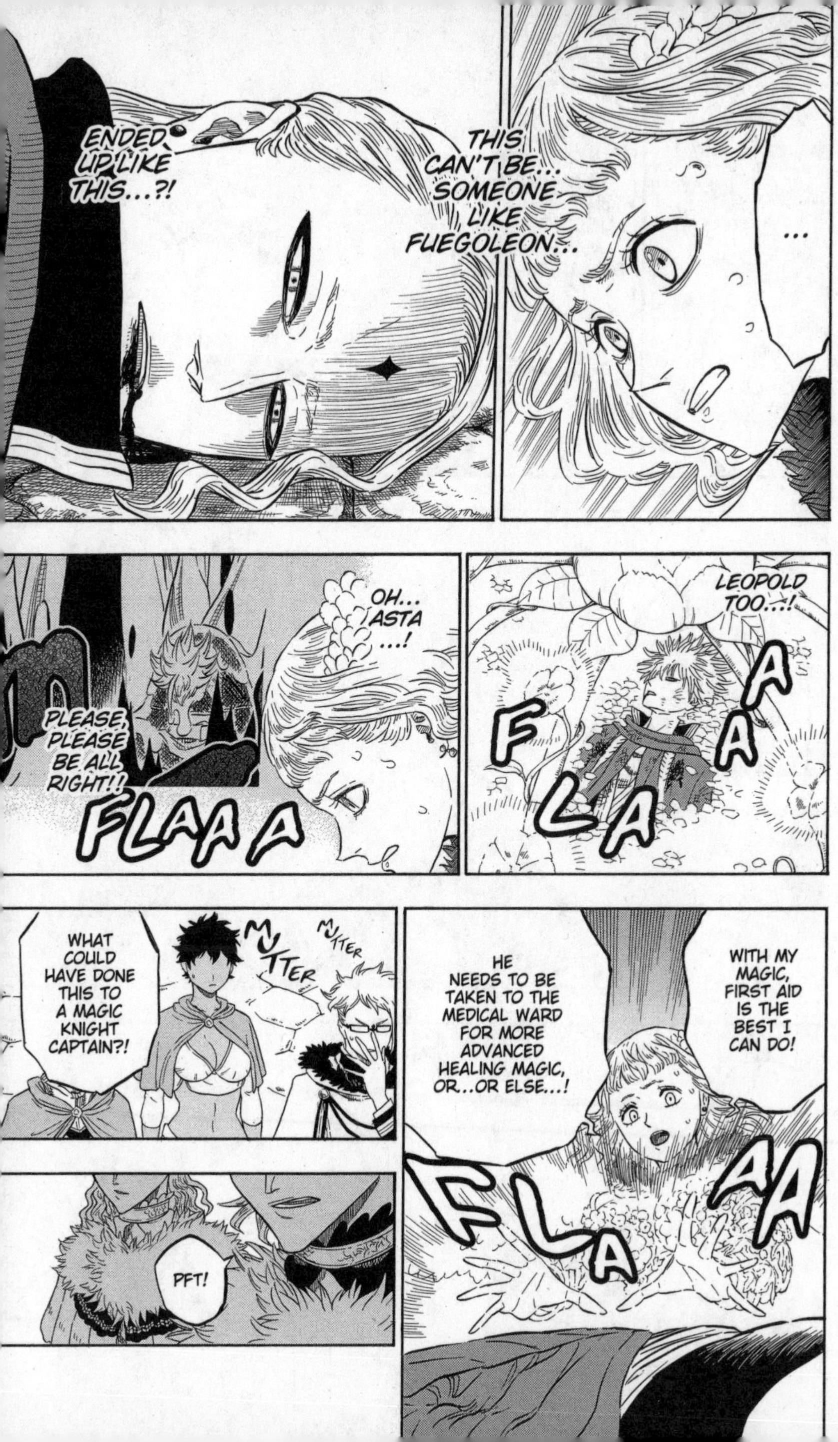
...
THIS CAN'T BE... SOMEONE LIKE FUEGOLEON...
ENDED UP LIKE THIS...?!
LEOPOLD TOO...!
FLAAA
OH... ASTA ...!
PLEASE, PLEASE BE ALL RIGHT!!
FLAAA A
WITH MY MAGIC, FIRST AID IS THE BEST I CAN DO!
HE NEEDS TO BE TAKEN TO THE MEDICAL WARD FOR MORE ADVANCED HEALING MAGIC, OR...OR ELSE...!
FLAAA
MUTTER
MUTTER
WHAT COULD HAVE DONE THIS TO A MAGIC KNIGHT CAPTAIN?!
PFT!

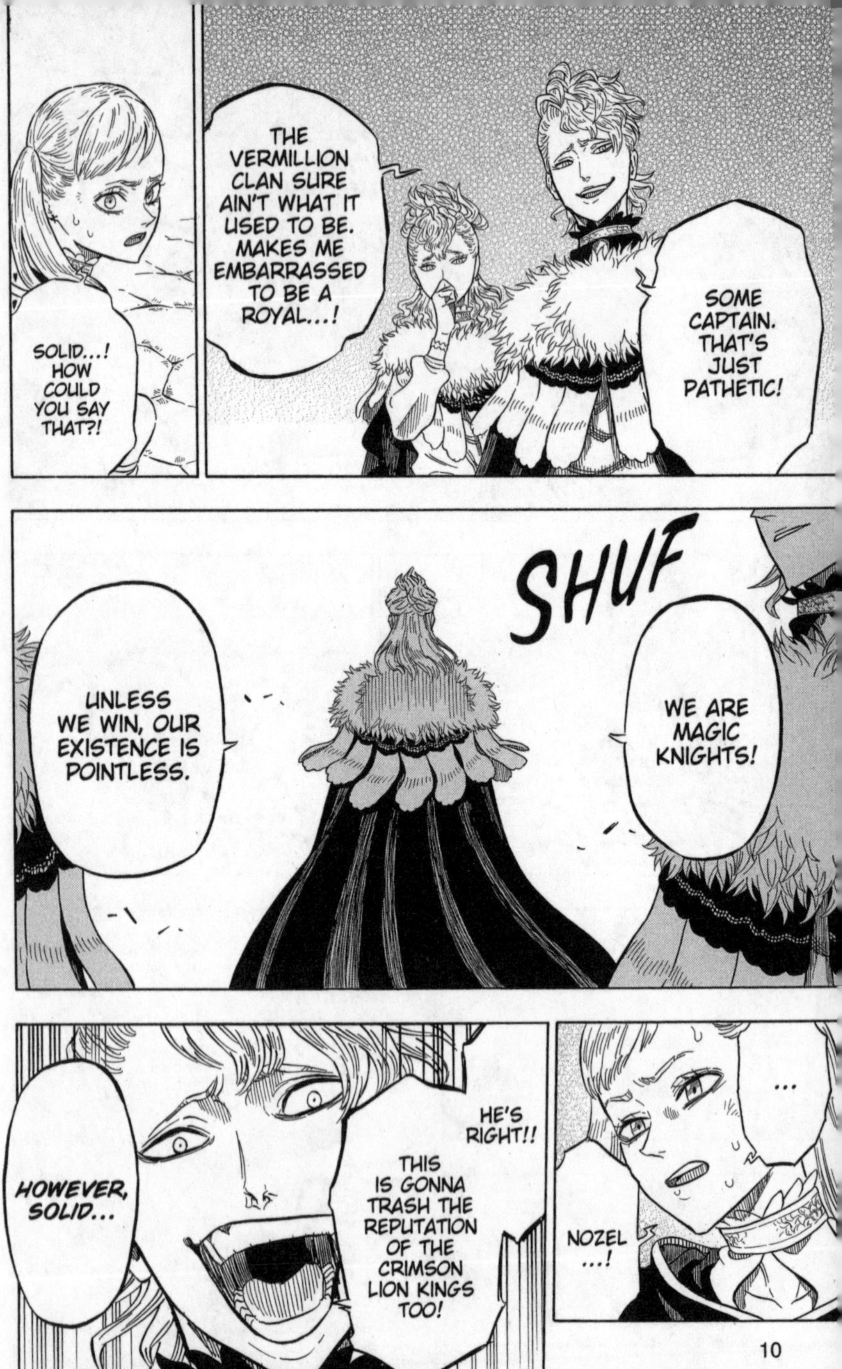
SOME CAPTAIN. THAT'S JUST PATHETIC!
THE VERMILLION CLAN SURE AIN'T WHAT IT USED TO BE. MAKES ME EMBARRASSED TO BE A ROYAL...!
SOLID...! HOW COULD YOU SAY THAT?!
SHUF
WE ARE MAGIC KNIGHTS!
UNLESS WE WIN, OUR EXISTENCE IS POINTLESS.
...
NOZEL ...!
HE'S RIGHT!!
THIS IS GONNA TRASH THE REPUTATION OF THE CRIMSON LION KINGS TOO!
HOWEVER, SOLID...

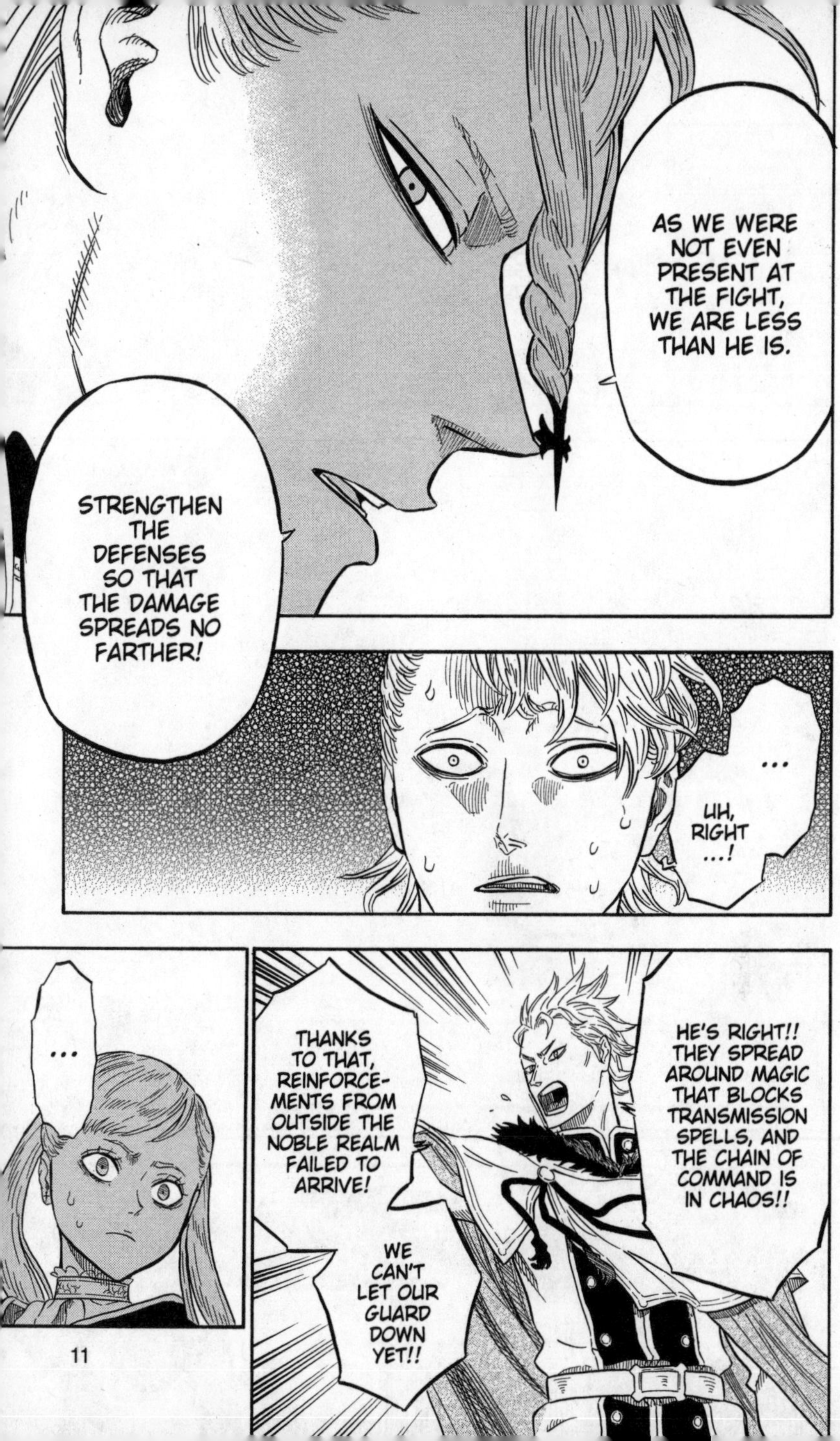
AS WE WERE NOT EVEN PRESENT AT THE FIGHT, WE ARE LESS THAN HE IS.
STRENGTHEN THE DEFENSES SO THAT THE DAMAGE SPREADS NO FARTHER!
...
UH, RIGHT ...!
HE'S RIGHT!! THEY SPREAD AROUND MAGIC THAT BLOCKS TRANSMISSION SPELLS, AND THE CHAIN OF COMMAND IS IN CHAOS!!
THANKS TO THAT, REINFORCE-MENTS FROM OUTSIDE THE NOBLE REALM FAILED TO ARRIVE!
WE CAN'T LET OUR GUARD DOWN YET!!
...

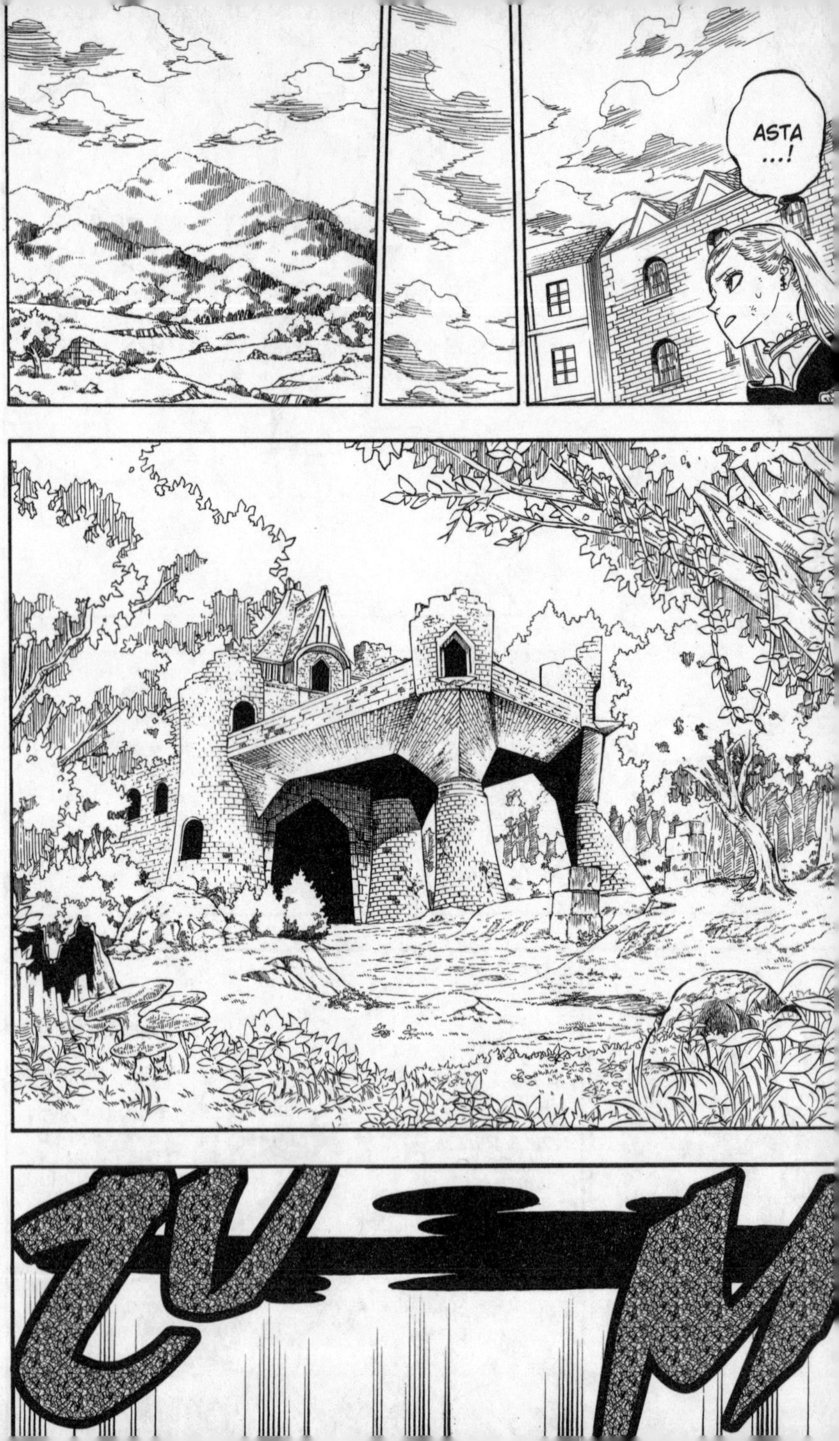
ASTA ...!

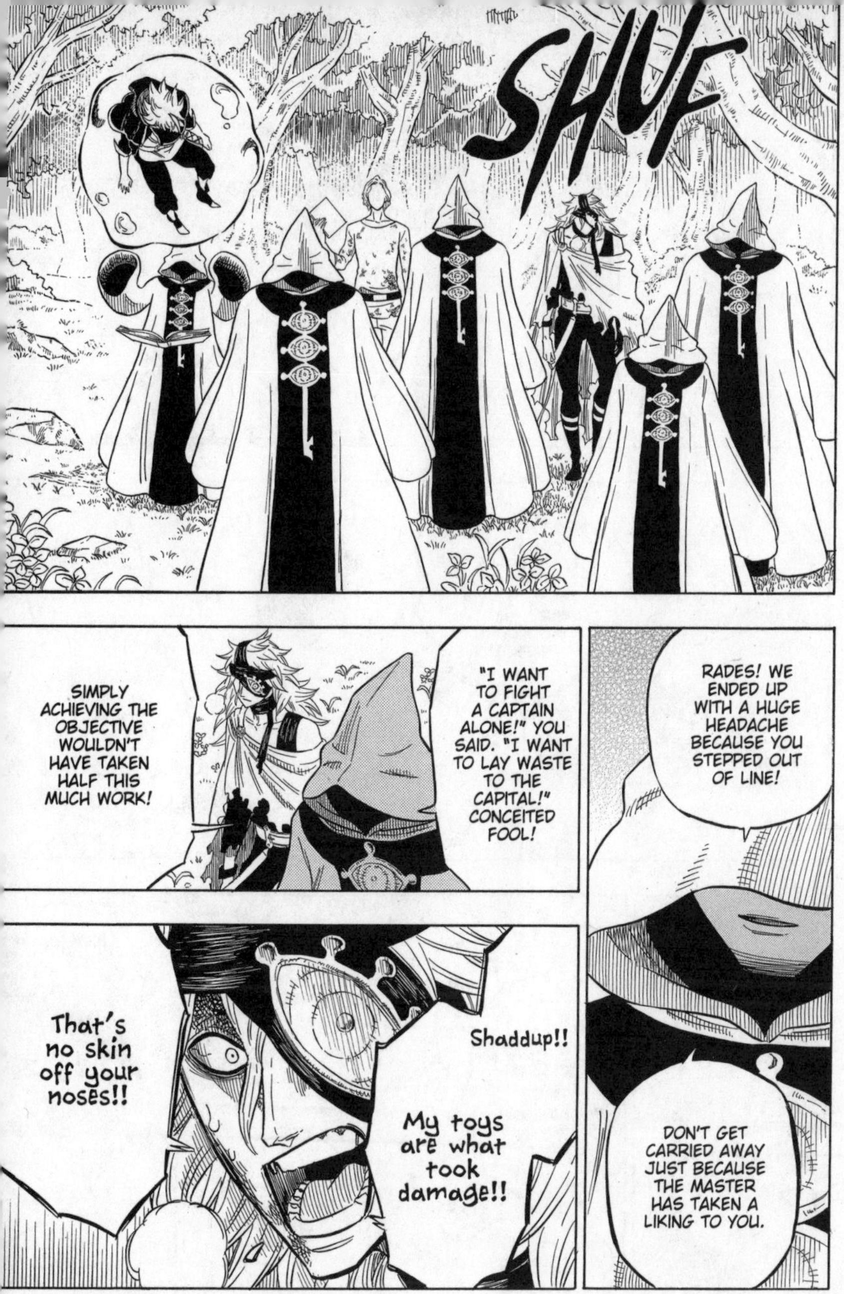
SHUF
RADES! WE ENDED UP WITH A HUGE HEADACHE BECAUSE YOU STEPPED OUT OF LINE!
DON'T GET CARRIED AWAY JUST BECAUSE THE MASTER HAS TAKEN A LIKING TO YOU.
"I WANT TO FIGHT A CAPTAIN ALONE!" YOU SAID. "I WANT TO LAY WASTE TO THE CAPITAL!" CONCEITED FOOL!
SIMPLY ACHIEVING THE OBJECTIVE WOULDN'T HAVE TAKEN HALF THIS MUCH WORK!
Shaddup!!
That's no skin off your noses!!
My toys are what took damage!!

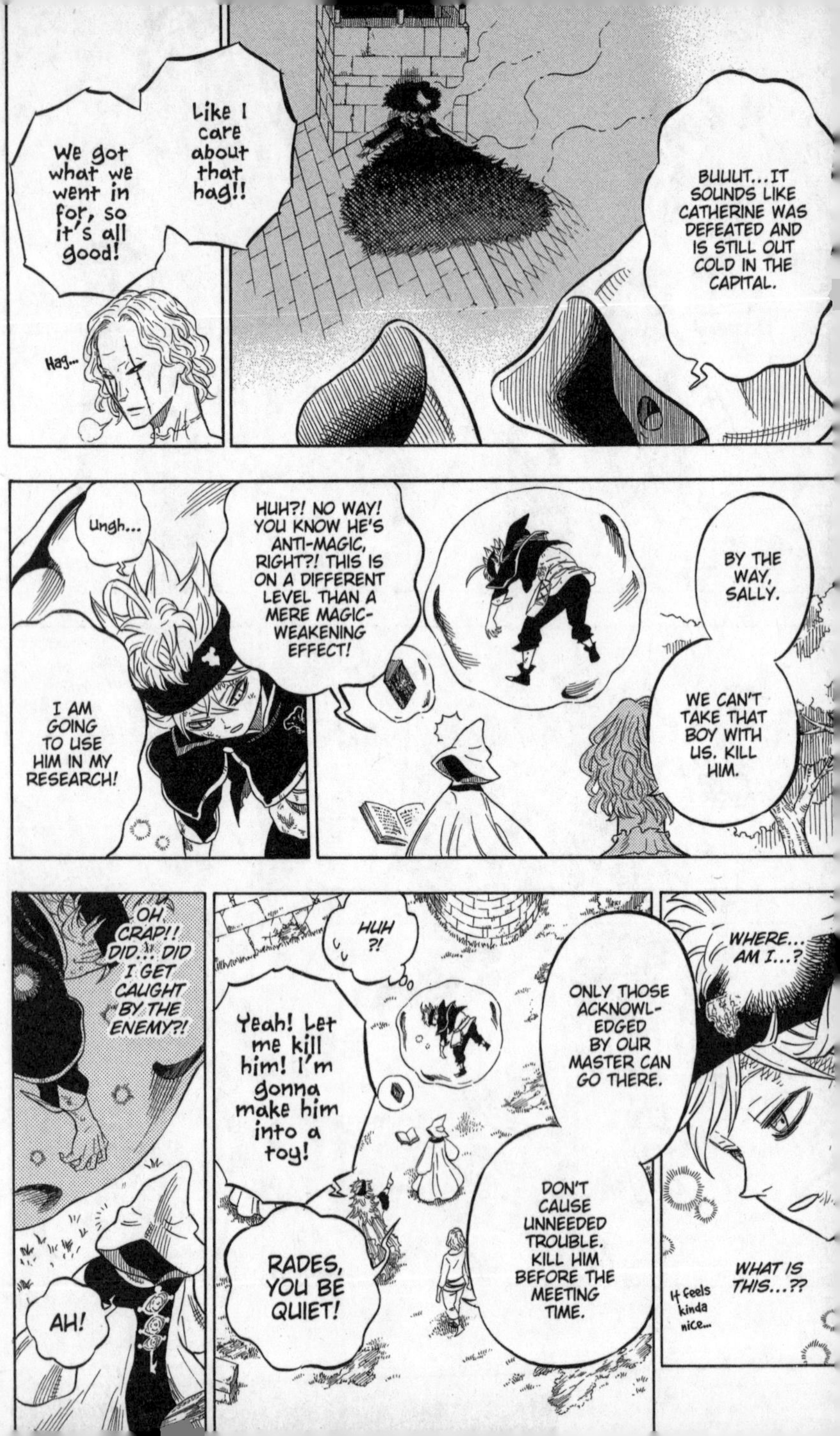
BUUUT...IT SOUNDS LIKE CATHERINE WAS DEFEATED AND IS STILL OUT COLD IN THE CAPITAL.
Like I care about that hag!!
We got what we went in for, so it's all good!
Hag...
BY THE WAY, SALLY.
WE CAN'T TAKE THAT BOY WITH US. KILL HIM.
HUH?! NO WAY! YOU KNOW HE'S ANTI-MAGIC, RIGHT?! THIS IS ON A DIFFERENT LEVEL THAN A MERE MAGIC-WEAKENING EFFECT!
I AM GOING TO USE HIM IN MY RESEARCH!
Ungh...
WHERE... AM I...?
WHAT IS THIS...??
It feels kinda nice...
ONLY THOSE ACKNOWL-EDGED BY OUR MASTER CAN GO THERE.
DON'T CAUSE UNNEEDED TROUBLE. KILL HIM BEFORE THE MEETING TIME.
HUH?!
Yeah! Let me kill him! I'm gonna make him into a toy!
RADES, YOU BE QUIET!
OH CRAP!! DID... DID I GET CAUGHT BY THE ENEMY?!
AH!

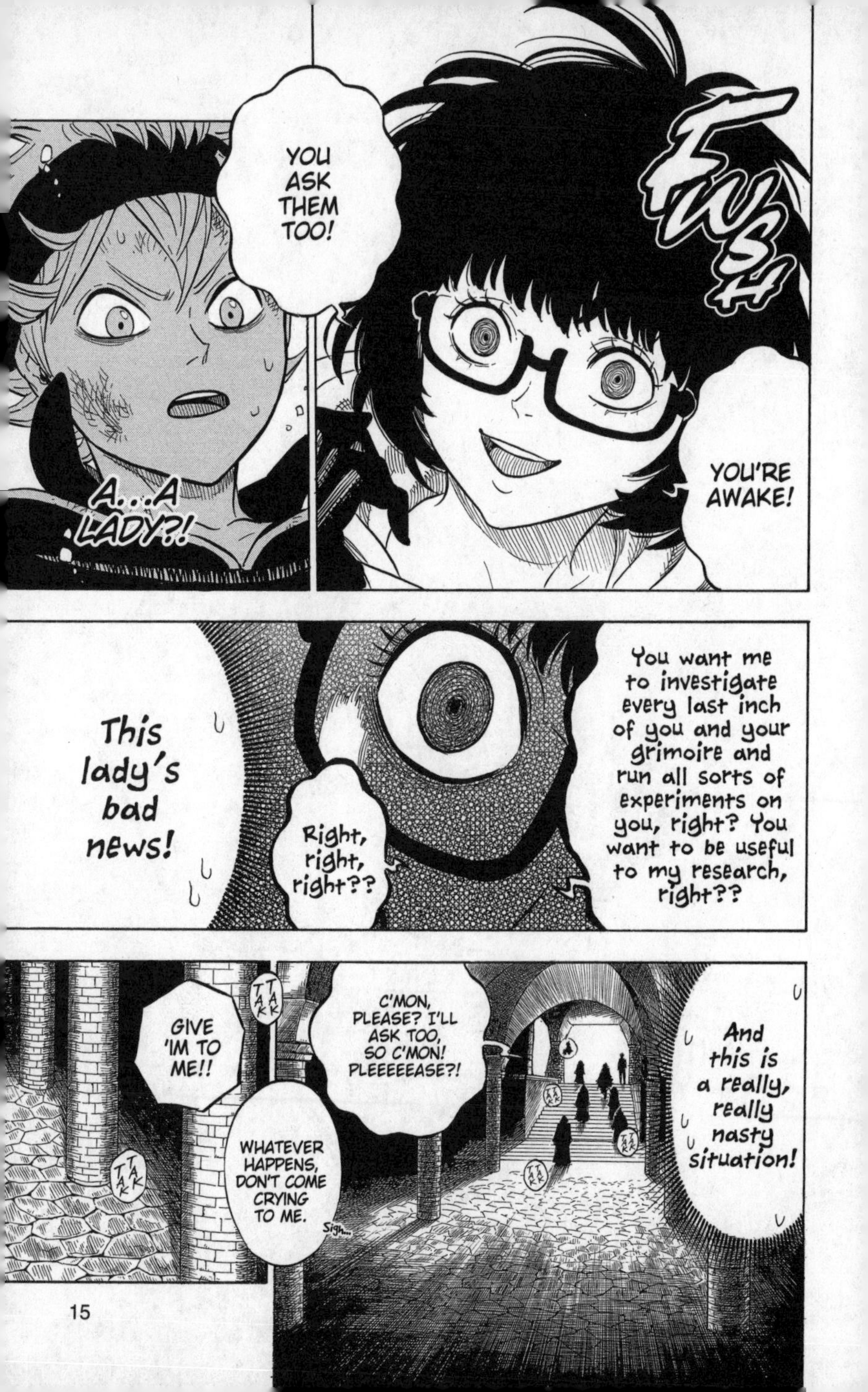
FWSH
YOU ASK THEM TOO!
YOU'RE AWAKE!
A...A LADY?!
You want me to investigate every last inch of you and your grimoire and run all sorts of experiments on you, right? You want to be useful to my research, right??
Right, right, right??
This lady's bad news!
And this is a really, really nasty situation!
C'MON, PLEASE? I'LL ASK TOO, SO C'MON! PLEEEEEASE?!
TTAKK
TTAKK
TTAKK
TTAKK
WHATEVER HAPPENS, DON'T COME CRYING TO ME.
Sigh...
TTAKK
GIVE 'IM TO ME!!
TTAKK

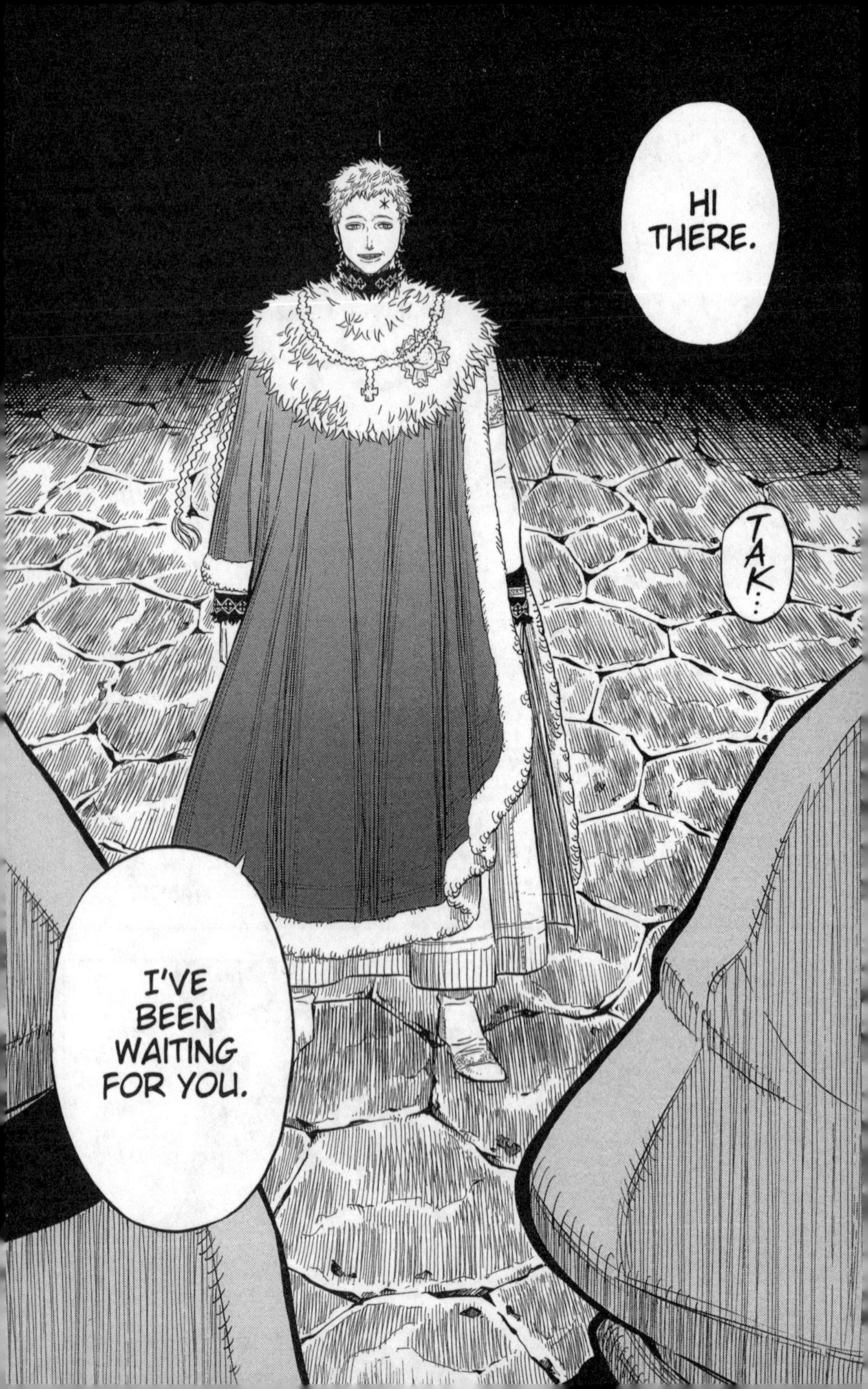
HI THERE.
TAK...
I'VE BEEN WAITING FOR YOU.

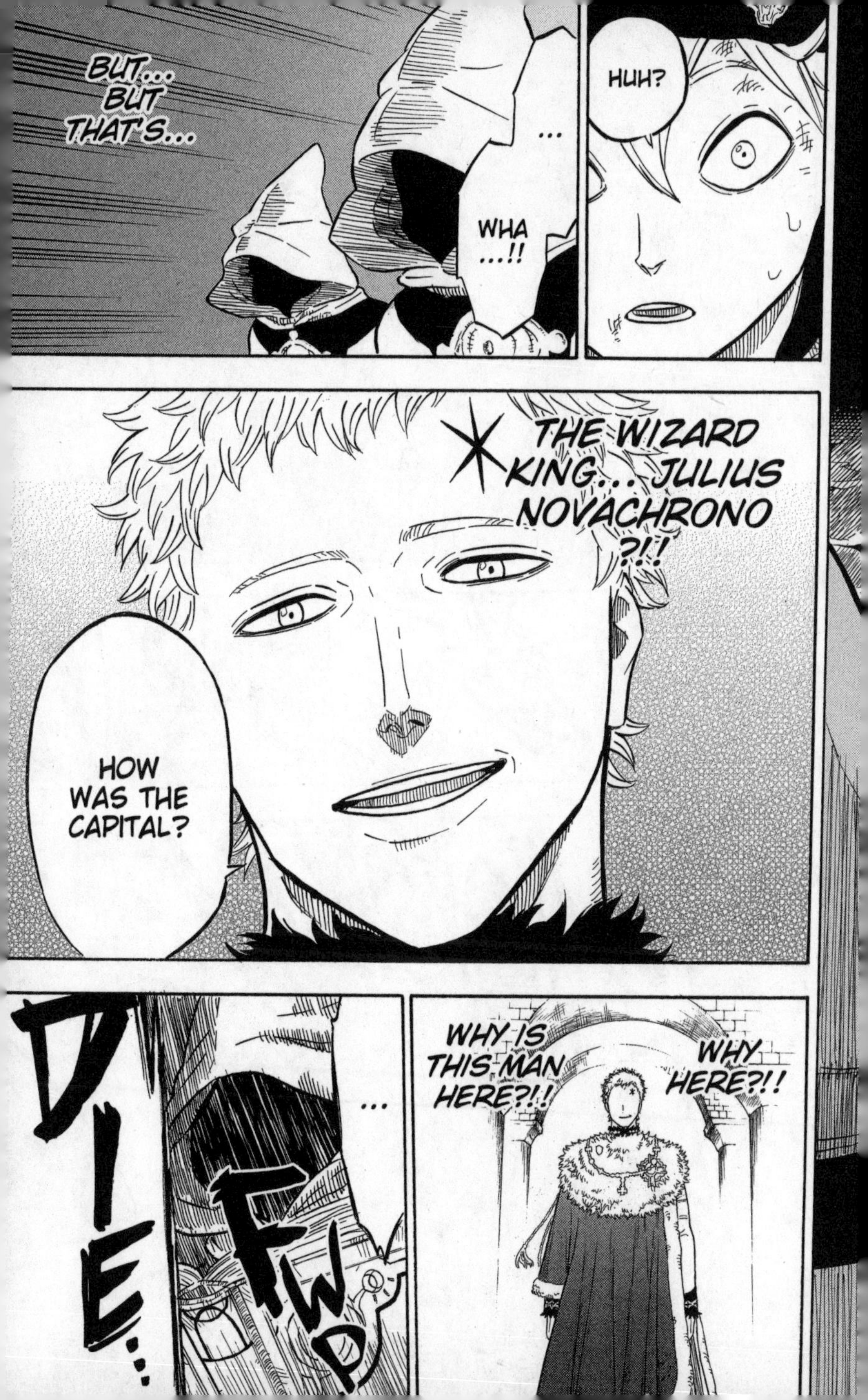
HUH?
...
WHA ...!!
BUT... BUT THAT'S...
THE WIZARD KING... JULIUS NOVACHRONO?!!
HOW WAS THE CAPITAL?
WHY HERE?!!
WHY IS THIS MAN HERE?!!
...
FWP
DIE...

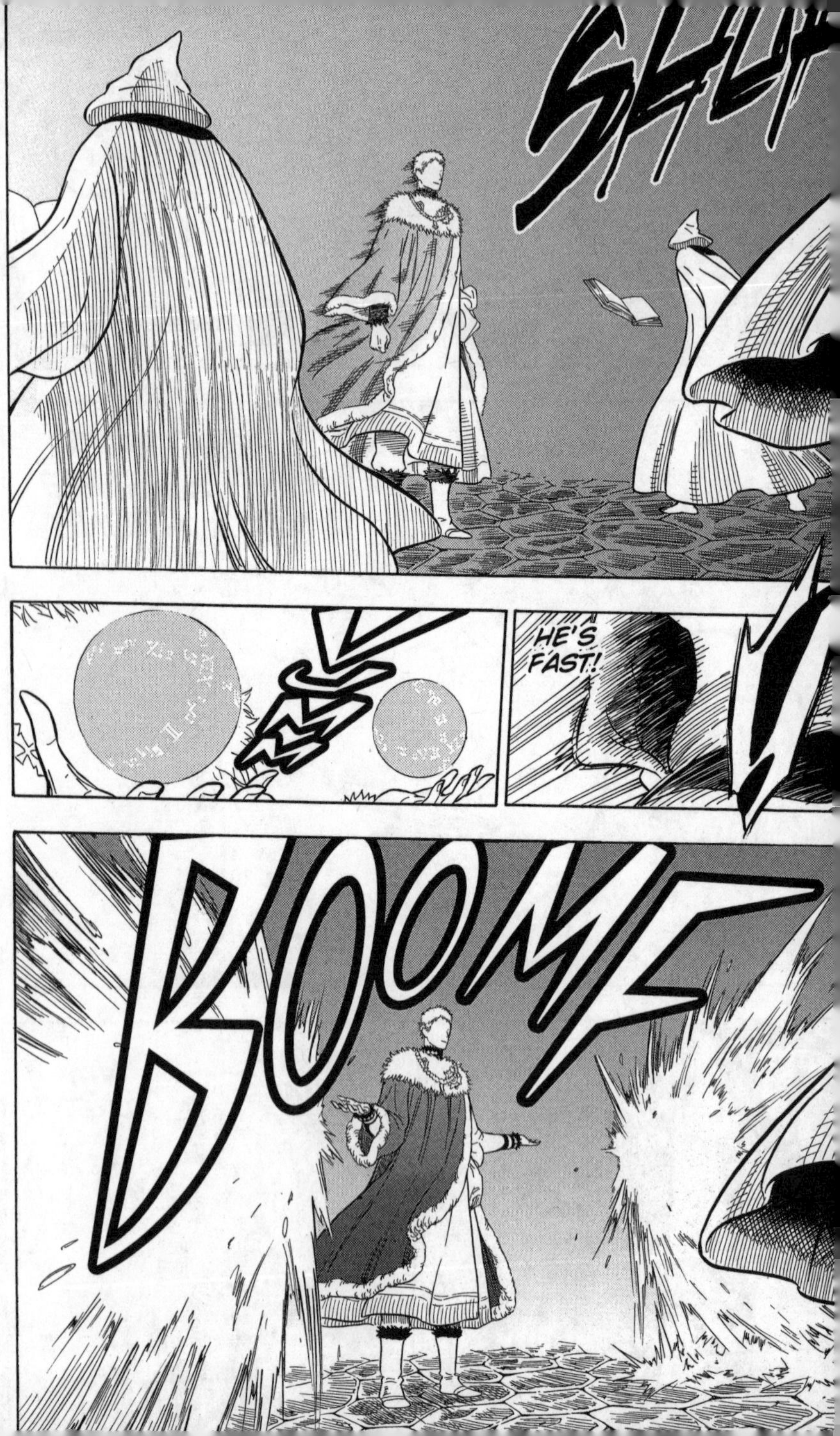
SHU
HE'S FAST!
BOOM

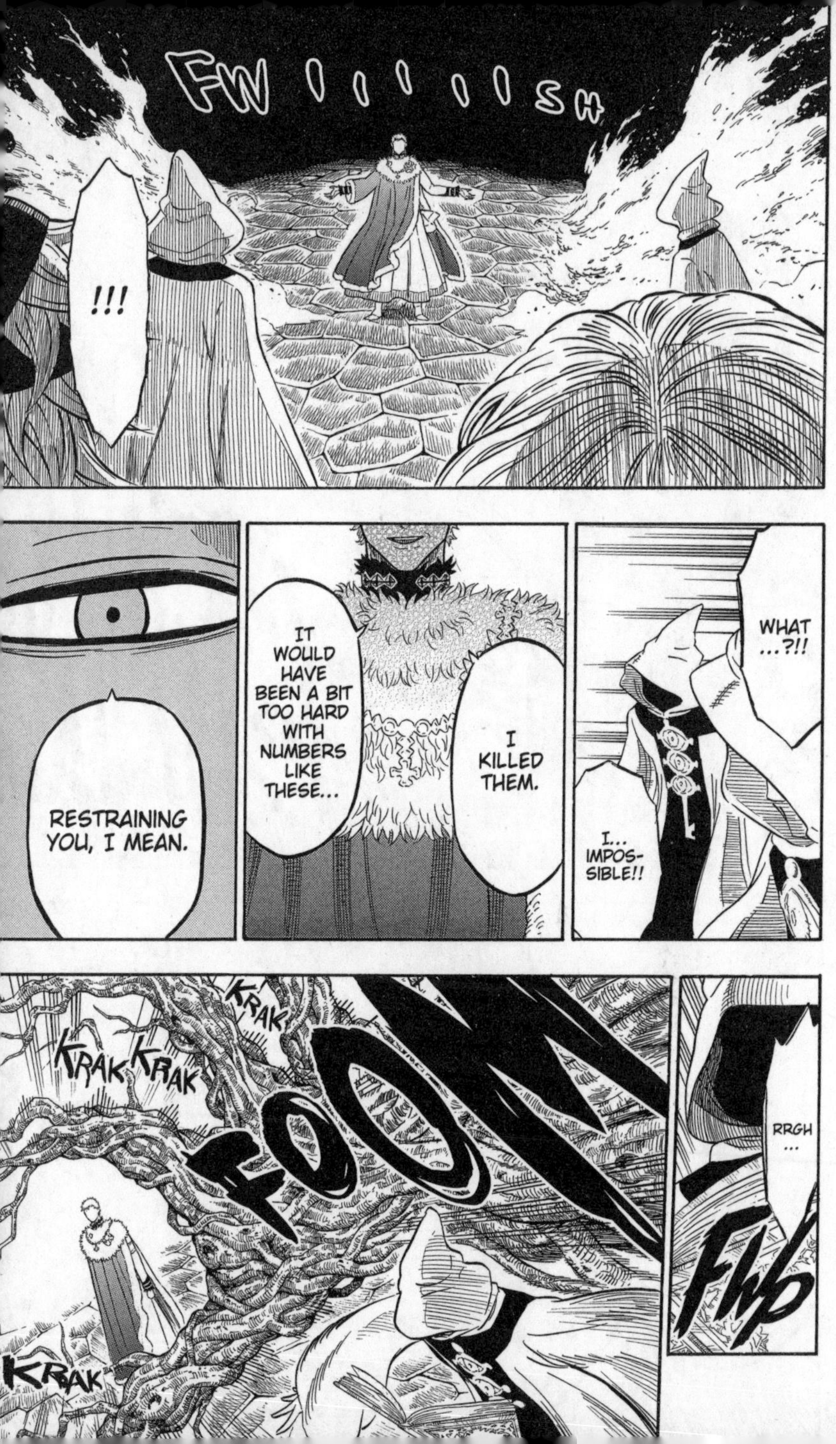
FWIIIIISH
!!!
WHAT ...?!!
I... IMPOSSIBLE!!
I KILLED THEM.
IT WOULD HAVE BEEN A BIT TOO HARD WITH NUMBERS LIKE THESE...
RESTRAINING YOU, I MEAN.
RRGH ...
FWP
KRAK
FOOM
KRAK KRAK
KRAK

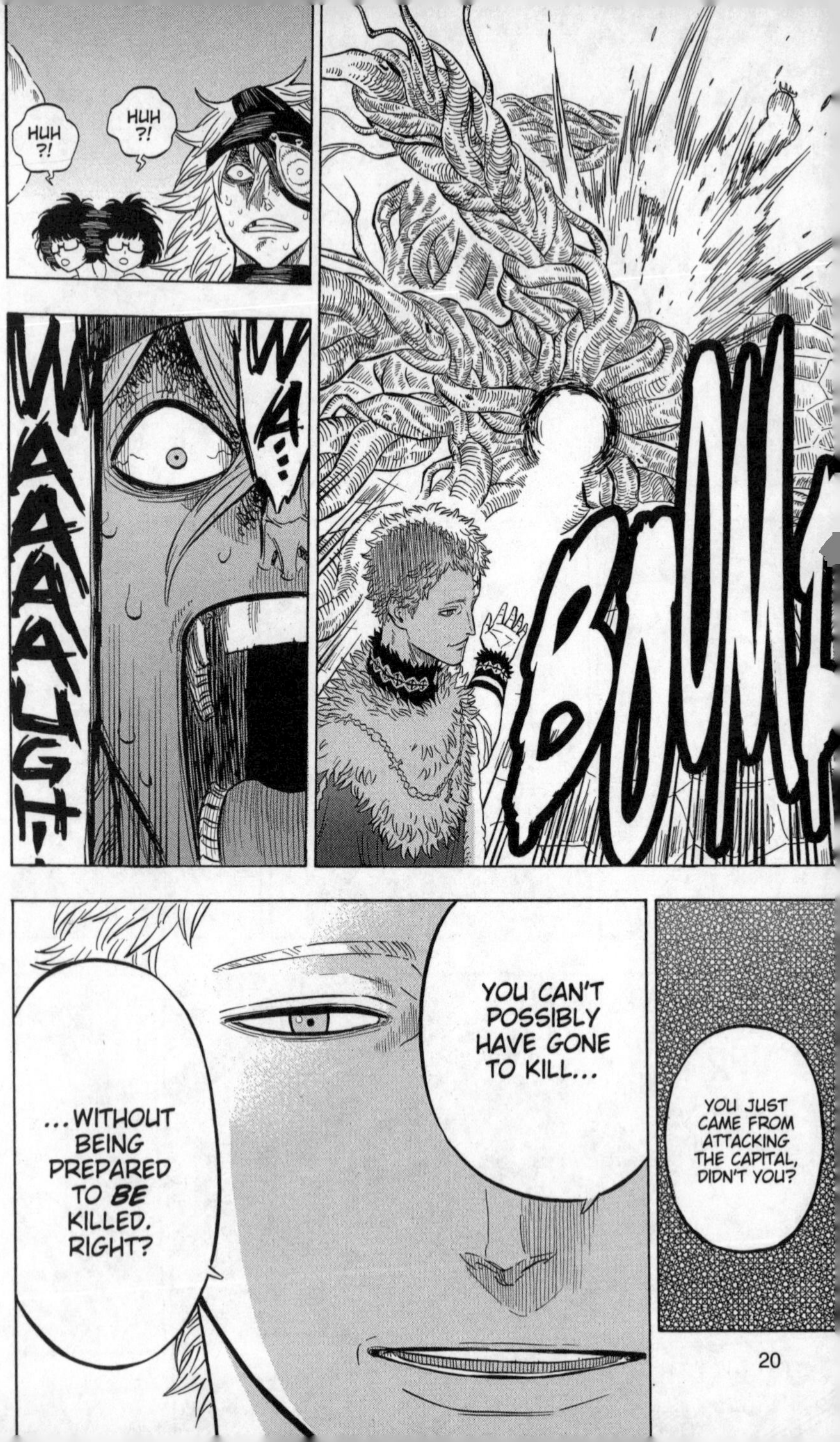
BOOM
HUH ?!
HUH ?!
WAAAAUGH!!
WA...!
YOU JUST CAME FROM ATTACKING THE CAPITAL, DIDN'T YOU?
YOU CAN'T POSSIBLY HAVE GONE TO KILL...
...WITHOUT BEING PREPARED TO *BE* KILLED. RIGHT?

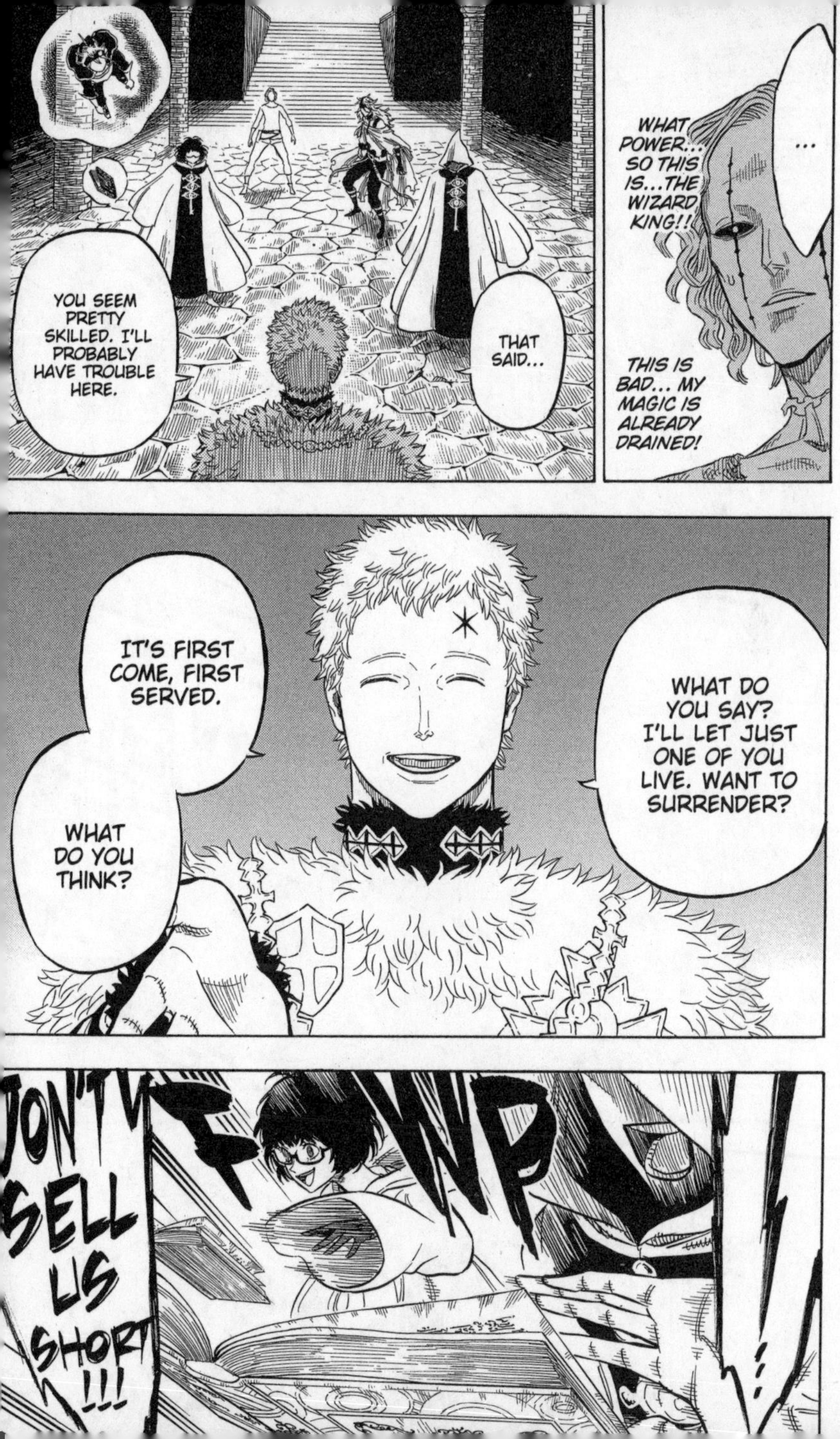

WHAT POWER... SO THIS IS...THE WIZARD KING!!
...
THIS IS BAD... MY MAGIC IS ALREADY DRAINED!
YOU SEEM PRETTY SKILLED. I'LL PROBABLY HAVE TROUBLE HERE.
THAT SAID...
WHAT DO YOU SAY? I'LL LET JUST ONE OF YOU LIVE. WANT TO SURRENDER?
IT'S FIRST COME, FIRST SERVED.
WHAT DO YOU THINK?
DON'T SELL US SHORT!!!

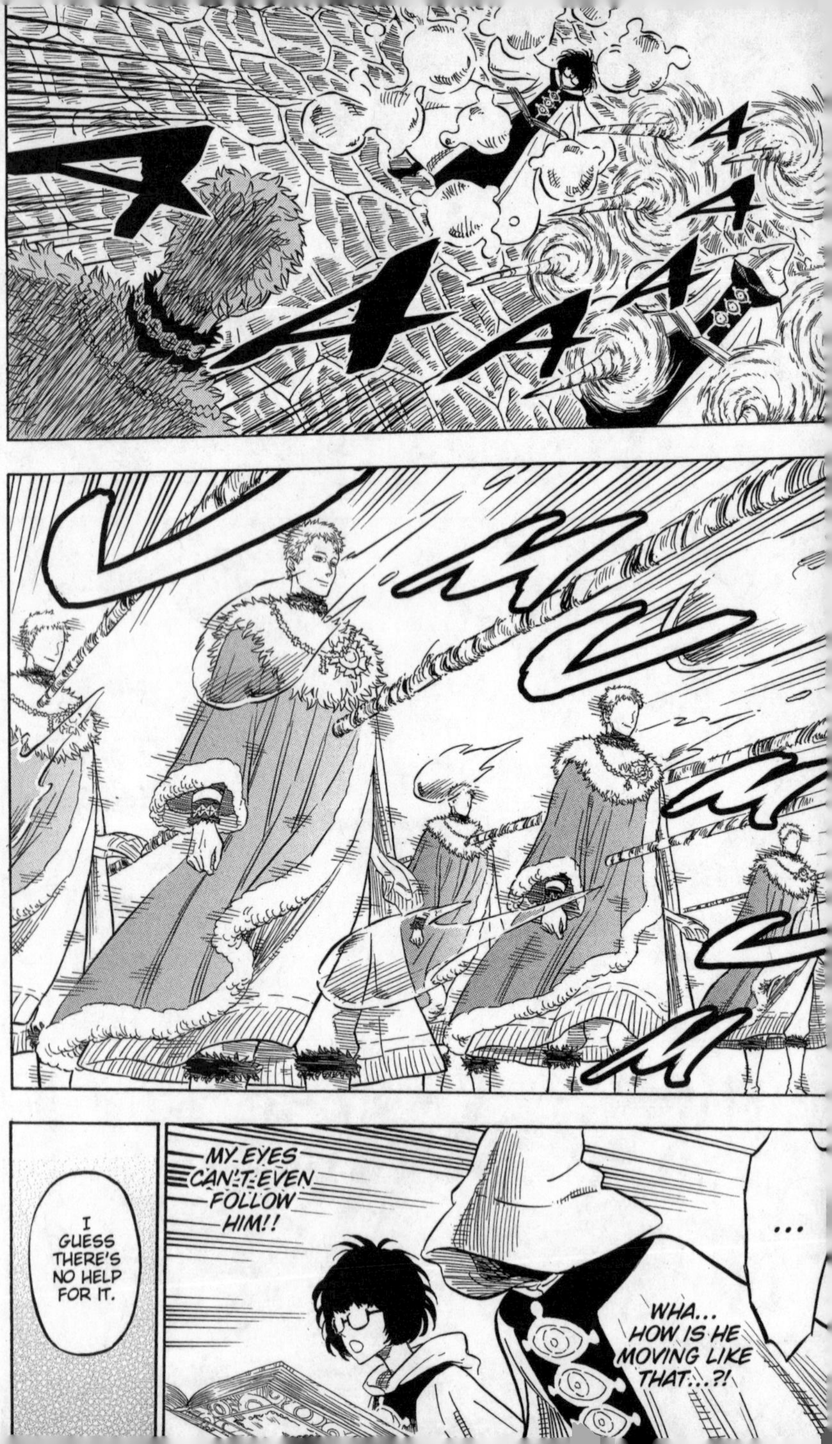
...
MY EYES CAN'T EVEN FOLLOW HIM!!
WHA... HOW IS HE MOVING LIKE THAT...?!
I GUESS THERE'S NO HELP FOR IT.

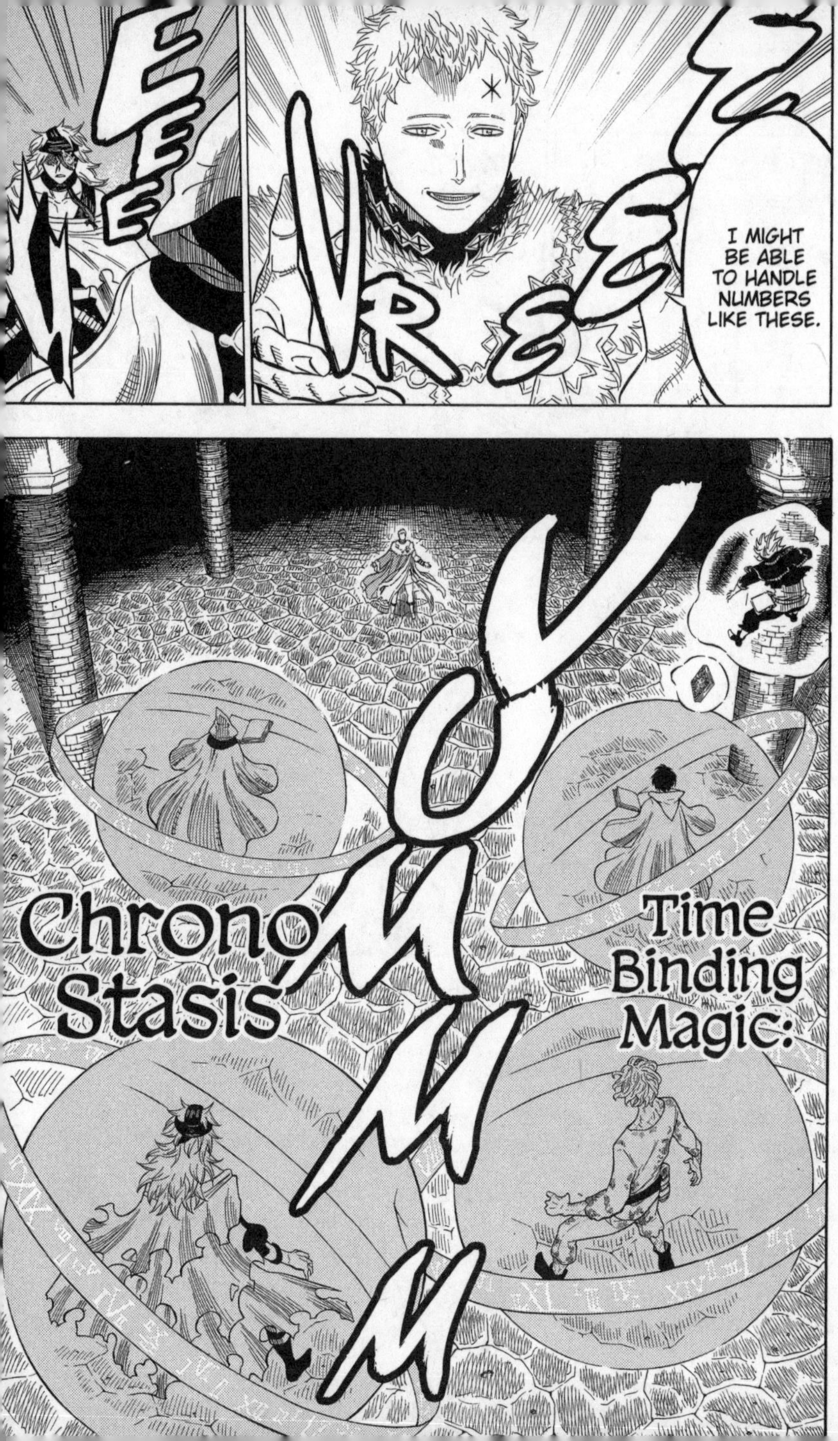
I MIGHT BE ABLE TO HANDLE NUMBERS LIKE THESE.
VOMMM
Time Binding Magic:
Chrono Stasis

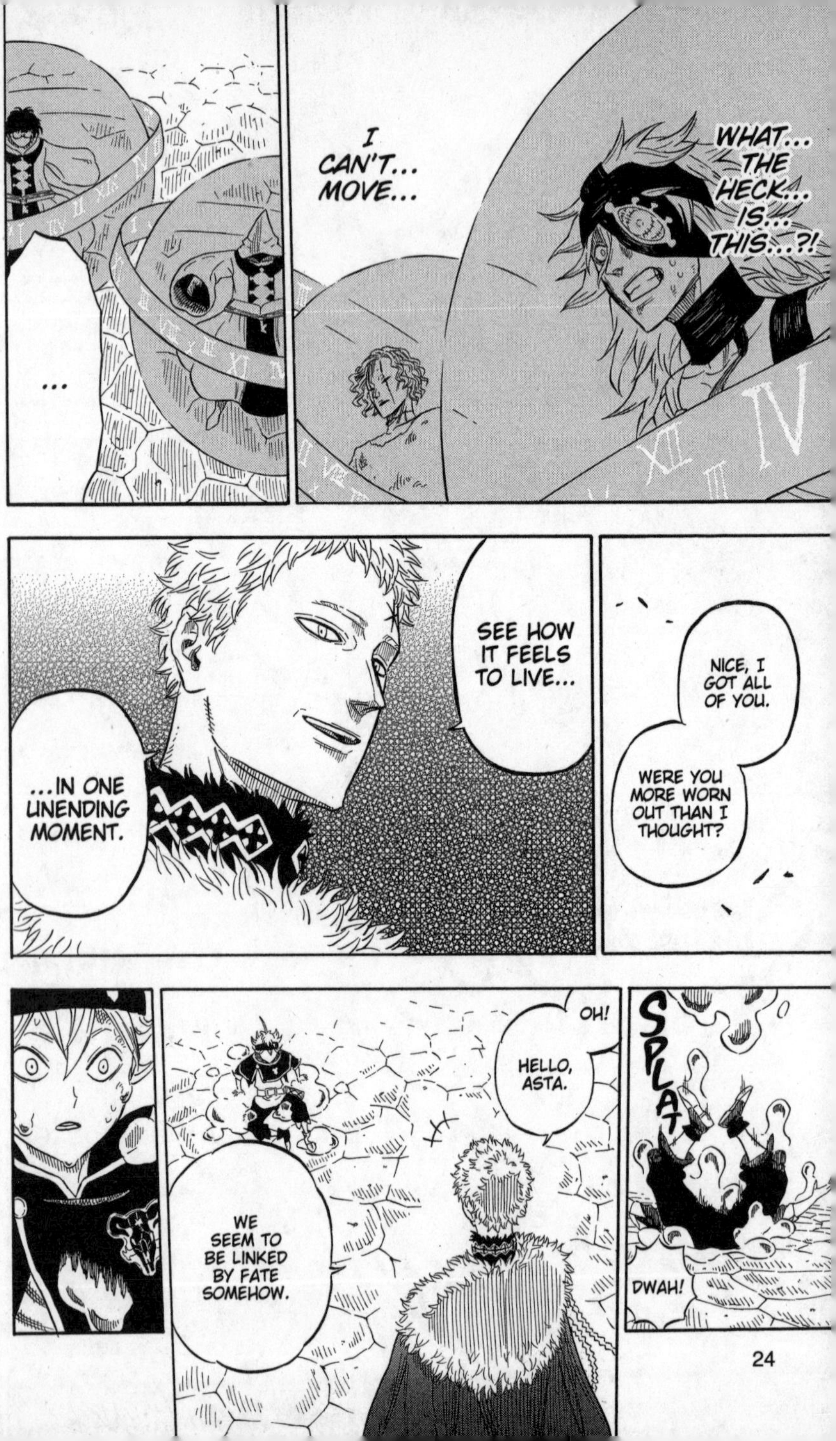
WHAT... THE HECK... IS... THIS...?!
I CAN'T... MOVE...
...
NICE, I GOT ALL OF YOU.
WERE YOU MORE WORN OUT THAN I THOUGHT?
SEE HOW IT FEELS TO LIVE...
...IN ONE UNENDING MOMENT.
SPLAT
DWAH!
OH!
HELLO, ASTA.
WE SEEM TO BE LINKED BY FATE SOMEHOW.

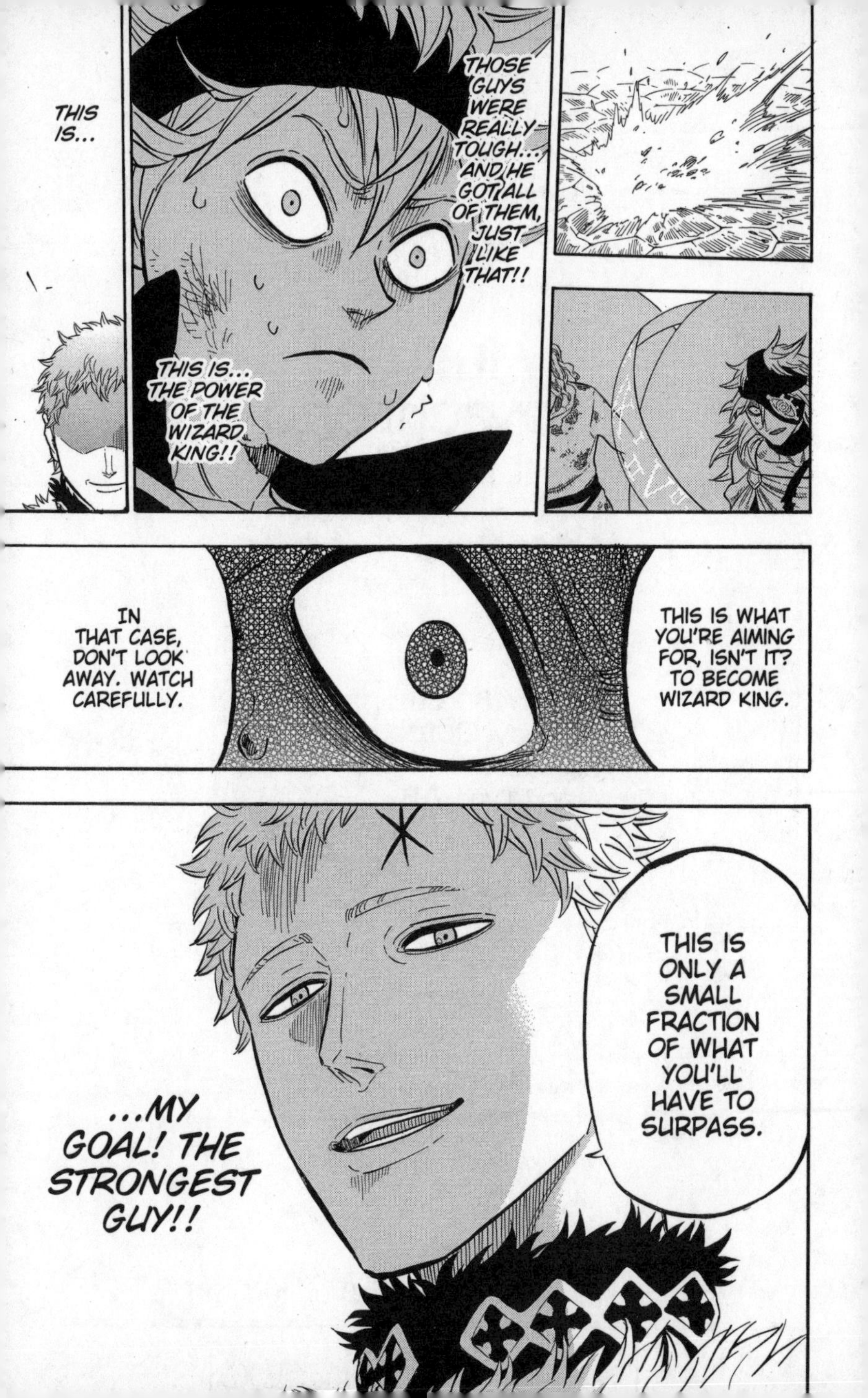
THOSE GUYS WERE REALLY TOUGH... AND HE GOT ALL OF THEM, JUST LIKE THAT!!
THIS IS...
THIS IS... THE POWER OF THE WIZARD KING!!
THIS IS WHAT YOU'RE AIMING FOR, ISN'T IT? TO BECOME WIZARD KING.
IN THAT CASE, DON'T LOOK AWAY. WATCH CAREFULLY.
THIS IS ONLY A SMALL FRACTION OF WHAT YOU'LL HAVE TO SURPASS.
...MY GOAL! THE STRONGEST GUY!!

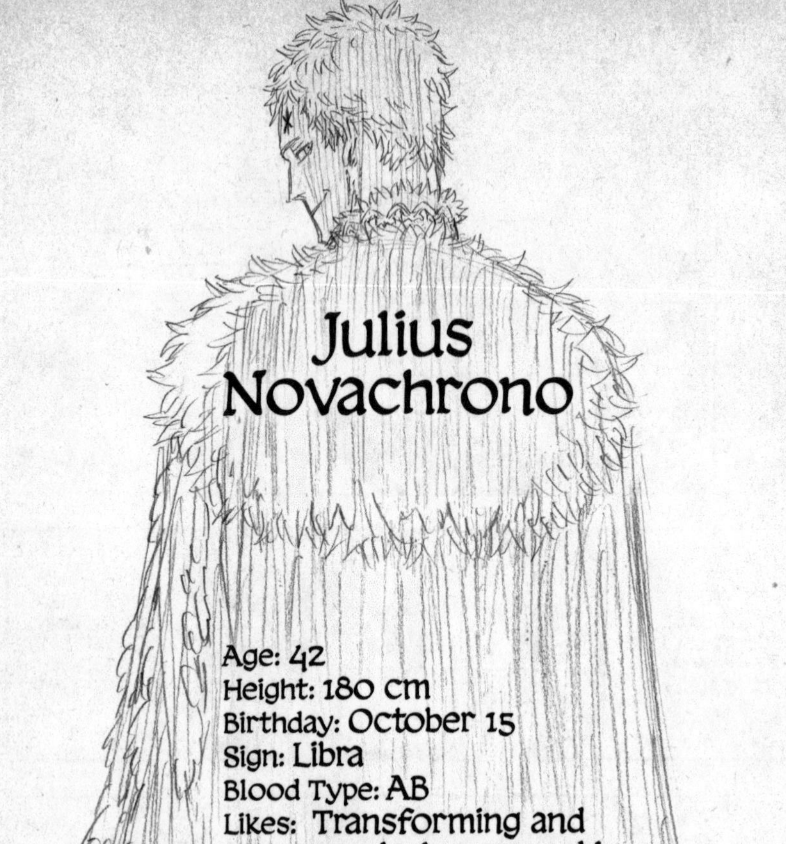

Julius Novachrono

Age: 42
Height: 180 cm
Birthday: October 15
Sign: Libra
Blood Type: AB
Likes: Transforming and wandering around in search of new spells.

Character Profile

✽Page 36: Light

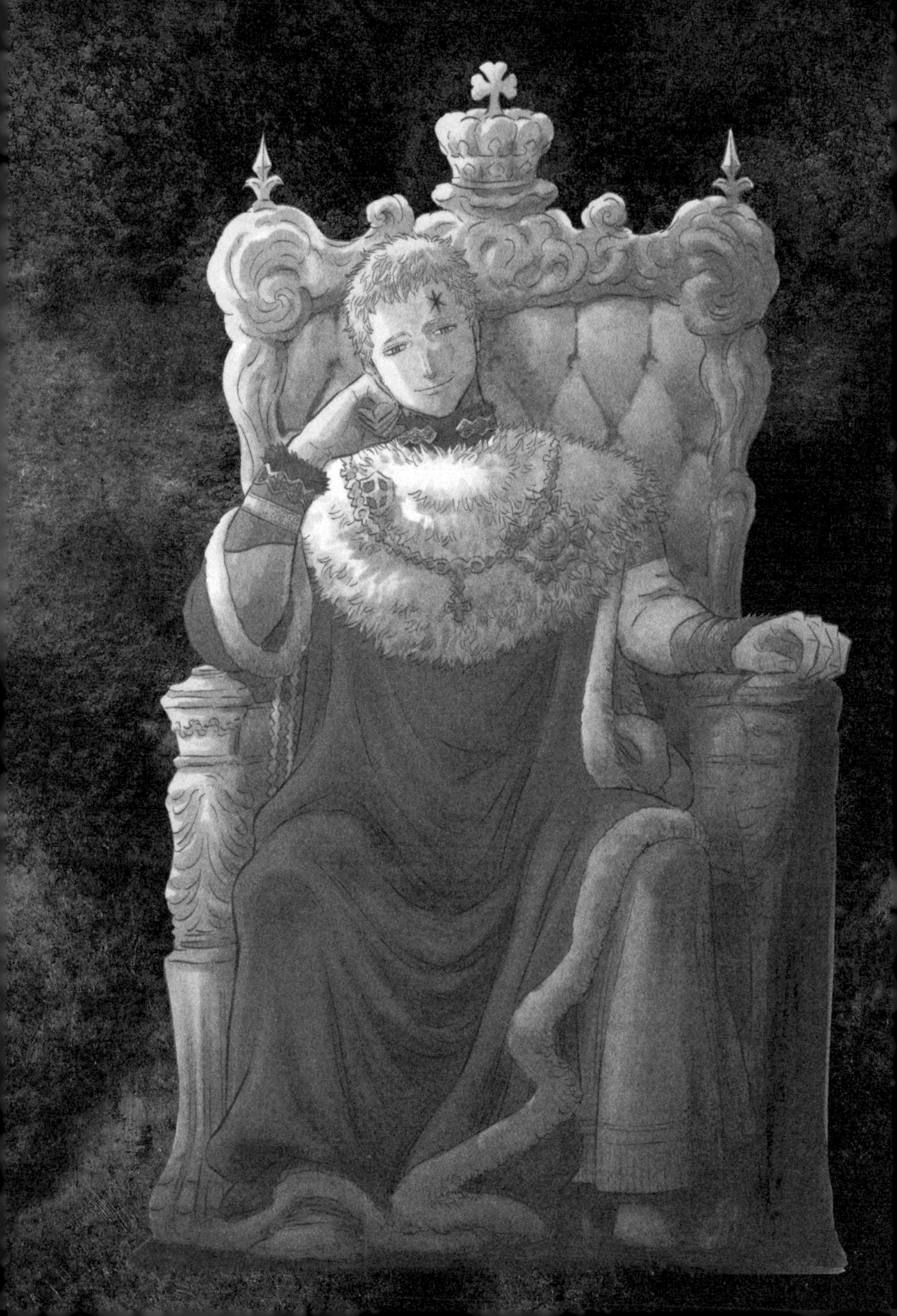

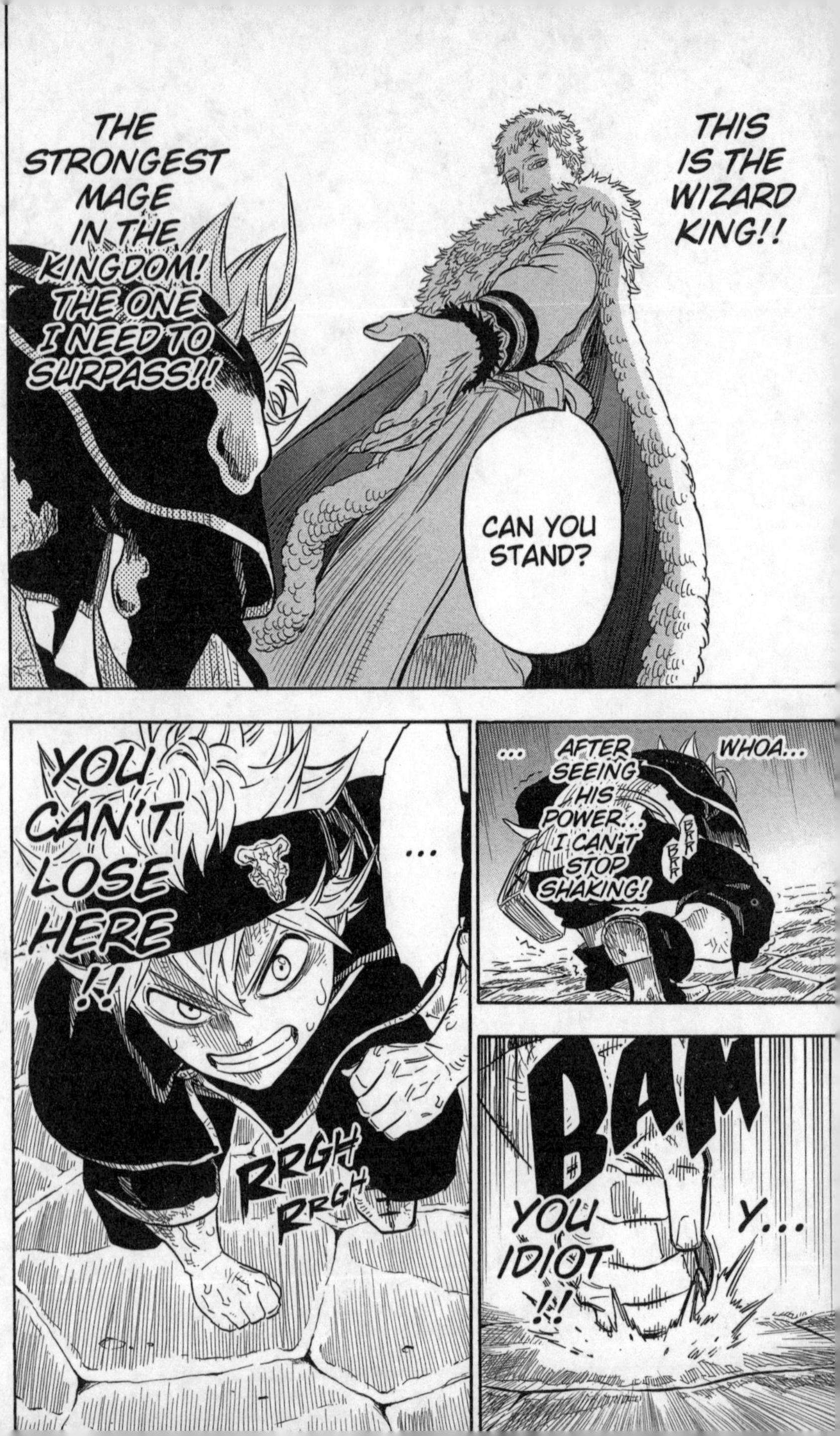
THIS IS THE WIZARD KING!!
THE STRONGEST MAGE IN THE KINGDOM! THE ONE I NEED TO SURPASS!!
CAN YOU STAND?
WHOA...
BRR BRR BRR
AFTER SEEING HIS POWER... I CAN'T STOP SHAKING!
...
BAM
Y...
YOU IDIOT!?!
...
YOU CAN'T LOSE HERE!!
RRGH RRGH

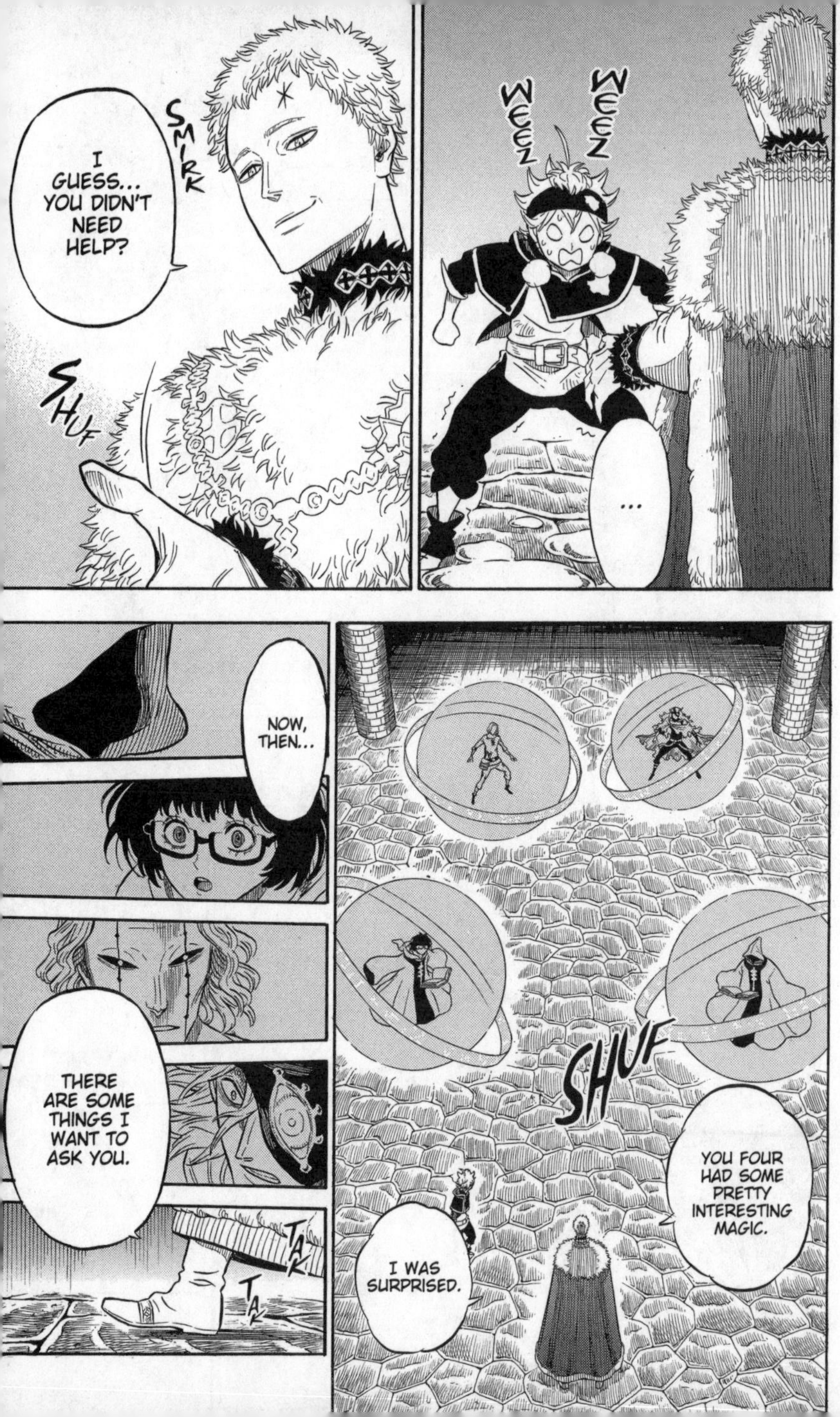
WEEZ WEEZ
...
SMIRK
I GUESS... YOU DIDN'T NEED HELP?
SHUF
SHUF
YOU FOUR HAD SOME PRETTY INTERESTING MAGIC.
I WAS SURPRISED.
NOW, THEN...
THERE ARE SOME THINGS I WANT TO ASK YOU.
TAK
TAK

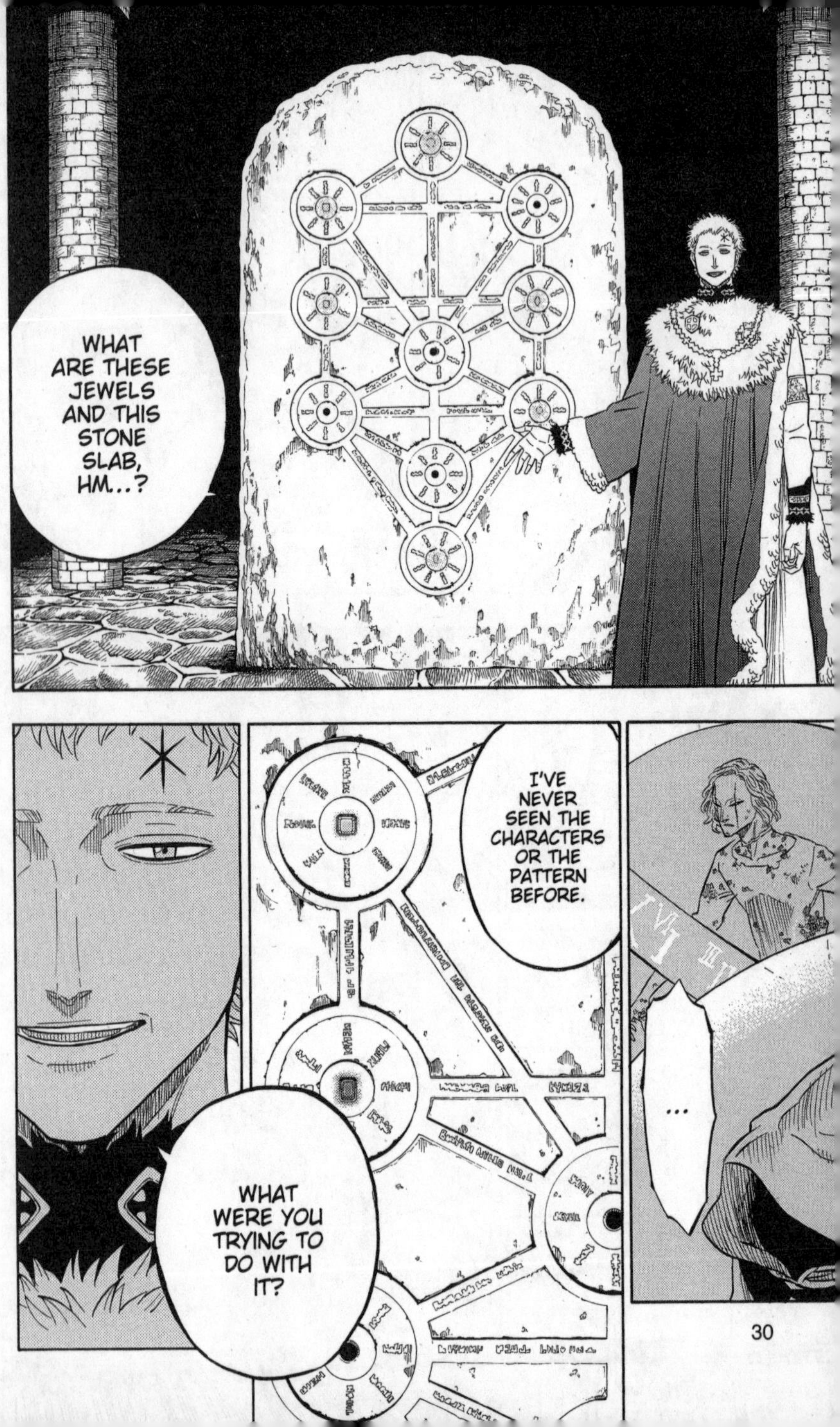
WHAT ARE THESE JEWELS AND THIS STONE SLAB, HM...?
...
I'VE NEVER SEEN THE CHARACTERS OR THE PATTERN BEFORE.
WHAT WERE YOU TRYING TO DO WITH IT?

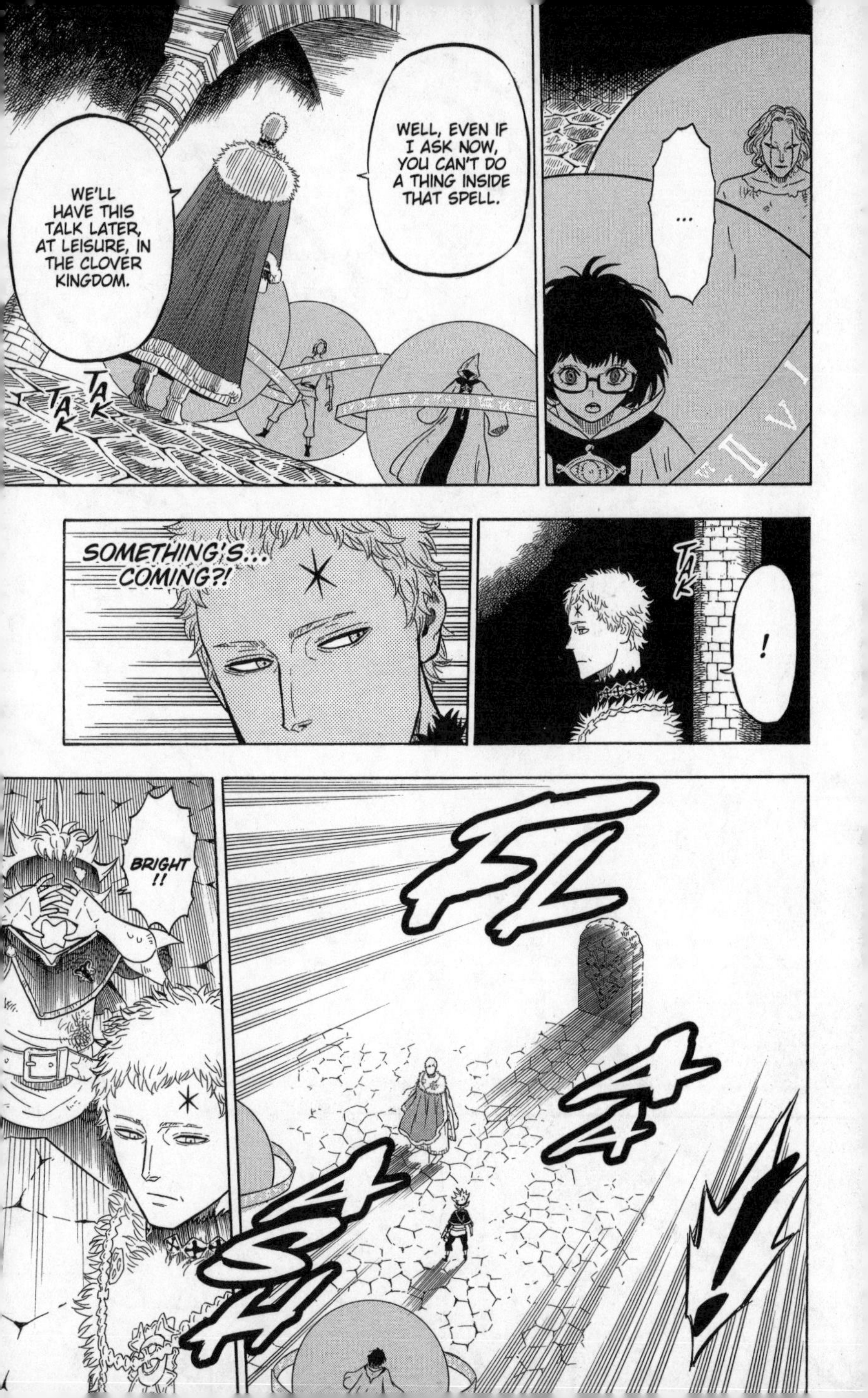
...
WELL, EVEN IF I ASK NOW, YOU CAN'T DO A THING INSIDE THAT SPELL.
WE'LL HAVE THIS TALK LATER, AT LEISURE, IN THE CLOVER KINGDOM.
TAK TAK
TAK
!
SOMETHING'S... COMING?!
BRIGHT!!

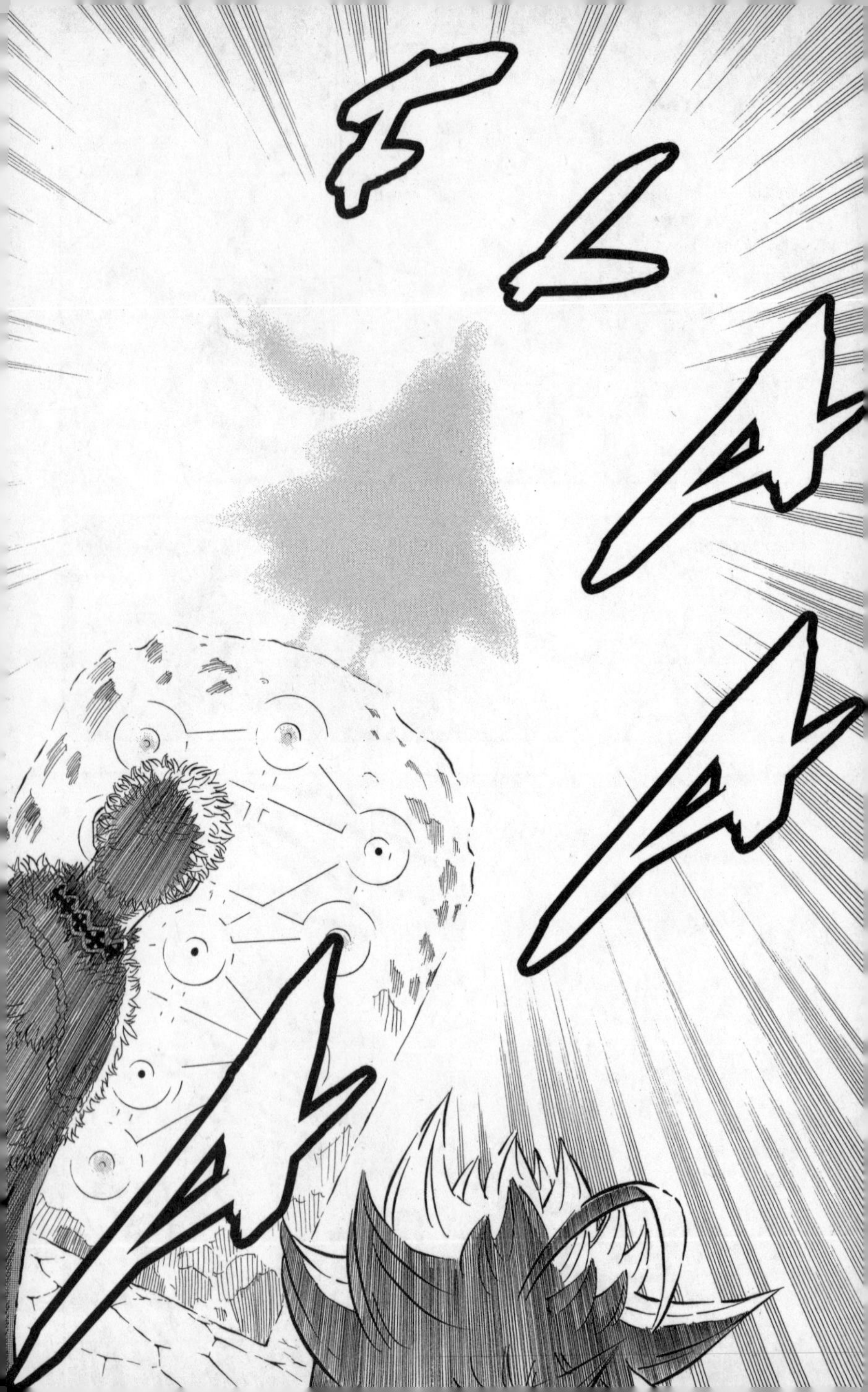

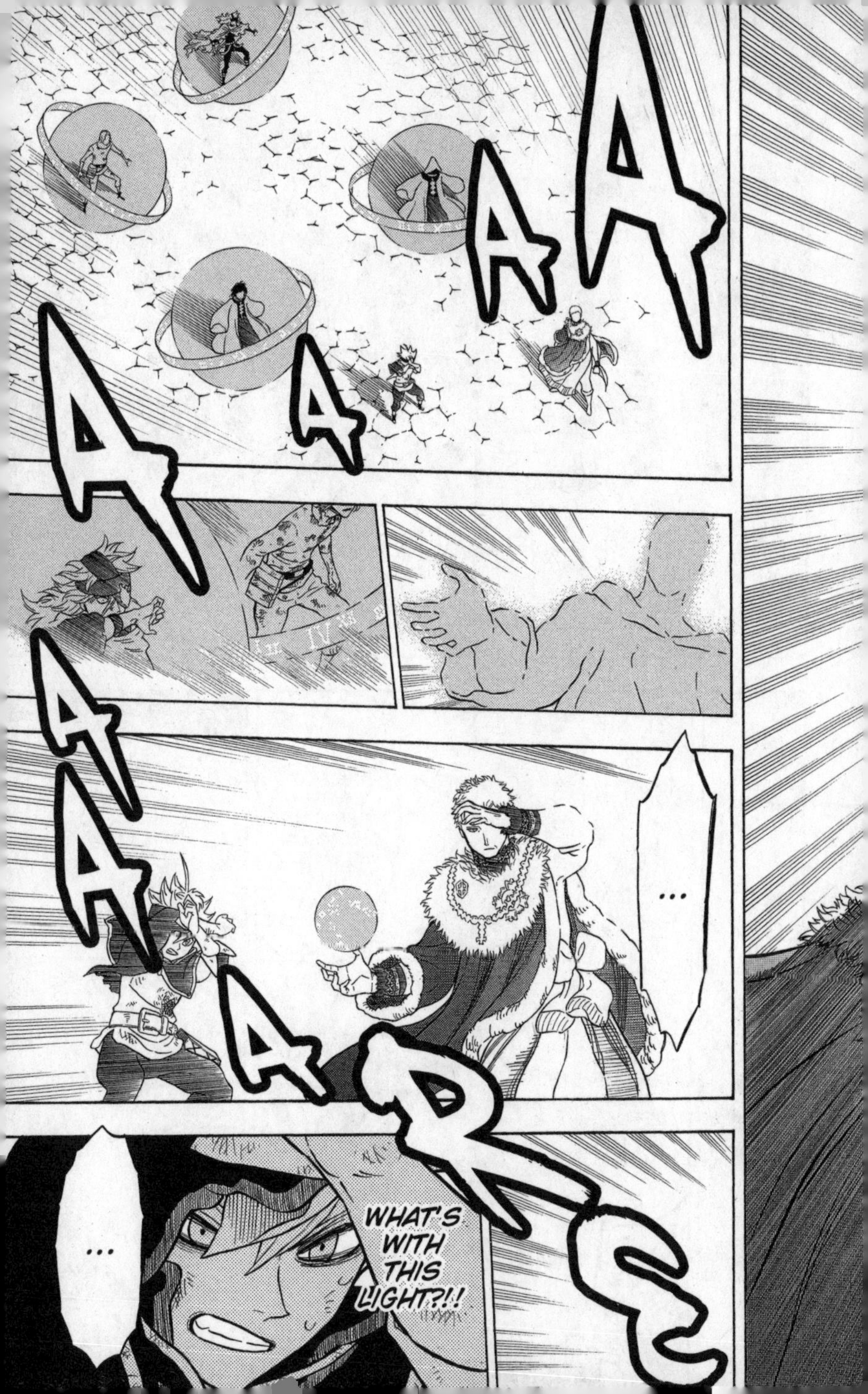
AAAAAAARG
...
WHAT'S WITH THIS LIGHT?!!
...

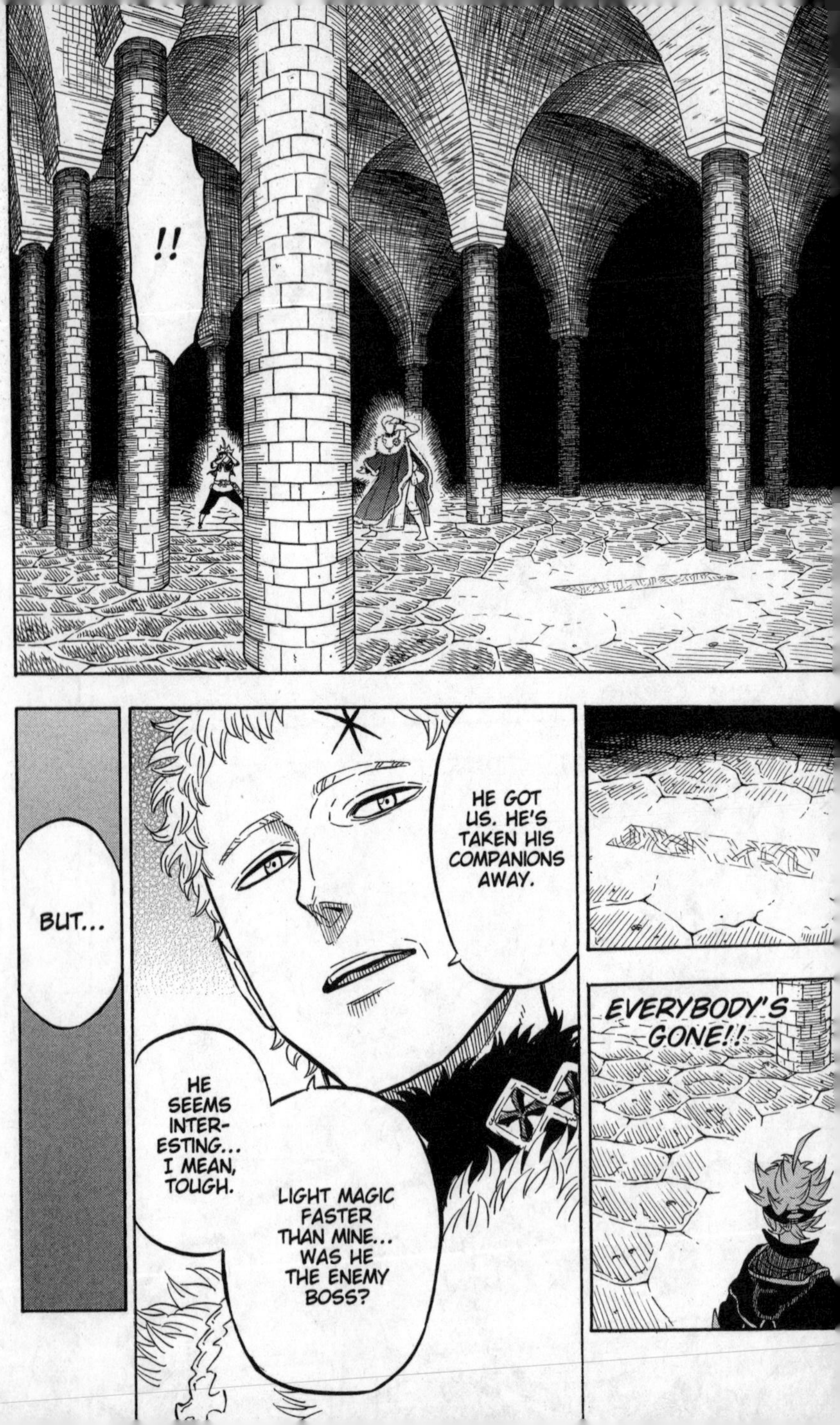
!!
EVERYBODY'S GONE!!
HE GOT US. HE'S TAKEN HIS COMPANIONS AWAY.
LIGHT MAGIC FASTER THAN MINE... WAS HE THE ENEMY BOSS?
HE SEEMS INTER-ESTING... I MEAN, TOUGH.
BUT...

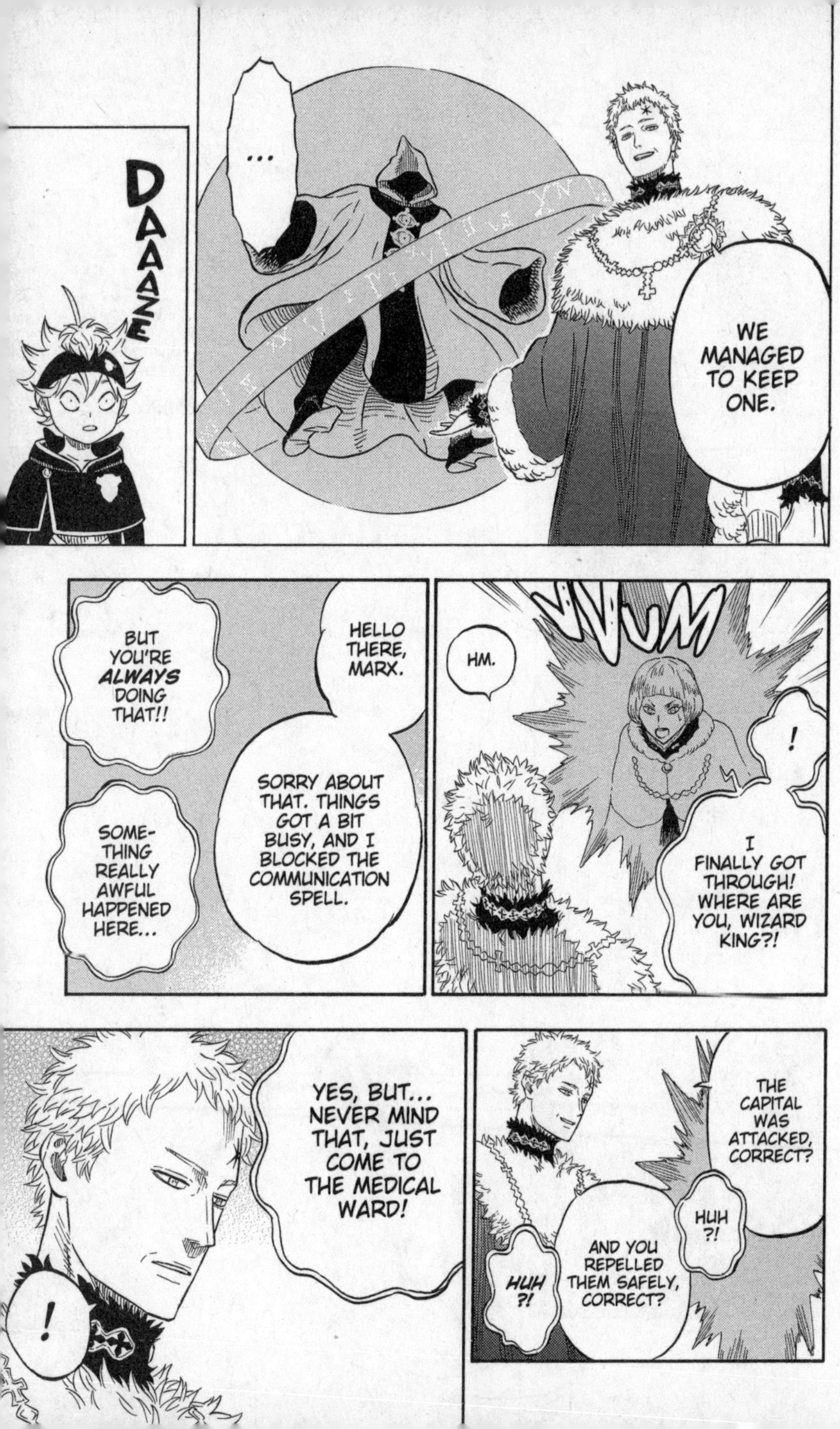
WE MANAGED TO KEEP ONE.
...
DAAAZE
VVUM
HM.
!
I FINALLY GOT THROUGH! WHERE ARE YOU, WIZARD KING?!
HELLO THERE, MARX.
SORRY ABOUT THAT. THINGS GOT A BIT BUSY, AND I BLOCKED THE COMMUNICATION SPELL.
BUT YOU'RE *ALWAYS* DOING THAT!!
SOME-THING REALLY AWFUL HAPPENED HERE...
THE CAPITAL WAS ATTACKED, CORRECT?
HUH ?!
AND YOU REPELLED THEM SAFELY, CORRECT?
HUH ?!
YES, BUT... NEVER MIND THAT, JUST COME TO THE MEDICAL WARD!
!

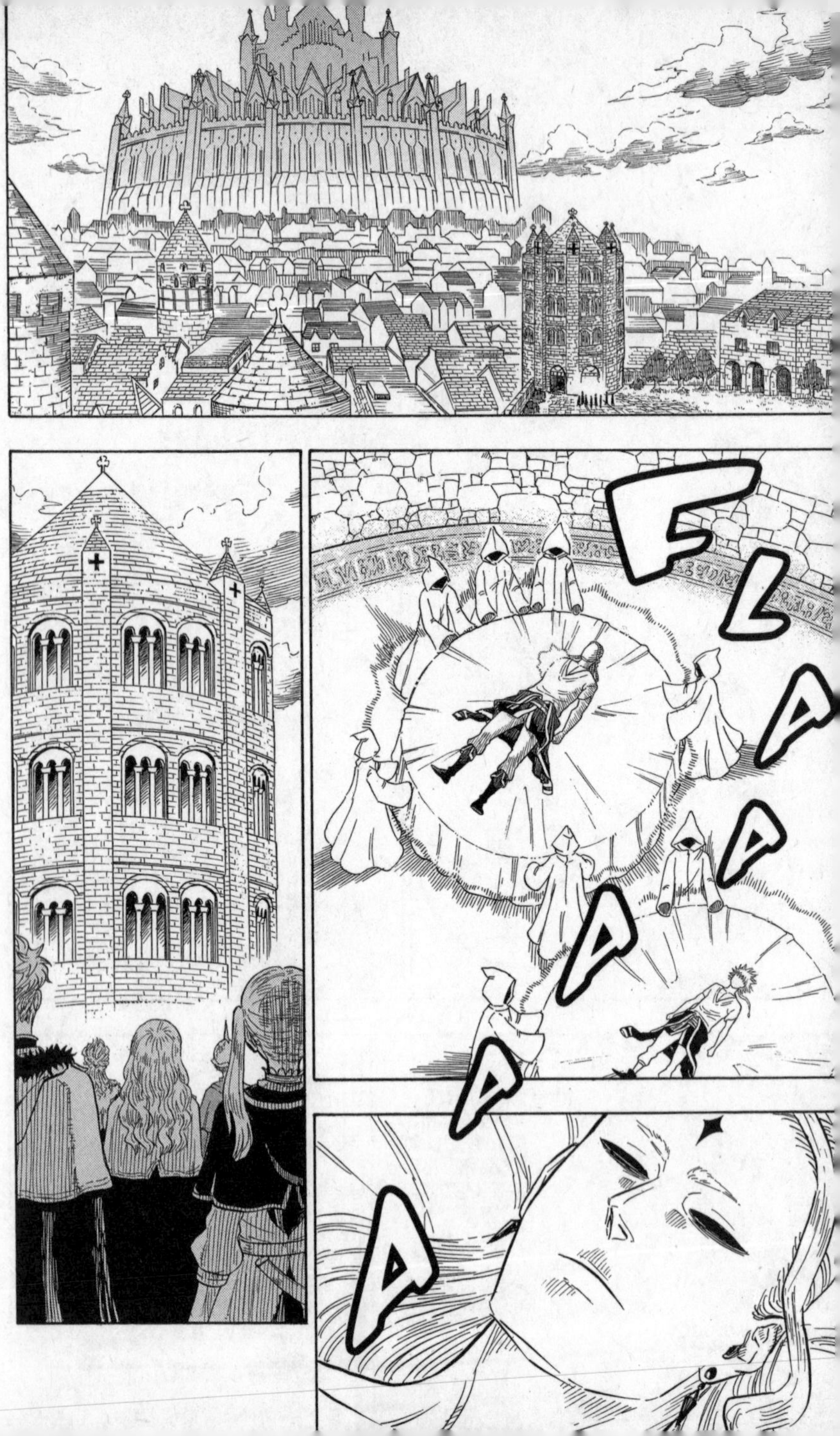
FLAAAAA

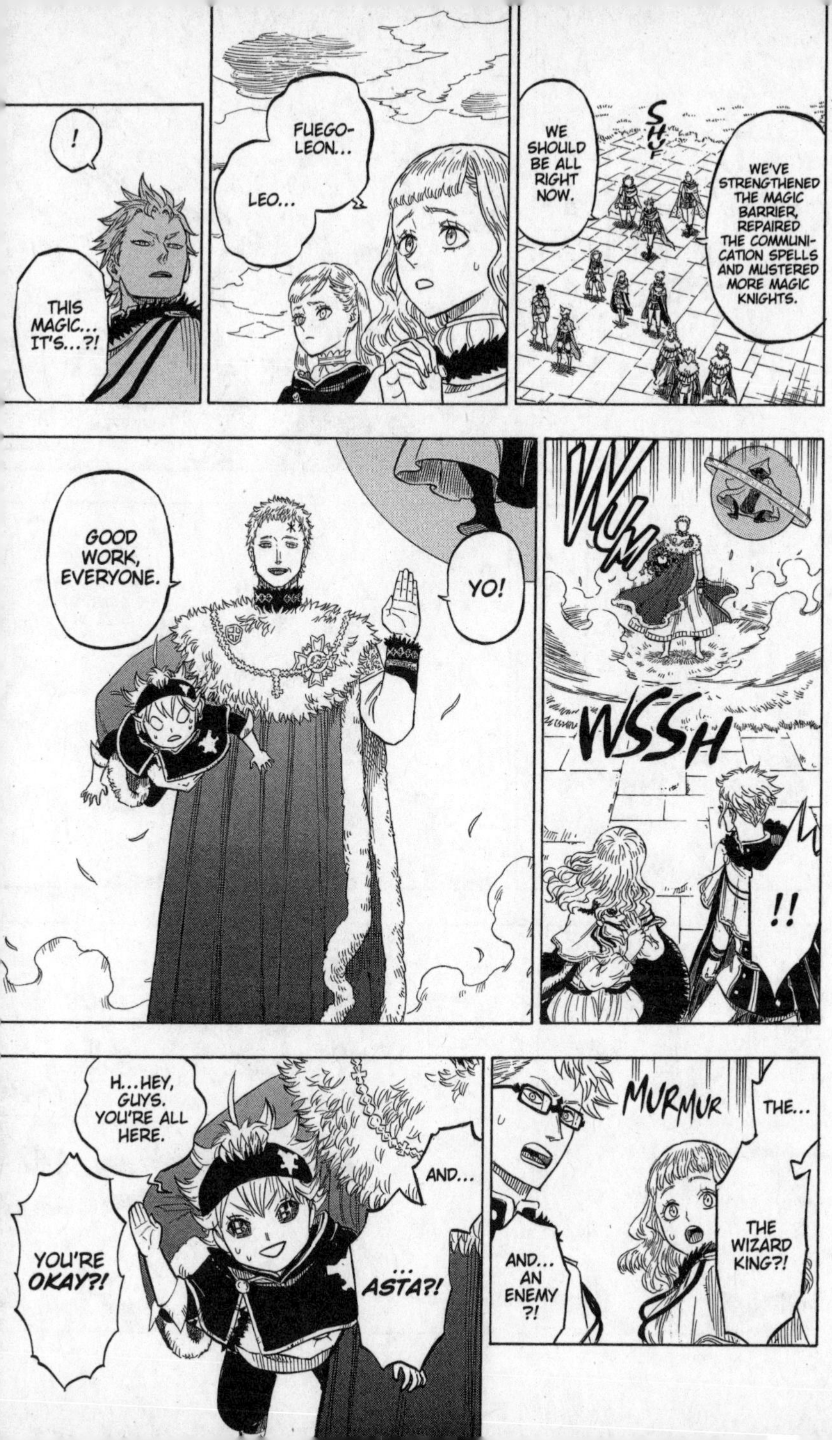
WE'VE STRENGTHENED THE MAGIC BARRIER, REPAIRED THE COMMUNICATION SPELLS AND MUSTERED MORE MAGIC KNIGHTS.
SHUF
WE SHOULD BE ALL RIGHT NOW.
FUEGO-LEON...
LEO...
!
THIS MAGIC... IT'S...?!
WUM
WSSH
!!
YO!
GOOD WORK, EVERYONE.
THE...
MURMUR
THE WIZARD KING?!
AND... AN ENEMY ?!
AND...
...ASTA?!
H...HEY, GUYS. YOU'RE ALL HERE.
YOU'RE OKAY?!

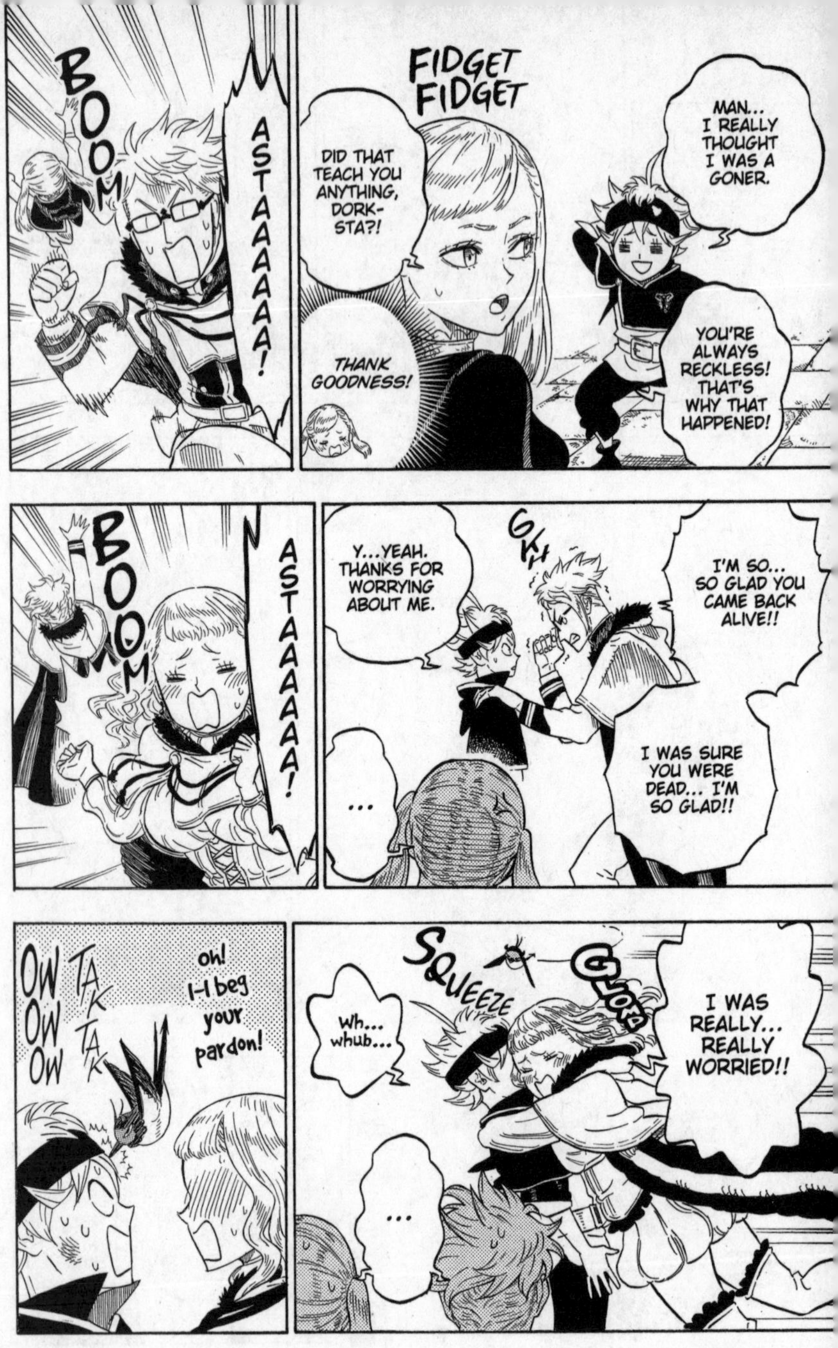
MAN... I REALLY THOUGHT I WAS A GONER.
FIDGET FIDGET
DID THAT TEACH YOU ANYTHING, DORK-STA?!
YOU'RE ALWAYS RECKLESS! THAT'S WHY THAT HAPPENED!
THANK GOODNESS!
BOOM
ASTAAAAAAAA!
I'M SO... SO GLAD YOU CAME BACK ALIVE!!
GKH
Y...YEAH. THANKS FOR WORRYING ABOUT ME.
I WAS SURE YOU WERE DEAD... I'M SO GLAD!!
...
BOOM
ASTAAAAAAAA!
I WAS REALLY... REALLY WORRIED!!
GLOMP
SQUEEZE
Wh... whub...
...
oh! I-I beg your pardon!
TAK TAK
OW OW OW

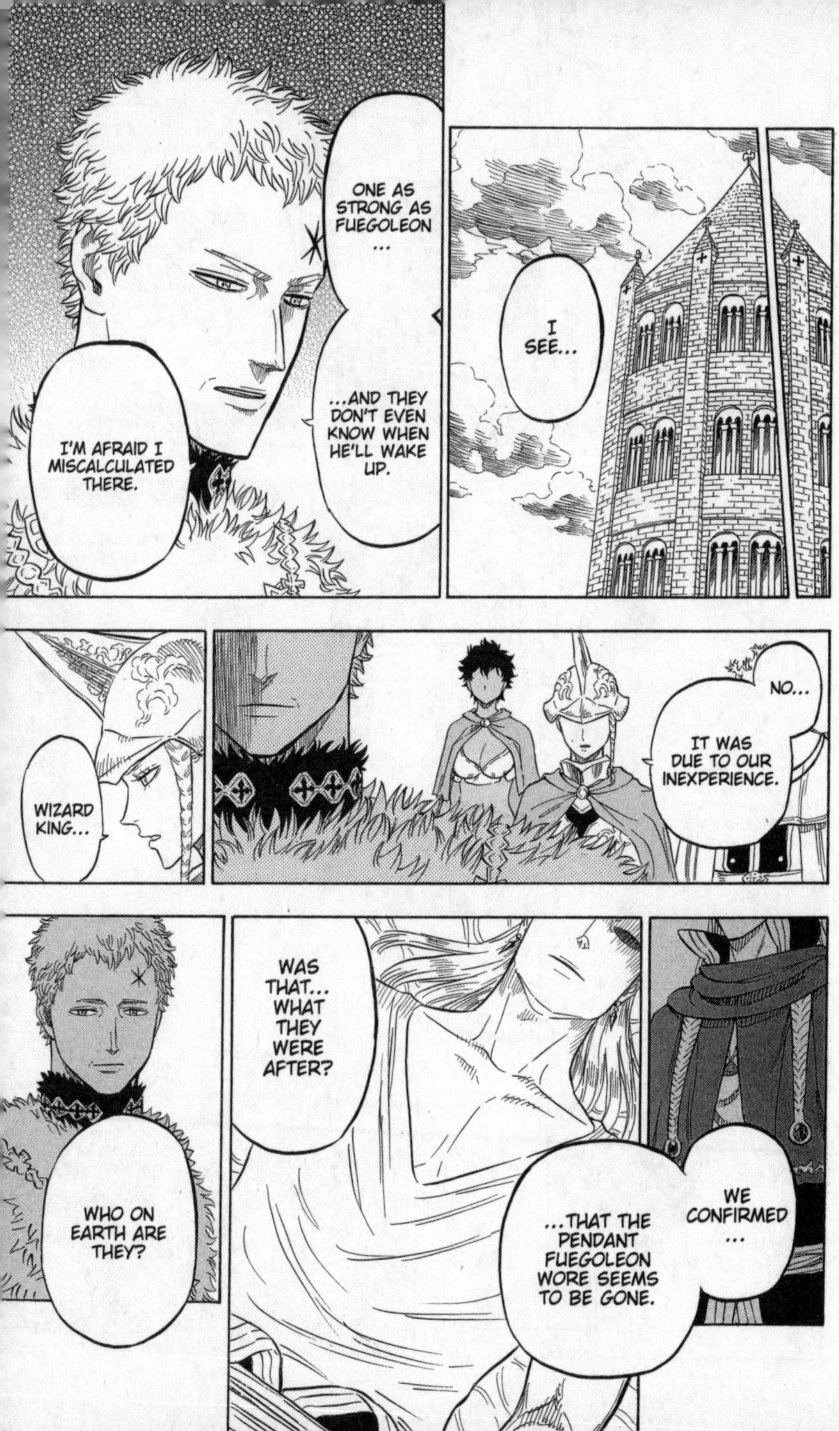
I SEE...
ONE AS STRONG AS FUEGOLEON ...
...AND THEY DON'T EVEN KNOW WHEN HE'LL WAKE UP.
I'M AFRAID I MISCALCULATED THERE.
NO...
IT WAS DUE TO OUR INEXPERIENCE.
WIZARD KING...
WE CONFIRMED ...
...THAT THE PENDANT FUEGOLEON WORE SEEMS TO BE GONE.
WAS THAT... WHAT THEY WERE AFTER?
WHO ON EARTH ARE THEY?

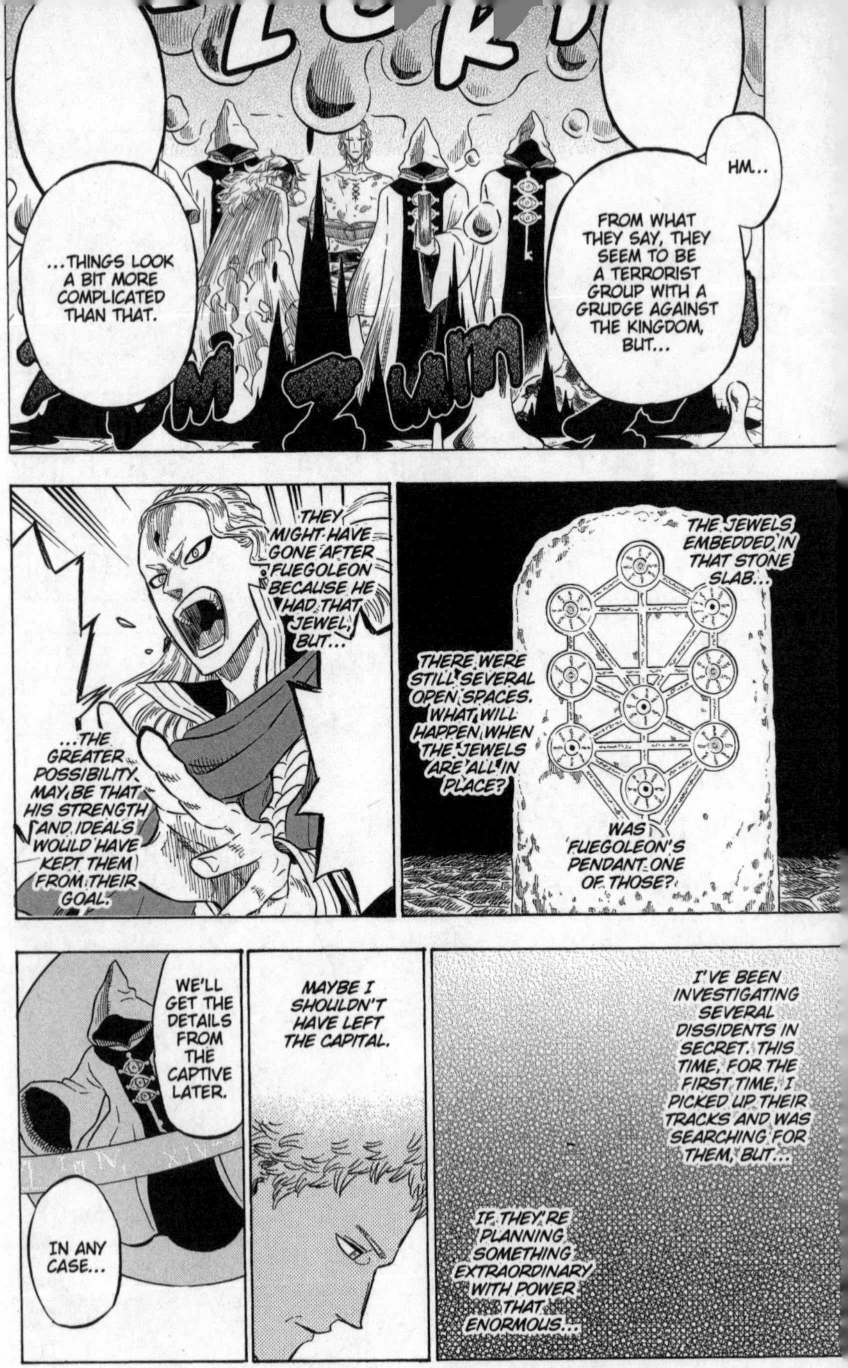
HM...
FROM WHAT THEY SAY, THEY SEEM TO BE A TERRORIST GROUP WITH A GRUDGE AGAINST THE KINGDOM, BUT...
...THINGS LOOK A BIT MORE COMPLICATED THAN THAT.
THE JEWELS EMBEDDED IN THAT STONE SLAB...
THERE WERE STILL SEVERAL OPEN SPACES. WHAT WILL HAPPEN WHEN THE JEWELS ARE ALL IN PLACE?
WAS FUEGOLEON'S PENDANT ONE OF THOSE?
THEY MIGHT HAVE GONE AFTER FUEGOLEON BECAUSE HE HAD THAT JEWEL, BUT...
...THE GREATER POSSIBILITY MAY BE THAT HIS STRENGTH AND IDEALS WOULD HAVE KEPT THEM FROM THEIR GOAL.
I'VE BEEN INVESTIGATING SEVERAL DISSIDENTS IN SECRET. THIS TIME, FOR THE FIRST TIME, I PICKED UP THEIR TRACKS AND WAS SEARCHING FOR THEM, BUT...
IF THEY'RE PLANNING SOMETHING EXTRAORDINARY WITH POWER THAT ENORMOUS...
MAYBE I SHOULDN'T HAVE LEFT THE CAPITAL.
WE'LL GET THE DETAILS FROM THE CAPTIVE LATER.
IN ANY CASE...

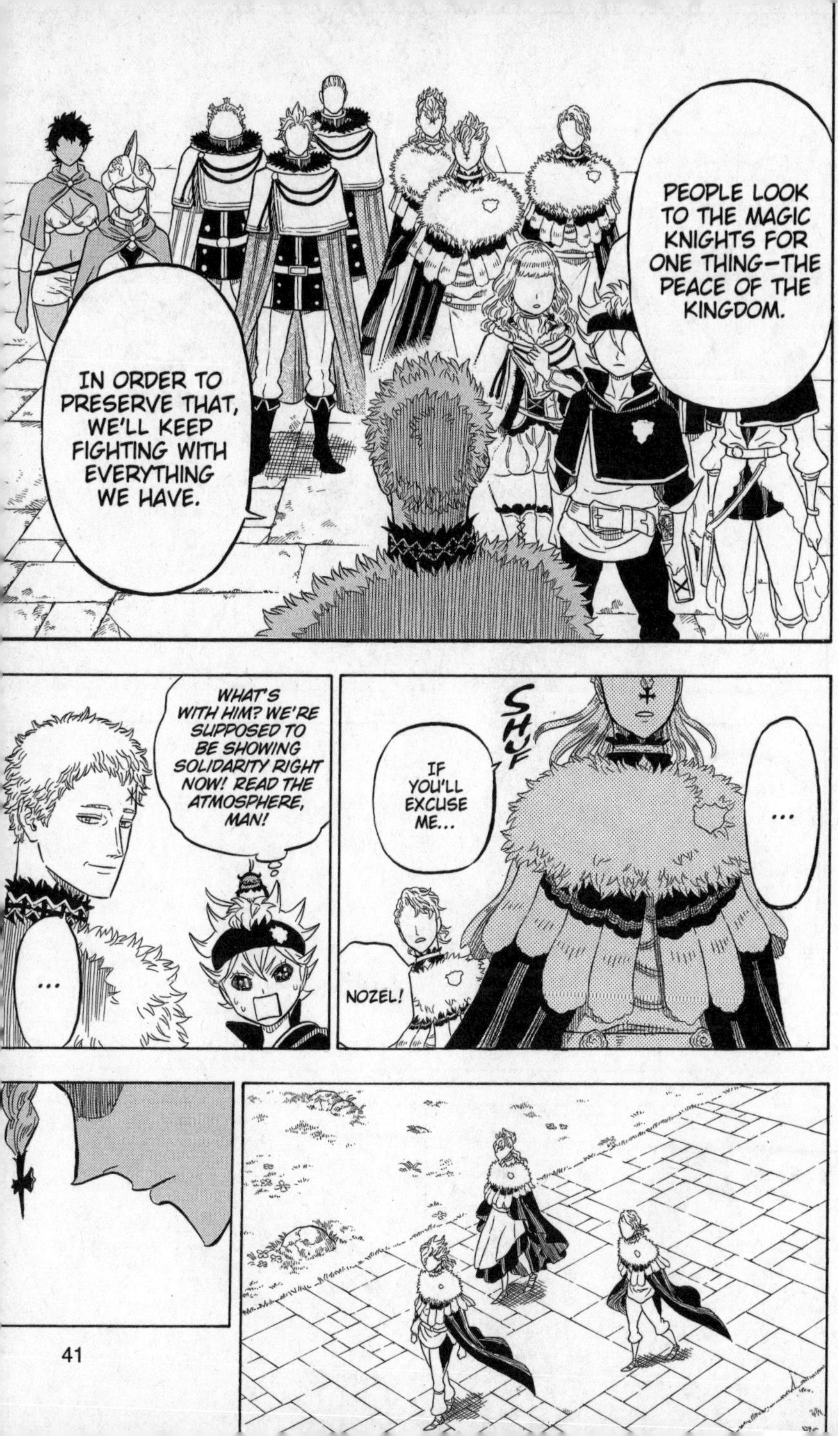
PEOPLE LOOK TO THE MAGIC KNIGHTS FOR ONE THING—THE PEACE OF THE KINGDOM.
IN ORDER TO PRESERVE THAT, WE'LL KEEP FIGHTING WITH EVERYTHING WE HAVE.
...
SHUF
IF YOU'LL EXCUSE ME...
NOZEL!
WHAT'S WITH HIM? WE'RE SUPPOSED TO BE SHOWING SOLIDARITY RIGHT NOW! READ THE ATMOSPHERE, MAN!
...

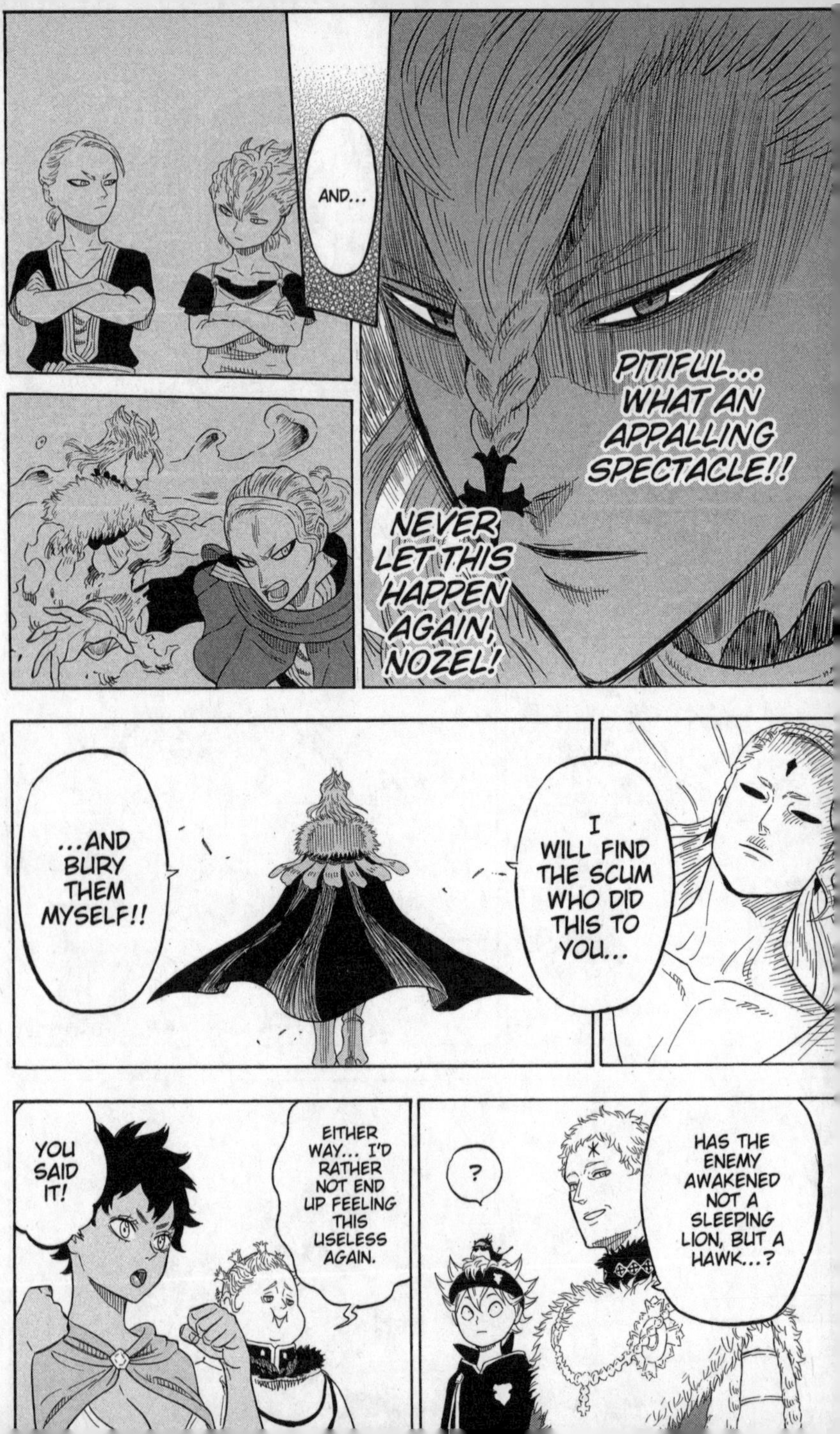
PITIFUL... WHAT AN APPALLING SPECTACLE!!
NEVER LET THIS HAPPEN AGAIN, NOZEL!
AND...
I WILL FIND THE SCUM WHO DID THIS TO YOU...
...AND BURY THEM MYSELF!!
HAS THE ENEMY AWAKENED NOT A SLEEPING LION, BUT A HAWK...?
?
EITHER WAY... I'D RATHER NOT END UP FEELING THIS USELESS AGAIN.
YOU SAID IT!

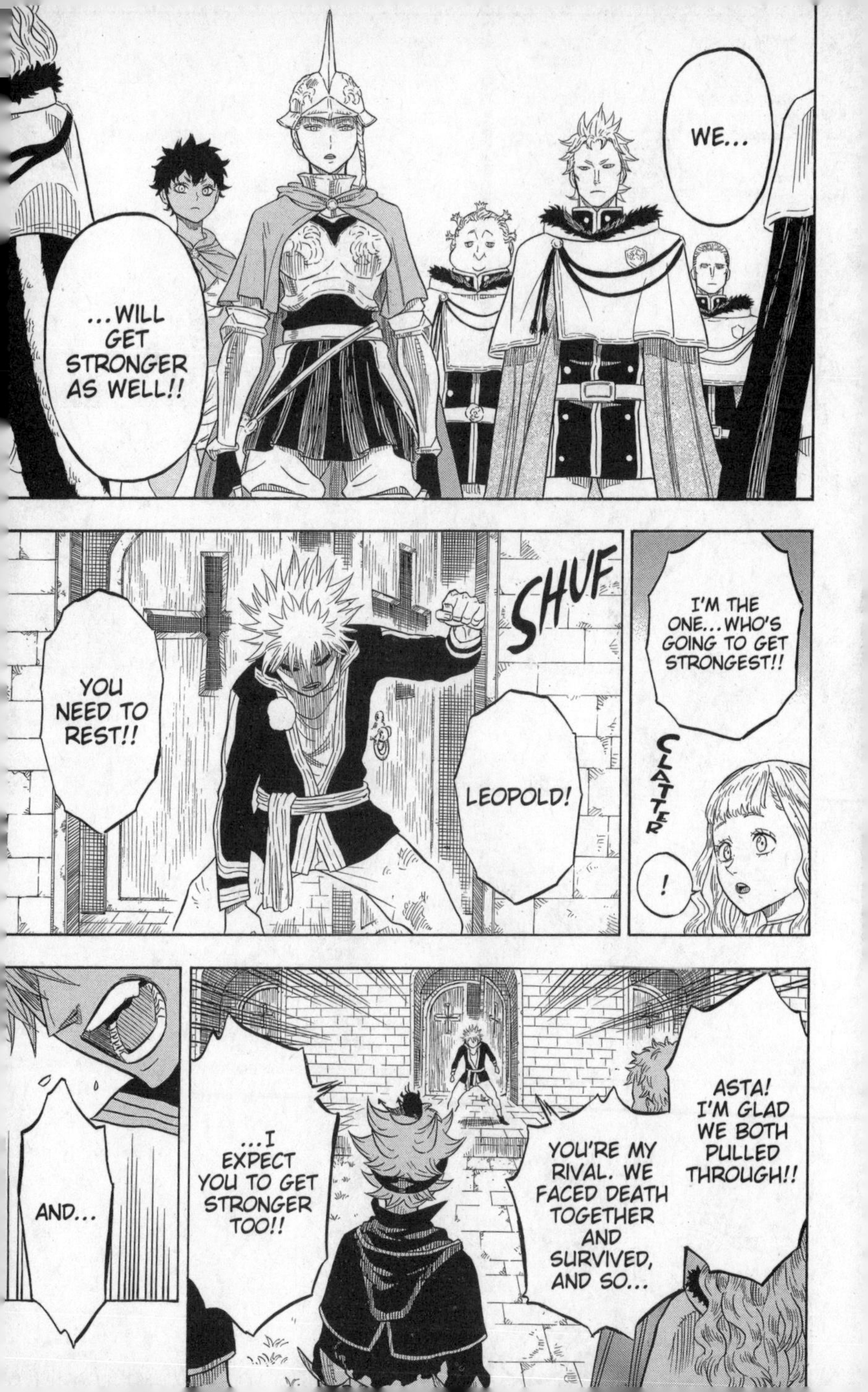
WE...
...WILL GET STRONGER AS WELL!!
I'M THE ONE...WHO'S GOING TO GET STRONGEST!!
CLATTER
!
SHUF
LEOPOLD!
YOU NEED TO REST!!
ASTA! I'M GLAD WE BOTH PULLED THROUGH!!
YOU'RE MY RIVAL. WE FACED DEATH TOGETHER AND SURVIVED, AND SO...
...I EXPECT YOU TO GET STRONGER TOO!!
AND...

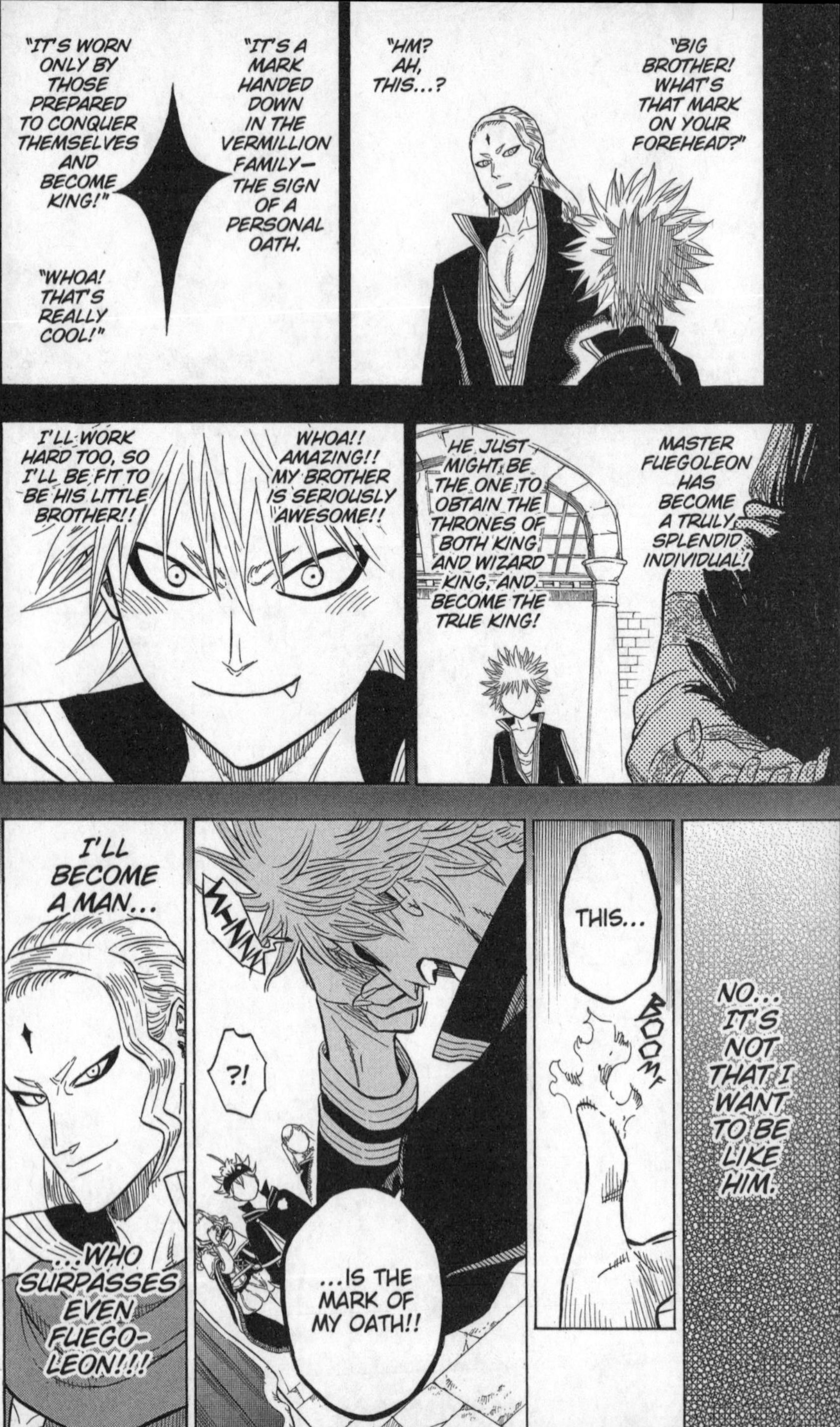
"BIG BROTHER! WHAT'S THAT MARK ON YOUR FOREHEAD?"
"HM? AH, THIS...?
"IT'S A MARK HANDED DOWN IN THE VERMILLION FAMILY—THE SIGN OF A PERSONAL OATH.
"IT'S WORN ONLY BY THOSE PREPARED TO CONQUER THEMSELVES AND BECOME KING!"
"WHOA! THAT'S REALLY COOL!"
MASTER FUEGOLEON HAS BECOME A TRULY SPLENDID INDIVIDUAL!
HE JUST MIGHT BE THE ONE TO OBTAIN THE THRONES OF BOTH KING AND WIZARD KING, AND BECOME THE TRUE KING!
WHOA!! AMAZING!! MY BROTHER IS SERIOUSLY AWESOME!!
I'LL WORK HARD TOO, SO I'LL BE FIT TO BE HIS LITTLE BROTHER!!
NO... IT'S NOT THAT I WANT TO BE LIKE HIM.
THIS...
BOOM
?!
...IS THE MARK OF MY OATH!!
I'LL BECOME A MAN...
...WHO SURPASSES EVEN FUEGO-LEON!!!

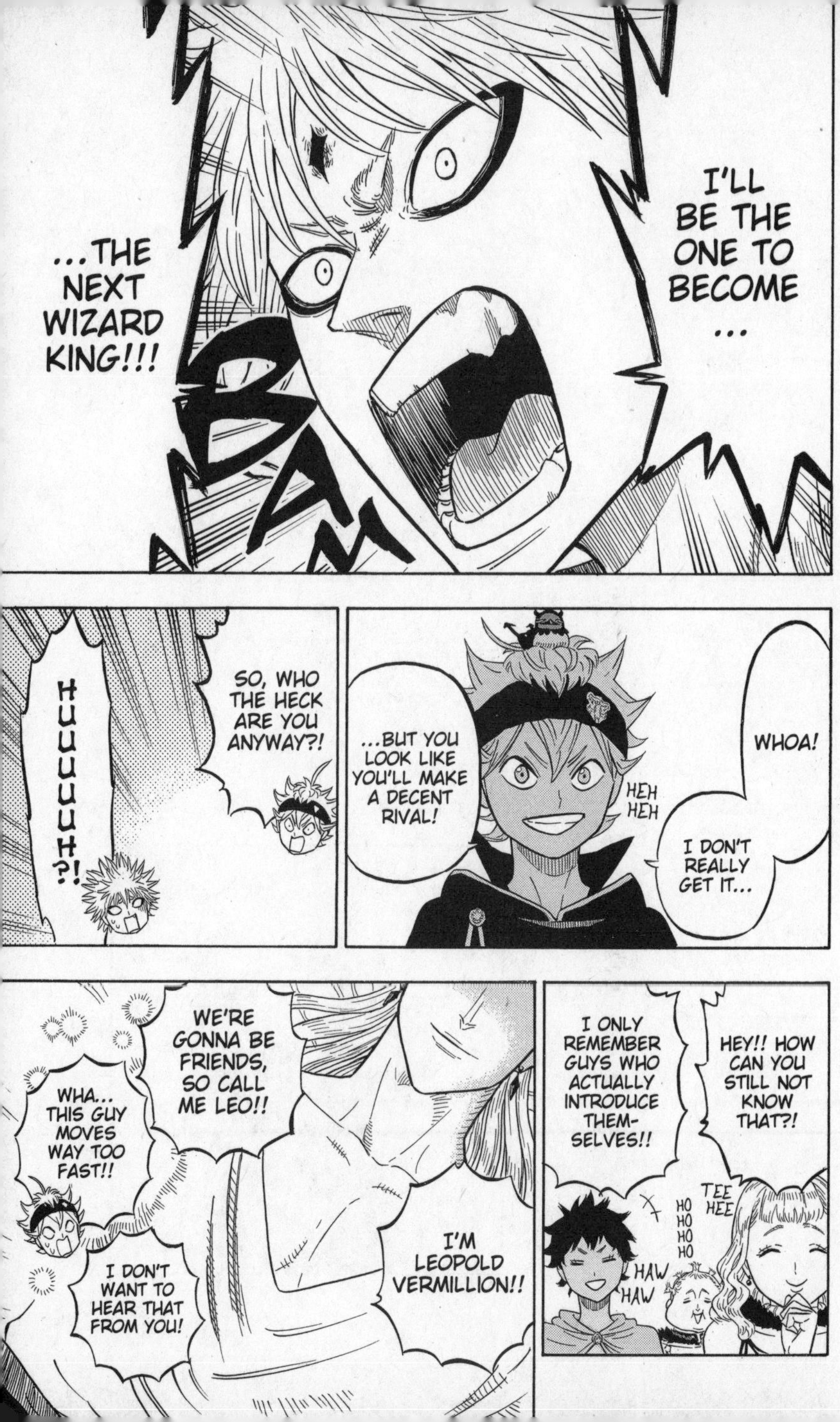
I'LL BE THE ONE TO BECOME ...
BAM
...THE NEXT WIZARD KING!!!
WHOA!
I DON'T REALLY GET IT...
HEH HEH
...BUT YOU LOOK LIKE YOU'LL MAKE A DECENT RIVAL!
SO, WHO THE HECK ARE YOU ANYWAY?!
HUUUUUH?!
HEY!! HOW CAN YOU STILL NOT KNOW THAT?!
I ONLY REMEMBER GUYS WHO ACTUALLY INTRODUCE THEM-SELVES!!
TEE HEE
HO HO HO HO
HAW HAW
I'M LEOPOLD VERMILLION!!
WE'RE GONNA BE FRIENDS, SO CALL ME LEO!!
WHA... THIS GUY MOVES WAY TOO FAST!!
I DON'T WANT TO HEAR THAT FROM YOU!

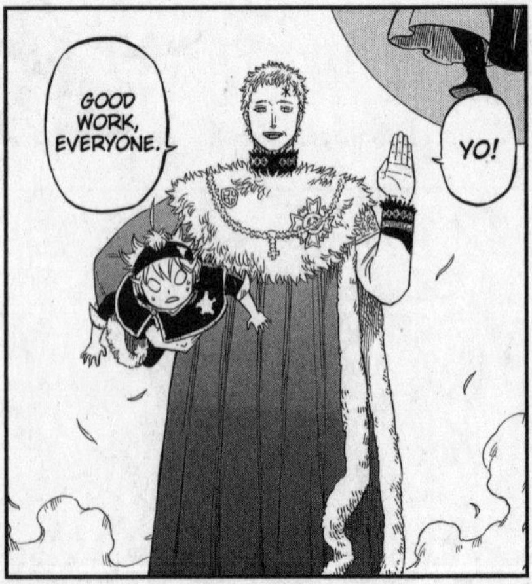
YO!
GOOD WORK, EVERYONE.

Page 37: Next Time We Meet

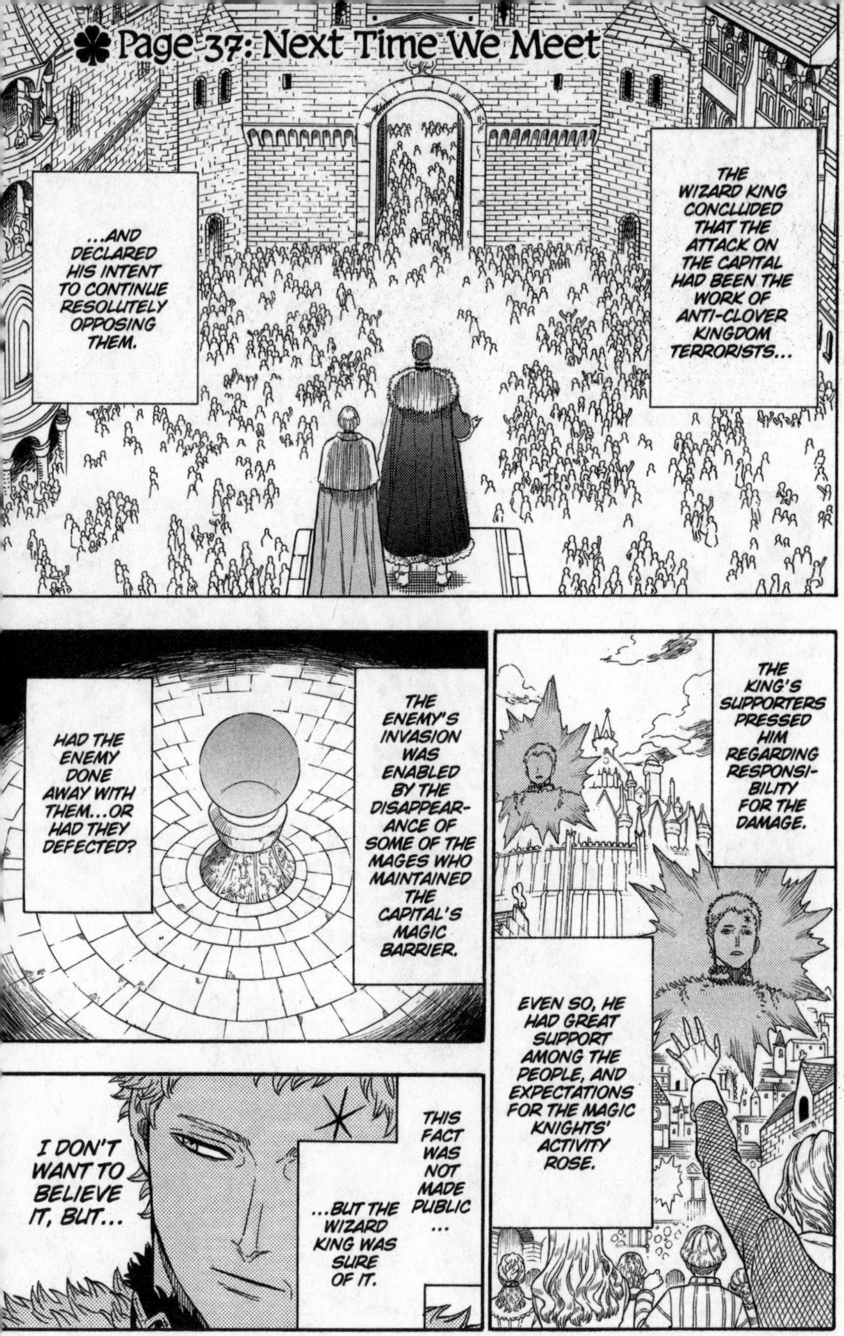
THE WIZARD KING CONCLUDED THAT THE ATTACK ON THE CAPITAL HAD BEEN THE WORK OF ANTI-CLOVER KINGDOM TERRORISTS...
...AND DECLARED HIS INTENT TO CONTINUE RESOLUTELY OPPOSING THEM.
THE KING'S SUPPORTERS PRESSED HIM REGARDING RESPONSI-BILITY FOR THE DAMAGE.
EVEN SO, HE HAD GREAT SUPPORT AMONG THE PEOPLE, AND EXPECTATIONS FOR THE MAGIC KNIGHTS' ACTIVITY ROSE.
THE ENEMY'S INVASION WAS ENABLED BY THE DISAPPEAR-ANCE OF SOME OF THE MAGES WHO MAINTAINED THE CAPITAL'S MAGIC BARRIER.
HAD THE ENEMY DONE AWAY WITH THEM...OR HAD THEY DEFECTED?
THIS FACT WAS NOT MADE PUBLIC...
...BUT THE WIZARD KING WAS SURE OF IT.
I DON'T WANT TO BELIEVE IT, BUT...

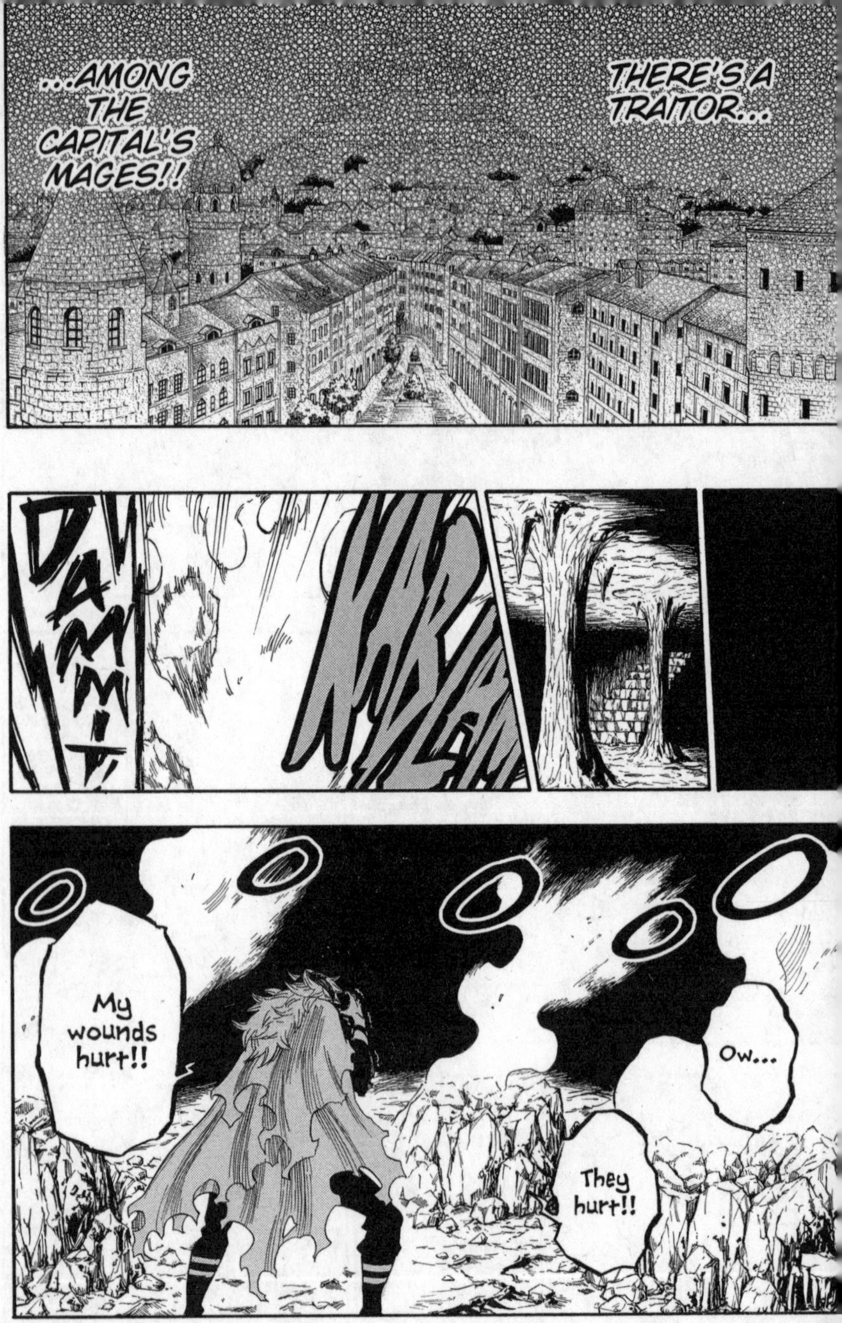
THERE'S A TRAITOR...
...AMONG THE CAPITAL'S MAGES!!
DAMMIT!
Ow...
They hurt!!
My wounds hurt!!

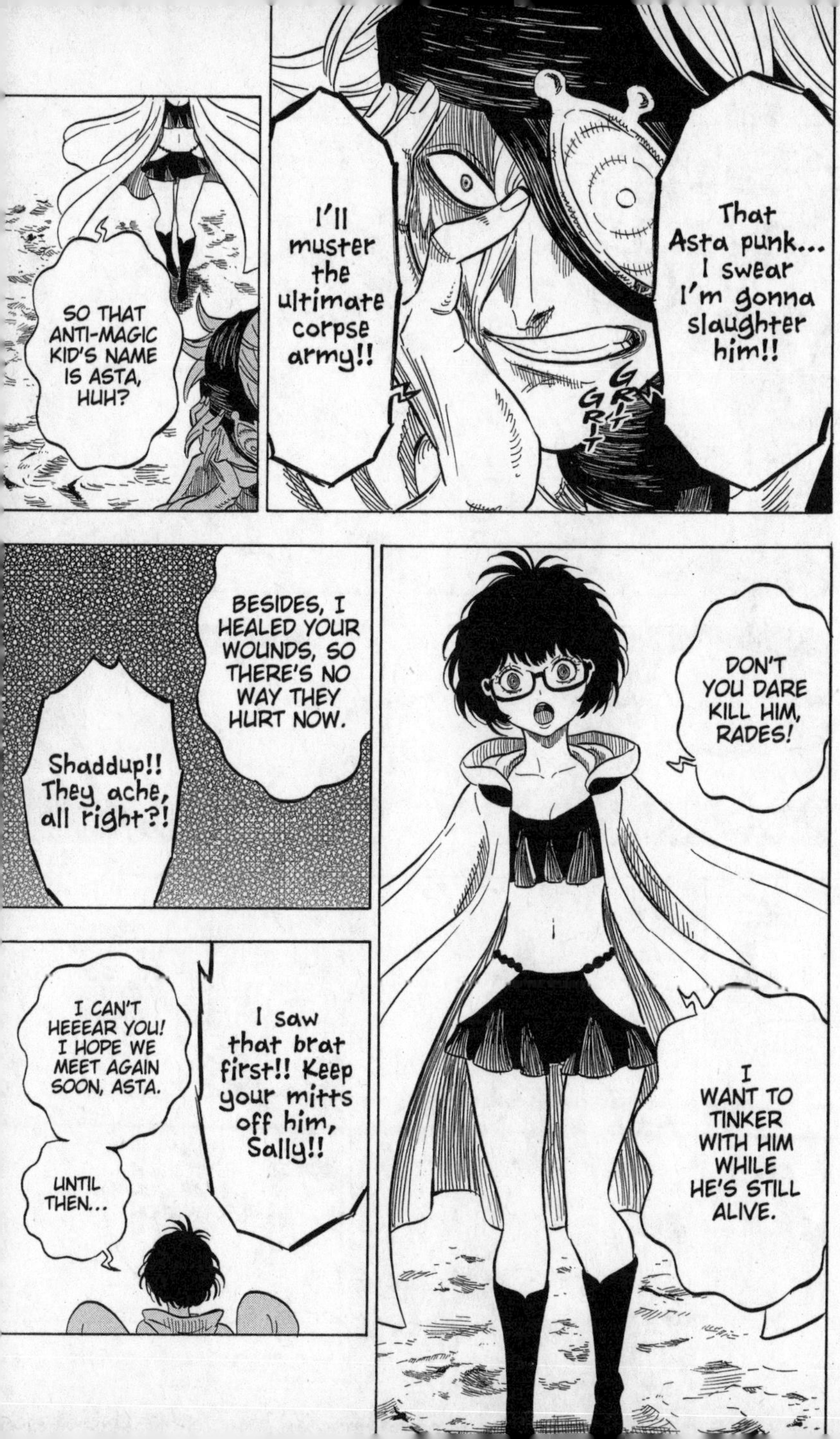

That Asta punk... I swear I'm gonna slaughter him!!
GRIT GRIT
I'll muster the ultimate corpse army!!
SO THAT ANTI-MAGIC KID'S NAME IS ASTA, HUH?
DON'T YOU DARE KILL HIM, RADES!
I WANT TO TINKER WITH HIM WHILE HE'S STILL ALIVE.
BESIDES, I HEALED YOUR WOUNDS, SO THERE'S NO WAY THEY HURT NOW.
Shaddup!! They ache, all right?!
I saw that brat first!! Keep your mitts off him, Sally!!
I CAN'T HEEEAR YOU! I HOPE WE MEET AGAIN SOON, ASTA.
UNTIL THEN...

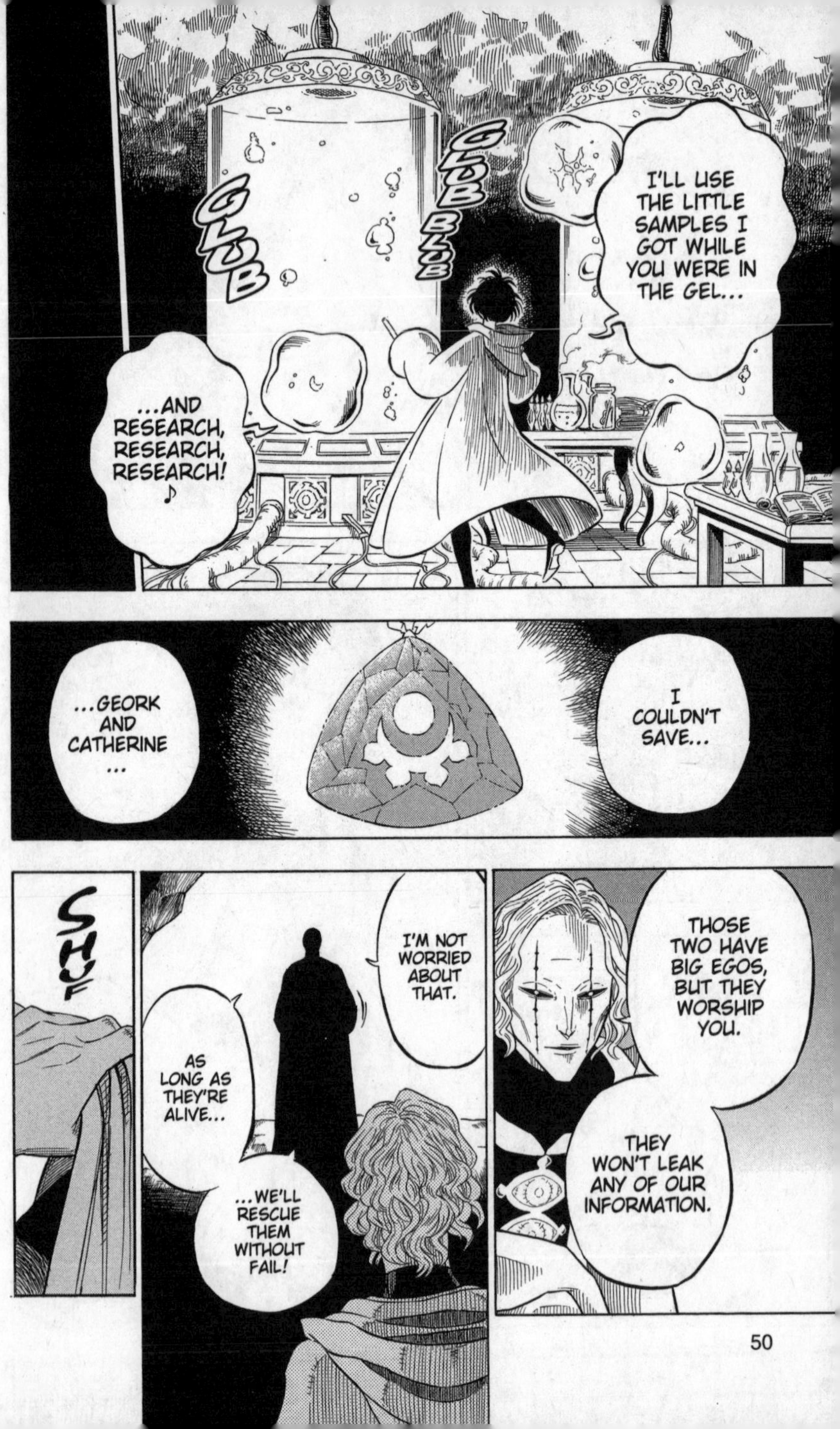
I'LL USE THE LITTLE SAMPLES I GOT WHILE YOU WERE IN THE GEL...
GLUB BLUB
GLUB
...AND RESEARCH, RESEARCH, RESEARCH! ♪
I COULDN'T SAVE...
...GEORK AND CATHERINE ...
THOSE TWO HAVE BIG EGOS, BUT THEY WORSHIP YOU.
THEY WON'T LEAK ANY OF OUR INFORMATION.
I'M NOT WORRIED ABOUT THAT.
AS LONG AS THEY'RE ALIVE...
...WE'LL RESCUE THEM WITHOUT FAIL!
SHUF

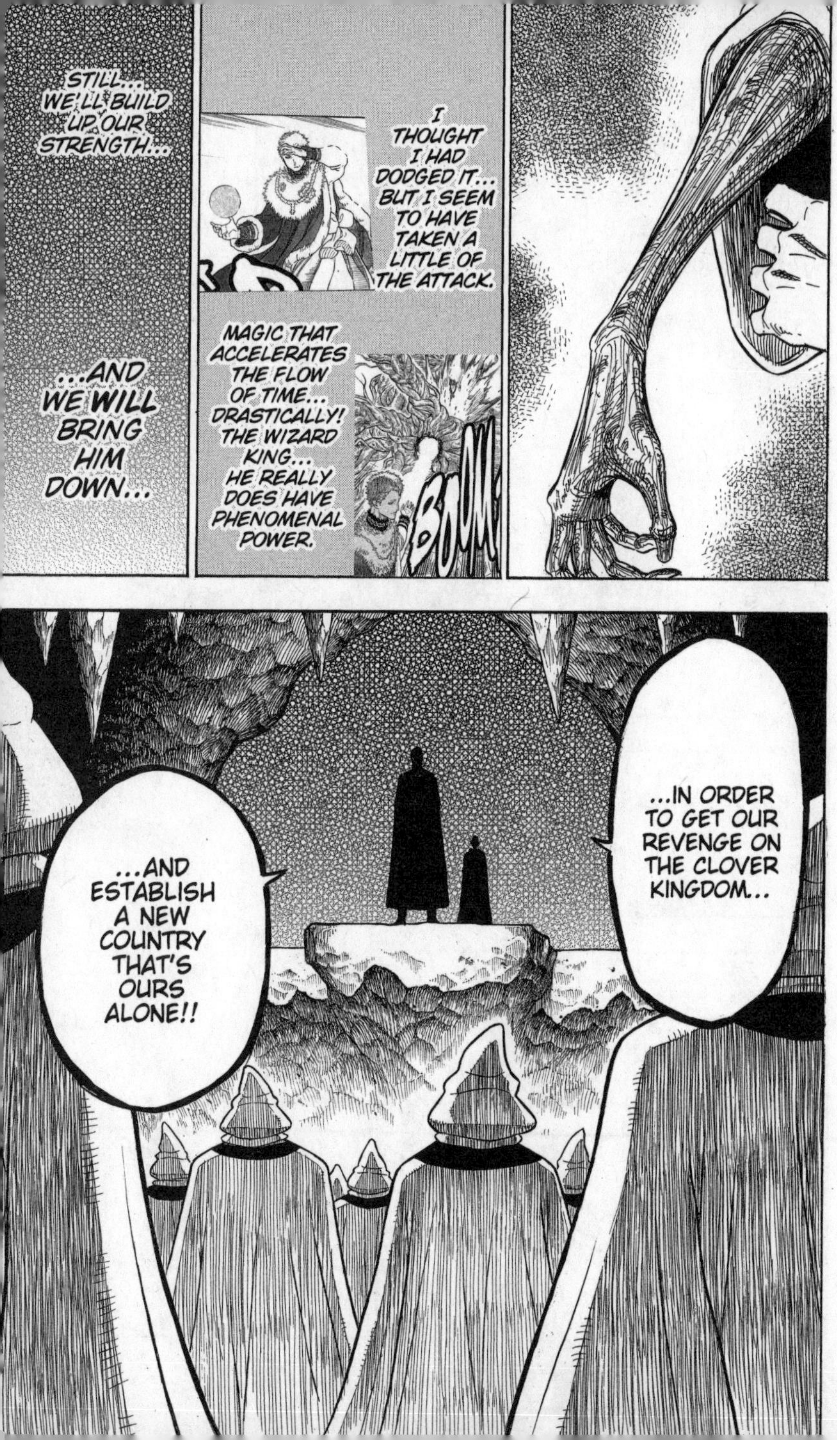
I THOUGHT I HAD DODGED IT... BUT I SEEM TO HAVE TAKEN A LITTLE OF THE ATTACK.
MAGIC THAT ACCELERATES THE FLOW OF TIME... DRASTICALLY! THE WIZARD KING... HE REALLY DOES HAVE PHENOMENAL POWER.
BOOM
STILL... WE'LL BUILD UP OUR STRENGTH...
...AND WE WILL BRING HIM DOWN...
...IN ORDER TO GET OUR REVENGE ON THE CLOVER KINGDOM...
...AND ESTABLISH A NEW COUNTRY THAT'S OURS ALONE!!

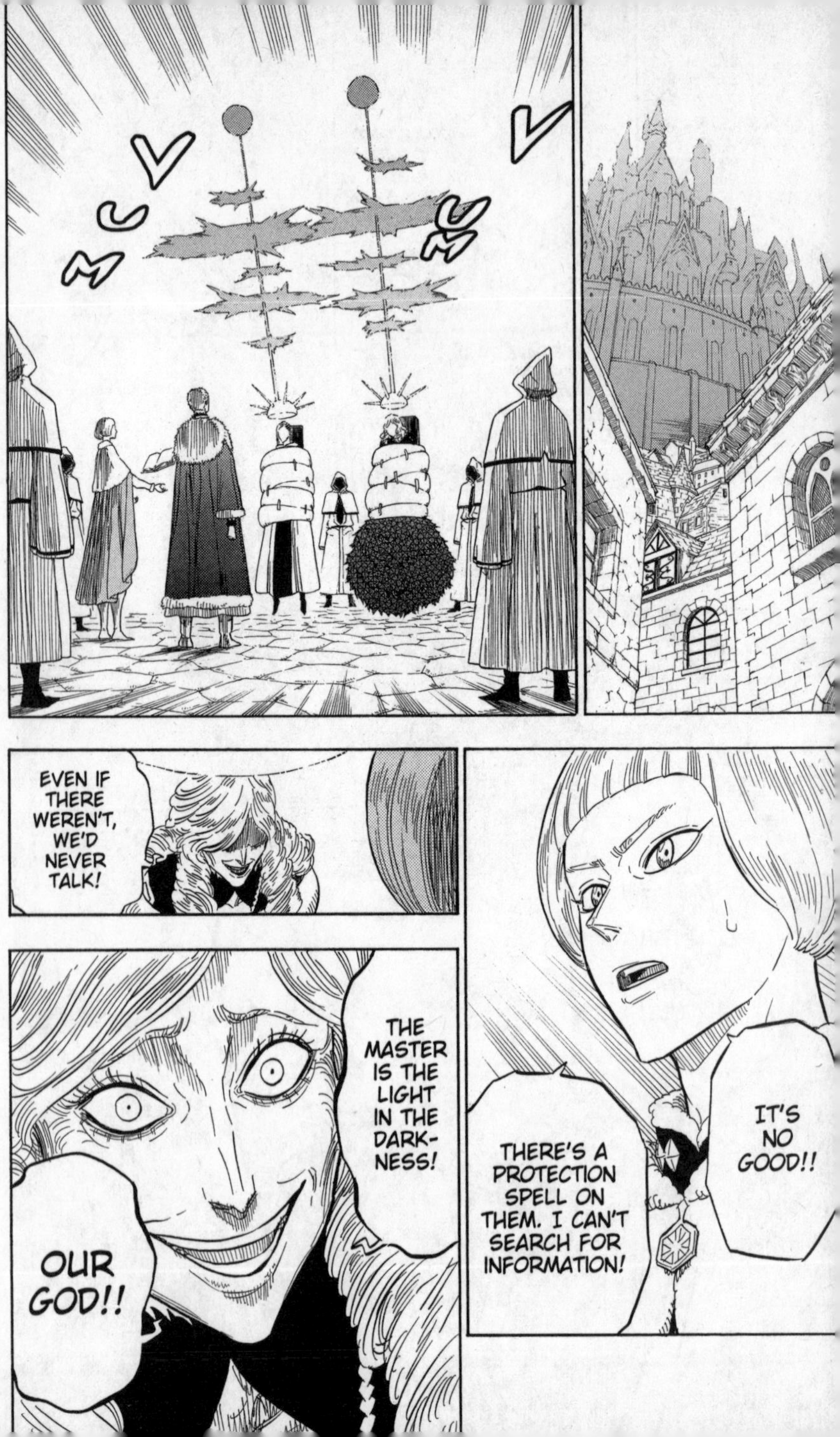
VUM
VUM
IT'S NO GOOD!!
THERE'S A PROTECTION SPELL ON THEM. I CAN'T SEARCH FOR INFORMATION!
EVEN IF THERE WEREN'T, WE'D NEVER TALK!
THE MASTER IS THE LIGHT IN THE DARK-NESS!
OUR GOD!!

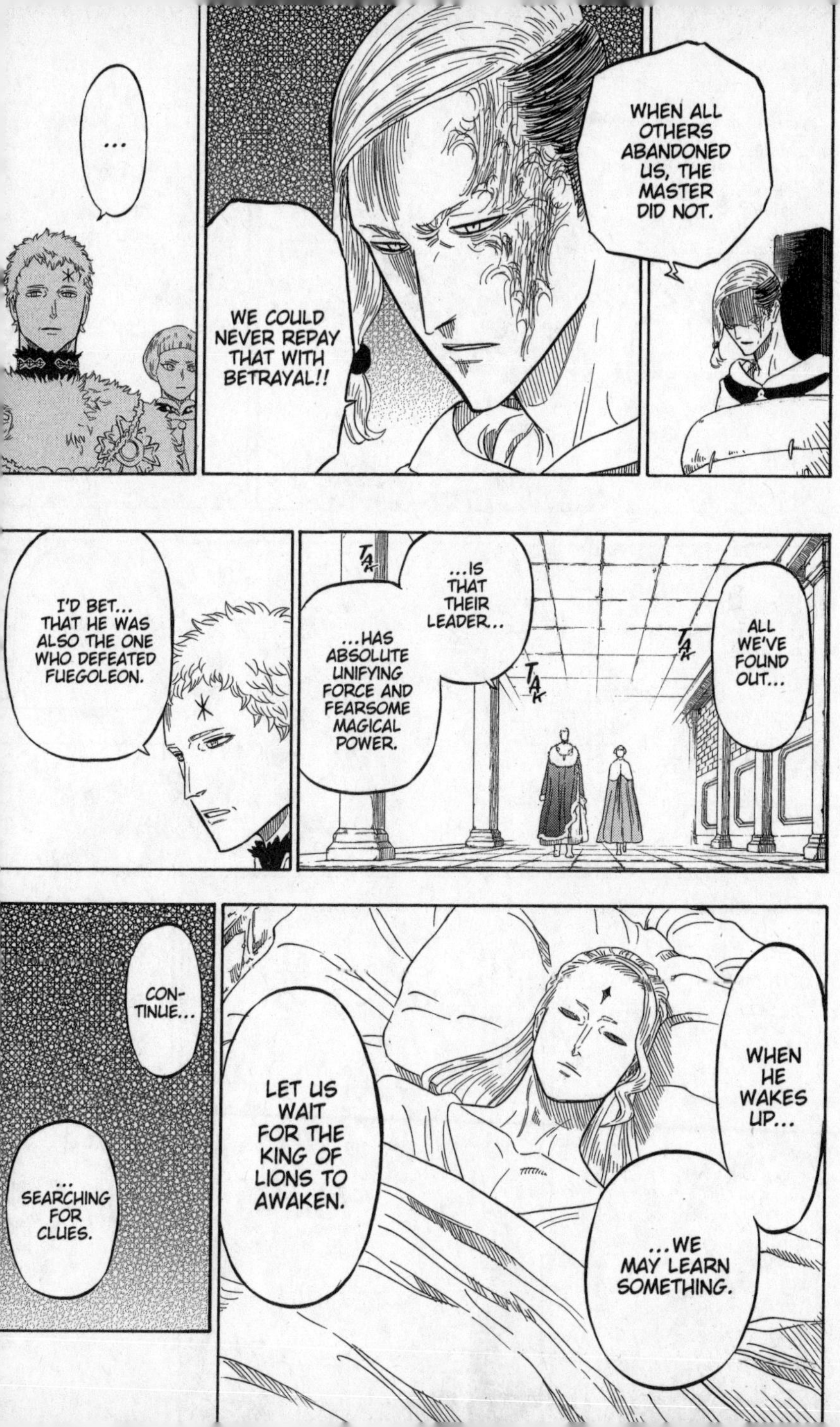
WHEN ALL OTHERS ABANDONED US, THE MASTER DID NOT.
WE COULD NEVER REPAY THAT WITH BETRAYAL!!
...
ALL WE'VE FOUND OUT...
TAK
TAK
...IS THAT THEIR LEADER...
...HAS ABSOLUTE UNIFYING FORCE AND FEARSOME MAGICAL POWER.
TAK
I'D BET... THAT HE WAS ALSO THE ONE WHO DEFEATED FUEGOLEON.
WHEN HE WAKES UP...
...WE MAY LEARN SOMETHING.
LET US WAIT FOR THE KING OF LIONS TO AWAKEN.
CON-TINUE...
... SEARCHING FOR CLUES.

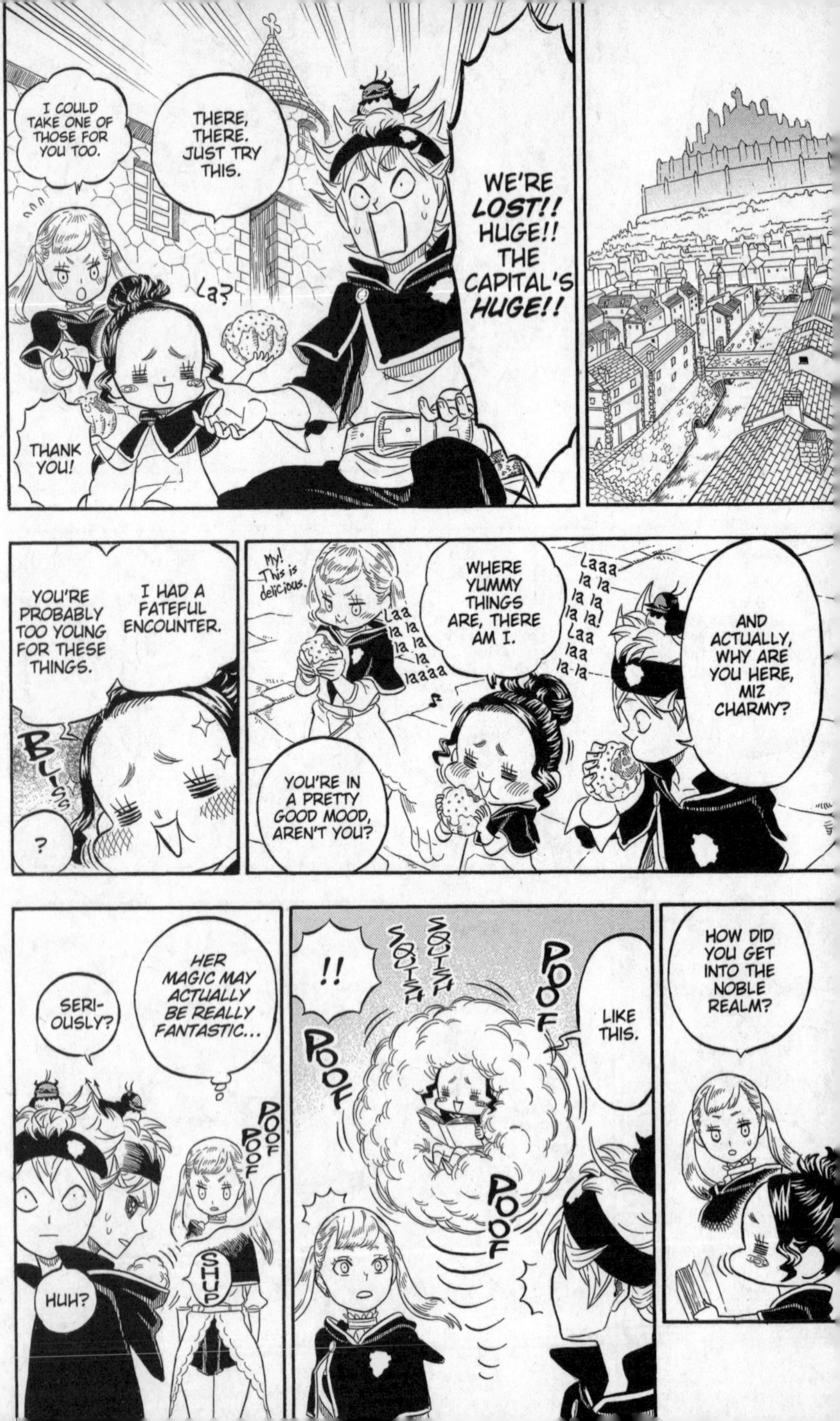
WE'RE *LOST!!* HUGE!! THE CAPITAL'S *HUGE!!*
THERE, THERE. JUST TRY THIS.
I COULD TAKE ONE OF THOSE FOR YOU TOO.
La?
THANK YOU!
AND ACTUALLY, WHY ARE YOU HERE, MIZ CHARMY?
WHERE YUMMY THINGS ARE, THERE AM I.
Laaa la la la la la la! Laa laa la-la
Laa la la la la la laaaa
My! This is delicious.
YOU'RE IN A PRETTY GOOD MOOD, AREN'T YOU?
I HAD A FATEFUL ENCOUNTER.
YOU'RE PROBABLY TOO YOUNG FOR THESE THINGS.
BLISS
?
HOW DID YOU GET INTO THE NOBLE REALM?
LIKE THIS.
POOF
SQUISH SQUISH
!!
POOF
POOF
HER MAGIC MAY ACTUALLY BE REALLY FANTASTIC...
SERI-OUSLY?
POOF POOF
SHUP
HUH?

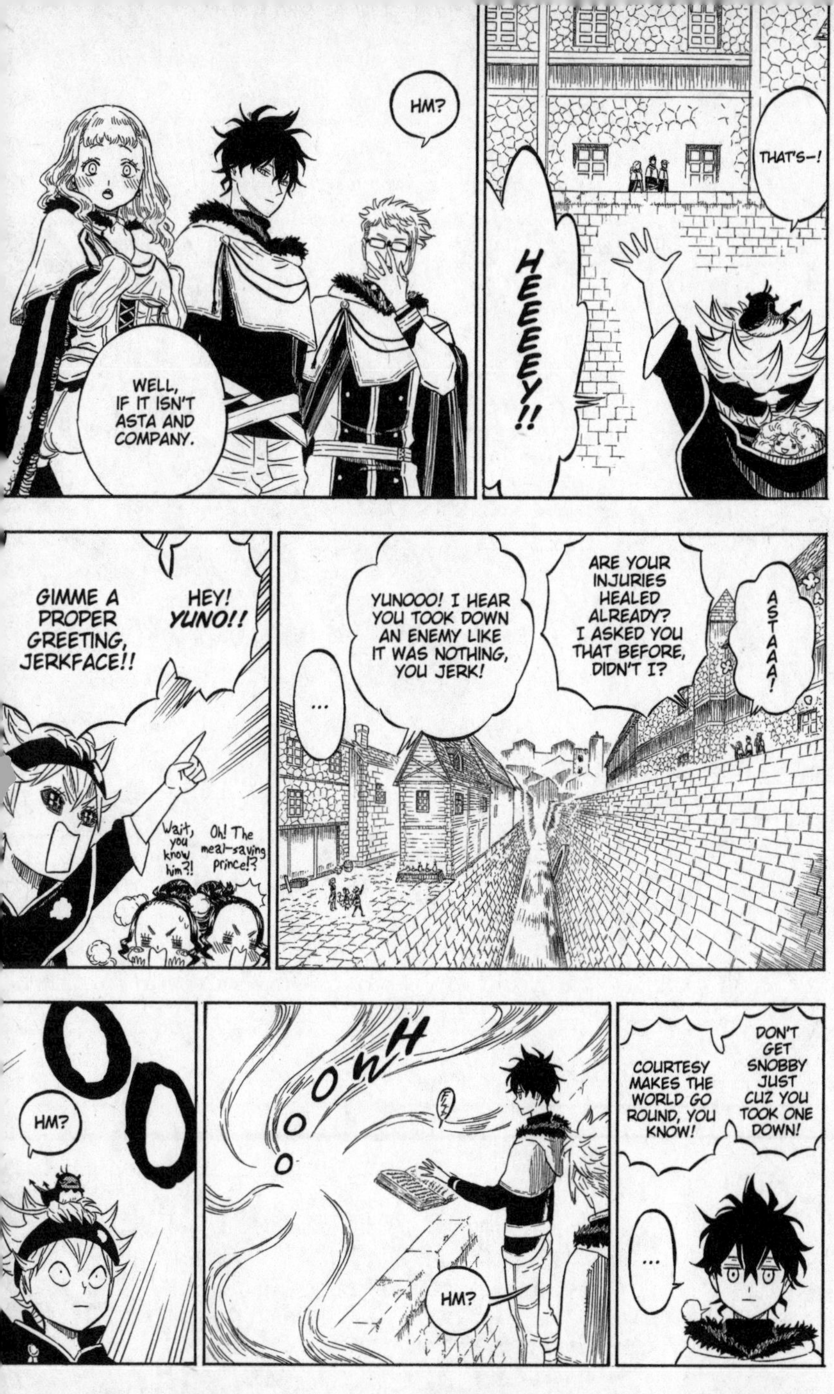
THAT'S—!
HEEEEEY!!
HM?
WELL, IF IT ISN'T ASTA AND COMPANY.
ASTAAA!
ARE YOUR INJURIES HEALED ALREADY? I ASKED YOU THAT BEFORE, DIDN'T I?
YUNOOO! I HEAR YOU TOOK DOWN AN ENEMY LIKE IT WAS NOTHING, YOU JERK!
...
HEY! YUNO!!
GIMME A PROPER GREETING, JERKFACE!!
Oh! The meal-saving prince!?
Wait, you know him?!
DON'T GET SNOBBY JUST CUZ YOU TOOK ONE DOWN!
COURTESY MAKES THE WORLD GO ROUND, YOU KNOW!
...
OOOWH
HM?
HM?

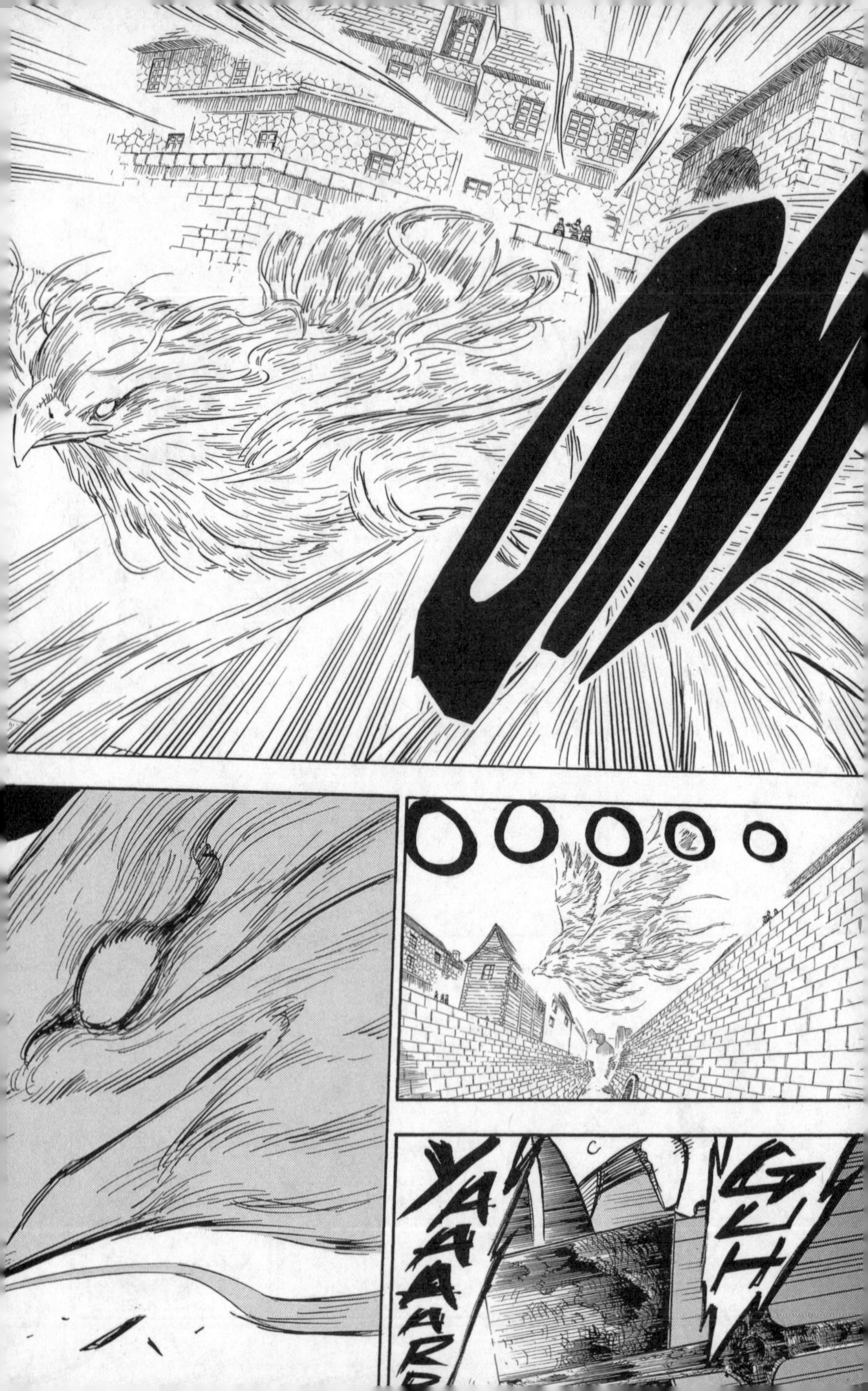
OOOOO
GUH
YAAAAR

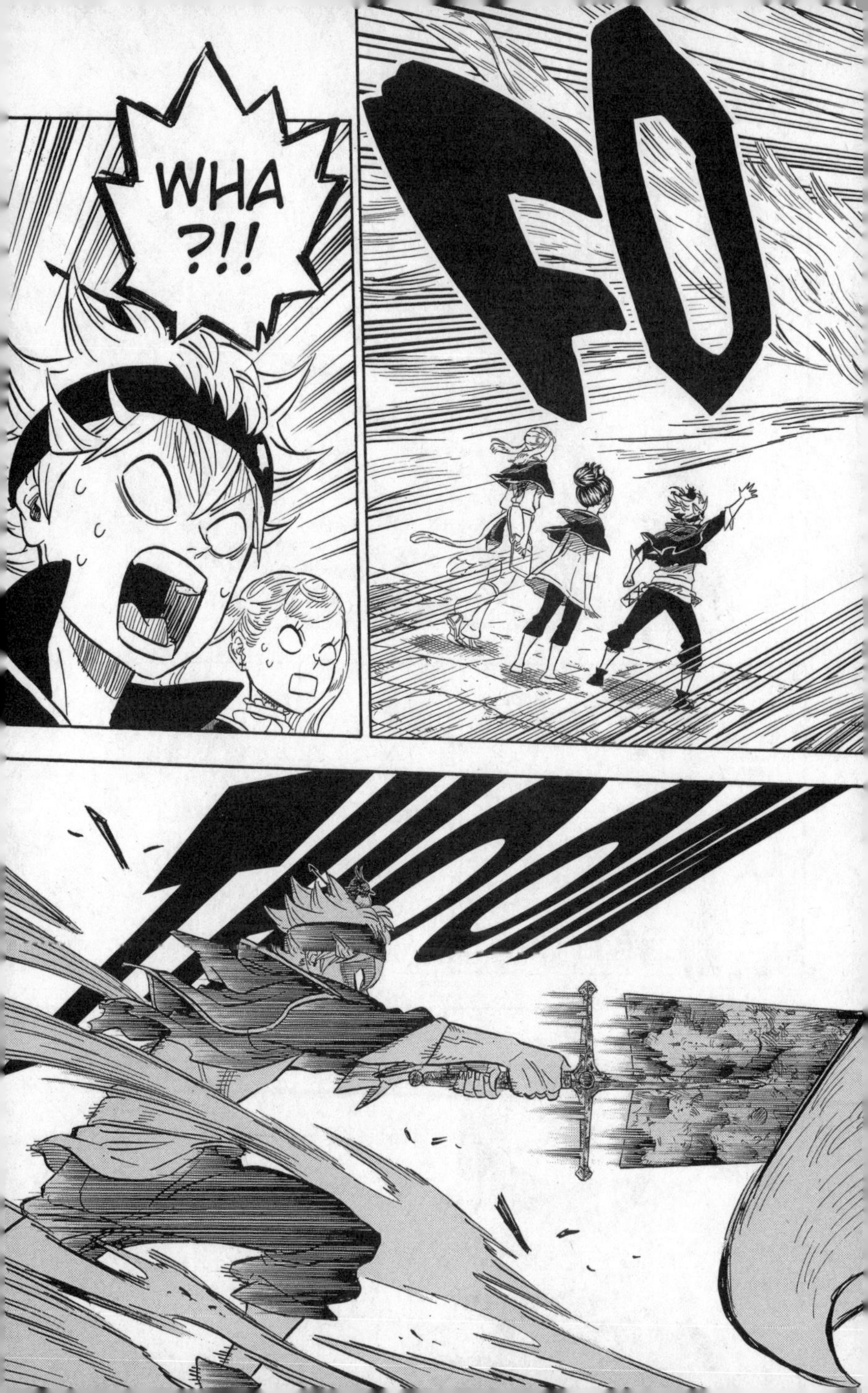
WHA ?!!

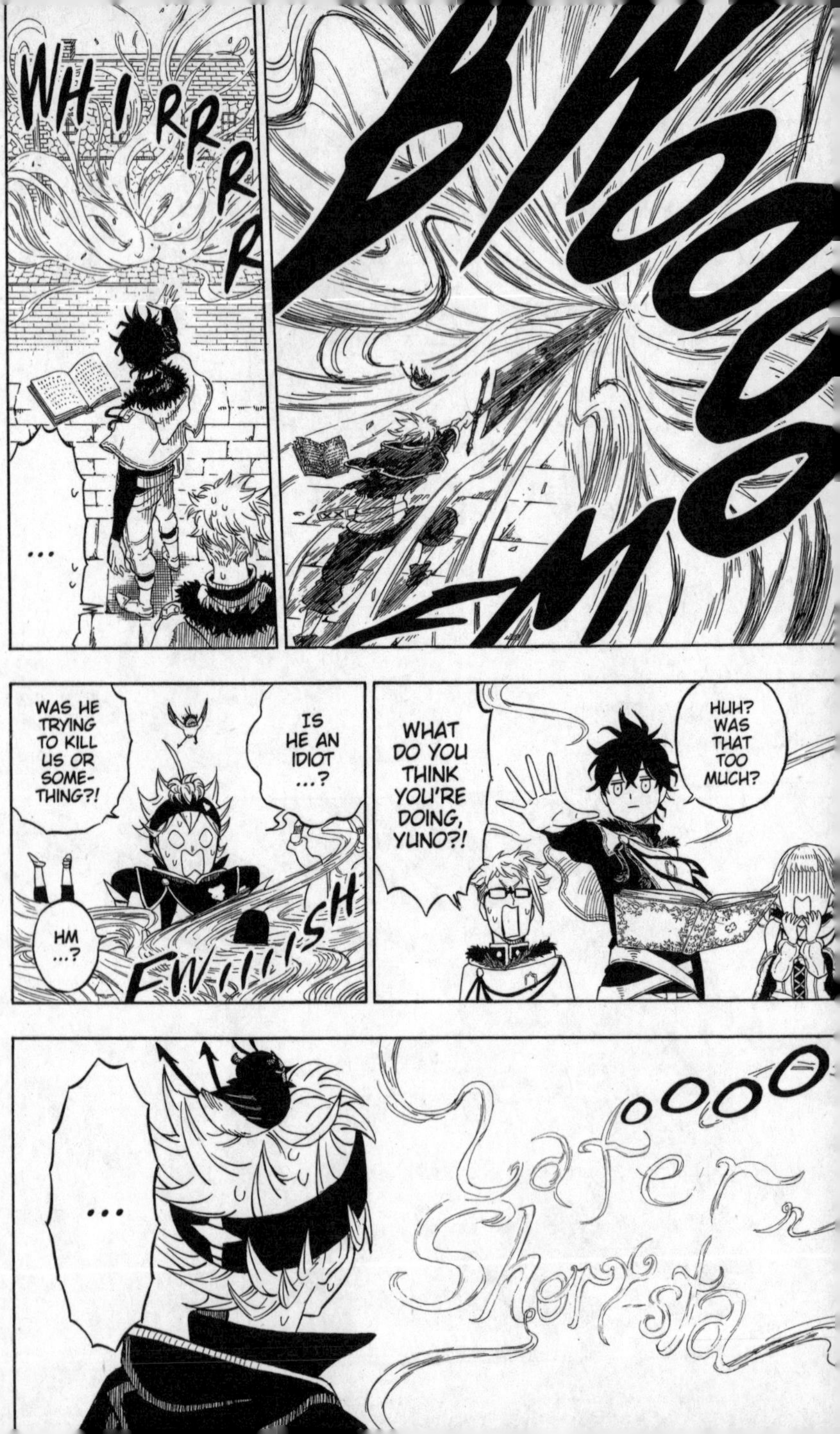
BWOOOOM
WHIRRRR
...
HUH? WAS THAT TOO MUCH?
WHAT DO YOU THINK YOU'RE DOING, YUNO?!
IS HE AN IDIOT ...?
WAS HE TRYING TO KILL US OR SOMETHING?!
HM ...?
FWIIIISH
OOOOO
Laterr
Shorr-sta
...

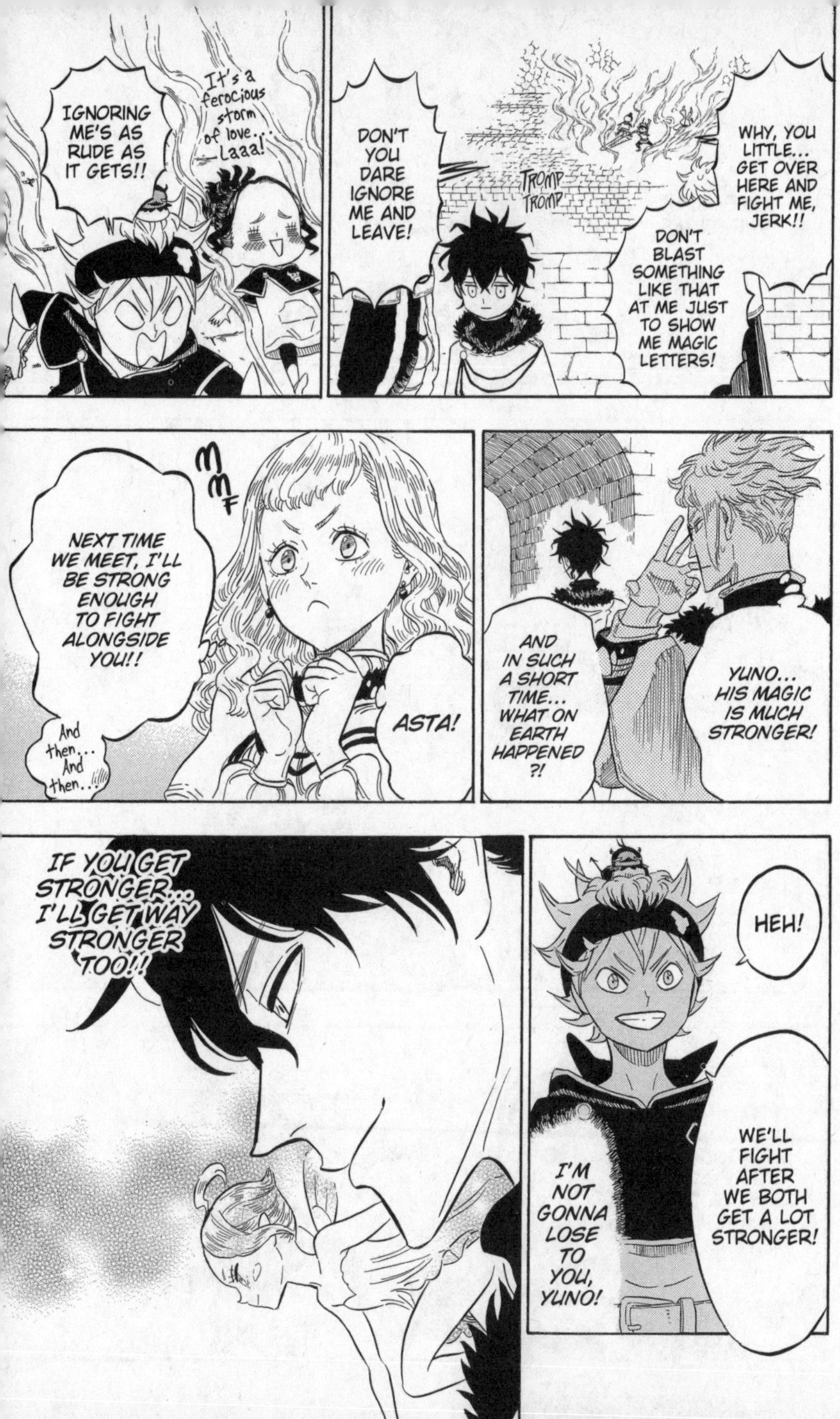
WHY, YOU LITTLE... GET OVER HERE AND FIGHT ME, JERK!!
DON'T BLAST SOMETHING LIKE THAT AT ME JUST TO SHOW ME MAGIC LETTERS!
TROMP TROMP
DON'T YOU DARE IGNORE ME AND LEAVE!
IGNORING ME'S AS RUDE AS IT GETS!!
It's a ferocious storm of love... Laaa!
YUNO... HIS MAGIC IS MUCH STRONGER!
AND IN SUCH A SHORT TIME... WHAT ON EARTH HAPPENED?!
ASTA!
MMF
NEXT TIME WE MEET, I'LL BE STRONG ENOUGH TO FIGHT ALONGSIDE YOU!!
And then... And then...
HEH!
WE'LL FIGHT AFTER WE BOTH GET A LOT STRONGER!
I'M NOT GONNA LOSE TO YOU, YUNO!
IF YOU GET STRONGER... I'LL GET WAY STRONGER TOO!!

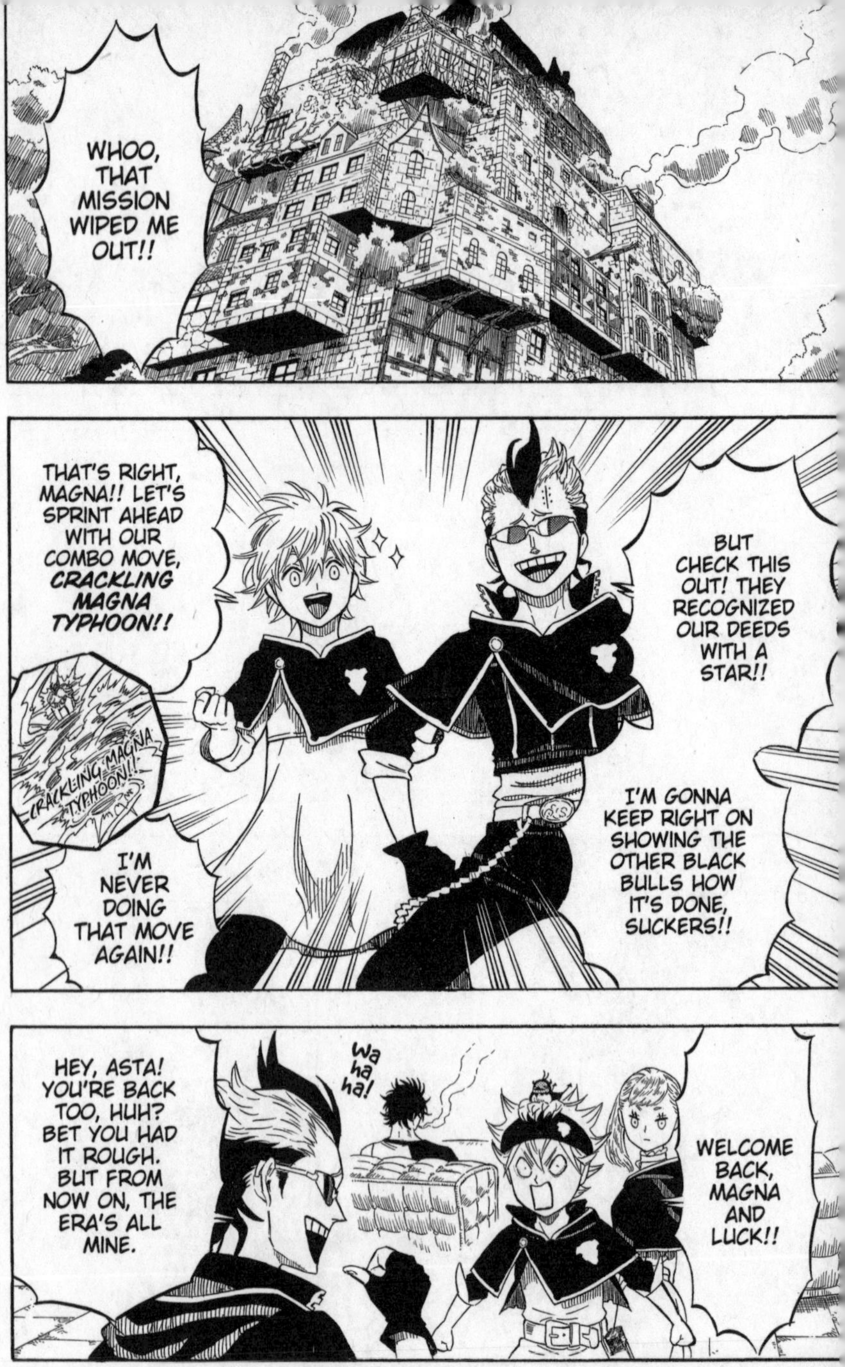
WHOO, THAT MISSION WIPED ME OUT!!
BUT CHECK THIS OUT! THEY RECOGNIZED OUR DEEDS WITH A STAR!!
THAT'S RIGHT, MAGNA!! LET'S SPRINT AHEAD WITH OUR COMBO MOVE, ***CRACKLING MAGNA TYPHOON!!***
I'M GONNA KEEP RIGHT ON SHOWING THE OTHER BLACK BULLS HOW IT'S DONE, SUCKERS!!
CRACKLING MAGNA TYPHOON!!
I'M NEVER DOING THAT MOVE AGAIN!!
WELCOME BACK, MAGNA AND LUCK!!
Wa ha ha!
HEY, ASTA! YOU'RE BACK TOO, HUH? BET YOU HAD IT ROUGH. BUT FROM NOW ON, THE ERA'S ALL MINE.

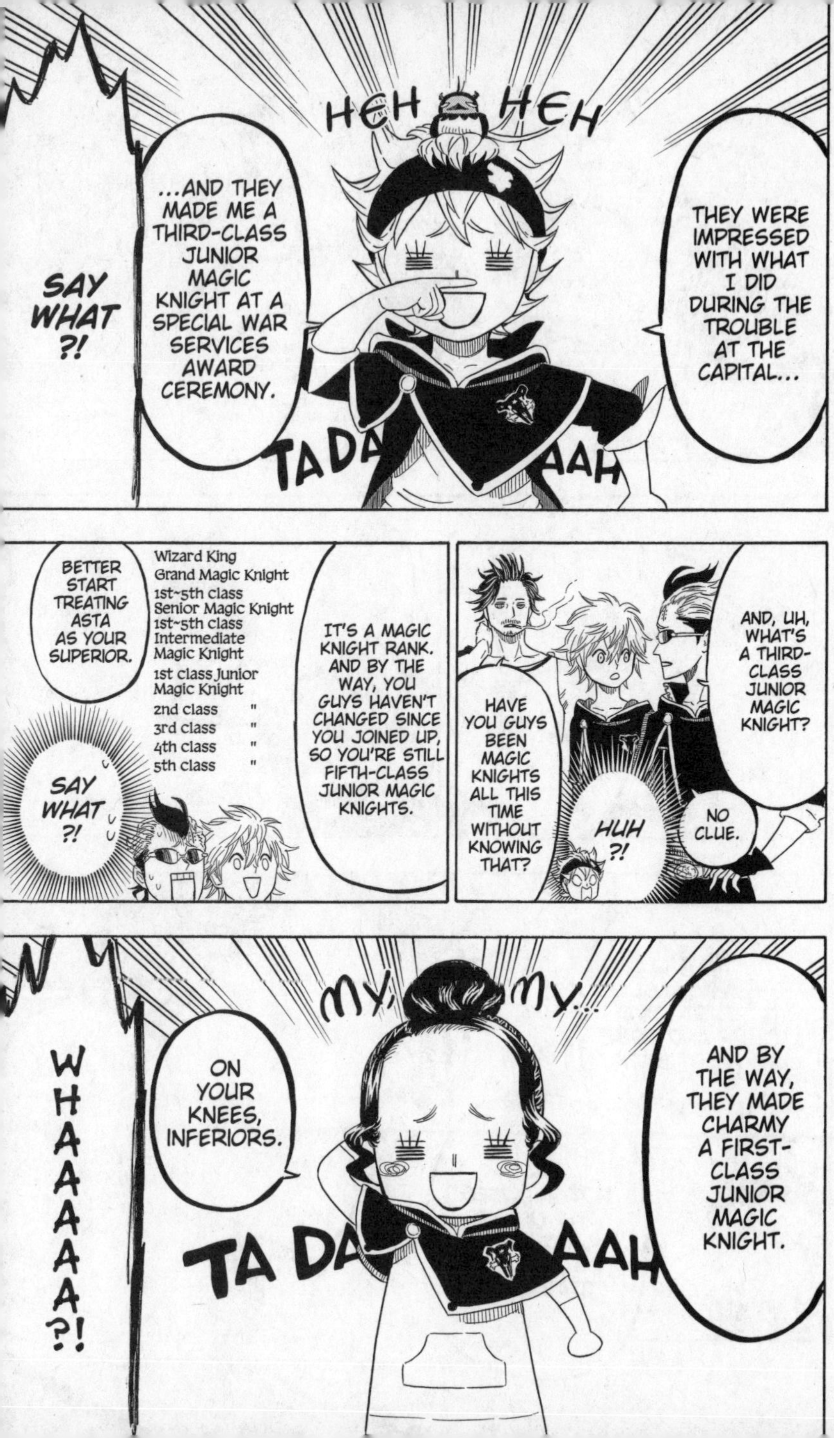
THEY WERE IMPRESSED WITH WHAT I DID DURING THE TROUBLE AT THE CAPITAL...
HEH HEH
...AND THEY MADE ME A THIRD-CLASS JUNIOR MAGIC KNIGHT AT A SPECIAL WAR SERVICES AWARD CEREMONY.
TA DA AAH
SAY WHAT ?!
AND, UH, WHAT'S A THIRD-CLASS JUNIOR MAGIC KNIGHT?
NO CLUE.
HAVE YOU GUYS BEEN MAGIC KNIGHTS ALL THIS TIME WITHOUT KNOWING THAT?
HUH ?!
IT'S A MAGIC KNIGHT RANK. AND BY THE WAY, YOU GUYS HAVEN'T CHANGED SINCE YOU JOINED UP, SO YOU'RE STILL FIFTH-CLASS JUNIOR MAGIC KNIGHTS.
Wizard King
Grand Magic Knight
1st~5th class Senior Magic Knight
1st~5th class Intermediate Magic Knight
1st class Junior Magic Knight
2nd class "
3rd class "
4th class "
5th class "
BETTER START TREATING ASTA AS YOUR SUPERIOR.
SAY WHAT ?!
AND BY THE WAY, THEY MADE CHARMY A FIRST-CLASS JUNIOR MAGIC KNIGHT.
MY, MY...
ON YOUR KNEES, INFERIORS.
TA DA AAH
WHAAAAAA ?!

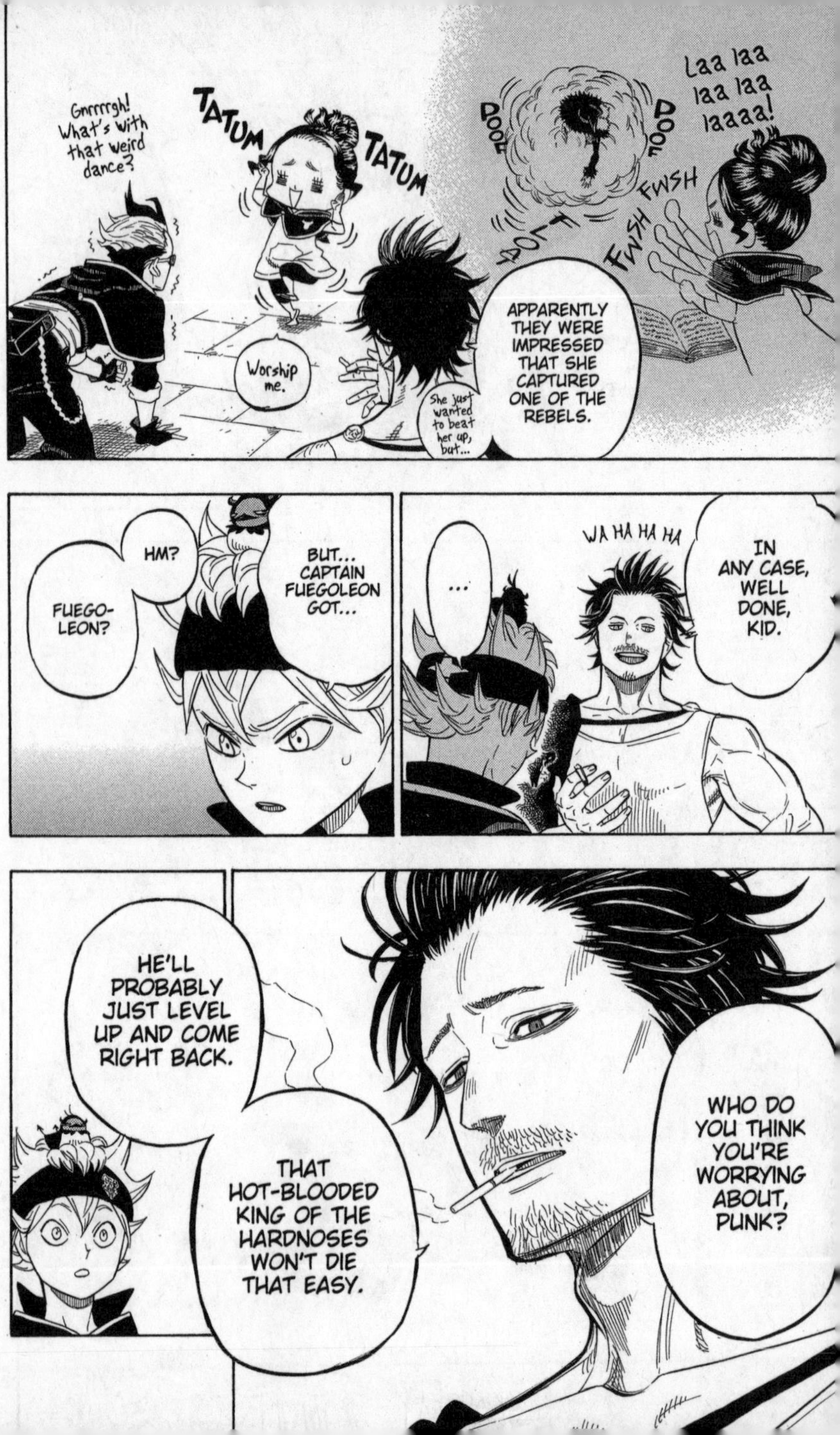
Laa laa laa laa laaaa!
FWSH FWSH
DOOF DOOF
JOLT
APPARENTLY THEY WERE IMPRESSED THAT SHE CAPTURED ONE OF THE REBELS.
She just wanted to beat her up, but...
TATUM TATUM
Worship me.
Gnrrrrgh! What's with that weird dance?
IN ANY CASE, WELL DONE, KID.
WA HA HA HA
...
BUT... CAPTAIN FUEGOLEON GOT...
HM?
FUEGO-LEON?
WHO DO YOU THINK YOU'RE WORRYING ABOUT, PUNK?
THAT HOT-BLOODED KING OF THE HARDNOSES WON'T DIE THAT EASY.
HE'LL PROBABLY JUST LEVEL UP AND COME RIGHT BACK.

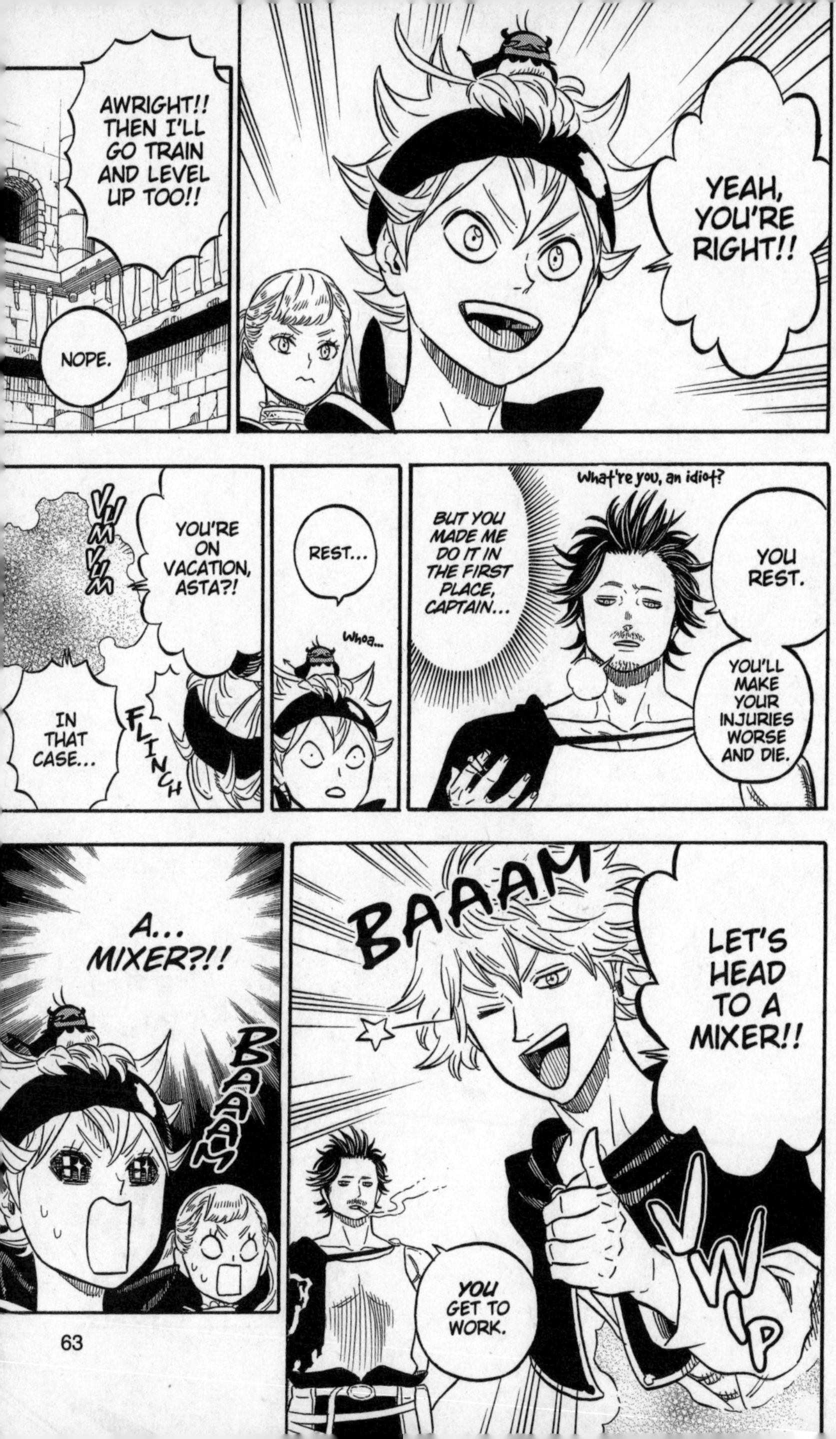
YEAH, YOU'RE RIGHT!!
AWRIGHT!! THEN I'LL GO TRAIN AND LEVEL UP TOO!!
NOPE.
What're you, an idiot?
YOU REST.
BUT YOU MADE ME DO IT IN THE FIRST PLACE, CAPTAIN...
YOU'LL MAKE YOUR INJURIES WORSE AND DIE.
REST...
Whoa...
YOU'RE ON VACATION, ASTA?!
VMMVMM
FLINCH
IN THAT CASE...
BAAAM
LET'S HEAD TO A MIXER!!
VWIP
YOU GET TO WORK.
A... MIXER?!!
BAAAM

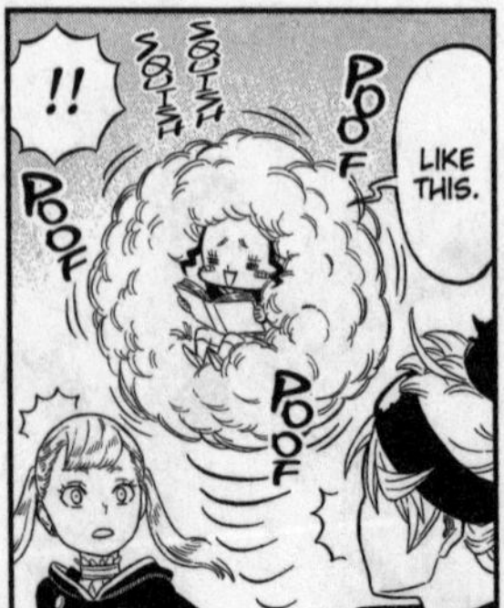
LIKE THIS.
POOF
SQUISH SQUISH
!!
POOF
POOF

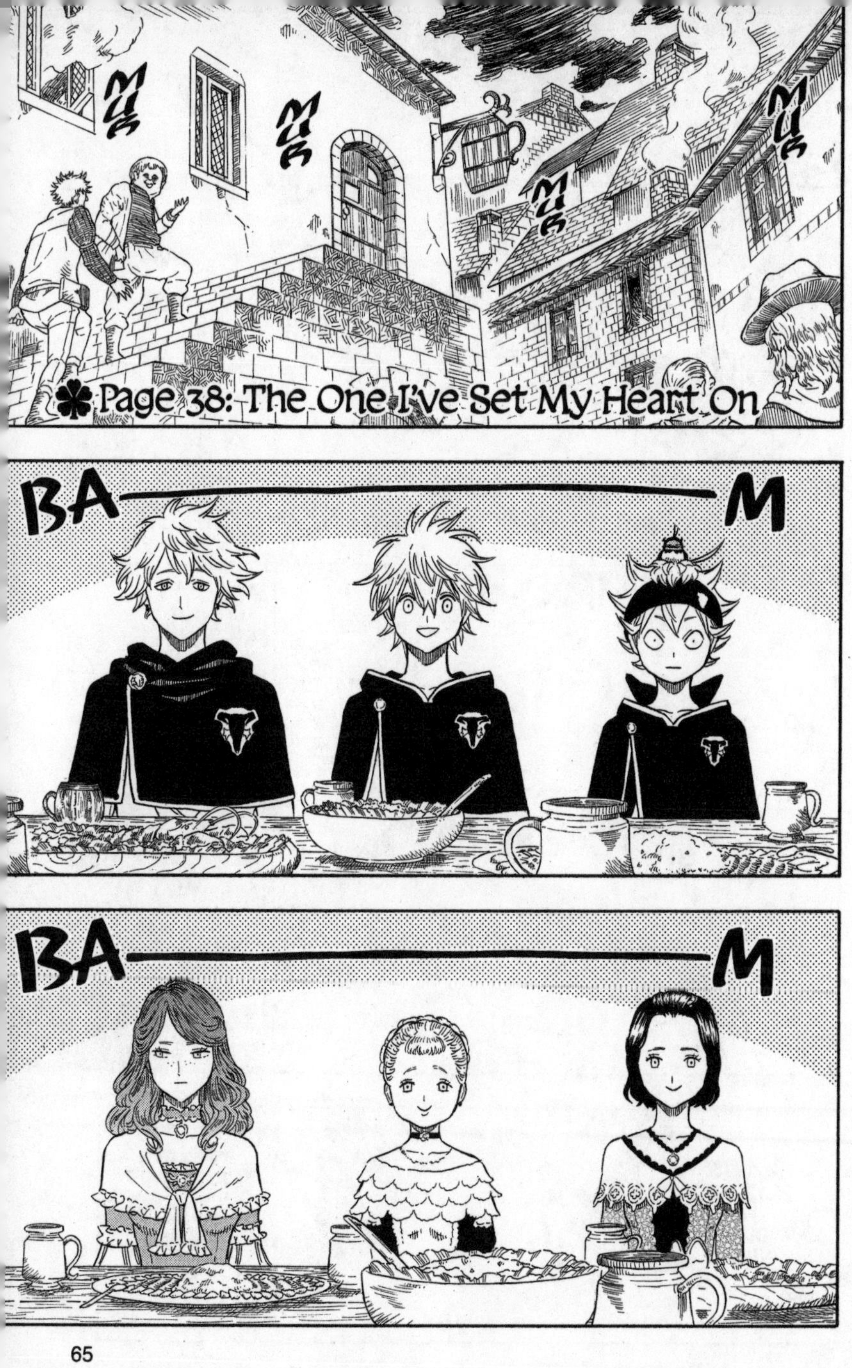
MUR
MUR
MUR
MUR
Page 38: The One I've Set My Heart On
BA———M
BA———M

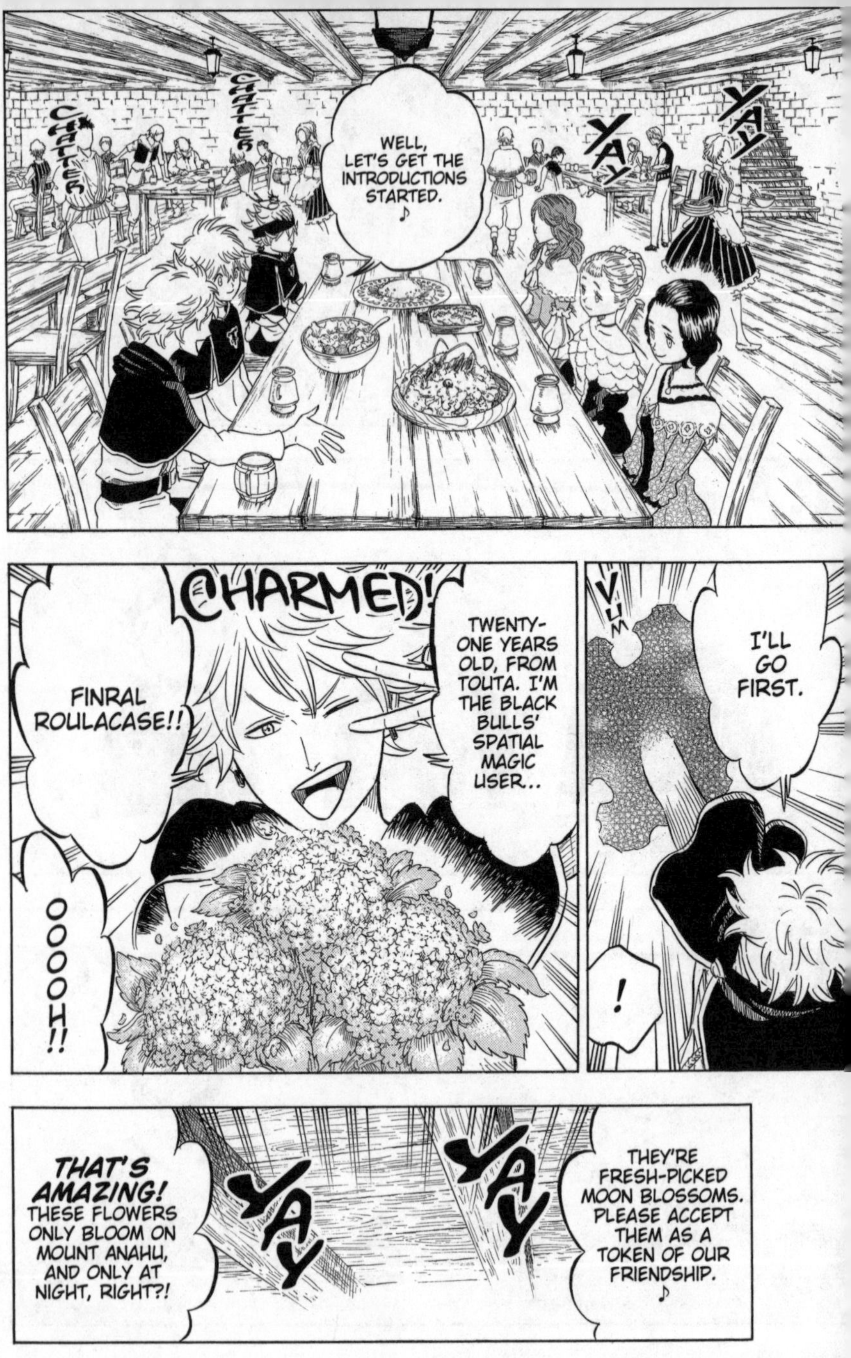
YAY
YAY
WELL, LET'S GET THE INTRODUCTIONS STARTED. ♪
CHATTER
CHATTER
I'LL GO FIRST.
VUM
!
TWENTY-ONE YEARS OLD, FROM TOUTA. I'M THE BLACK BULLS' SPATIAL MAGIC USER...
CHARMED!
FINRAL ROULACASE!!
OOOOOH!!
THEY'RE FRESH-PICKED MOON BLOSSOMS. PLEASE ACCEPT THEM AS A TOKEN OF OUR FRIENDSHIP. ♪
YAY
YAY
THAT'S AMAZING! THESE FLOWERS ONLY BLOOM ON MOUNT ANAHU, AND ONLY AT NIGHT, RIGHT?!

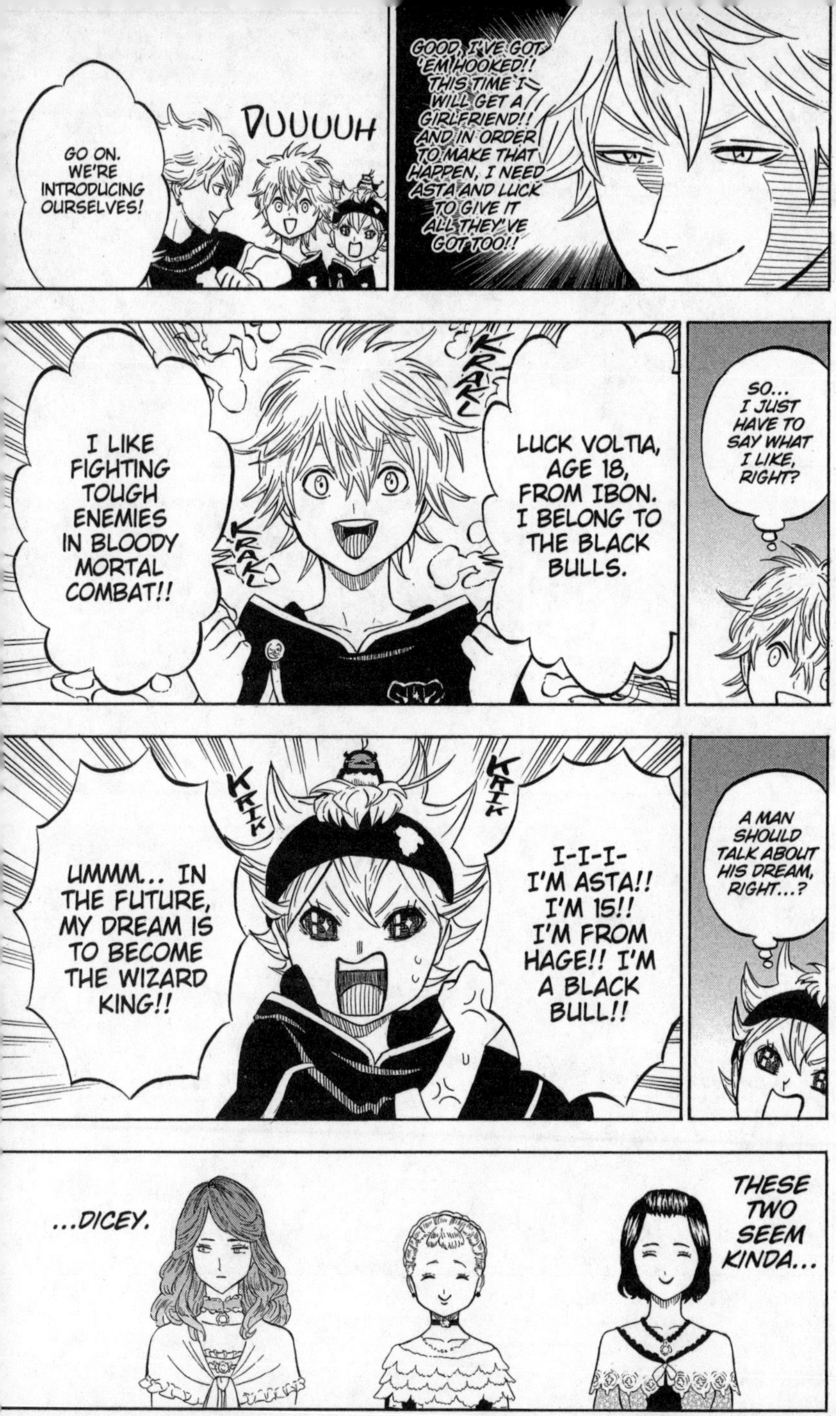
GOOD, I'VE GOT 'EM HOOKED!! THIS TIME I WILL GET A GIRLFRIEND!! AND IN ORDER TO MAKE THAT HAPPEN, I NEED ASTA AND LUCK TO GIVE IT ALL THEY'VE GOT TOO!!
DUUUUH
GO ON. WE'RE INTRODUCING OURSELVES!
SO... I JUST HAVE TO SAY WHAT I LIKE, RIGHT?
KRAKL
LUCK VOLTIA, AGE 18, FROM IBON. I BELONG TO THE BLACK BULLS.
KRAKL
I LIKE FIGHTING TOUGH ENEMIES IN BLOODY MORTAL COMBAT!!
A MAN SHOULD TALK ABOUT HIS DREAM, RIGHT...?
KRIK
I-I-I- I'M ASTA!! I'M 15!! I'M FROM HAGE!! I'M A BLACK BULL!!
KRIK
UMMM... IN THE FUTURE, MY DREAM IS TO BECOME THE WIZARD KING!!
THESE TWO SEEM KINDA...
...DICEY.

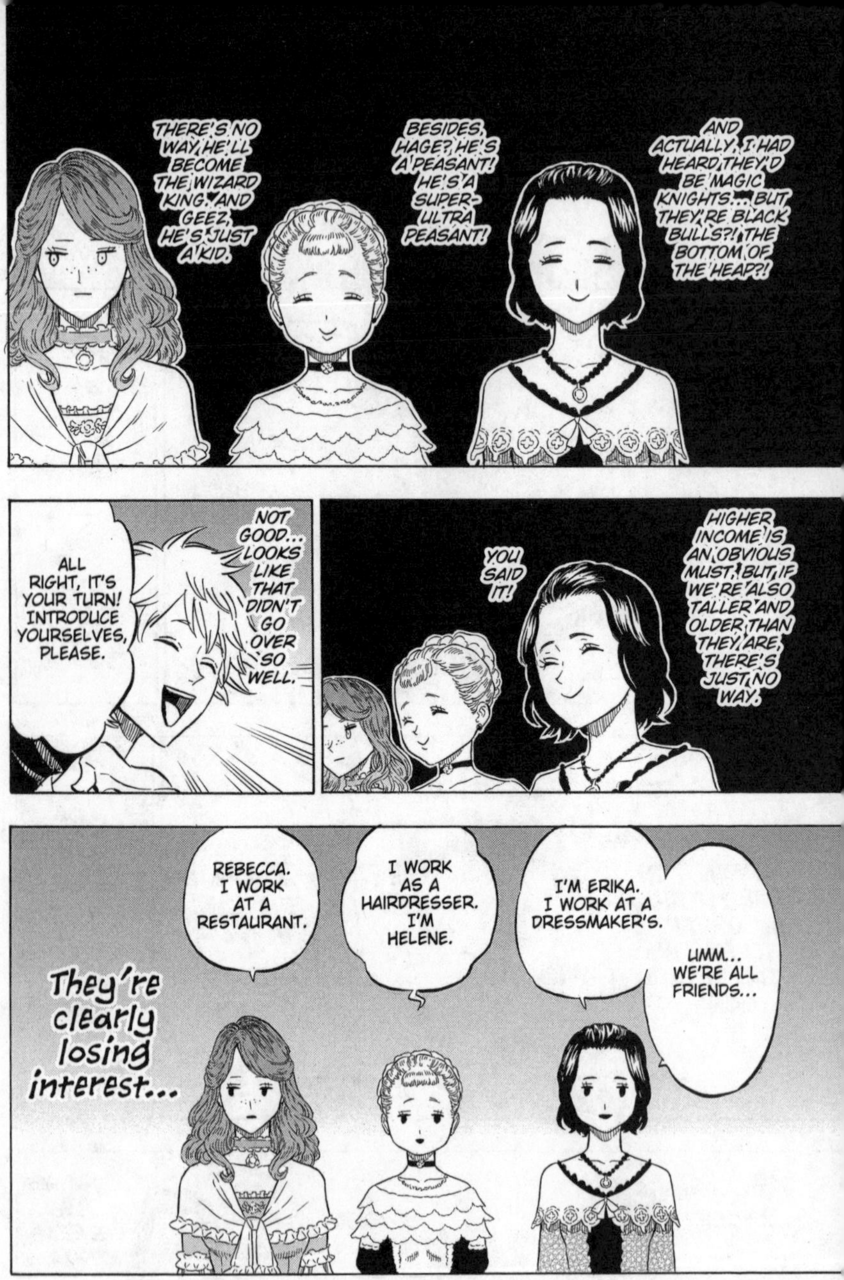
AND ACTUALLY, I HAD HEARD THEY'D BE MAGIC KNIGHTS... BUT THEY'RE BLACK BULLS?! THE BOTTOM OF THE HEAP?!
BESIDES, HAGE? HE'S A PEASANT! HE'S A SUPER-ULTRA PEASANT!
THERE'S NO WAY HE'LL BECOME THE WIZARD KING. AND GEEZ, HE'S JUST A KID.
HIGHER INCOME IS AN OBVIOUS MUST, BUT IF WE'RE ALSO TALLER AND OLDER THAN THEY ARE, THERE'S JUST NO WAY.
YOU SAID IT!
NOT GOOD... LOOKS LIKE THAT DIDN'T GO OVER SO WELL.
ALL RIGHT, IT'S YOUR TURN! INTRODUCE YOURSELVES, PLEASE.
I'M ERIKA. I WORK AT A DRESSMAKER'S.
UMM... WE'RE ALL FRIENDS...
I WORK AS A HAIRDRESSER. I'M HELENE.
REBECCA. I WORK AT A RESTAURANT.
They're clearly losing interest...

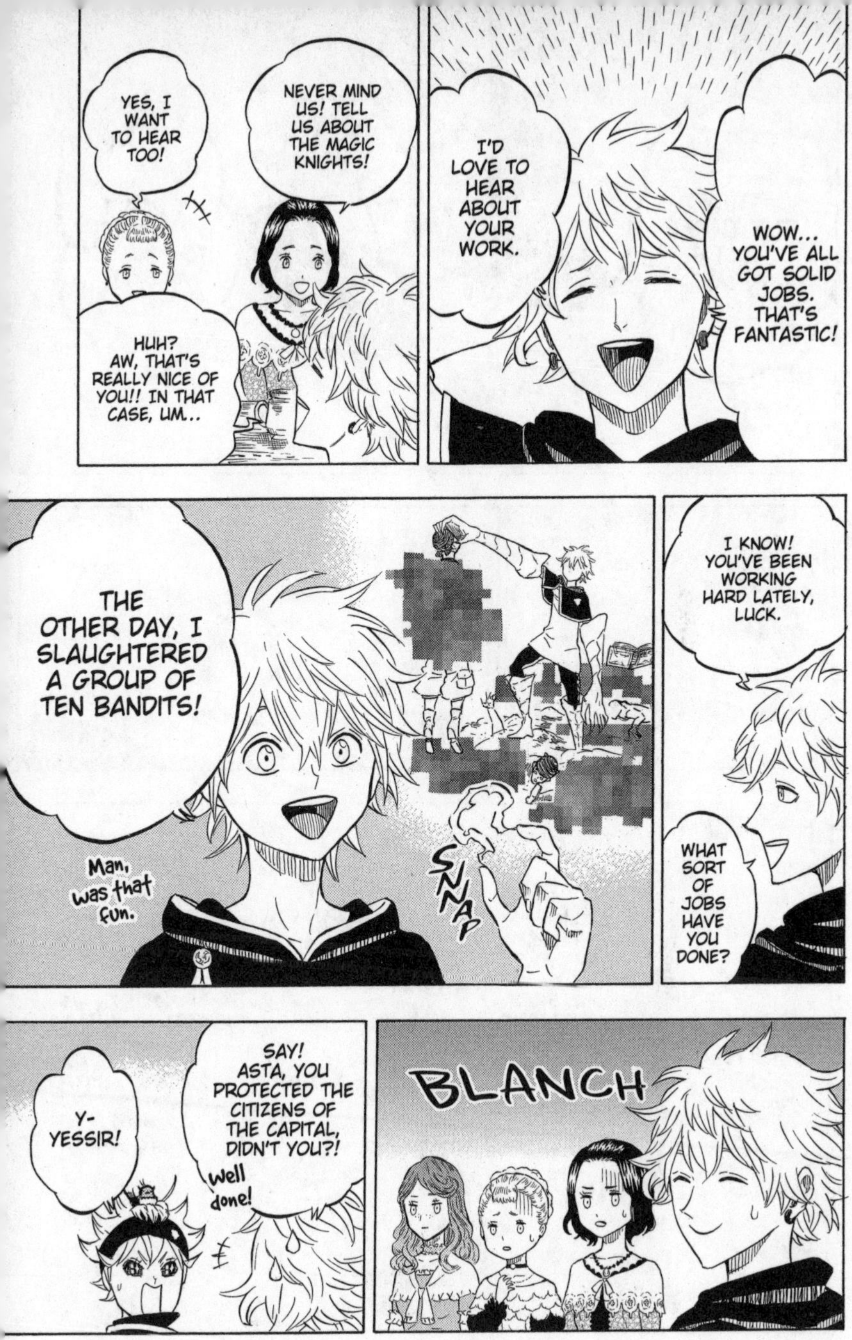
WOW... YOU'VE ALL GOT SOLID JOBS. THAT'S FANTASTIC!
I'D LOVE TO HEAR ABOUT YOUR WORK.
NEVER MIND US! TELL US ABOUT THE MAGIC KNIGHTS!
YES, I WANT TO HEAR TOO!
HUH? AW, THAT'S REALLY NICE OF YOU!! IN THAT CASE, UM...
I KNOW! YOU'VE BEEN WORKING HARD LATELY, LUCK.
WHAT SORT OF JOBS HAVE YOU DONE?
THE OTHER DAY, I SLAUGHTERED A GROUP OF TEN BANDITS!
SNNAP
Man, was that fun.
BLANCH
SAY! ASTA, YOU PROTECTED THE CITIZENS OF THE CAPITAL, DIDN'T YOU?!
Well done!
Y- YESSIR!

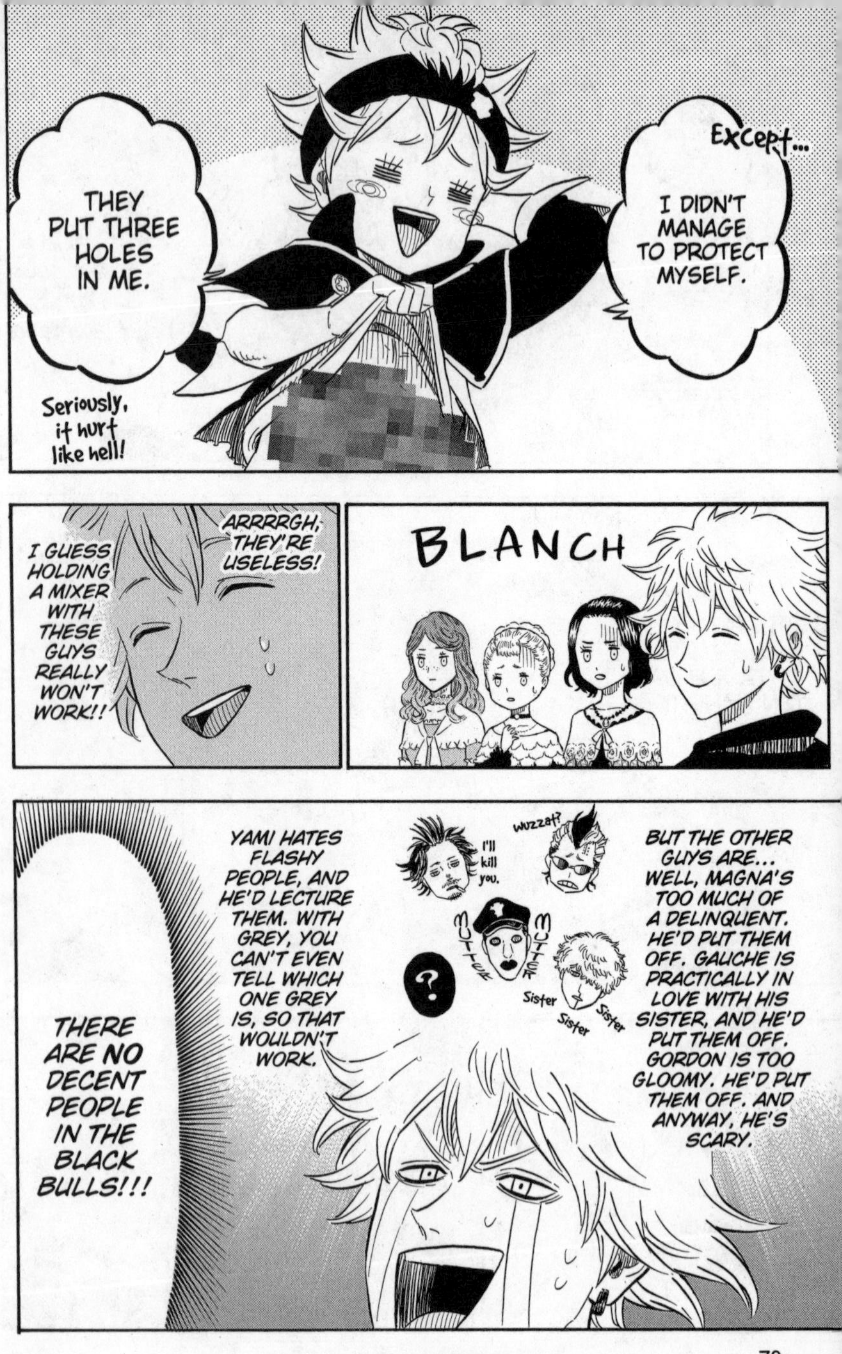
Except...
I DIDN'T MANAGE TO PROTECT MYSELF.
THEY PUT THREE HOLES IN ME.
Seriously, it hurt like hell!
BLANCH
ARRRRGH, THEY'RE USELESS!
I GUESS HOLDING A MIXER WITH THESE GUYS REALLY WON'T WORK!!
YAMI HATES FLASHY PEOPLE, AND HE'D LECTURE THEM. WITH GREY, YOU CAN'T EVEN TELL WHICH ONE GREY IS, SO THAT WOULDN'T WORK.
wuzzat?
I'll kill you.
MUTTER MUTTER
?
Sister Sister Sister
BUT THE OTHER GUYS ARE... WELL, MAGNA'S TOO MUCH OF A DELINQUENT. HE'D PUT THEM OFF. GAUCHE IS PRACTICALLY IN LOVE WITH HIS SISTER, AND HE'D PUT THEM OFF. GORDON IS TOO GLOOMY. HE'D PUT THEM OFF. AND ANYWAY, HE'S SCARY.
THERE ARE NO DECENT PEOPLE IN THE BLACK BULLS!!!

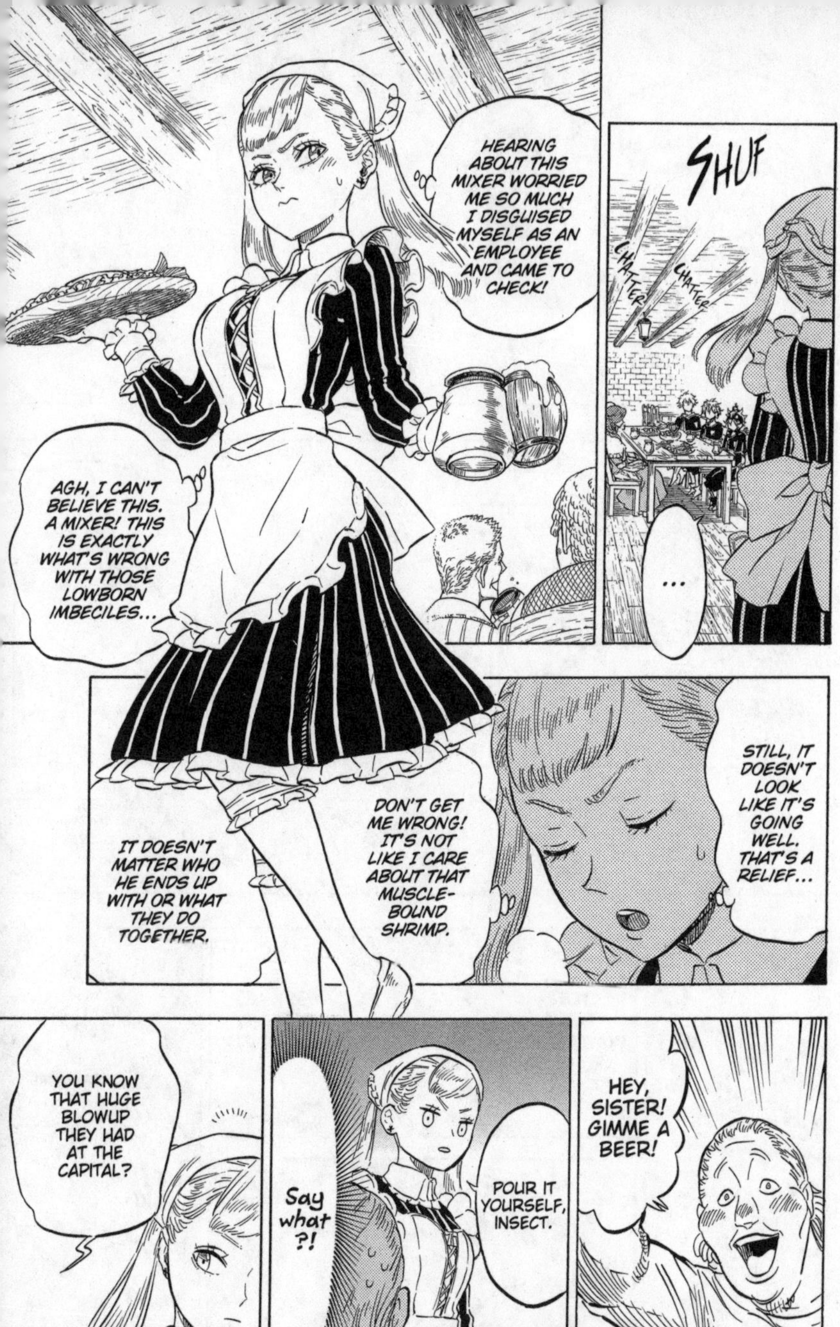
SHUF
CHATTER
CHATTER
...
HEARING ABOUT THIS MIXER WORRIED ME SO MUCH I DISGUISED MYSELF AS AN EMPLOYEE AND CAME TO CHECK!
AGH, I CAN'T BELIEVE THIS. A MIXER! THIS IS EXACTLY WHAT'S WRONG WITH THOSE LOWBORN IMBECILES...
STILL, IT DOESN'T LOOK LIKE IT'S GOING WELL. THAT'S A RELIEF...
DON'T GET ME WRONG! IT'S NOT LIKE I CARE ABOUT THAT MUSCLE-BOUND SHRIMP.
IT DOESN'T MATTER WHO HE ENDS UP WITH OR WHAT THEY DO TOGETHER.
HEY, SISTER! GIMME A BEER!
POUR IT YOURSELF, INSECT.
Say what?!
YOU KNOW THAT HUGE BLOWUP THEY HAD AT THE CAPITAL?

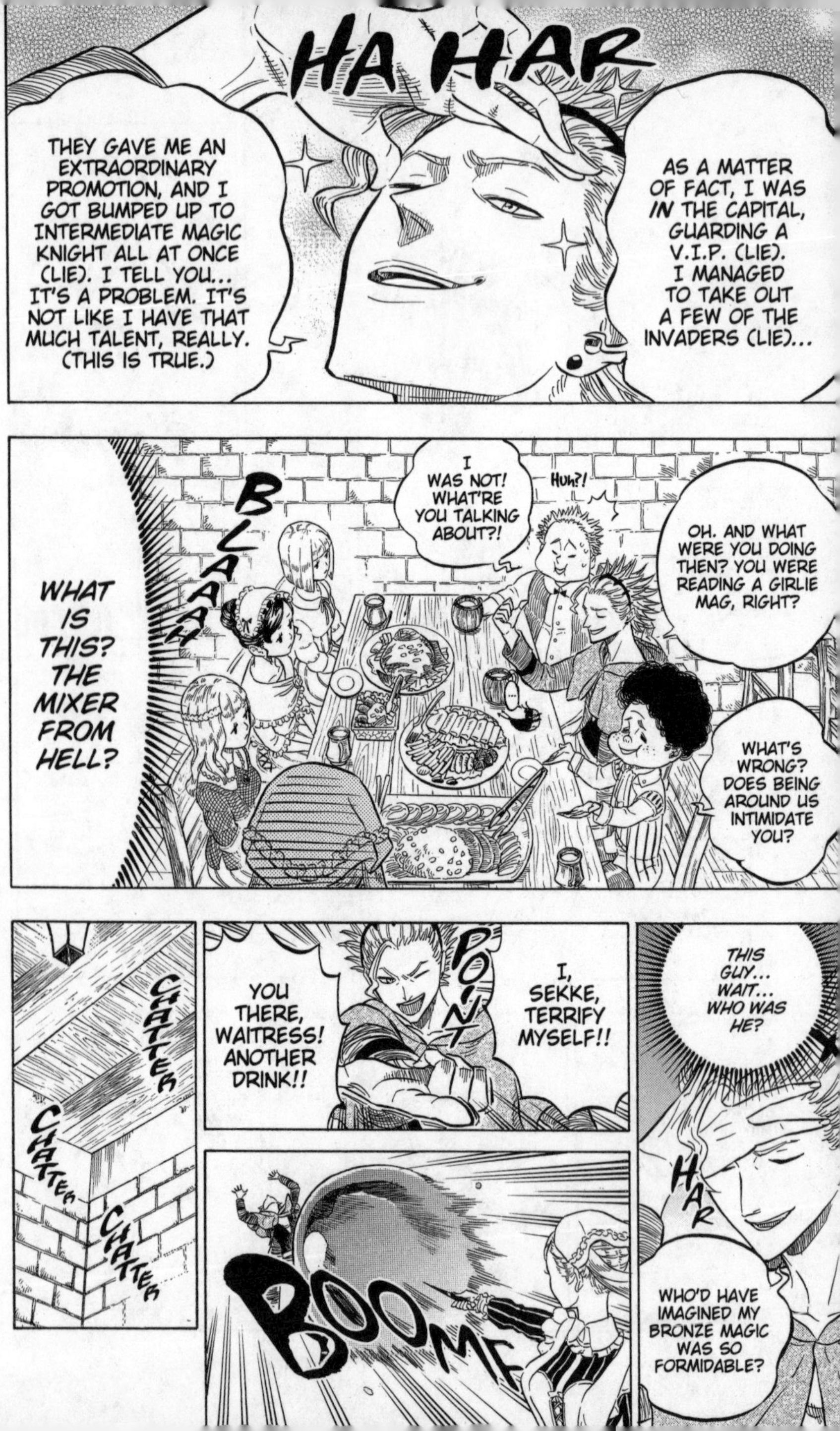
HA HAR
AS A MATTER OF FACT, I WAS *IN* THE CAPITAL, GUARDING A V.I.P. (LIE). I MANAGED TO TAKE OUT A FEW OF THE INVADERS (LIE)...
THEY GAVE ME AN EXTRAORDINARY PROMOTION, AND I GOT BUMPED UP TO INTERMEDIATE MAGIC KNIGHT ALL AT ONCE (LIE). I TELL YOU... IT'S A PROBLEM. IT'S NOT LIKE I HAVE THAT MUCH TALENT, REALLY. (THIS IS TRUE.)
OH. AND WHAT WERE YOU DOING THEN? YOU WERE READING A GIRLIE MAG, RIGHT?
Huh?!
I WAS NOT! WHAT'RE YOU TALKING ABOUT?!
WHAT'S WRONG? DOES BEING AROUND US INTIMIDATE YOU?
BLAAAAH
WHAT IS THIS? THE MIXER FROM HELL?
THIS GUY... WAIT... WHO WAS HE?
HAR
WHO'D HAVE IMAGINED MY BRONZE MAGIC WAS SO FORMIDABLE?
I, SEKKE, TERRIFY MYSELF!!
POINT
YOU THERE, WAITRESS! ANOTHER DRINK!!
BOOMF
CHATTER
CHATTER
CHATTER
CHATTER

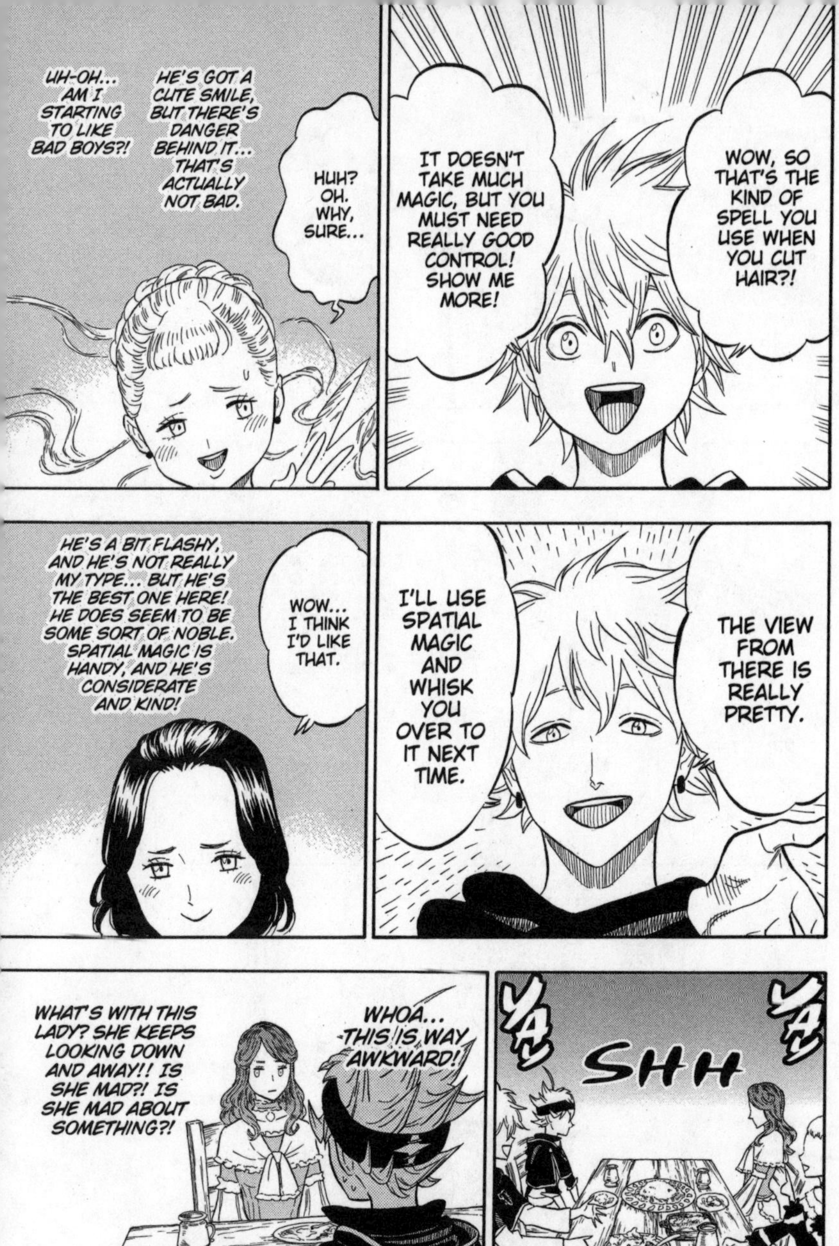
WOW, SO THAT'S THE KIND OF SPELL YOU USE WHEN YOU CUT HAIR?!
IT DOESN'T TAKE MUCH MAGIC, BUT YOU MUST NEED REALLY GOOD CONTROL! SHOW ME MORE!
HUH? OH. WHY, SURE...
HE'S GOT A CUTE SMILE, BUT THERE'S DANGER BEHIND IT... THAT'S ACTUALLY NOT BAD.
UH-OH... AM I STARTING TO LIKE BAD BOYS?!
THE VIEW FROM THERE IS REALLY PRETTY.
I'LL USE SPATIAL MAGIC AND WHISK YOU OVER TO IT NEXT TIME.
WOW... I THINK I'D LIKE THAT.
HE'S A BIT FLASHY, AND HE'S NOT REALLY MY TYPE... BUT HE'S THE BEST ONE HERE! HE DOES SEEM TO BE SOME SORT OF NOBLE. SPATIAL MAGIC IS HANDY, AND HE'S CONSIDERATE AND KIND!
YA
YA
SHH
WHOA... THIS IS WAY AWKWARD!
WHAT'S WITH THIS LADY? SHE KEEPS LOOKING DOWN AND AWAY!! IS SHE MAD?! IS SHE MAD ABOUT SOMETHING?!

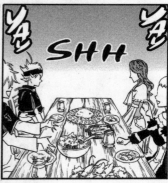

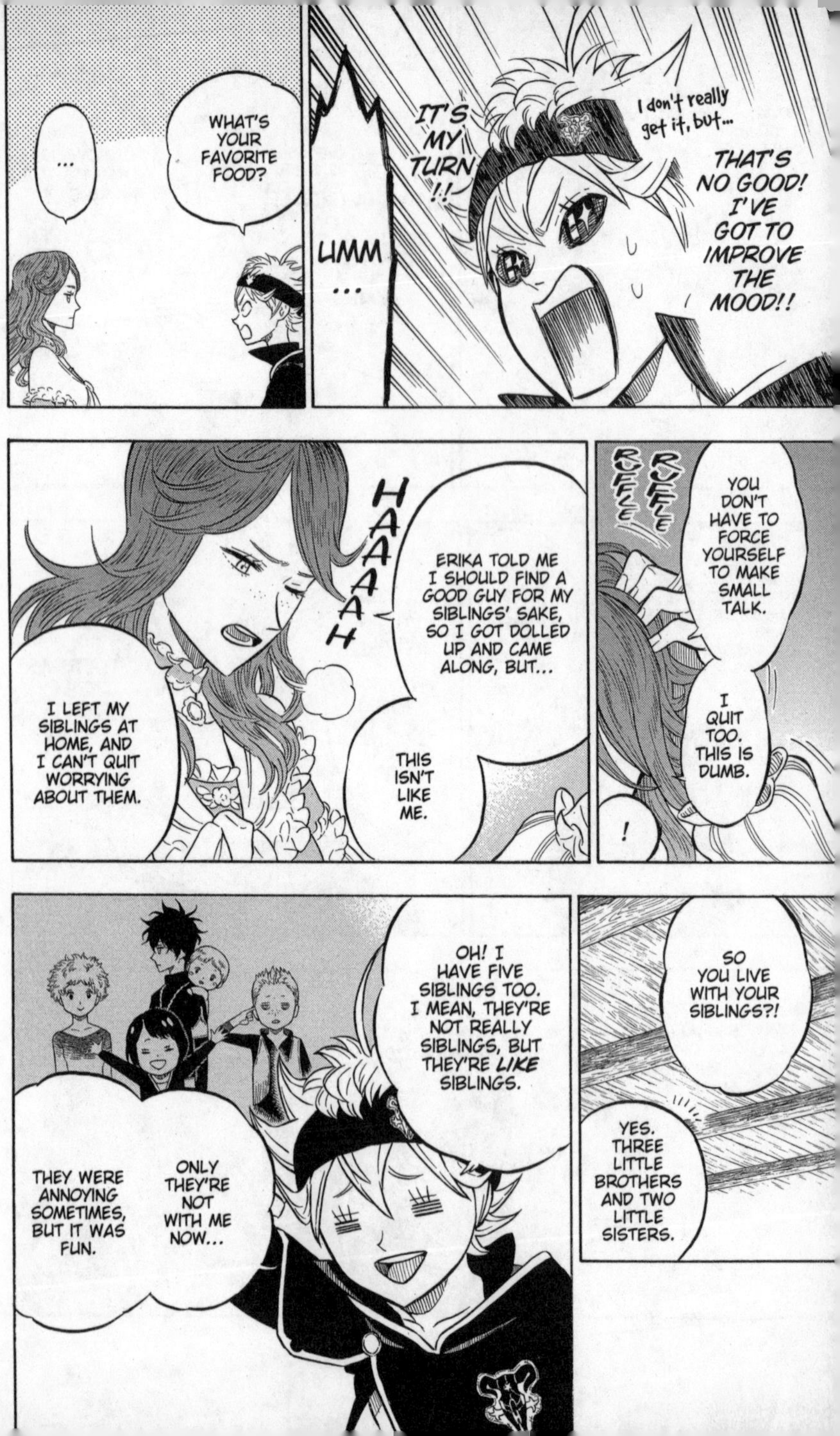
I don't really get it, but...
THAT'S NO GOOD! I'VE GOT TO IMPROVE THE MOOD!!
IT'S MY TURN!!
UMM...
WHAT'S YOUR FAVORITE FOOD?
...
RUFFLE RUFFLE
YOU DON'T HAVE TO FORCE YOURSELF TO MAKE SMALL TALK.
I QUIT TOO. THIS IS DUMB.
!
HAAAAAH
ERIKA TOLD ME I SHOULD FIND A GOOD GUY FOR MY SIBLINGS' SAKE, SO I GOT DOLLED UP AND CAME ALONG, BUT...
THIS ISN'T LIKE ME.
I LEFT MY SIBLINGS AT HOME, AND I CAN'T QUIT WORRYING ABOUT THEM.
SO YOU LIVE WITH YOUR SIBLINGS?!
YES. THREE LITTLE BROTHERS AND TWO LITTLE SISTERS.
OH! I HAVE FIVE SIBLINGS TOO. I MEAN, THEY'RE NOT REALLY SIBLINGS, BUT THEY'RE *LIKE* SIBLINGS.
ONLY THEY'RE NOT WITH ME NOW...
THEY WERE ANNOYING SOMETIMES, BUT IT WAS FUN.

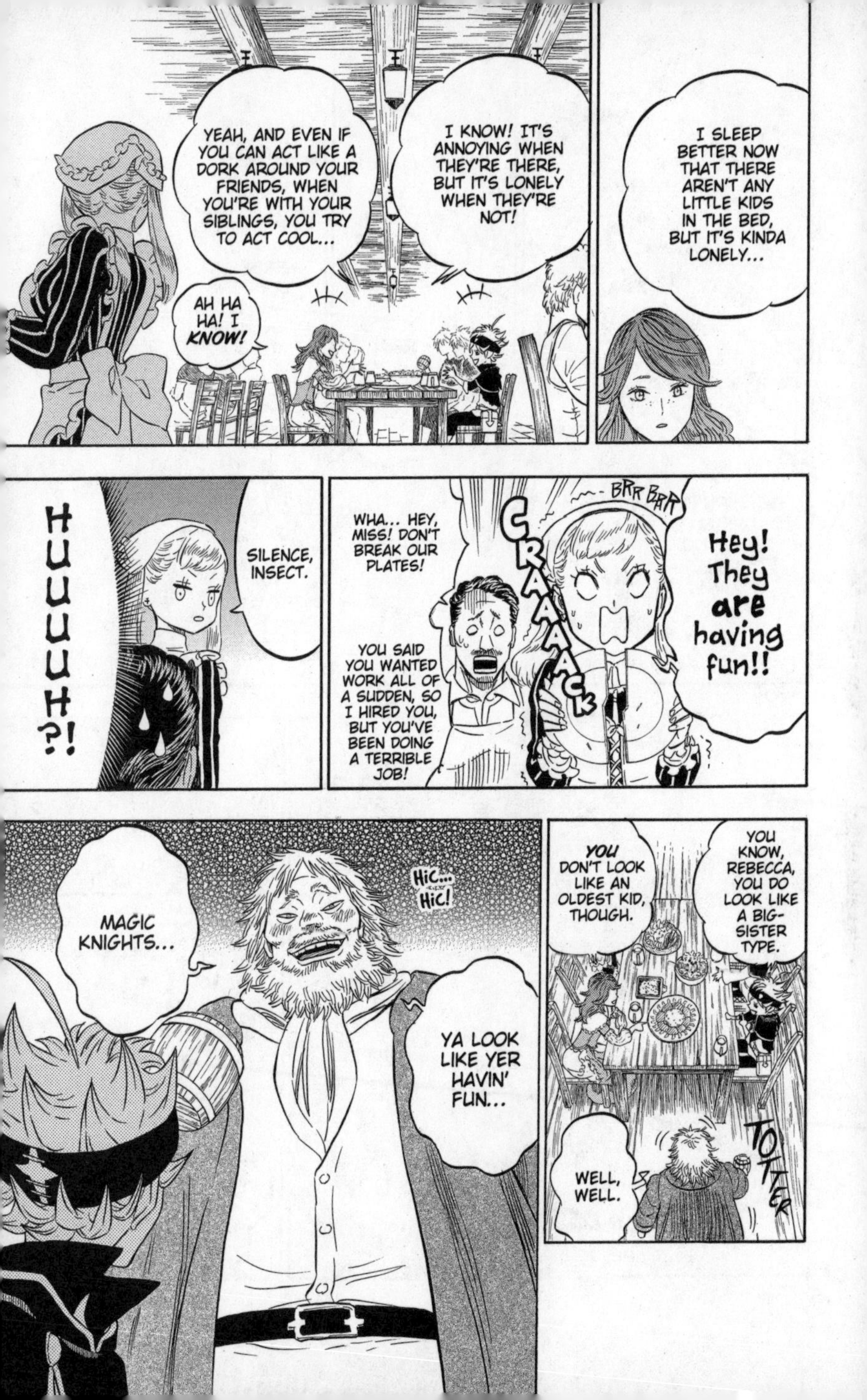
I SLEEP BETTER NOW THAT THERE AREN'T ANY LITTLE KIDS IN THE BED, BUT IT'S KINDA LONELY...
I KNOW! IT'S ANNOYING WHEN THEY'RE THERE, BUT IT'S LONELY WHEN THEY'RE NOT!
YEAH, AND EVEN IF YOU CAN ACT LIKE A DORK AROUND YOUR FRIENDS, WHEN YOU'RE WITH YOUR SIBLINGS, YOU TRY TO ACT COOL...
AH HA HA! I *KNOW!*
Hey! They **are** having fun!!
BRR BRR
CRAAAACK
WHA... HEY, MISS! DON'T BREAK OUR PLATES!
YOU SAID YOU WANTED WORK ALL OF A SUDDEN, SO I HIRED YOU, BUT YOU'VE BEEN DOING A TERRIBLE JOB!
SILENCE, INSECT.
HUUUUUH?!
YOU KNOW, REBECCA, YOU DO LOOK LIKE A BIG-SISTER TYPE.
YOU DON'T LOOK LIKE AN OLDEST KID, THOUGH.
TOTTER
WELL, WELL.
Hic... Hic!
MAGIC KNIGHTS...
YA LOOK LIKE YER HAVIN' FUN...

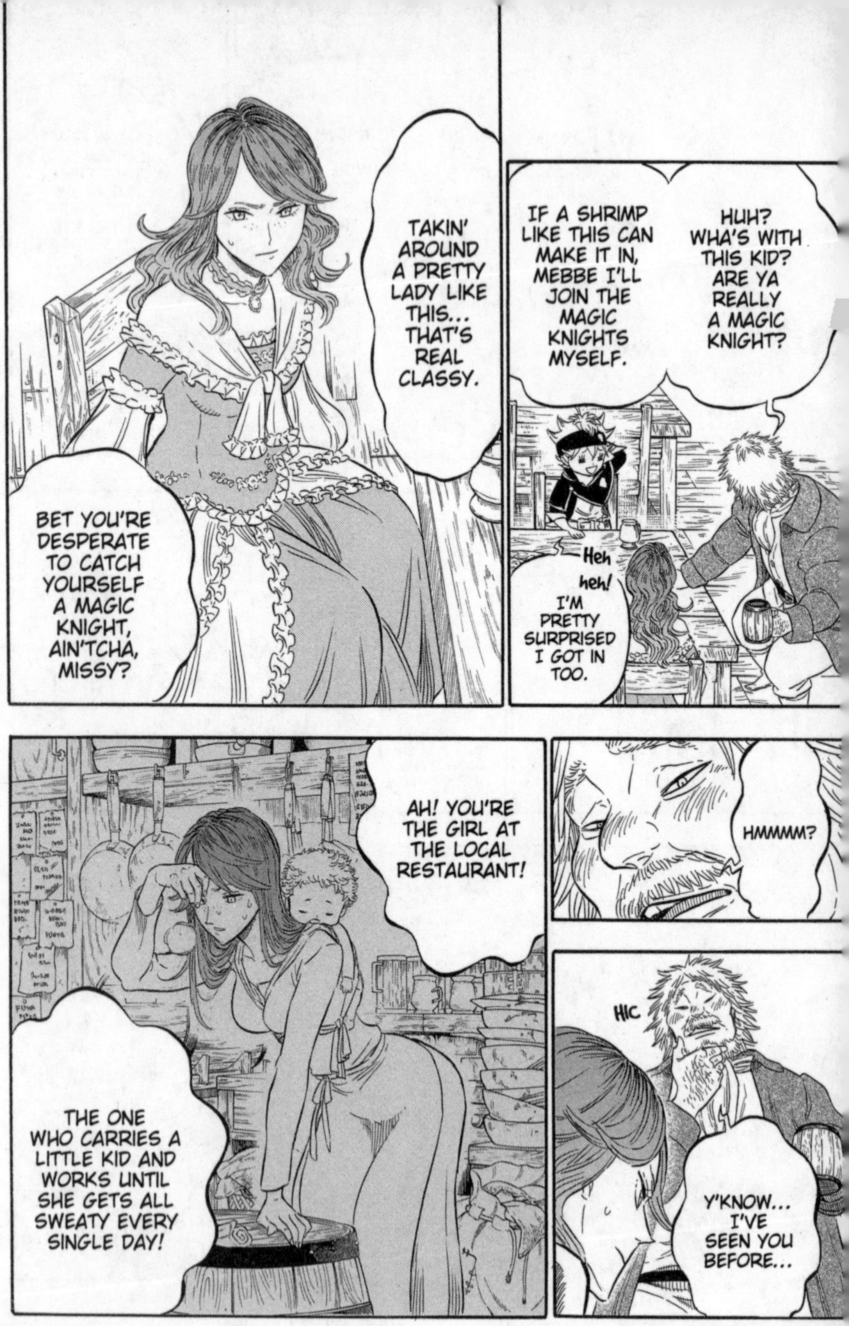
HUH? WHA'S WITH THIS KID? ARE YA REALLY A MAGIC KNIGHT?
IF A SHRIMP LIKE THIS CAN MAKE IT IN, MEBBE I'LL JOIN THE MAGIC KNIGHTS MYSELF.
Heh heh!
I'M PRETTY SURPRISED I GOT IN TOO.
TAKIN' AROUND A PRETTY LADY LIKE THIS... THAT'S REAL CLASSY.
BET YOU'RE DESPERATE TO CATCH YOURSELF A MAGIC KNIGHT, AIN'TCHA, MISSY?
HMMMM?
HIC
Y'KNOW... I'VE SEEN YOU BEFORE...
AH! YOU'RE THE GIRL AT THE LOCAL RESTAURANT!
THE ONE WHO CARRIES A LITTLE KID AND WORKS UNTIL SHE GETS ALL SWEATY EVERY SINGLE DAY!

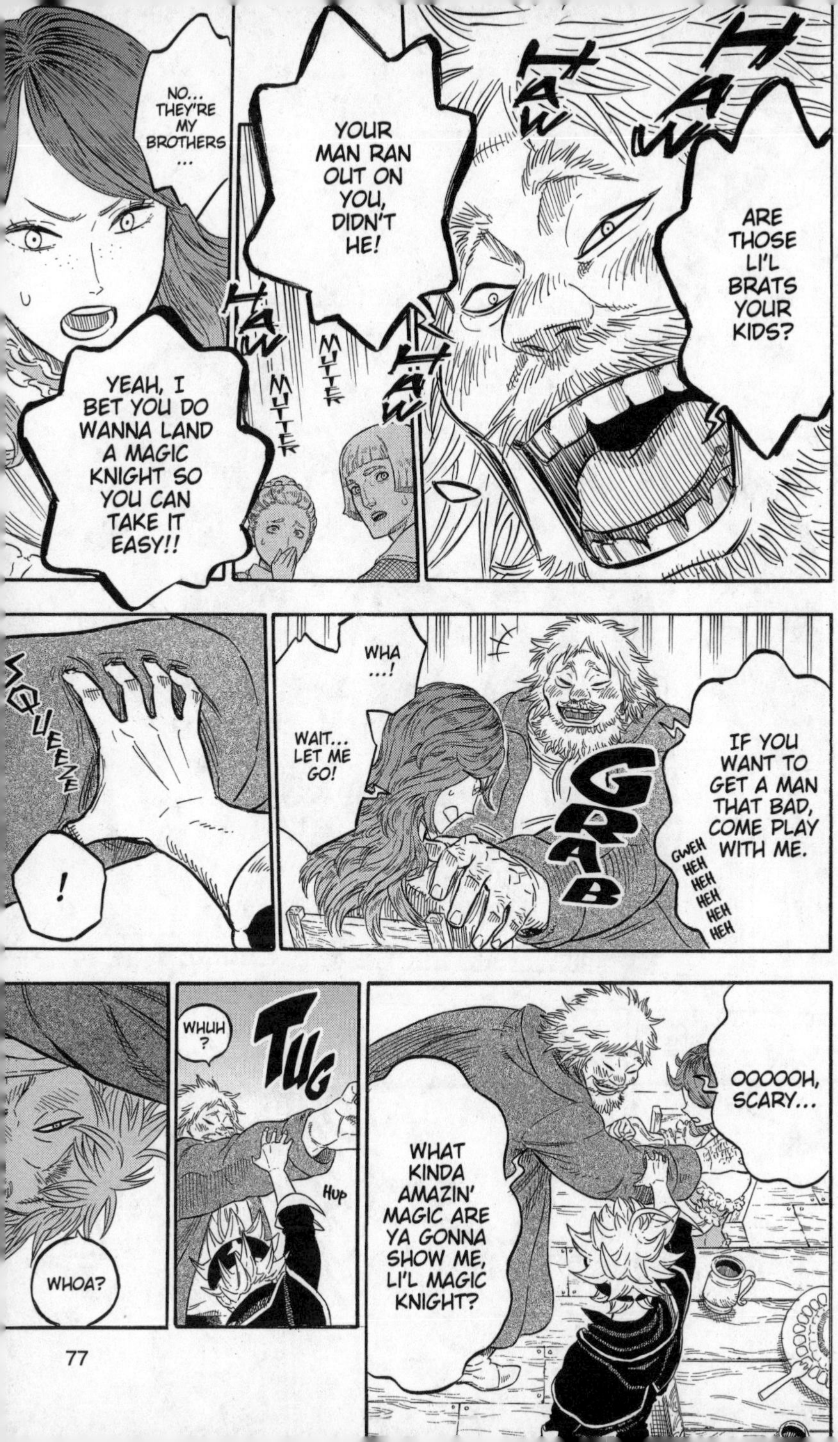
HAW HAW
ARE THOSE LI'L BRATS YOUR KIDS?
YOUR MAN RAN OUT ON YOU, DIDN'T HE!
HAW HAW
HAW HAW
MUTTER MUTTER
NO... THEY'RE MY BROTHERS...
YEAH, I BET YOU DO WANNA LAND A MAGIC KNIGHT SO YOU CAN TAKE IT EASY!!
IF YOU WANT TO GET A MAN THAT BAD, COME PLAY WITH ME.
GWEH HEH HEH HEH HEH HEH
GRAB
WHA...!
WAIT... LET ME GO!
SQUEEZE
!
OOOOOH, SCARY...
WHAT KINDA AMAZIN' MAGIC ARE YA GONNA SHOW ME, LI'L MAGIC KNIGHT?
TUG
WHUH?
HUP
WHOA?

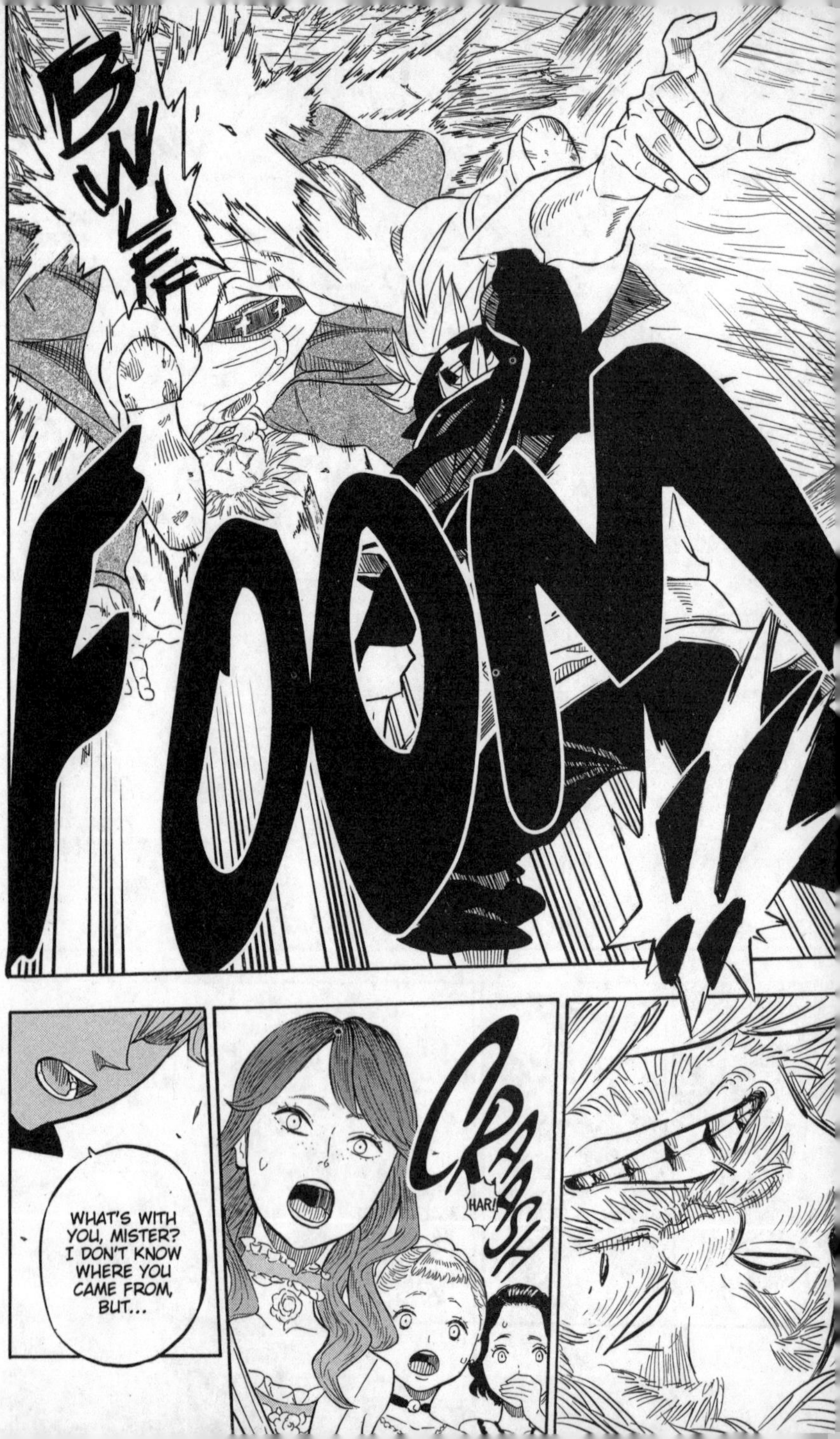
BWUFF
FOOM!!
CRASH
HAR!
WHAT'S WITH YOU, MISTER? I DON'T KNOW WHERE YOU CAME FROM, BUT...

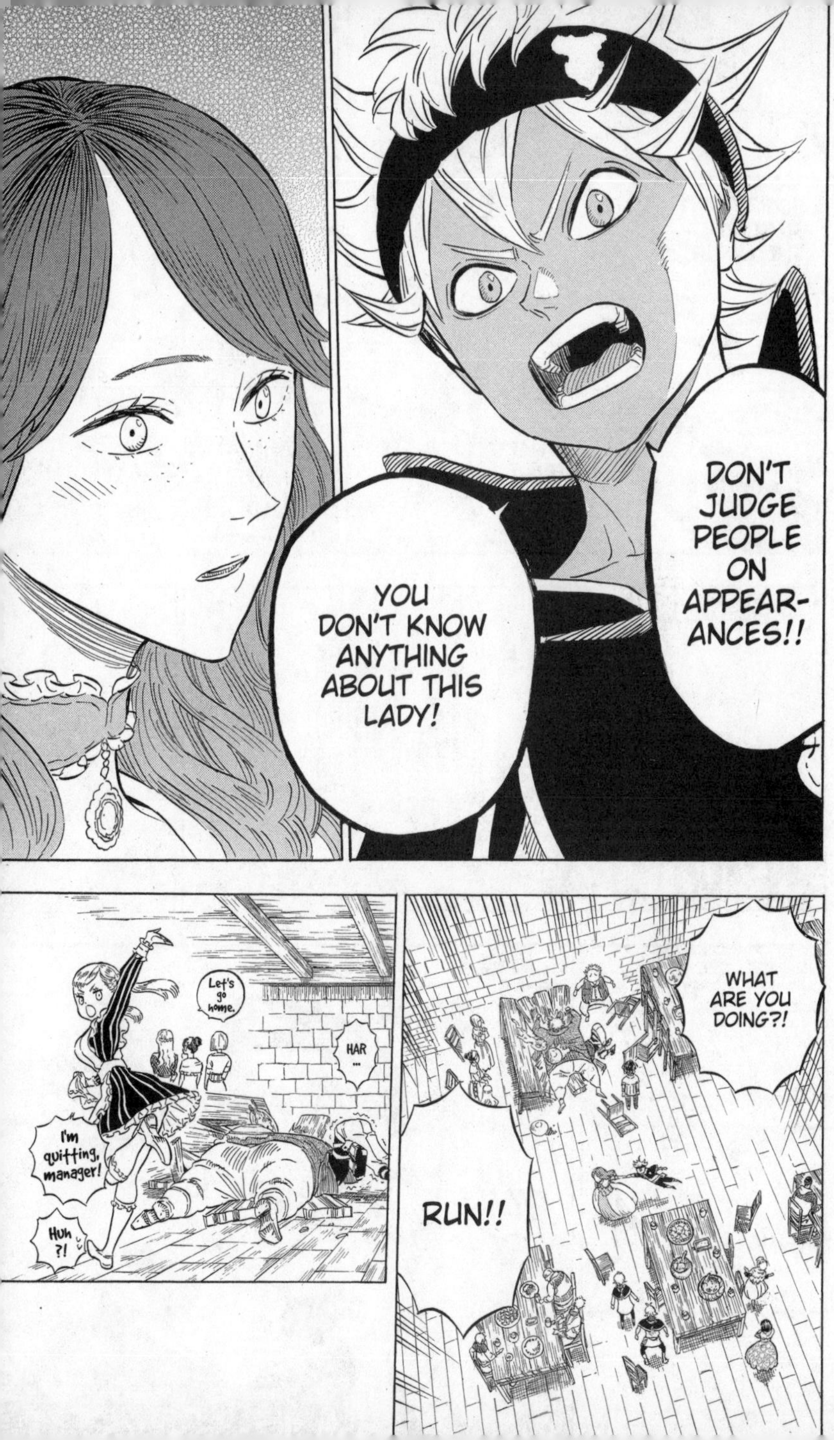
DON'T JUDGE PEOPLE ON APPEARANCES!!
YOU DON'T KNOW ANYTHING ABOUT THIS LADY!
WHAT ARE YOU DOING?!
RUN!!
Let's go home.
HAR ...
I'm quitting, manager!
Huh ?!

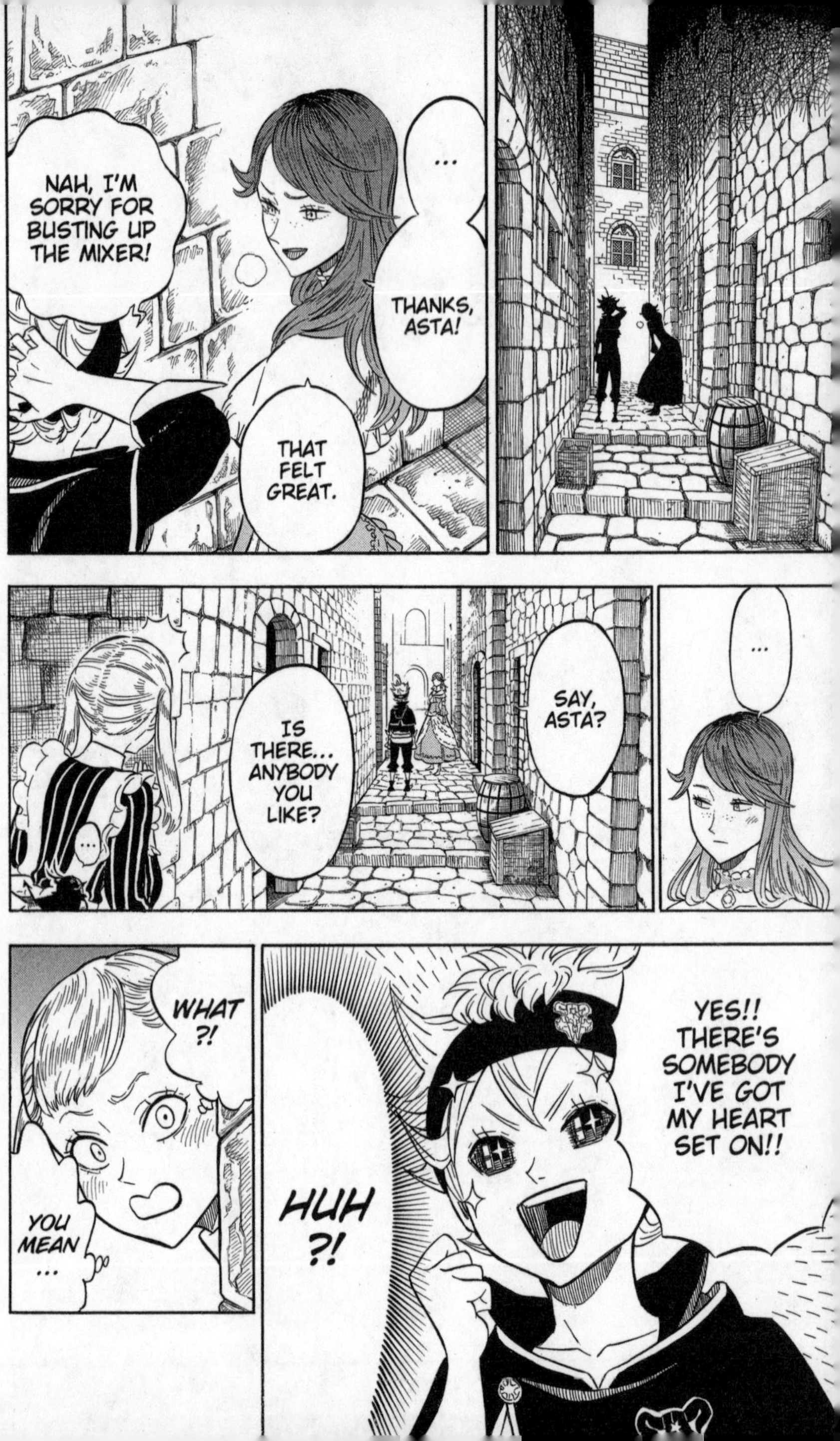
...
THANKS, ASTA!
THAT FELT GREAT.
NAH, I'M SORRY FOR BUSTING UP THE MIXER!
...
SAY, ASTA?
IS THERE... ANYBODY YOU LIKE?
...
YES!! THERE'S SOMEBODY I'VE GOT MY HEART SET ON!!
HUH ?!
WHAT ?!
YOU MEAN ...

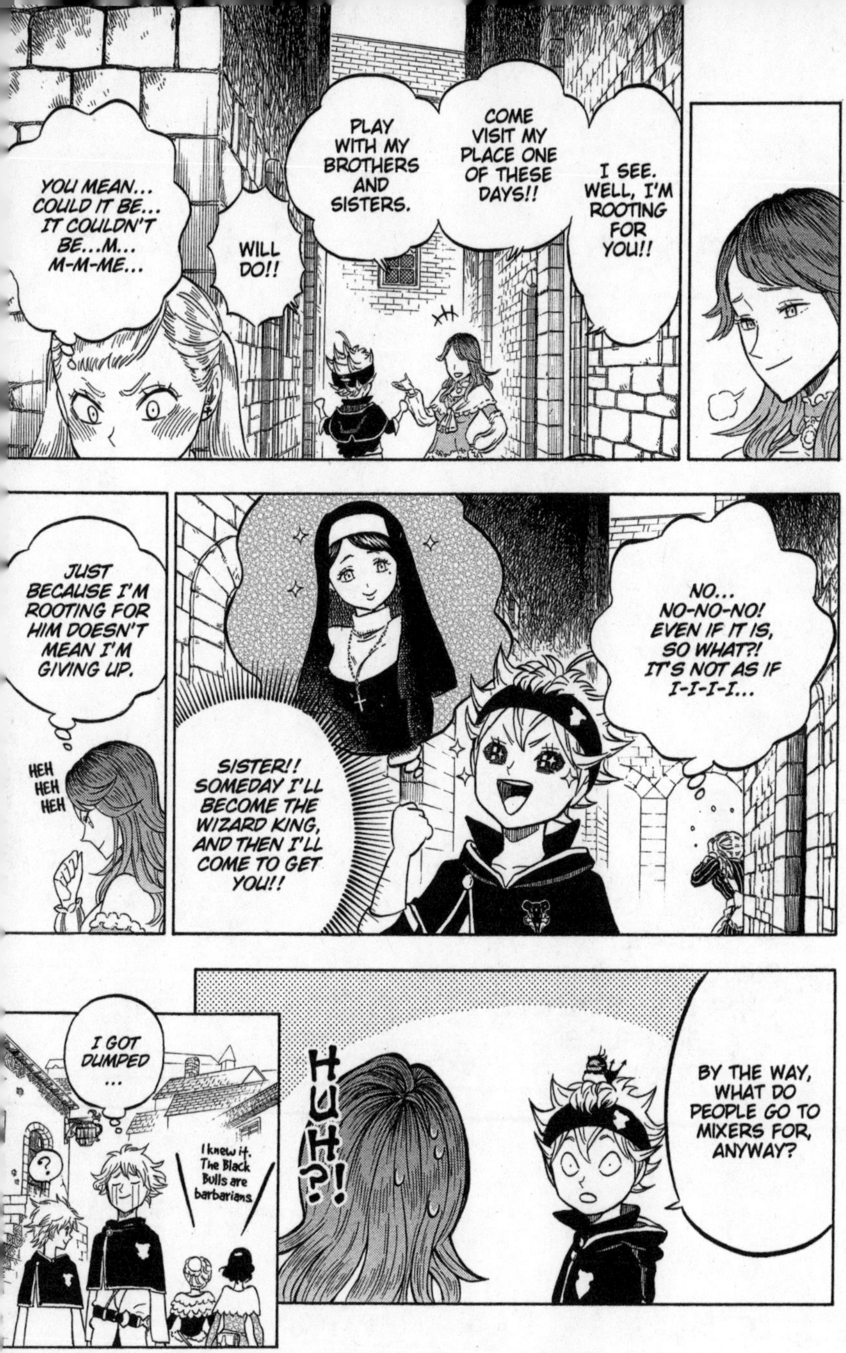
I SEE. WELL, I'M ROOTING FOR YOU!!
COME VISIT MY PLACE ONE OF THESE DAYS!!
PLAY WITH MY BROTHERS AND SISTERS.
WILL DO!!
YOU MEAN... COULD IT BE... IT COULDN'T BE...M... M-M-ME...
NO... NO-NO-NO! EVEN IF IT IS, SO WHAT?! IT'S NOT AS IF I-I-I-I...
SISTER!! SOMEDAY I'LL BECOME THE WIZARD KING, AND THEN I'LL COME TO GET YOU!!
JUST BECAUSE I'M ROOTING FOR HIM DOESN'T MEAN I'M GIVING UP.
HEH HEH HEH
BY THE WAY, WHAT DO PEOPLE GO TO MIXERS FOR, ANYWAY?
HUH?!
I GOT DUMPED ...
I knew it. The Black Bulls are barbarians.

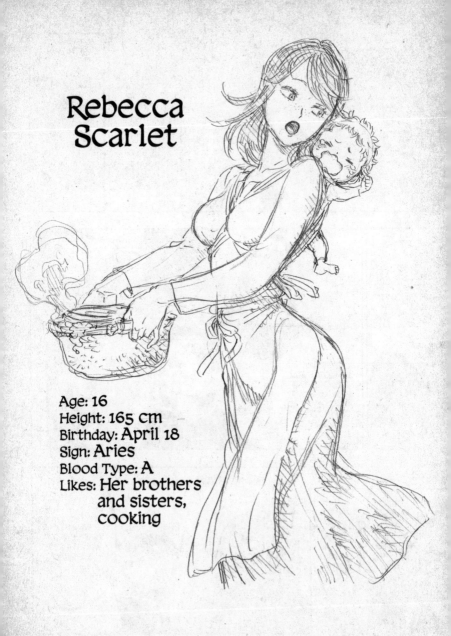

Rebecca Scarlet

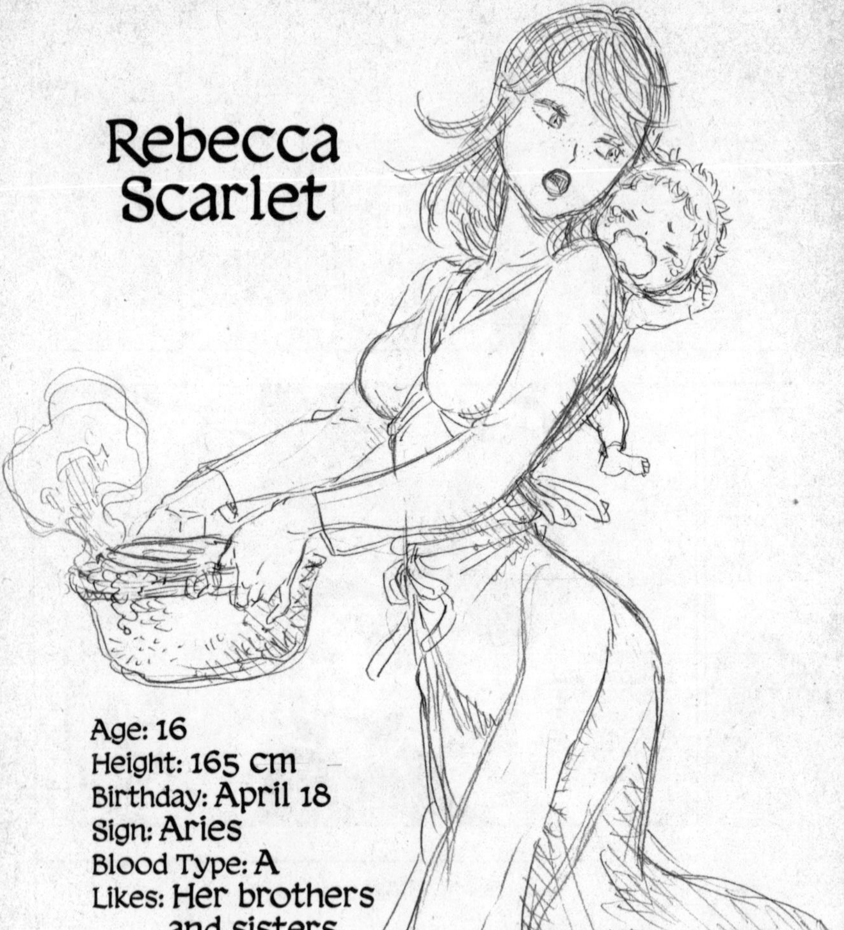

Age: 16
Height: 165 cm
Birthday: April 18
Sign: Aries
Blood Type: A
Likes: Her brothers and sisters, cooking

Character Profile

Page 39: The Mirror Mage

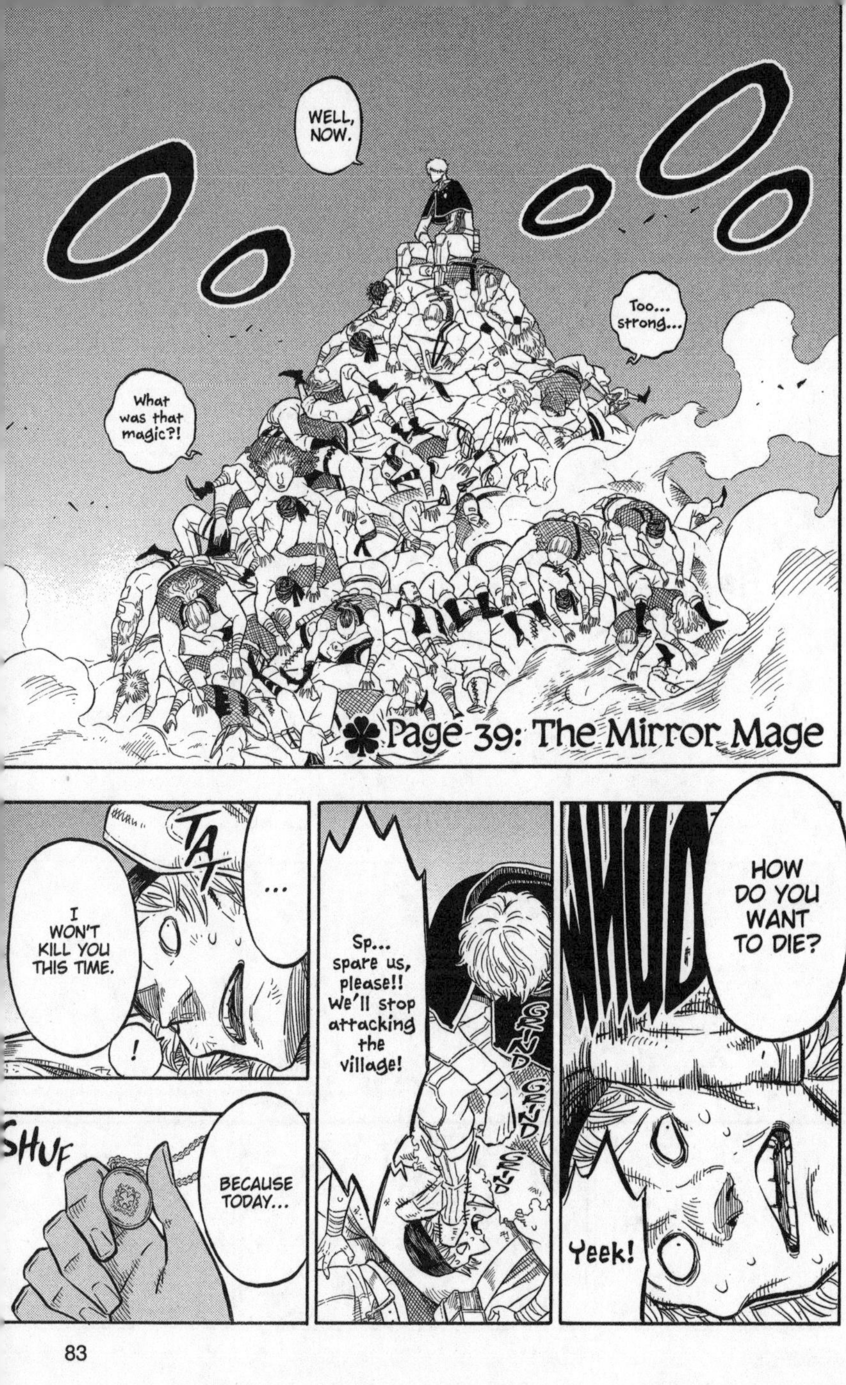
WELL, NOW.
Too... strong...
What was that magic?!
WHUD
HOW DO YOU WANT TO DIE?
Yeek!
Sp... spare us, please!! We'll stop attacking the village!
GRIND GRIND GRIND
...
TAT
I WON'T KILL YOU THIS TIME.
!
SHUF
BECAUSE TODAY...

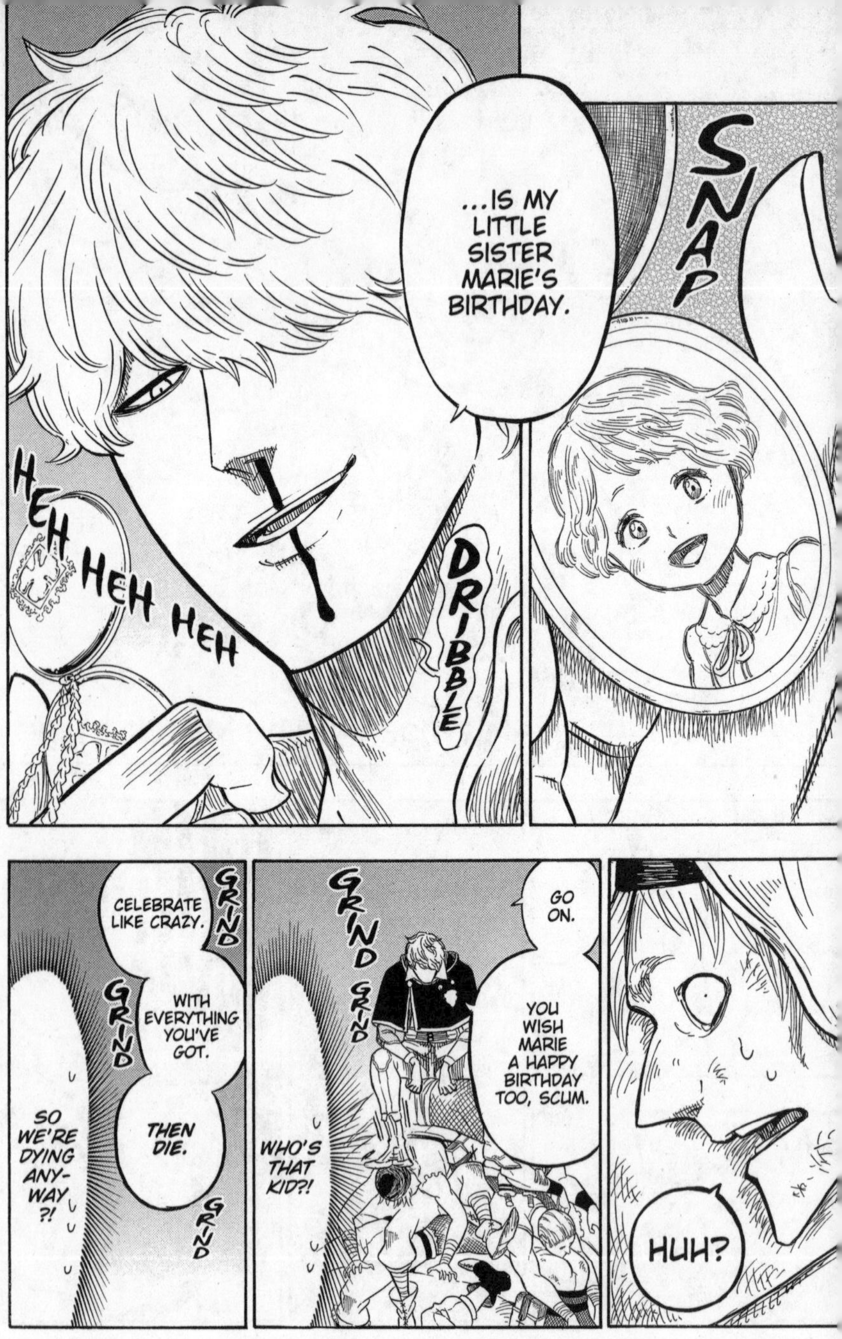
SNAP
...IS MY LITTLE SISTER MARIE'S BIRTHDAY.
HEH HEH HEH HEH
DRIBBLE
HUH?
GO ON.
YOU WISH MARIE A HAPPY BIRTHDAY TOO, SCUM.
GRIND GRIND
WHO'S THAT KID?!
CELEBRATE LIKE CRAZY.
GRIND
WITH EVERYTHING YOU'VE GOT.
GRIND
THEN DIE.
GRIND
SO WE'RE DYING ANY-WAY?!

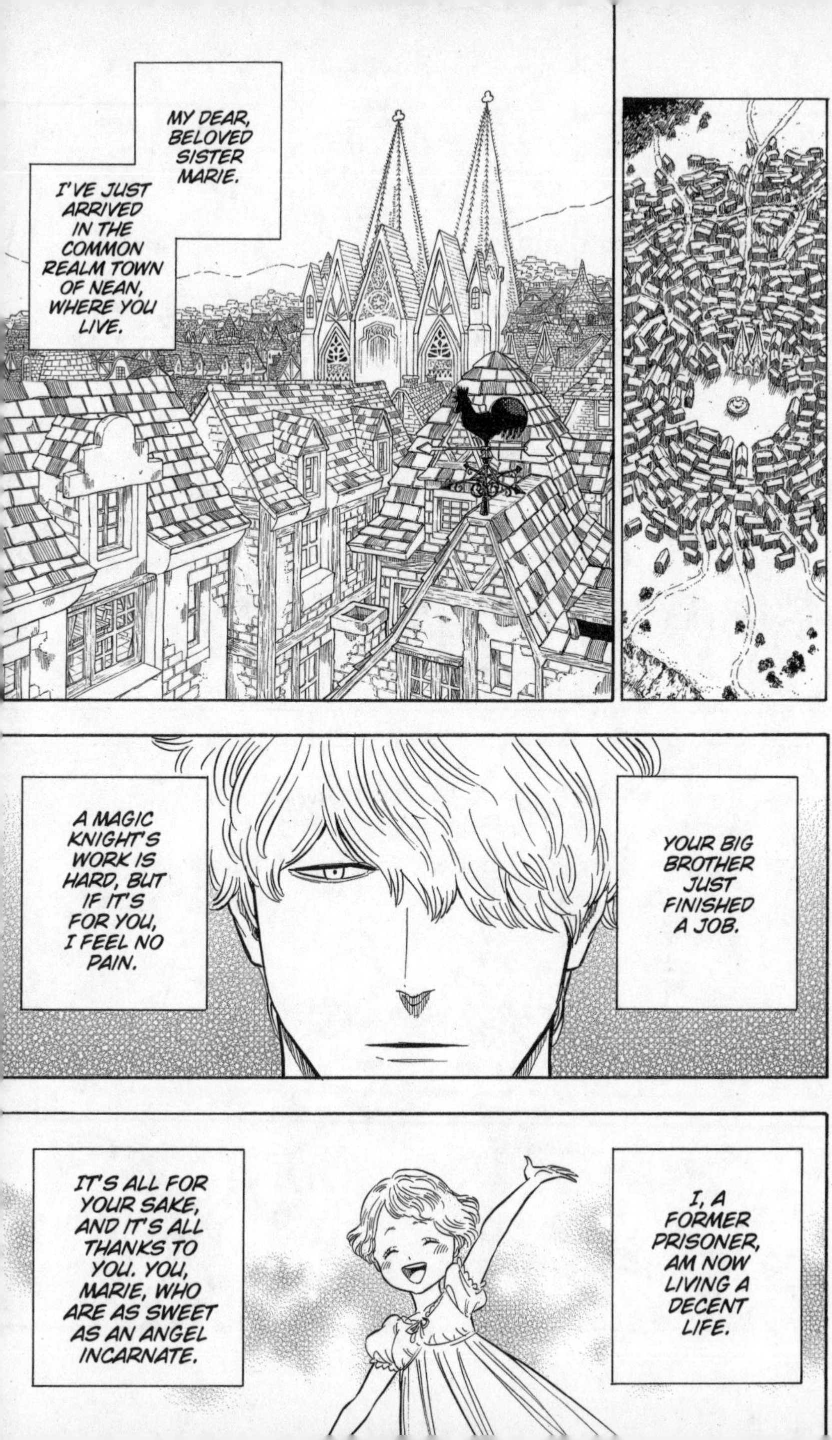
MY DEAR, BELOVED SISTER MARIE.
I'VE JUST ARRIVED IN THE COMMON REALM TOWN OF NEAN, WHERE YOU LIVE.
YOUR BIG BROTHER JUST FINISHED A JOB.
A MAGIC KNIGHT'S WORK IS HARD, BUT IF IT'S FOR YOU, I FEEL NO PAIN.
I, A FORMER PRISONER, AM NOW LIVING A DECENT LIFE.
IT'S ALL FOR YOUR SAKE, AND IT'S ALL THANKS TO YOU. YOU, MARIE, WHO ARE AS SWEET AS AN ANGEL INCARNATE.

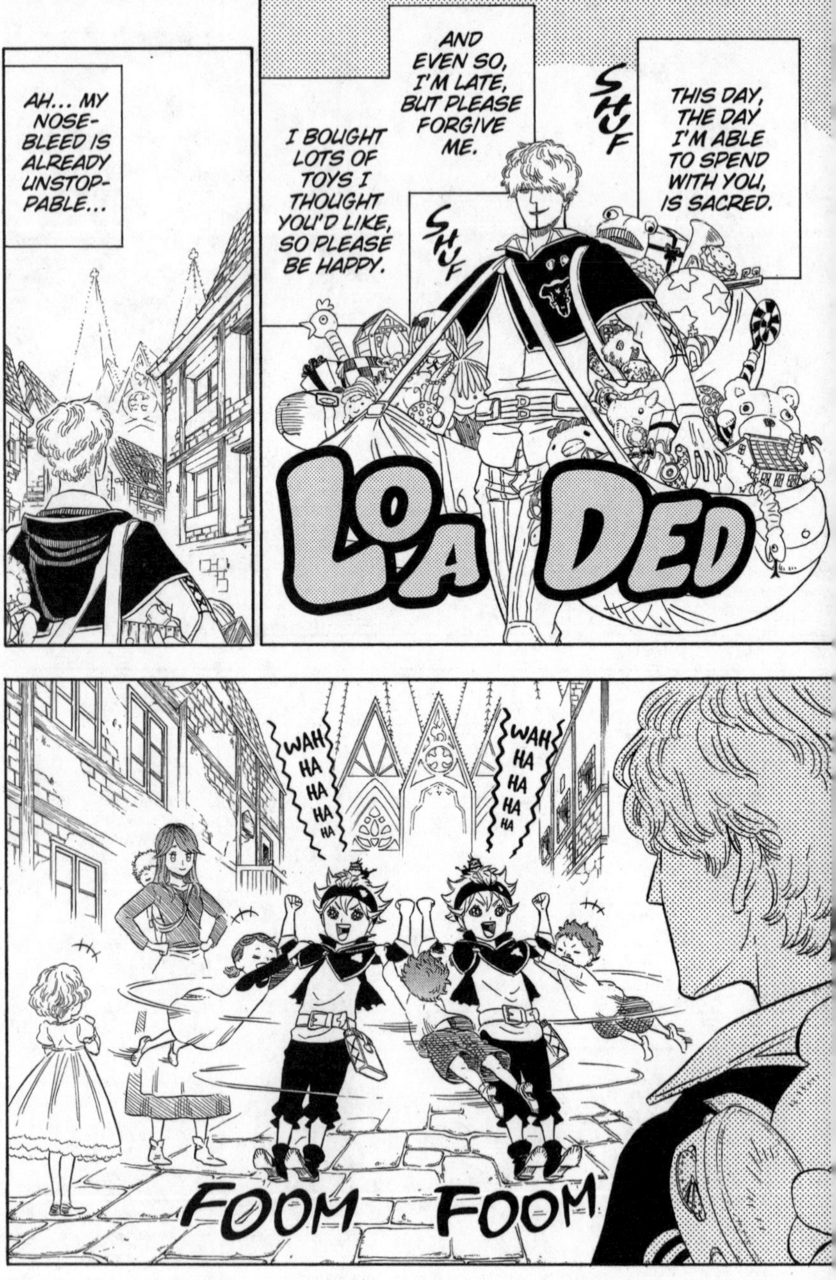

THIS DAY, THE DAY I'M ABLE TO SPEND WITH YOU, IS SACRED.
SHUF
AND EVEN SO, I'M LATE, BUT PLEASE FORGIVE ME.
I BOUGHT LOTS OF TOYS I THOUGHT YOU'D LIKE, SO PLEASE BE HAPPY.
SHUF
LOADED
AH... MY NOSE-BLEED IS ALREADY UNSTOP-PABLE...
WAH HA HA HA HA
WAH HA HA HA HA
FOOM FOOM

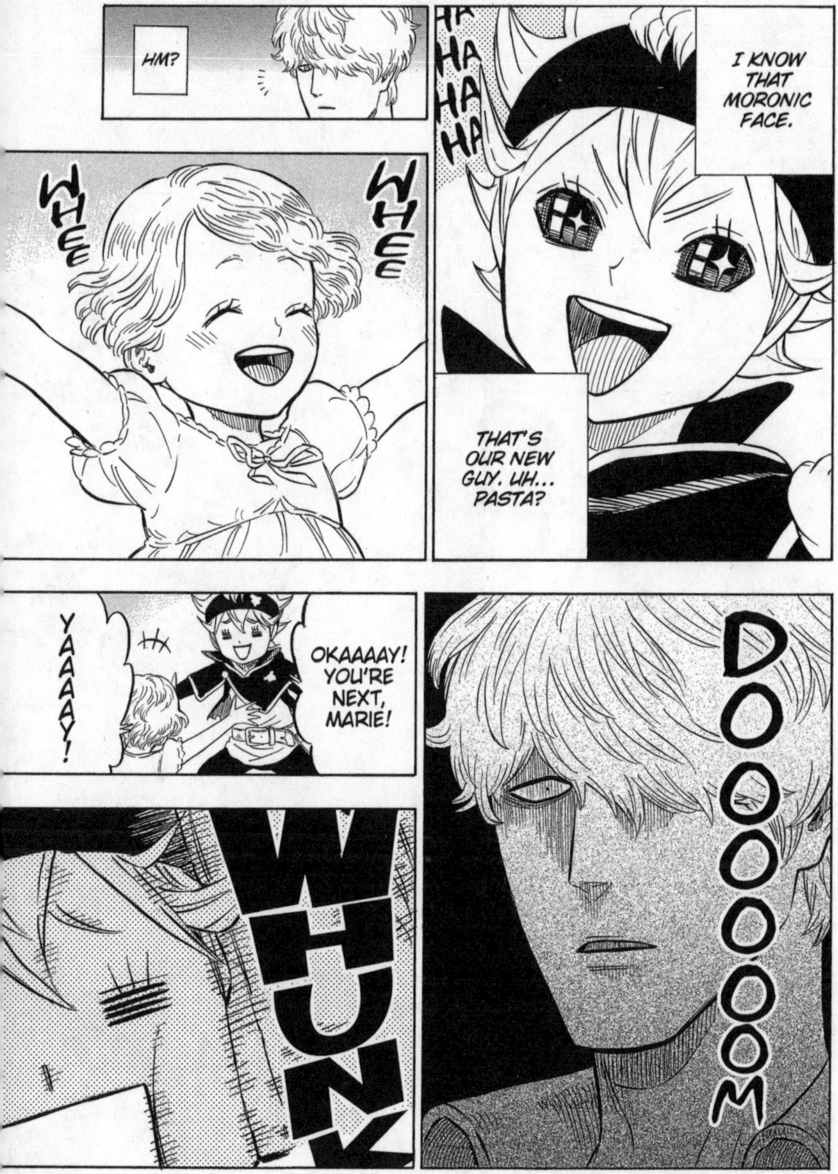
HAHAHAHA
I KNOW THAT MORONIC FACE.
THAT'S OUR NEW GUY. UH... PASTA?
HM?
WHEE
WHEE
DOOOOOOM
OKAAAAY! YOU'RE NEXT, MARIE!
YAAAAAY!
WHUNK

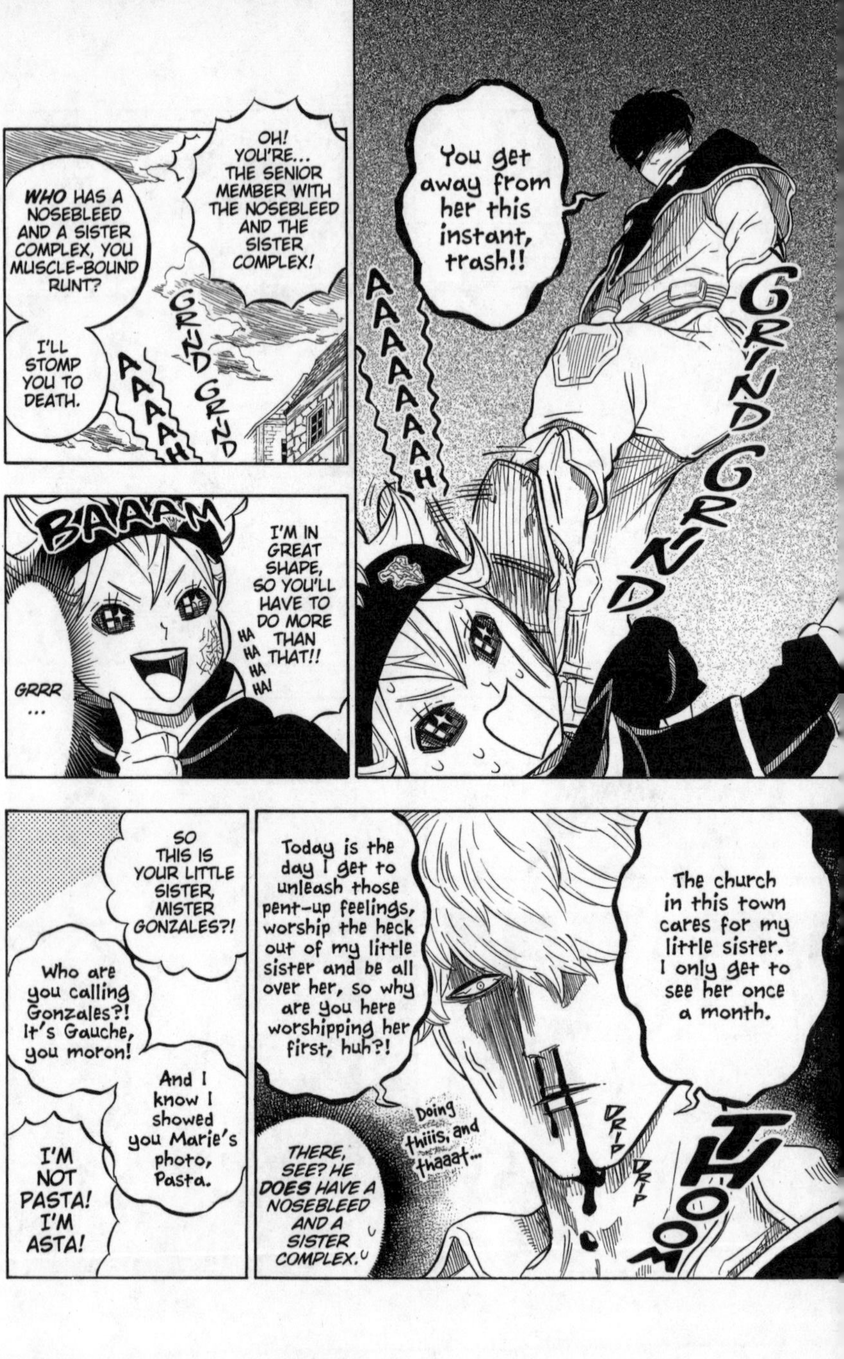
You get away from her this instant, trash!!
AAAAAAAAH
GRIND GRIND GRIND
OH! YOU'RE... THE SENIOR MEMBER WITH THE NOSEBLEED AND THE SISTER COMPLEX!
GRIND GRIND
AAAAH
WHO HAS A NOSEBLEED AND A SISTER COMPLEX, YOU MUSCLE-BOUND RUNT?
I'LL STOMP YOU TO DEATH.
BAAAM
I'M IN GREAT SHAPE, SO YOU'LL HAVE TO DO MORE THAN THAT!!
HA HA HA HA HA!
GRRR ...
The church in this town cares for my little sister. I only get to see her once a month.
THOOOM
Today is the day I get to unleash those pent-up feelings, worship the heck out of my little sister and be all over her, so why are you here worshipping her first, huh?!
DRIP DRIP
Doing thiiis, and thaaat...
*THERE, SEE? HE **DOES** HAVE A NOSEBLEED AND A SISTER COMPLEX.*
SO THIS IS YOUR LITTLE SISTER, MISTER GONZALES?!
Who are you calling Gonzales?! It's Gauche, you moron!
And I know I showed you Marie's photo, Pasta.
I'M NOT PASTA! I'M ASTA!

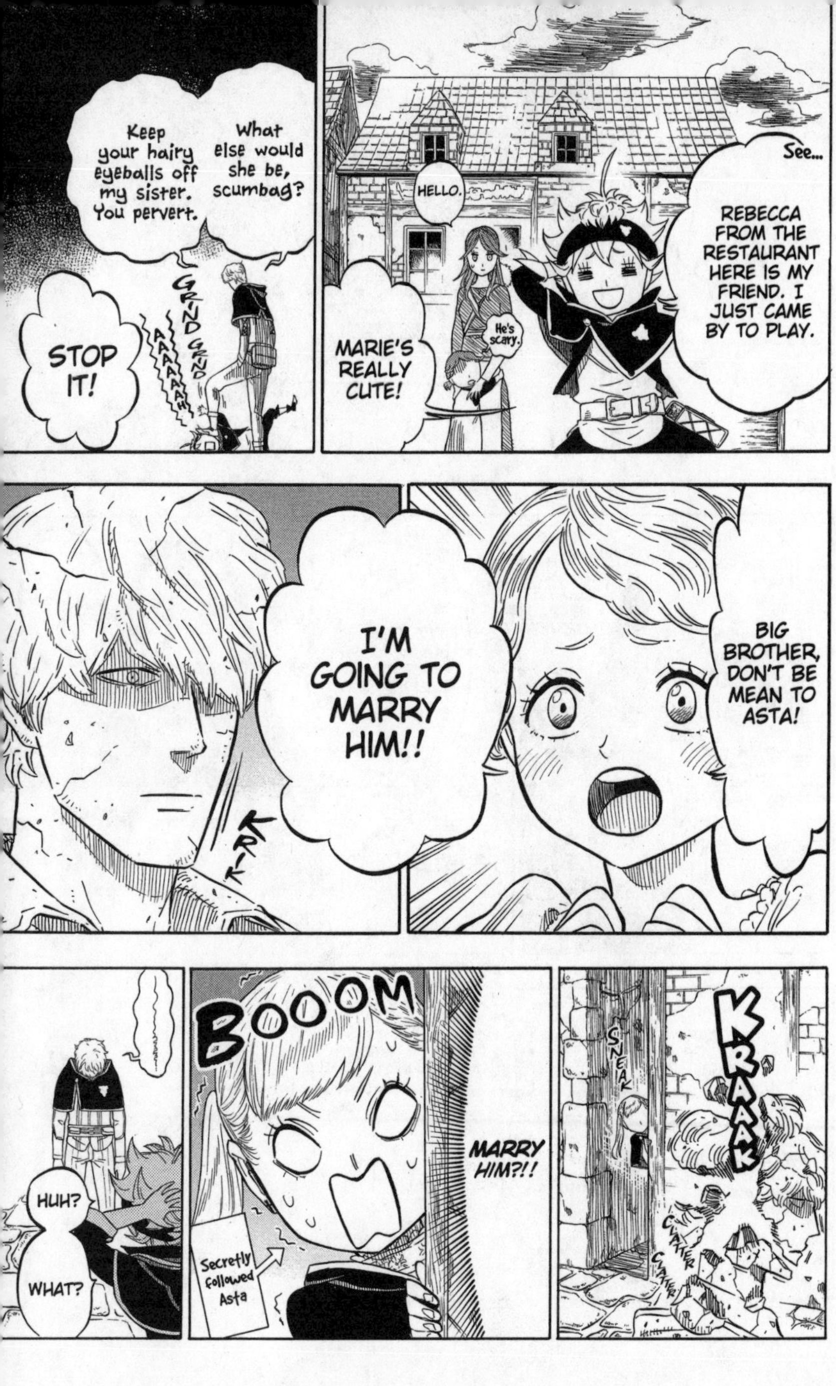
See...
REBECCA FROM THE RESTAURANT HERE IS MY FRIEND. I JUST CAME BY TO PLAY.
HELLO.
MARIE'S REALLY CUTE!
He's scary.
What else would she be, scumbag?
Keep your hairy eyeballs off my sister. You pervert.
GRIND GRIND
AAAAAAH
STOP IT!
BIG BROTHER, DON'T BE MEAN TO ASTA!
I'M GOING TO MARRY HIM!!
KRIK
KRAAAK
SNEAK
CLATTER
CLATTER
BOOOM
MARRY HIM?!!
Secretly followed Asta
HUH?
WHAT?

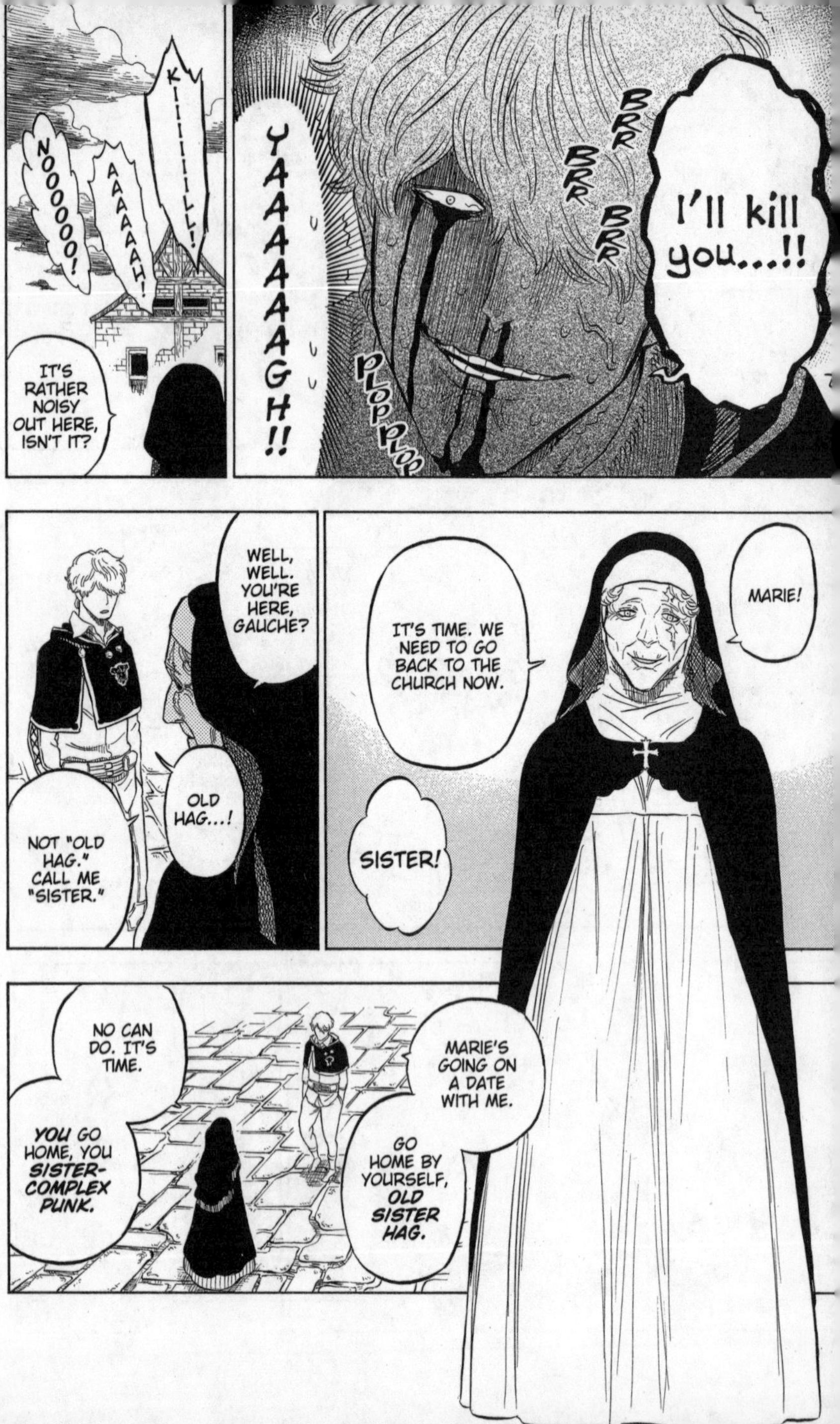
I'll kill you...!!
BRR BRR BRR
YAAAAAAAAAAGH!!
PLOP PLOP
KIIIIIIILL!
AAAAAAH!
NOOOOOOO!
IT'S RATHER NOISY OUT HERE, ISN'T IT?
MARIE!
IT'S TIME. WE NEED TO GO BACK TO THE CHURCH NOW.
SISTER!
WELL, WELL. YOU'RE HERE, GAUCHE?
OLD HAG...!
NOT "OLD HAG." CALL ME "SISTER."
MARIE'S GOING ON A DATE WITH ME.
GO HOME BY YOURSELF, OLD SISTER HAG.
NO CAN DO. IT'S TIME.
YOU GO HOME, YOU SISTER-COMPLEX PUNK.

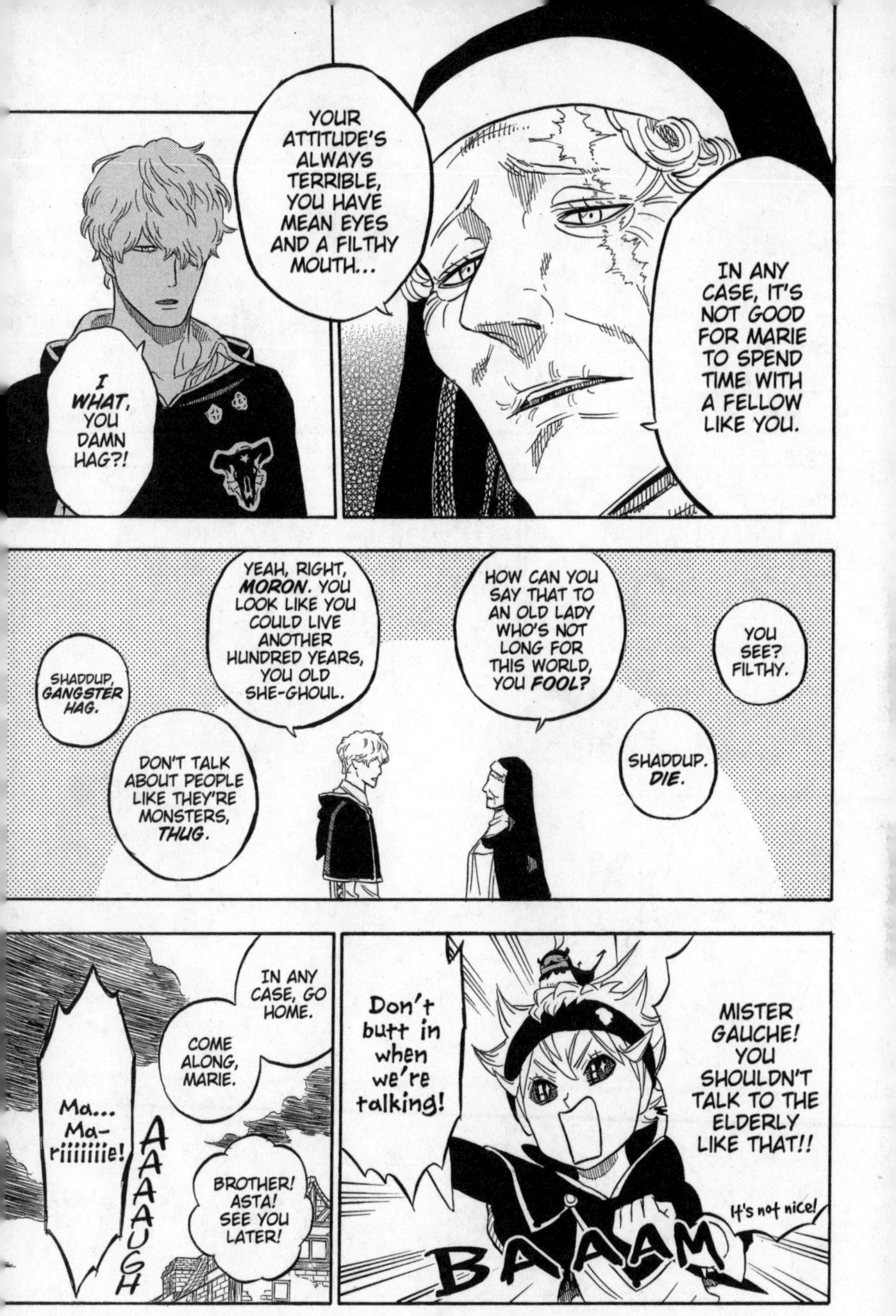
YOUR ATTITUDE'S ALWAYS TERRIBLE, YOU HAVE MEAN EYES AND A FILTHY MOUTH...
IN ANY CASE, IT'S NOT GOOD FOR MARIE TO SPEND TIME WITH A FELLOW LIKE YOU.
I *WHAT*, YOU DAMN HAG?!
YOU SEE? FILTHY.
SHADDUP. *DIE*.
HOW CAN YOU SAY THAT TO AN OLD LADY WHO'S NOT LONG FOR THIS WORLD, YOU *FOOL*?
YEAH, RIGHT, *MORON*. YOU LOOK LIKE YOU COULD LIVE ANOTHER HUNDRED YEARS, YOU OLD SHE-GHOUL.
DON'T TALK ABOUT PEOPLE LIKE THEY'RE MONSTERS, *THUG*.
SHADDUP, *GANGSTER HAG*.
MISTER GAUCHE! YOU SHOULDN'T TALK TO THE ELDERLY LIKE THAT!!
It's not nice!
Don't butt in when we're talking!
BAAAM
IN ANY CASE, GO HOME.
COME ALONG, MARIE.
BROTHER! ASTA! SEE YOU LATER!
AAAAAUGH
Ma... Ma-riiiiiiie!

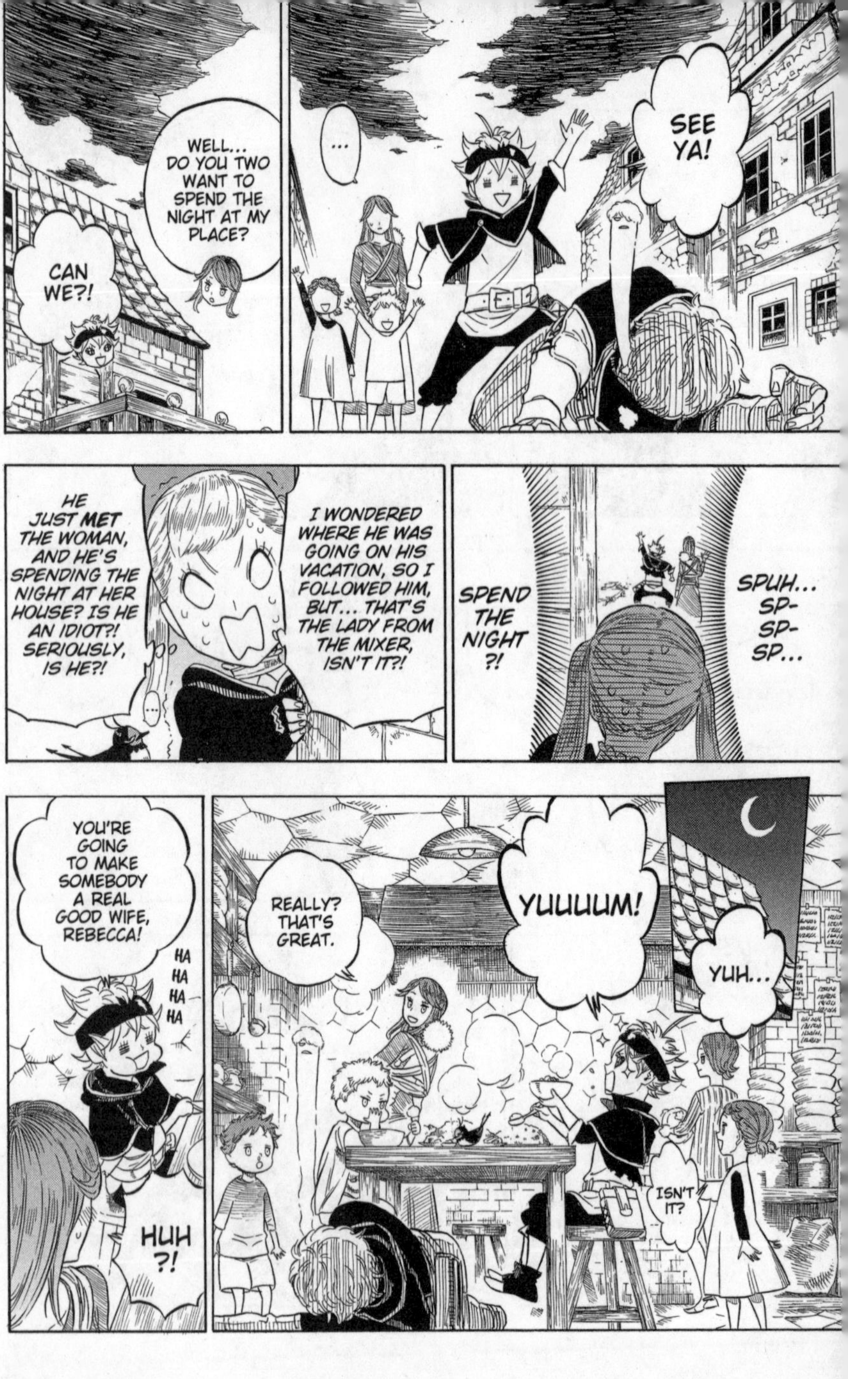
SEE YA!
...
WELL... DO YOU TWO WANT TO SPEND THE NIGHT AT MY PLACE?
CAN WE?!
SPUH... SP- SP- SP...
SPEND THE NIGHT?!
I WONDERED WHERE HE WAS GOING ON HIS VACATION, SO I FOLLOWED HIM, BUT... THAT'S THE LADY FROM THE MIXER, ISN'T IT?!
HE JUST MET THE WOMAN, AND HE'S SPENDING THE NIGHT AT HER HOUSE? IS HE AN IDIOT?! SERIOUSLY, IS HE?!
...
YUH...
YUUUUM!
REALLY? THAT'S GREAT.
ISN'T IT?
YOU'RE GOING TO MAKE SOMEBODY A REAL GOOD WIFE, REBECCA!
HA HA HA HA
HUH?!

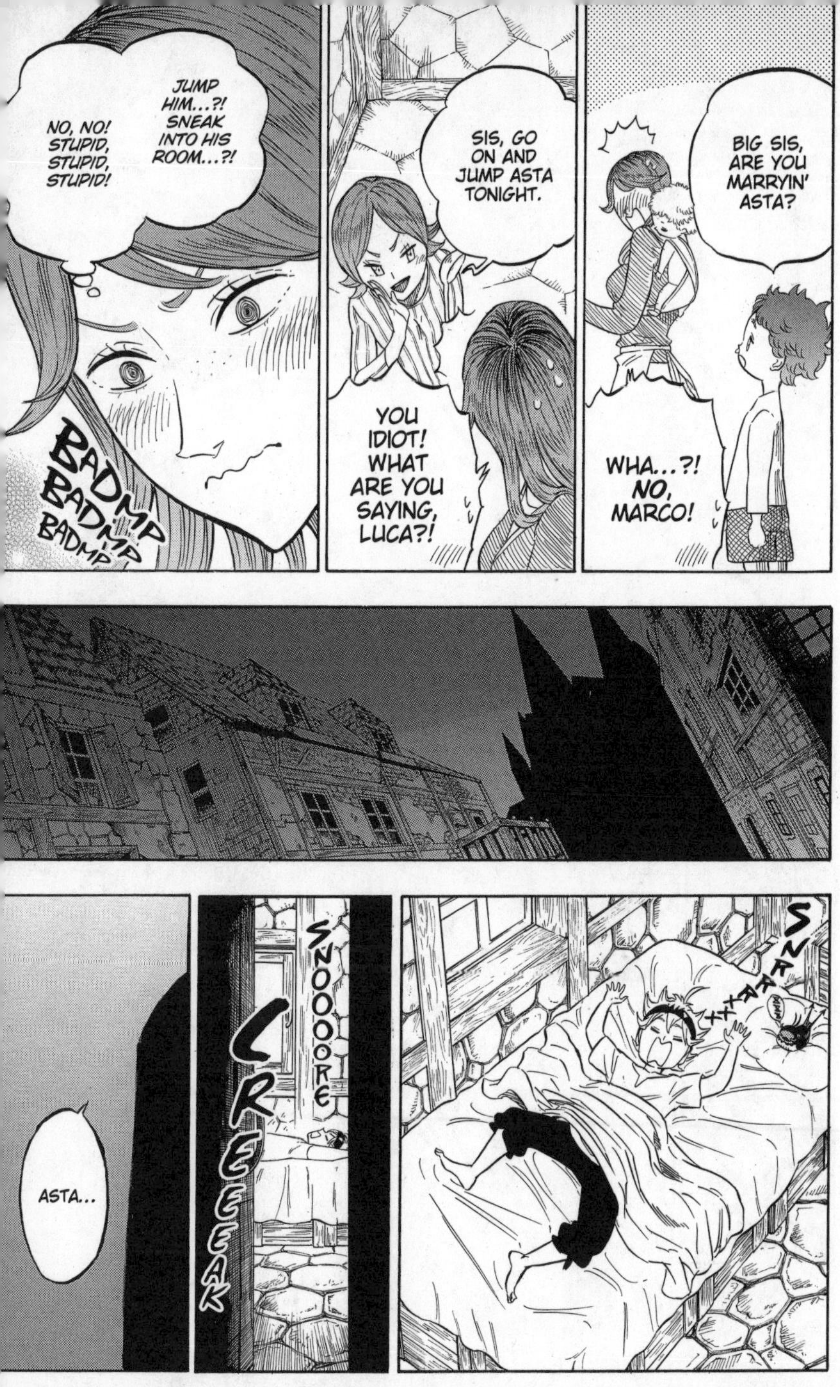

BIG SIS, ARE YOU MARRYIN' ASTA?
WHA...?! NO, MARCO!
SIS, GO ON AND JUMP ASTA TONIGHT.
YOU IDIOT! WHAT ARE YOU SAYING, LUCA?!
JUMP HIM...?! SNEAK INTO HIS ROOM...?!
NO, NO! STUPID, STUPID, STUPID!
BADMP BADMP BADMP
SNRRRXXX
MMM
SNOOOOORE
CREEEEAK
ASTA...

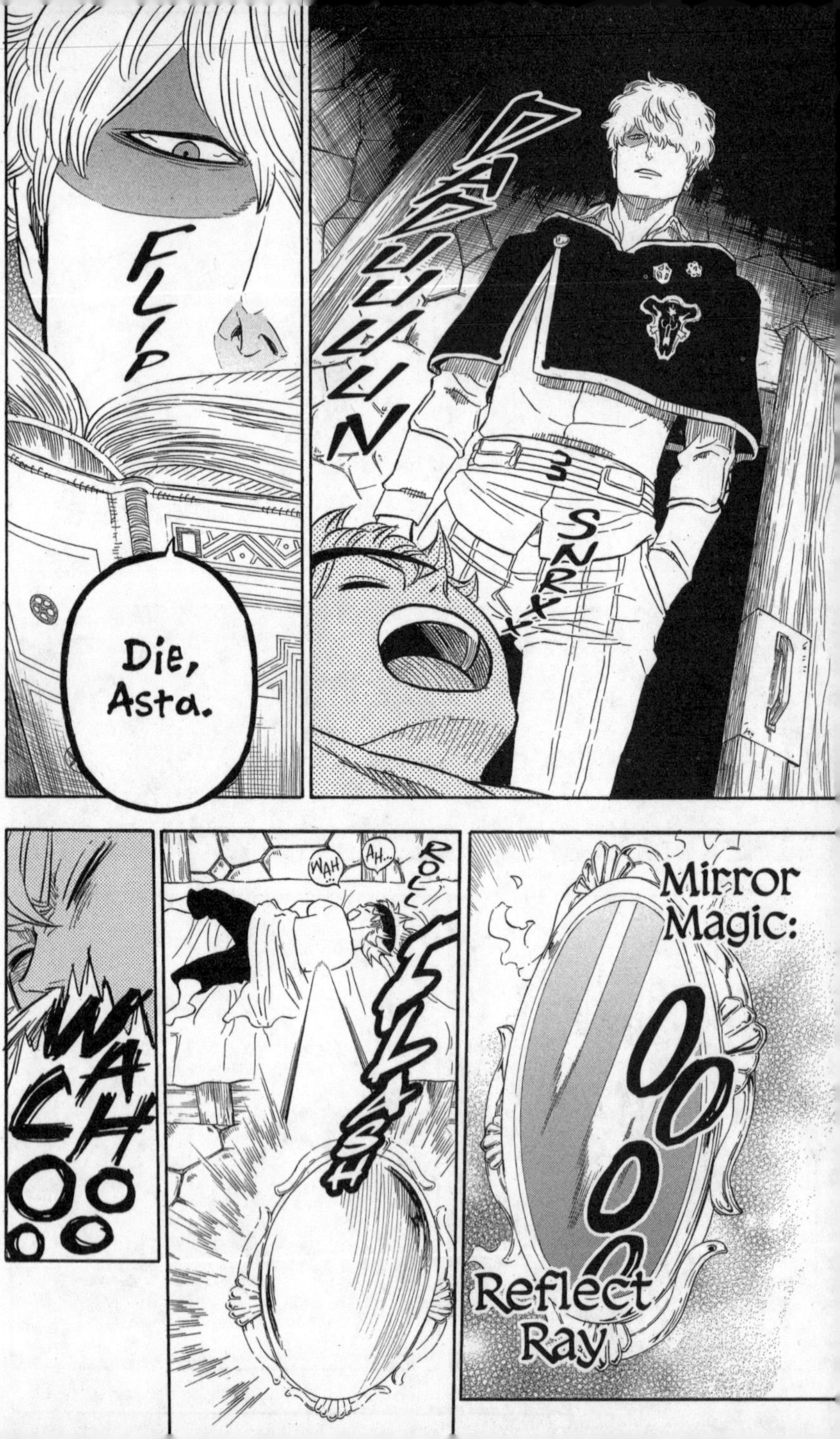
KAPUUUUN
SNRK
FLIP
Die, Asta.
Mirror Magic:
Reflect Ray
ROLL
AH...
WAH...
FLASH
WACHOOOO

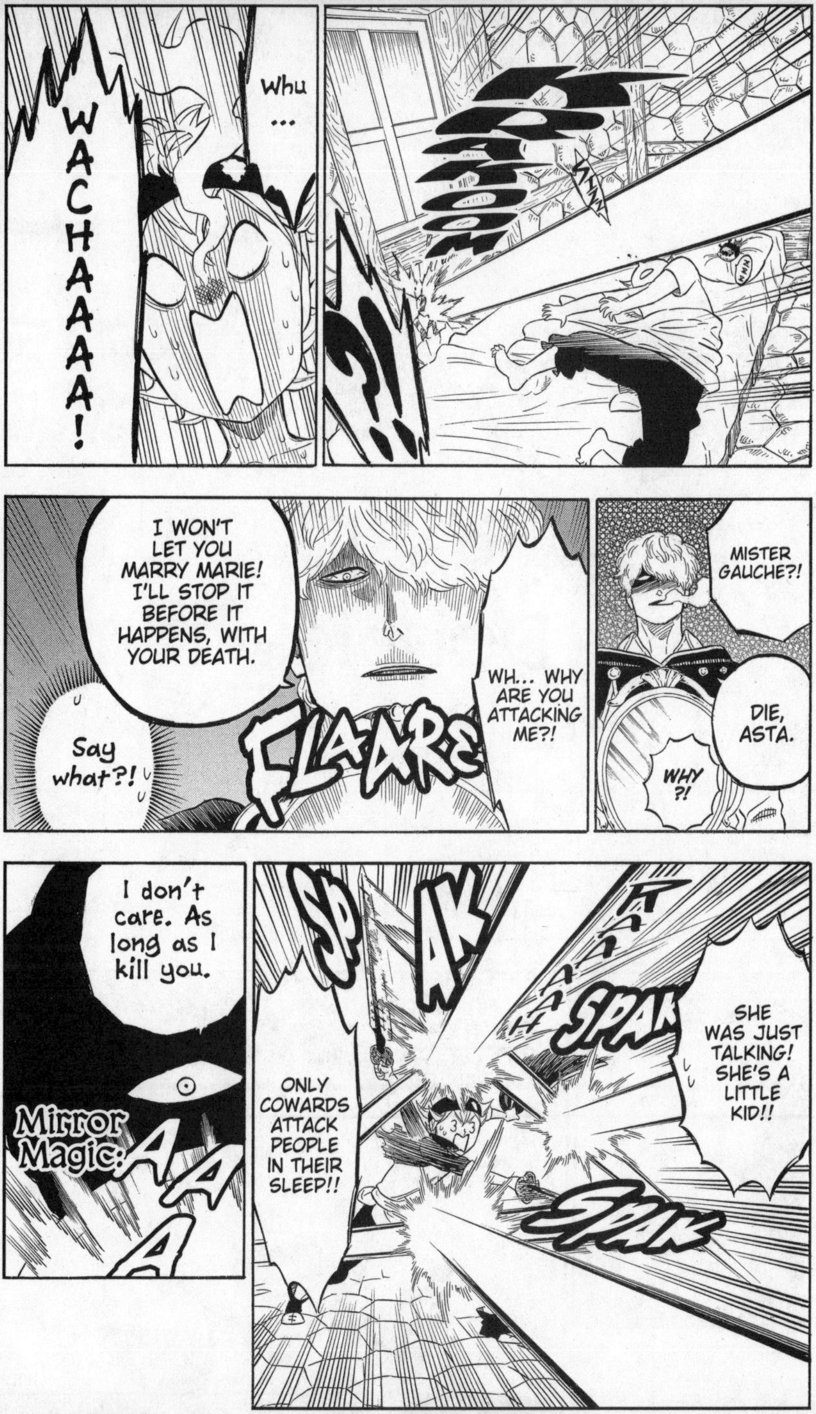
?!!
Whu
...
WACHAAAAAA!
MISTER GAUCHE?!
DIE, ASTA.
WHY ?!
WH... WHY ARE YOU ATTACKING ME?!
I WON'T LET YOU MARRY MARIE! I'LL STOP IT BEFORE IT HAPPENS, WITH YOUR DEATH.
FLAARE
Say what?!
SHE WAS JUST TALKING! SHE'S A LITTLE KID!!
SPAK
SPAK
SPAK
ONLY COWARDS ATTACK PEOPLE IN THEIR SLEEP!!
I don't care. As long as I kill you.
Mirror Magic: AAA
A

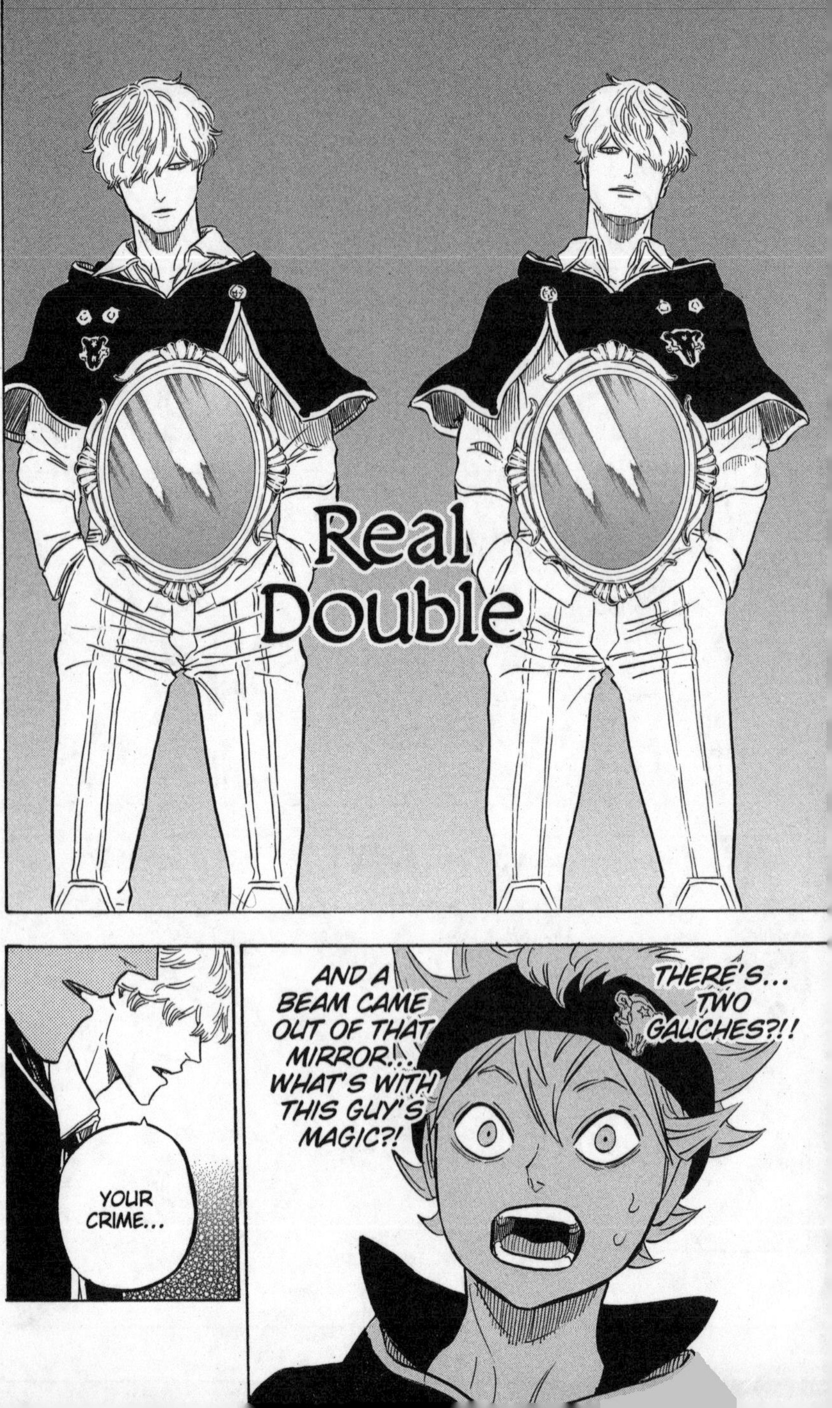
Real Double
THERE'S... TWO GAUCHES?!!
AND A BEAM CAME OUT OF THAT MIRROR... WHAT'S WITH THIS GUY'S MAGIC?!
YOUR CRIME...

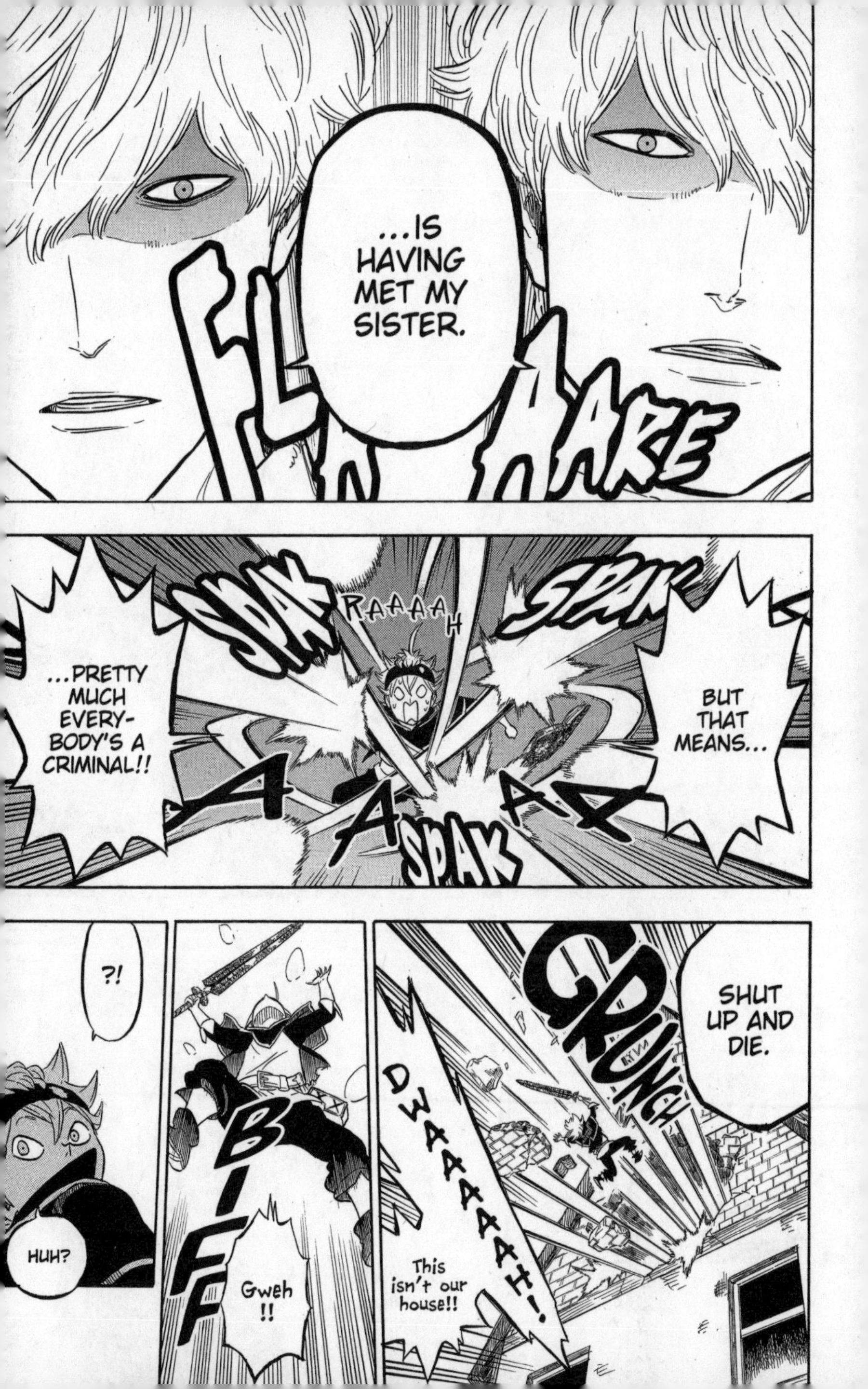
...IS HAVING MET MY SISTER.
FLAARE
SPAK
BUT THAT MEANS...
RAAAAAH
SPAK
...PRETTY MUCH EVERY-BODY'S A CRIMINAL!!
AAAA
SPAK
SHUT UP AND DIE.
CRUNCH
DWAAAAAAAH!
This isn't our house!!
BIFF
Gweh!!
?!
HUH?

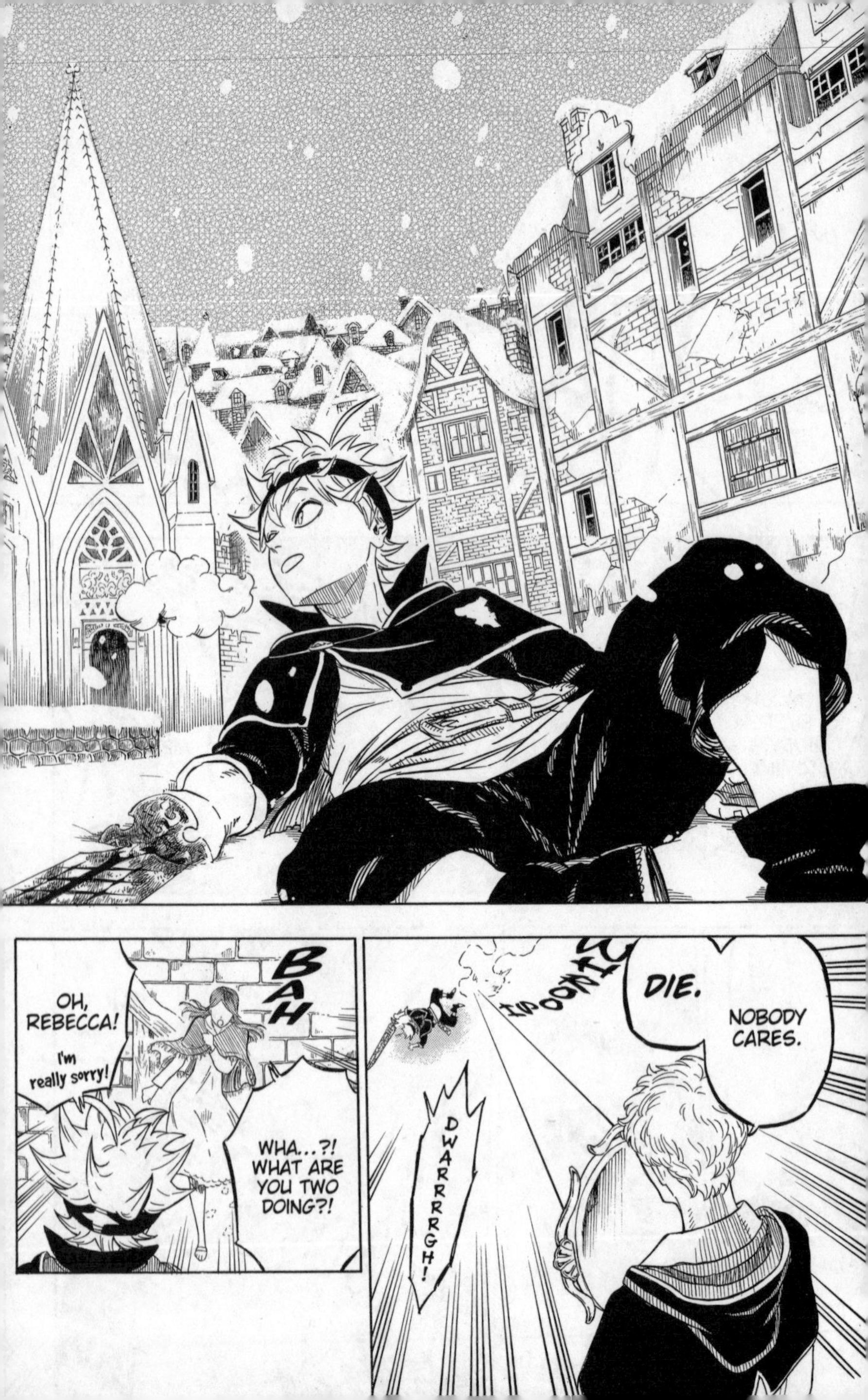
DIE.
NOBODY CARES.
DWARRRRGH!
BAH
OH, REBECCA!
I'm really sorry!
WHA...?! WHAT ARE YOU TWO DOING?!

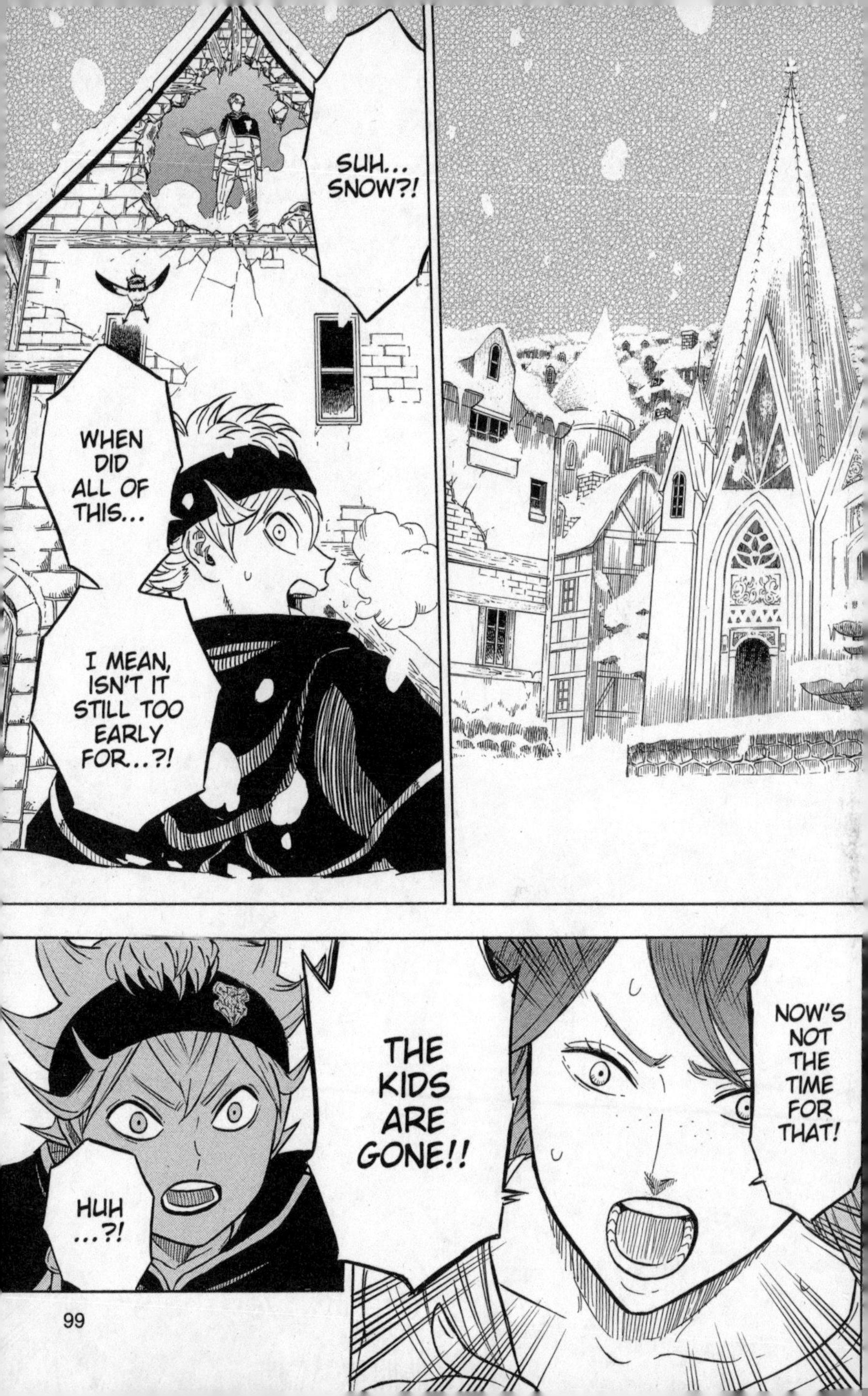
SUH... SNOW?!
WHEN DID ALL OF THIS...
I MEAN, ISN'T IT STILL TOO EARLY FOR..?!
NOW'S NOT THE TIME FOR THAT!
THE KIDS ARE GONE!!
HUH ...?!

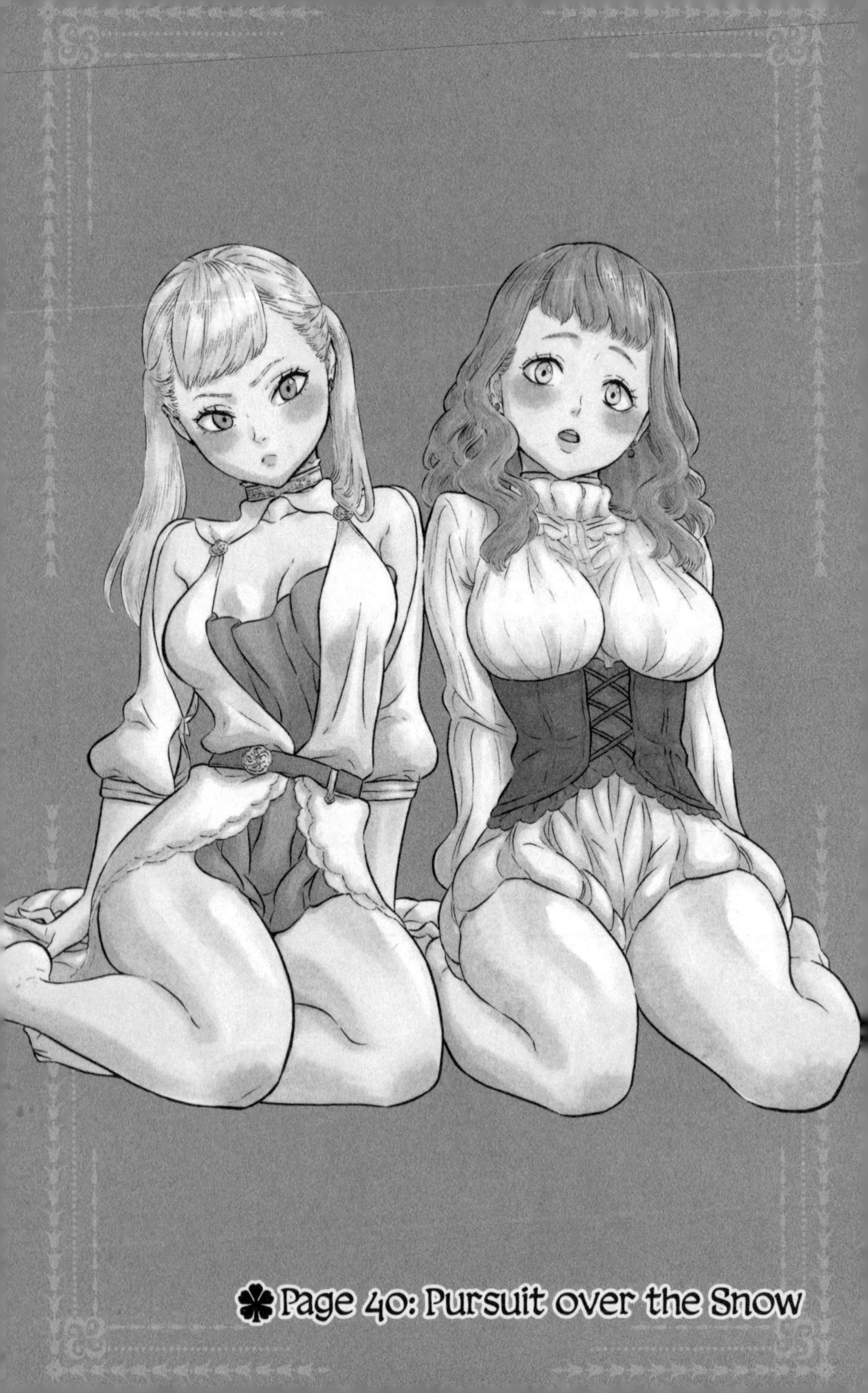

Page 40: Pursuit over the Snow

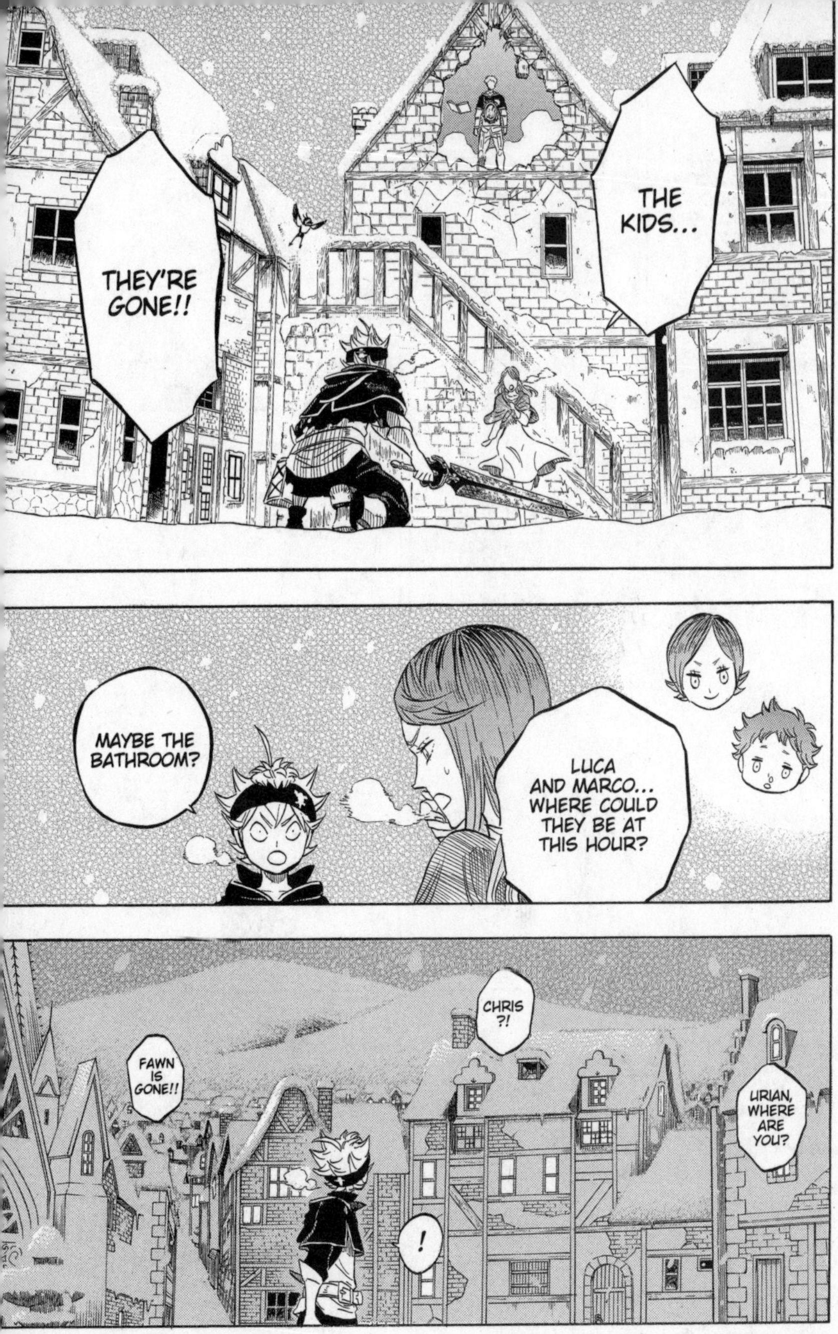
THE KIDS...
THEY'RE GONE!!
LUCA AND MARCO... WHERE COULD THEY BE AT THIS HOUR?
MAYBE THE BATHROOM?
URIAN, WHERE ARE YOU?
CHRIS ?!
FAWN IS GONE!!
!

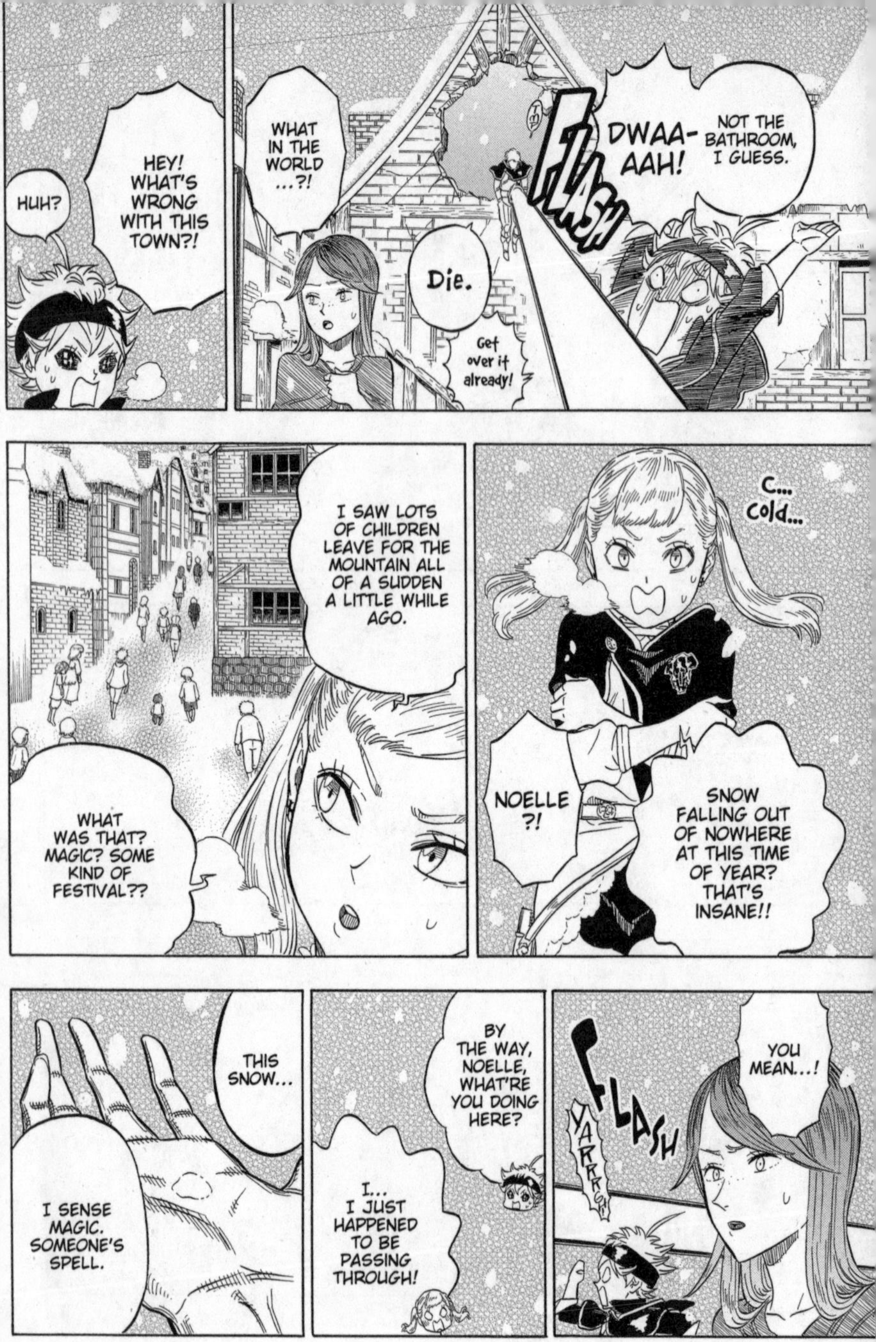
NOT THE BATHROOM, I GUESS.
DWAA-AAH!
FLASH
WHAT IN THE WORLD ...?!
Die.
Get over it already!
HEY! WHAT'S WRONG WITH THIS TOWN?!
HUH?
C... cold...
SNOW FALLING OUT OF NOWHERE AT THIS TIME OF YEAR? THAT'S INSANE!!
NOELLE ?!
I SAW LOTS OF CHILDREN LEAVE FOR THE MOUNTAIN ALL OF A SUDDEN A LITTLE WHILE AGO.
WHAT WAS THAT? MAGIC? SOME KIND OF FESTIVAL??
YOU MEAN...!
FLASH
YARRGH!
BY THE WAY, NOELLE, WHAT'RE YOU DOING HERE?
I... I JUST HAPPENED TO BE PASSING THROUGH!
THIS SNOW...
I SENSE MAGIC. SOMEONE'S SPELL.

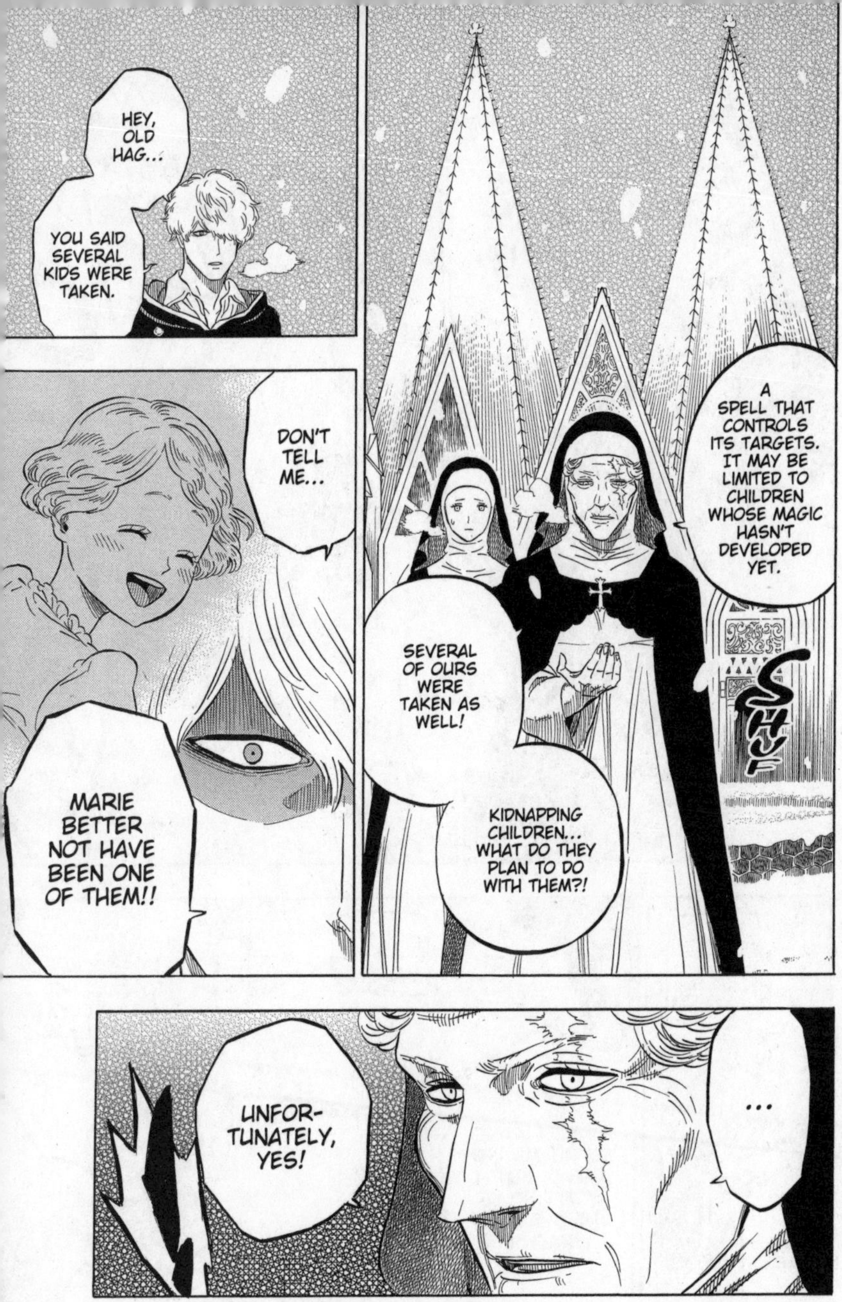
A SPELL THAT CONTROLS ITS TARGETS. IT MAY BE LIMITED TO CHILDREN WHOSE MAGIC HASN'T DEVELOPED YET.
SHUFF
SEVERAL OF OURS WERE TAKEN AS WELL!
KIDNAPPING CHILDREN... WHAT DO THEY PLAN TO DO WITH THEM?!
HEY, OLD HAG...
YOU SAID SEVERAL KIDS WERE TAKEN.
DON'T TELL ME...
MARIE BETTER NOT HAVE BEEN ONE OF THEM!!
...
UNFOR-TUNATELY, YES!

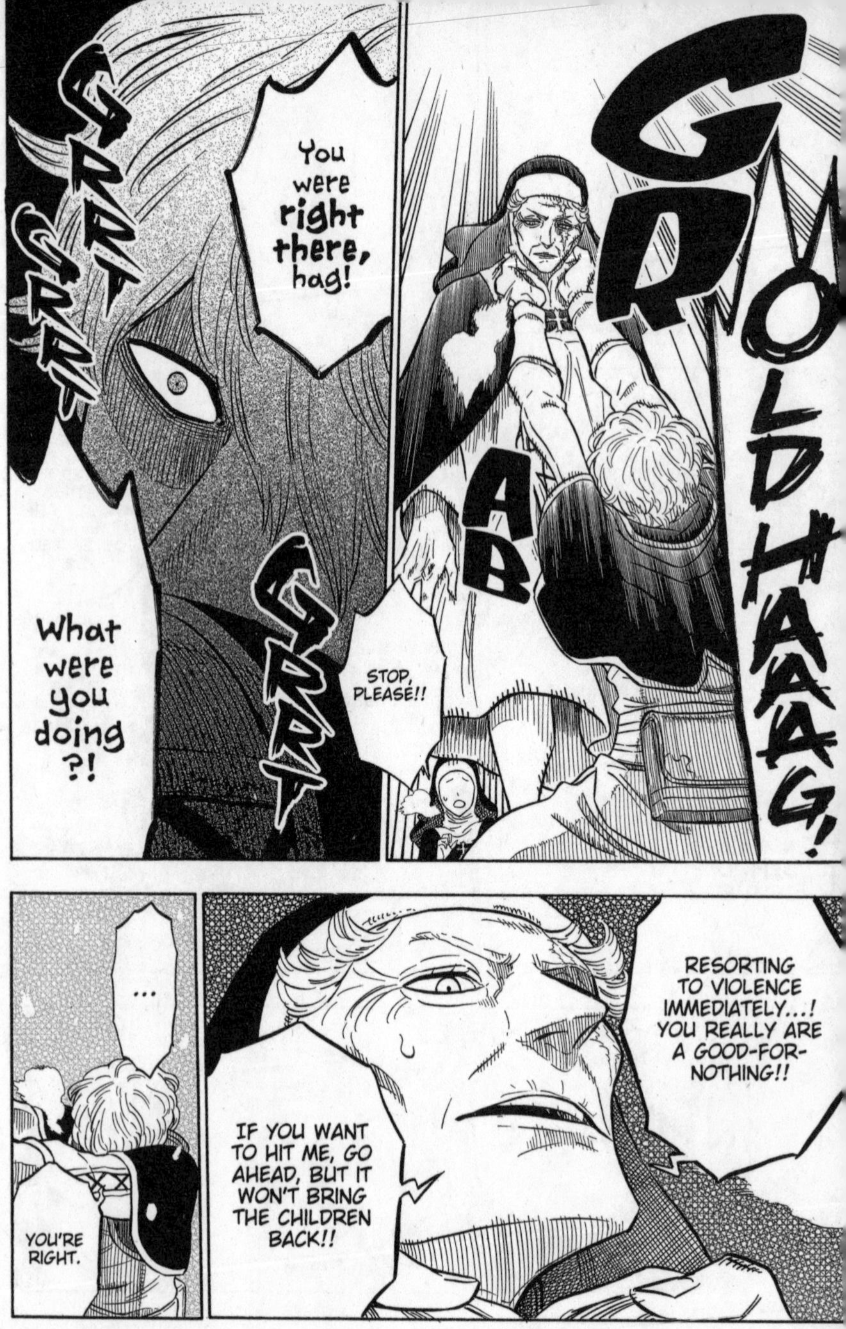
OLD HAAAG!
GRAB
STOP, PLEASE!!
GRRT GRRT
You were right there, hag!
GRRT
What were you doing?!
RESORTING TO VIOLENCE IMMEDIATELY...! YOU REALLY ARE A GOOD-FOR-NOTHING!!
IF YOU WANT TO HIT ME, GO AHEAD, BUT IT WON'T BRING THE CHILDREN BACK!!
...
YOU'RE RIGHT.

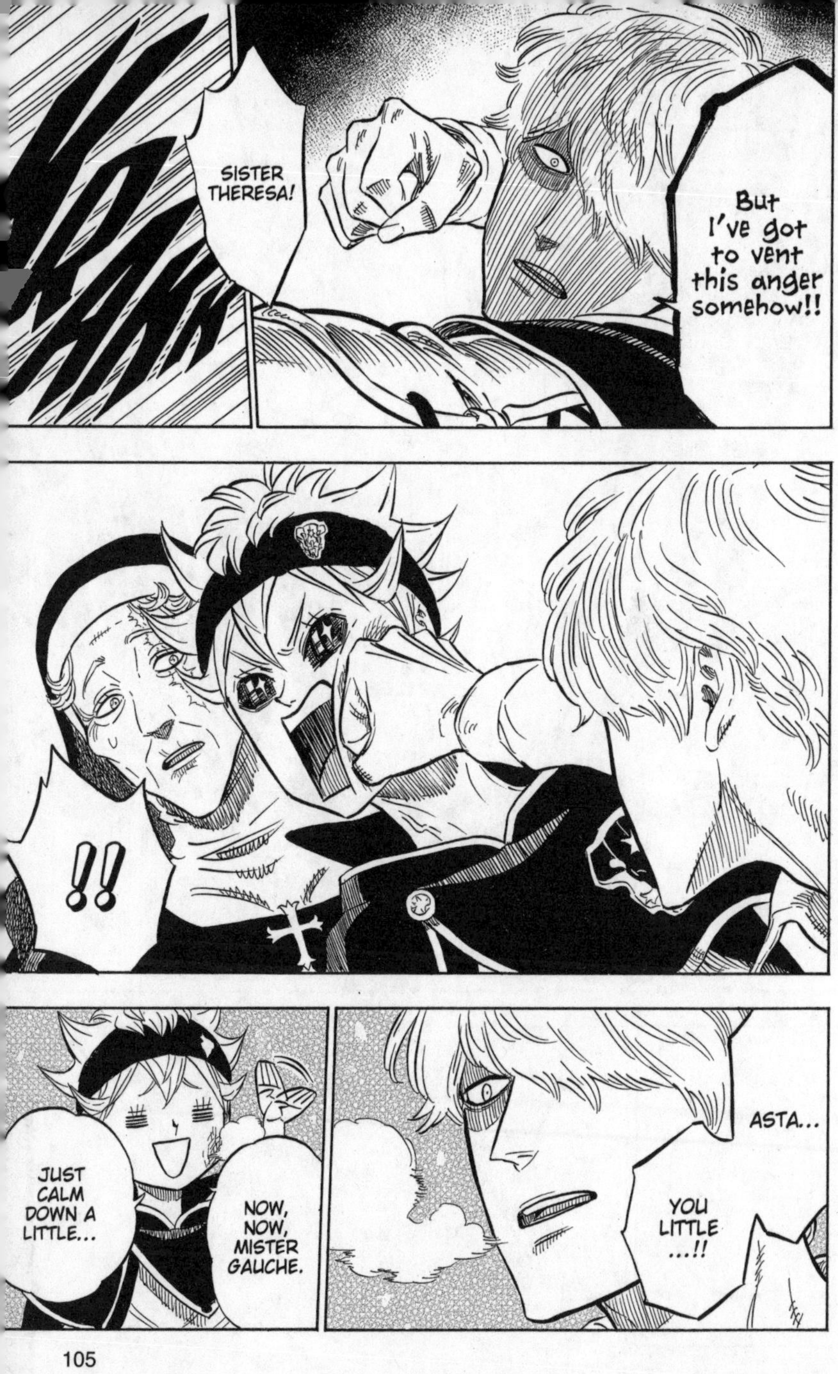
But I've got to vent this anger somehow!!
SISTER THERESA!
!!
ASTA...
YOU LITTLE ...!!
NOW, NOW, MISTER GAUCHE.
JUST CALM DOWN A LITTLE...

...ALL RIGHT ?!!

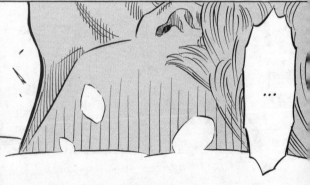

A MAGIC KNIGHT...

...

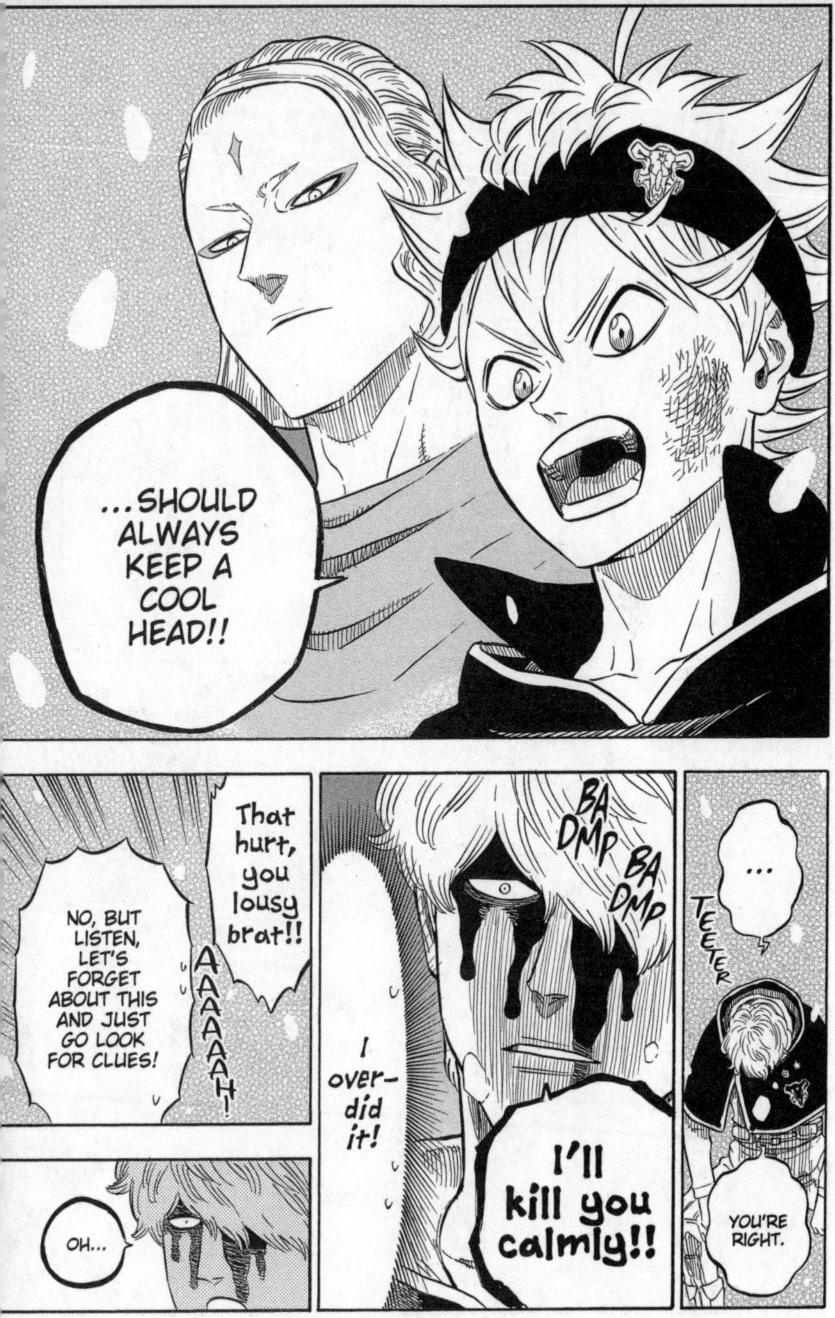
...SHOULD ALWAYS KEEP A COOL HEAD!!
...
TEETER
YOU'RE RIGHT.
BA DMP BA DMP
I'll kill you calmly!!
I over-did it!
That hurt, you lousy brat!!
AAAAAAH!
NO, BUT LISTEN, LET'S FORGET ABOUT THIS AND JUST GO LOOK FOR CLUES!
OH...

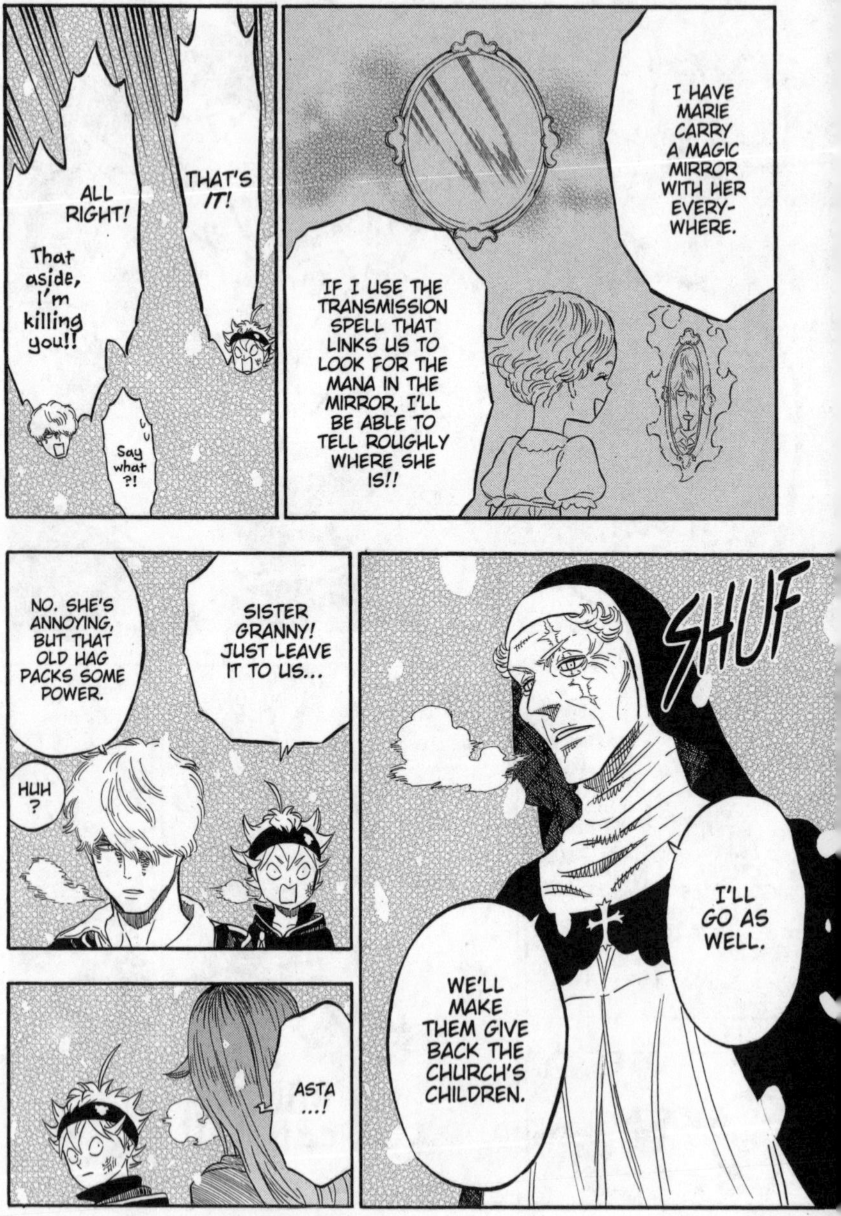
I HAVE MARIE CARRY A MAGIC MIRROR WITH HER EVERY-WHERE.
IF I USE THE TRANSMISSION SPELL THAT LINKS US TO LOOK FOR THE MANA IN THE MIRROR, I'LL BE ABLE TO TELL ROUGHLY WHERE SHE IS!!
THAT'S *IT!*
ALL RIGHT!
That aside, I'm killing you!!
Say what?!
SHUF
I'LL GO AS WELL.
WE'LL MAKE THEM GIVE BACK THE CHURCH'S CHILDREN.
SISTER GRANNY! JUST LEAVE IT TO US...
NO. SHE'S ANNOYING, BUT THAT OLD HAG PACKS SOME POWER.
HUH?
ASTA ...!

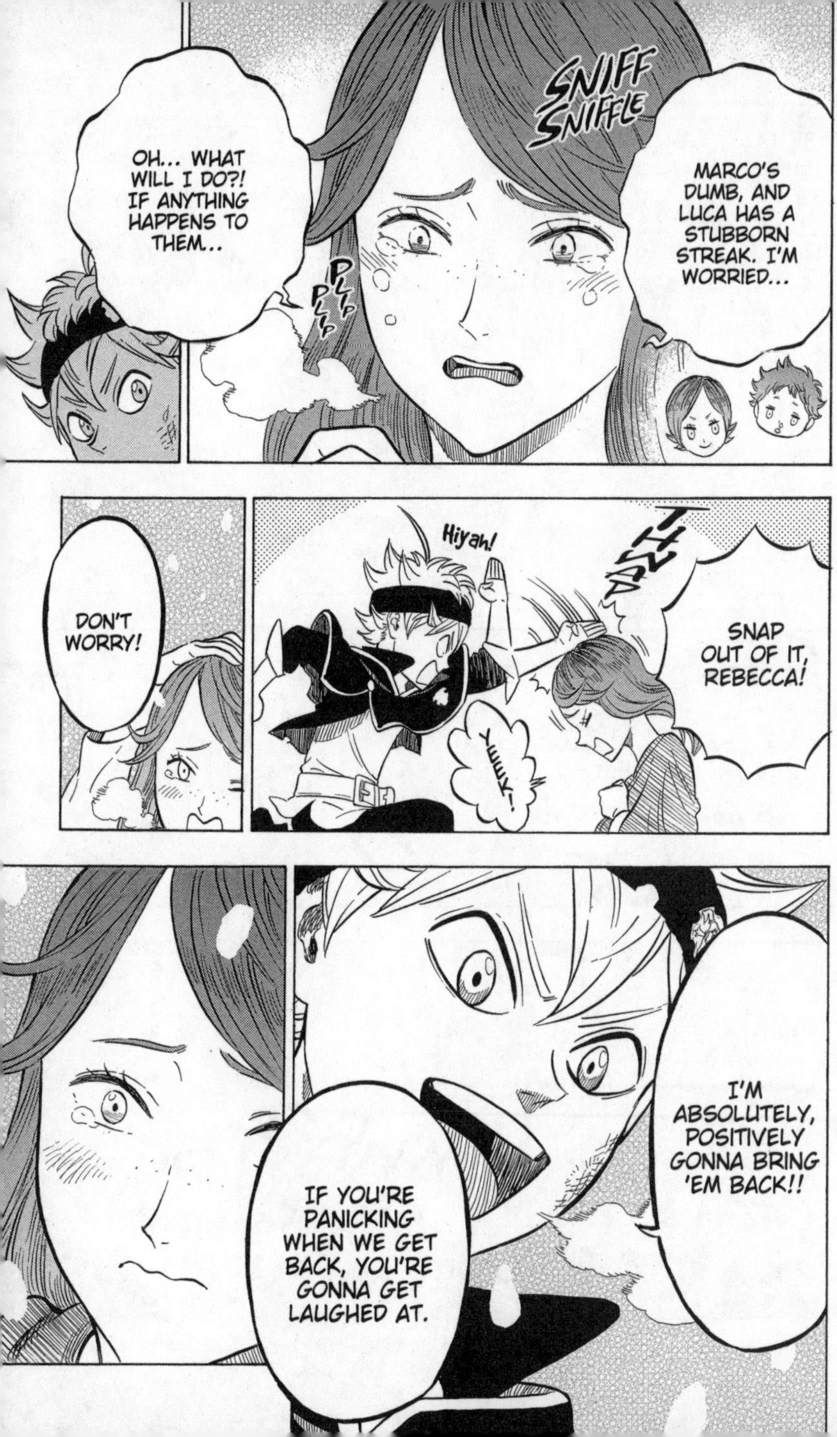
SNIFF SNIFFLE
MARCO'S DUMB, AND LUCA HAS A STUBBORN STREAK. I'M WORRIED...
OH... WHAT WILL I DO?! IF ANYTHING HAPPENS TO THEM...
PLIP PLIP PLIP
THWAP
SNAP OUT OF IT, REBECCA!
Hiyah!
YEEEK!
DON'T WORRY!
I'M ABSOLUTELY, POSITIVELY GONNA BRING 'EM BACK!!
IF YOU'RE PANICKING WHEN WE GET BACK, YOU'RE GONNA GET LAUGHED AT.

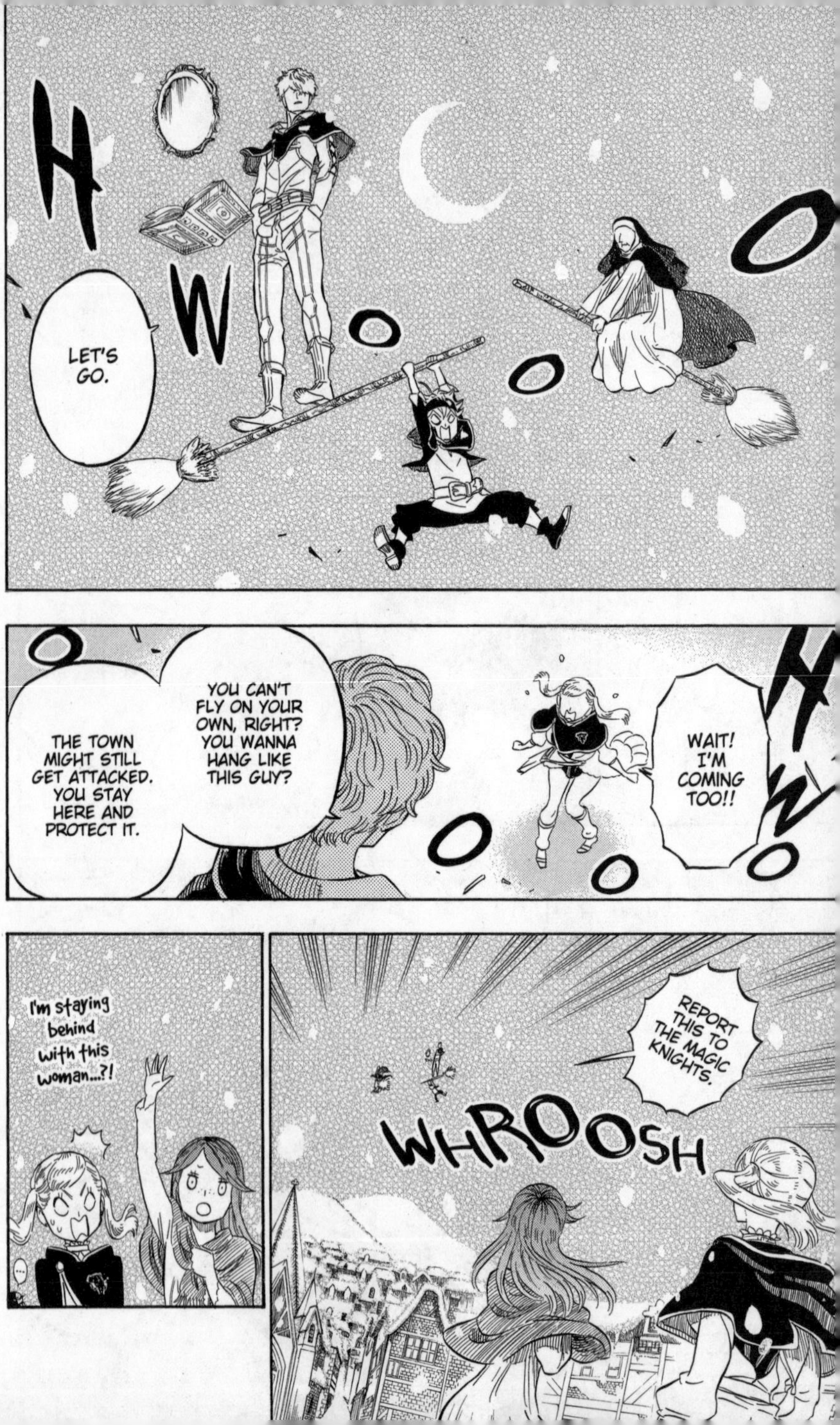
HWOOOO
LET'S GO.
WAIT! I'M COMING TOO!!
YOU CAN'T FLY ON YOUR OWN, RIGHT? YOU WANNA HANG LIKE THIS GUY?
THE TOWN MIGHT STILL GET ATTACKED. YOU STAY HERE AND PROTECT IT.
REPORT THIS TO THE MAGIC KNIGHTS.
WHROOSH
I'm staying behind with this woman...?!
...

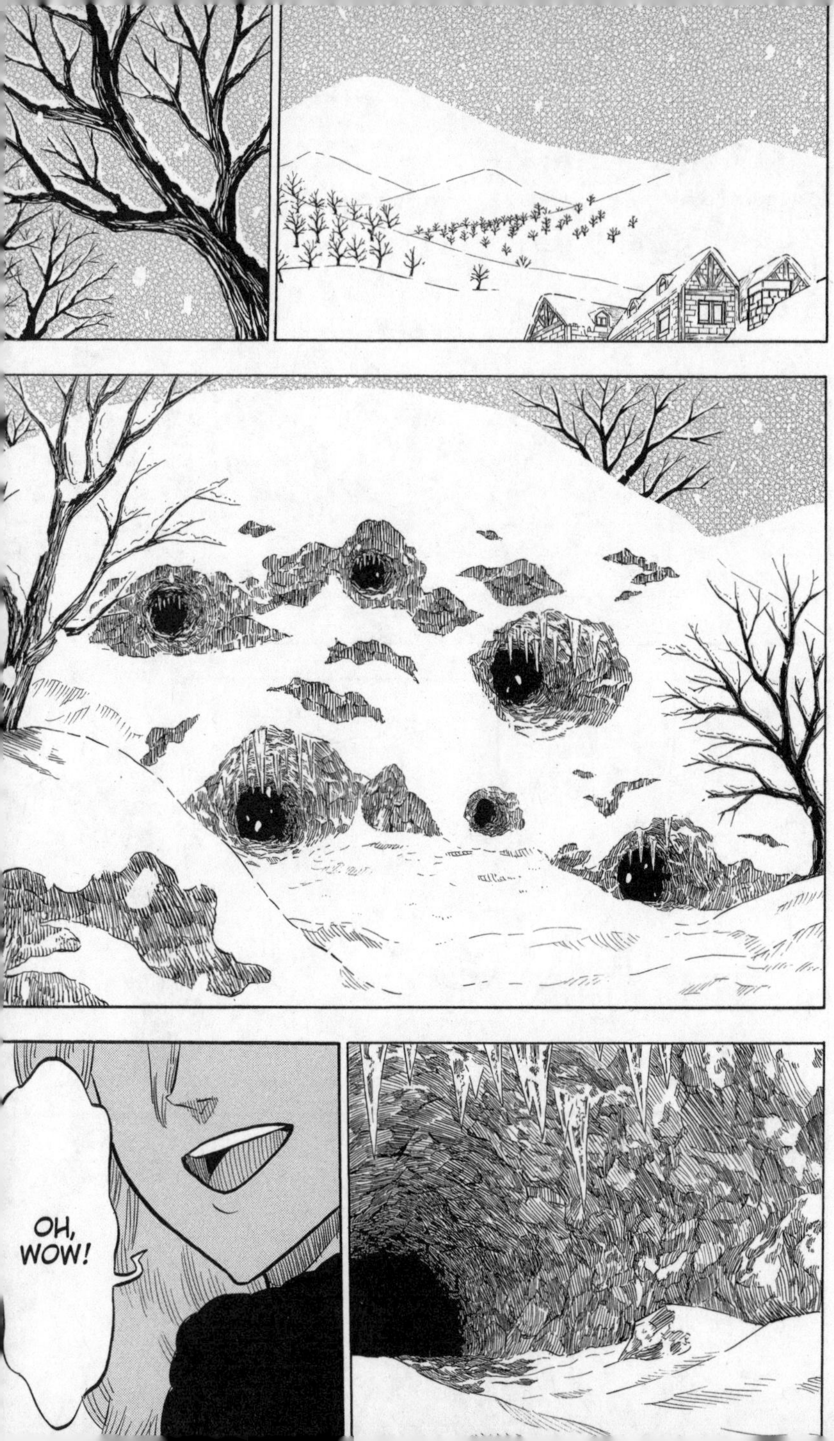
OH, WOW!

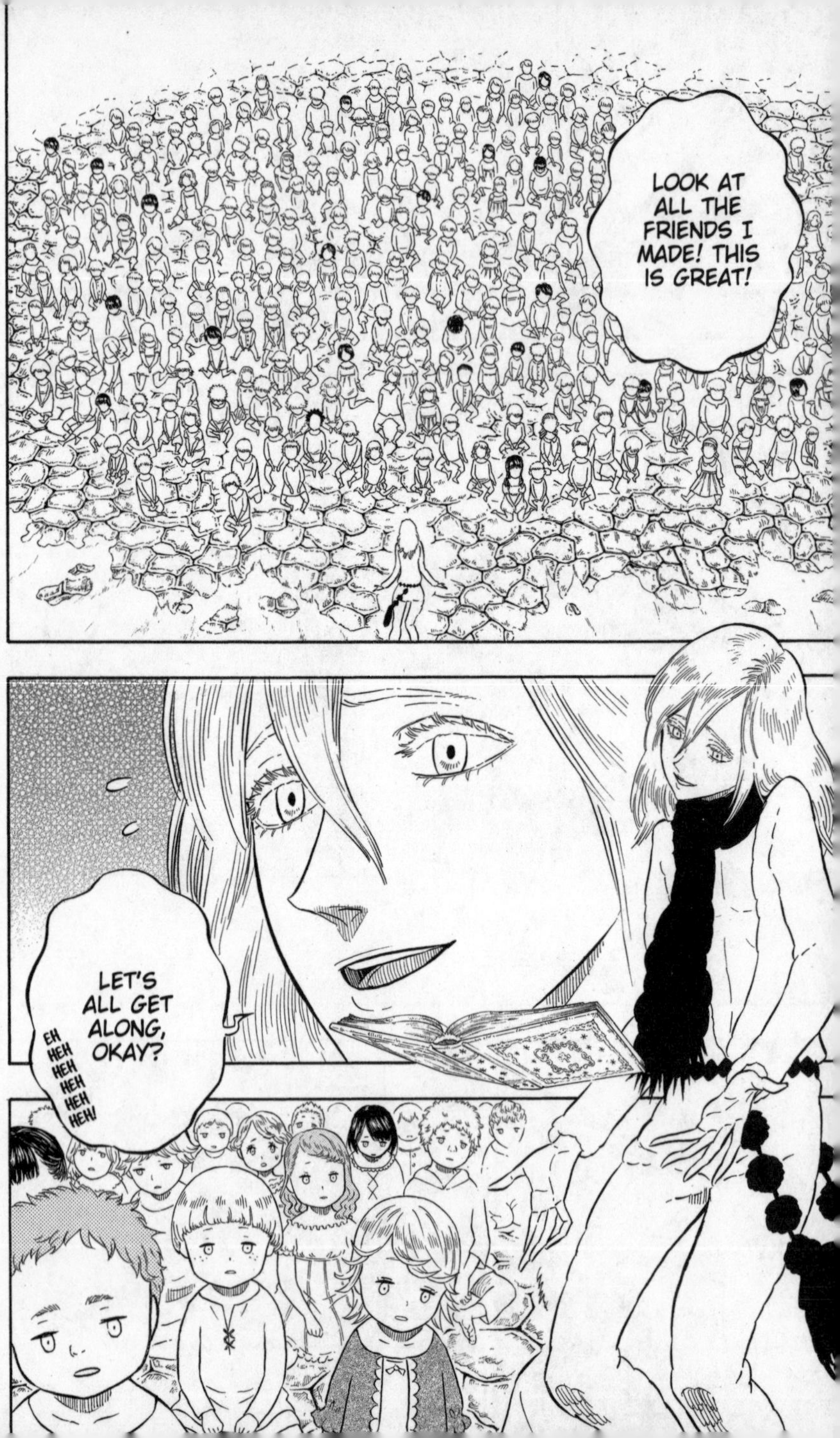
LOOK AT ALL THE FRIENDS I MADE! THIS IS GREAT!
LET'S ALL GET ALONG, OKAY?
EH HEH HEH HEH HEH HEH!

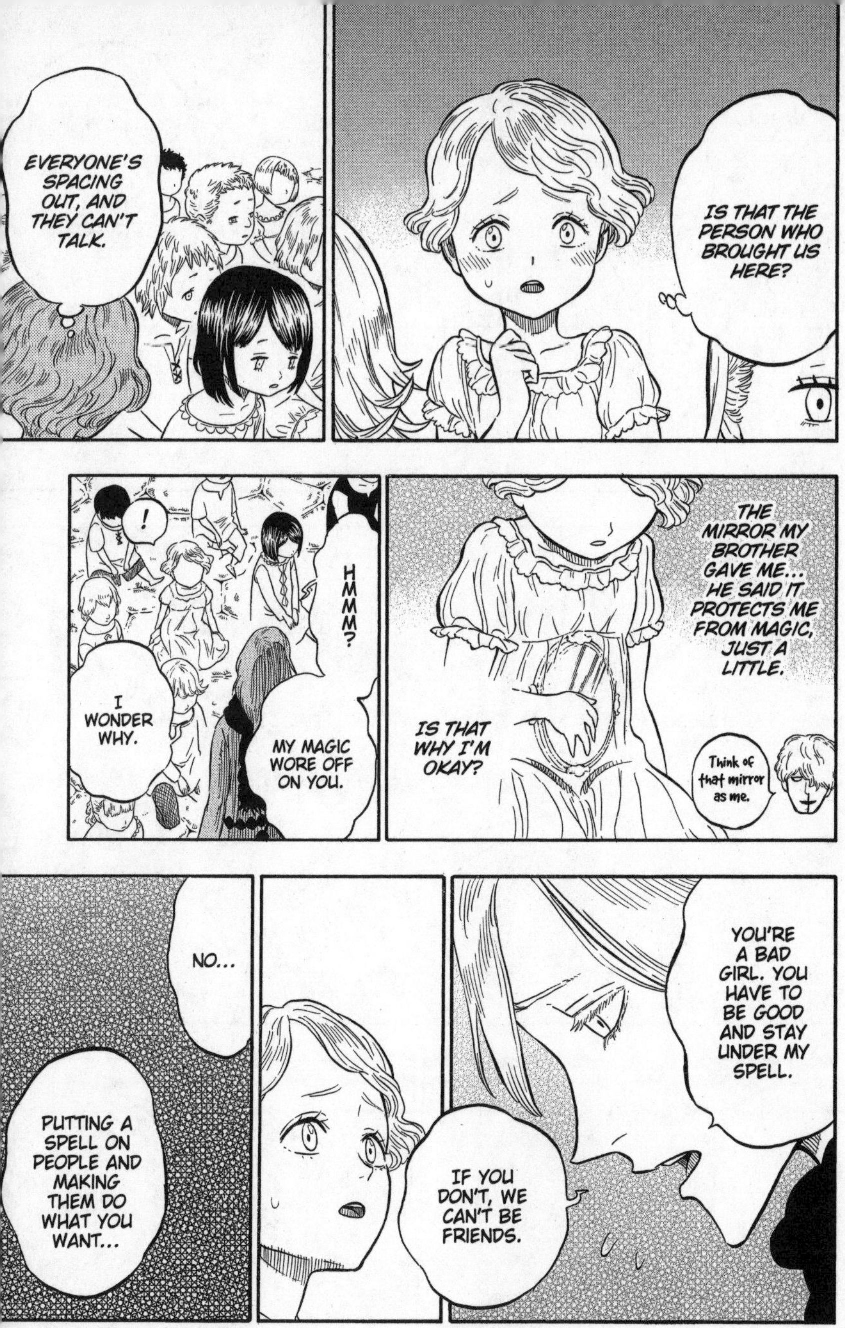
IS THAT THE PERSON WHO BROUGHT US HERE?
EVERYONE'S SPACING OUT, AND THEY CAN'T TALK.
THE MIRROR MY BROTHER GAVE ME... HE SAID IT PROTECTS ME FROM MAGIC, JUST A LITTLE.
Think of that mirror as me.
IS THAT WHY I'M OKAY?
!
HMMM?
MY MAGIC WORE OFF ON YOU.
I WONDER WHY.
YOU'RE A BAD GIRL. YOU HAVE TO BE GOOD AND STAY UNDER MY SPELL.
IF YOU DON'T, WE CAN'T BE FRIENDS.
NO...
PUTTING A SPELL ON PEOPLE AND MAKING THEM DO WHAT YOU WANT...

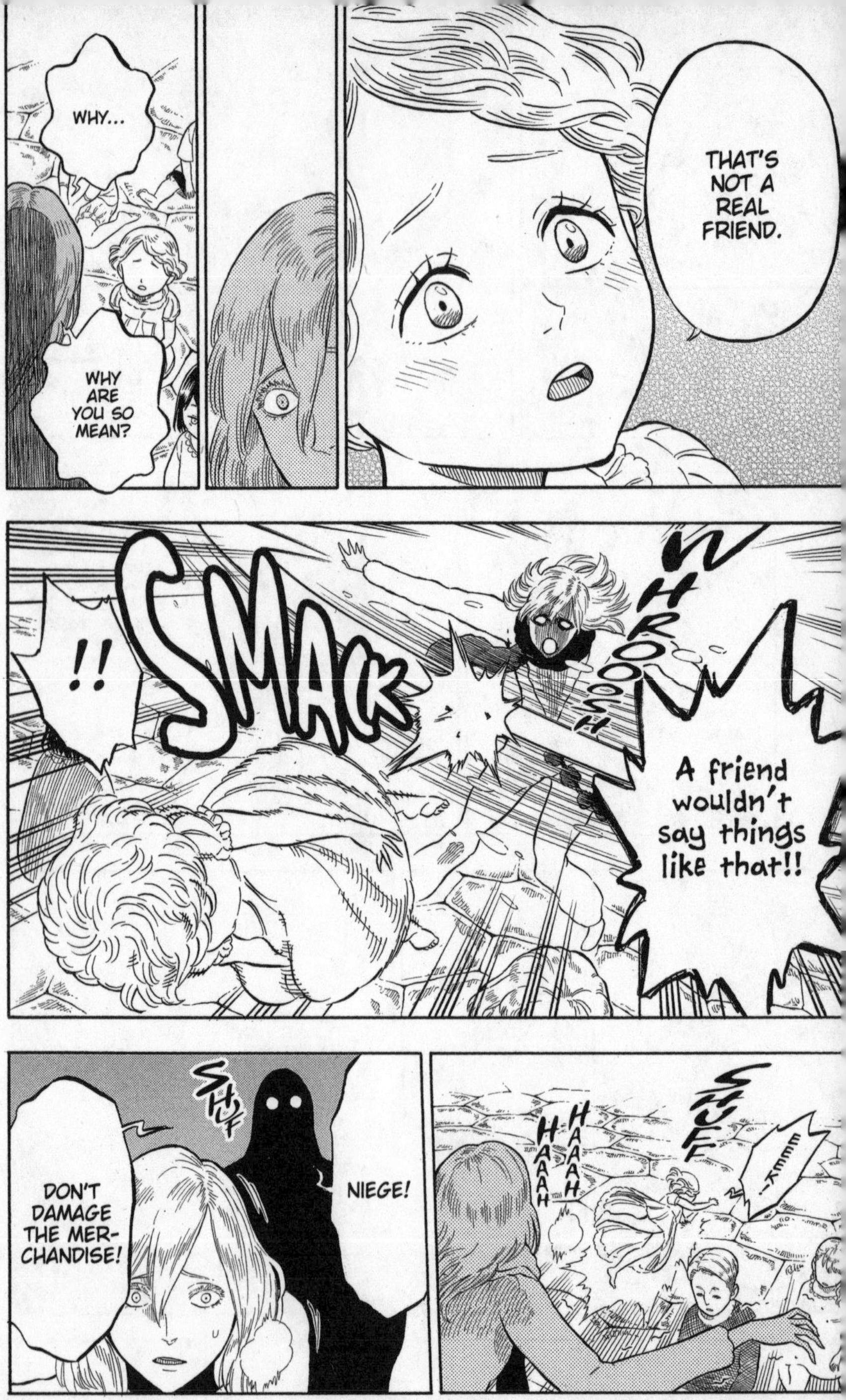
THAT'S NOT A REAL FRIEND.
WHY...
WHY ARE YOU SO MEAN?
WHROOOSH
A friend wouldn't say things like that!!
SMACK
!!
SHUFF
HAAAAH HAAAAH
NIEGE!
SHUF
DON'T DAMAGE THE MER-CHANDISE!

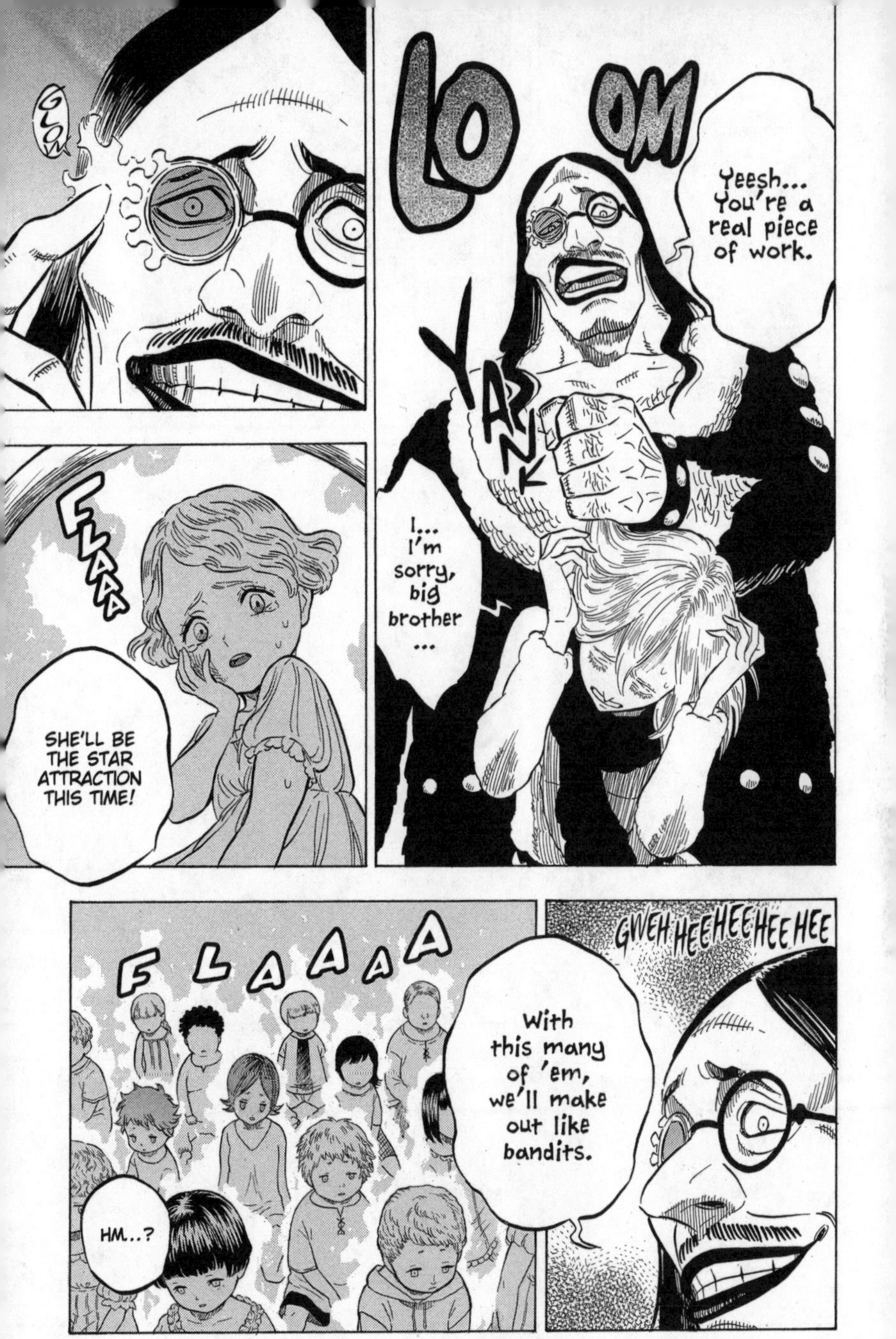
LOOM
Yeesh... You're a real piece of work.
YANK
I... I'm sorry, big brother...
GLOW
FLAAA
SHE'LL BE THE STAR ATTRACTION THIS TIME!
GWEH HEEHEE HEEHEE
With this many of 'em, we'll make out like bandits.
FLAAAA
HM...?

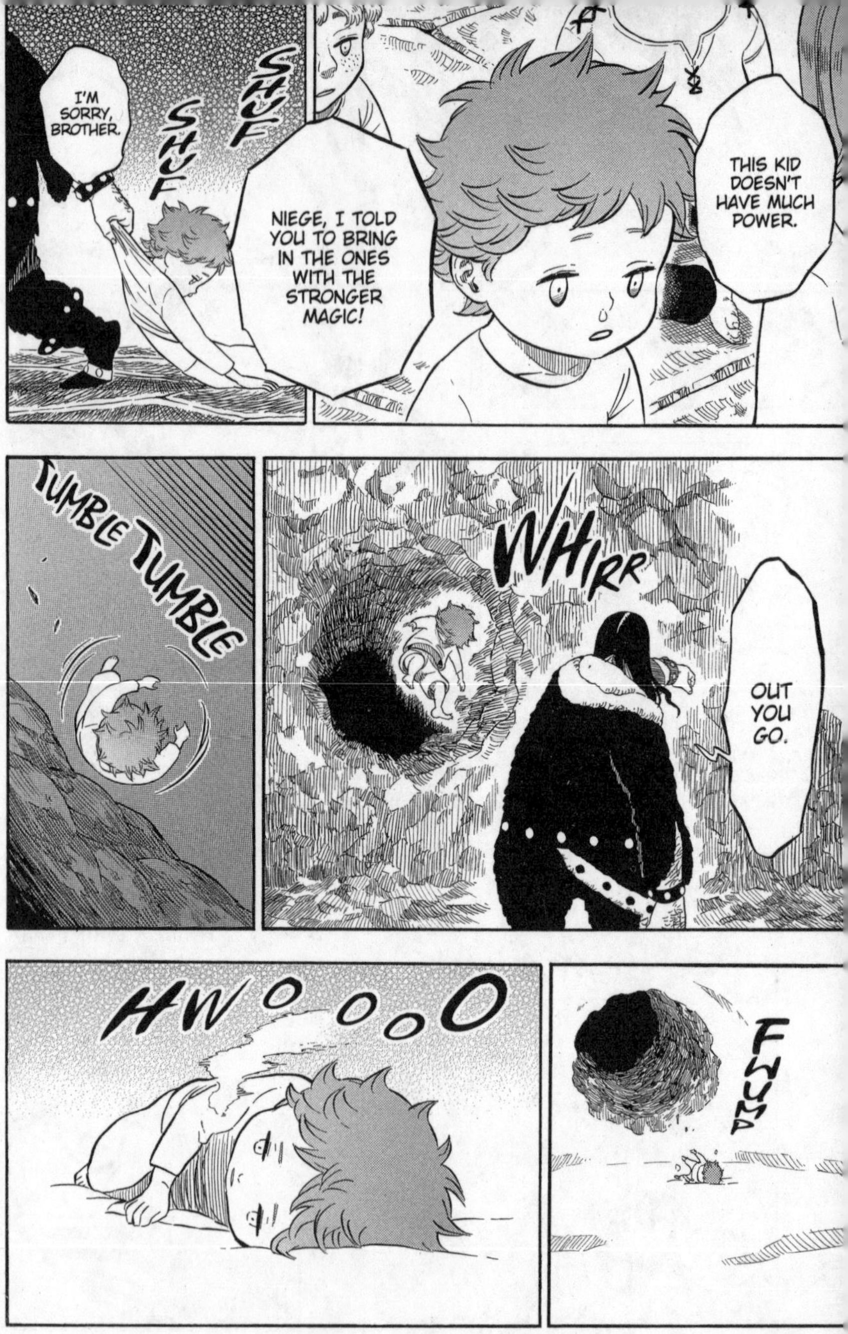
THIS KID DOESN'T HAVE MUCH POWER.
NIEGE, I TOLD YOU TO BRING IN THE ONES WITH THE STRONGER MAGIC!
SHUF
SHUF
I'M SORRY, BROTHER.
OUT YOU GO.
WHIRR
TUMBLE TUMBLE
FWUMP
HWOOOO

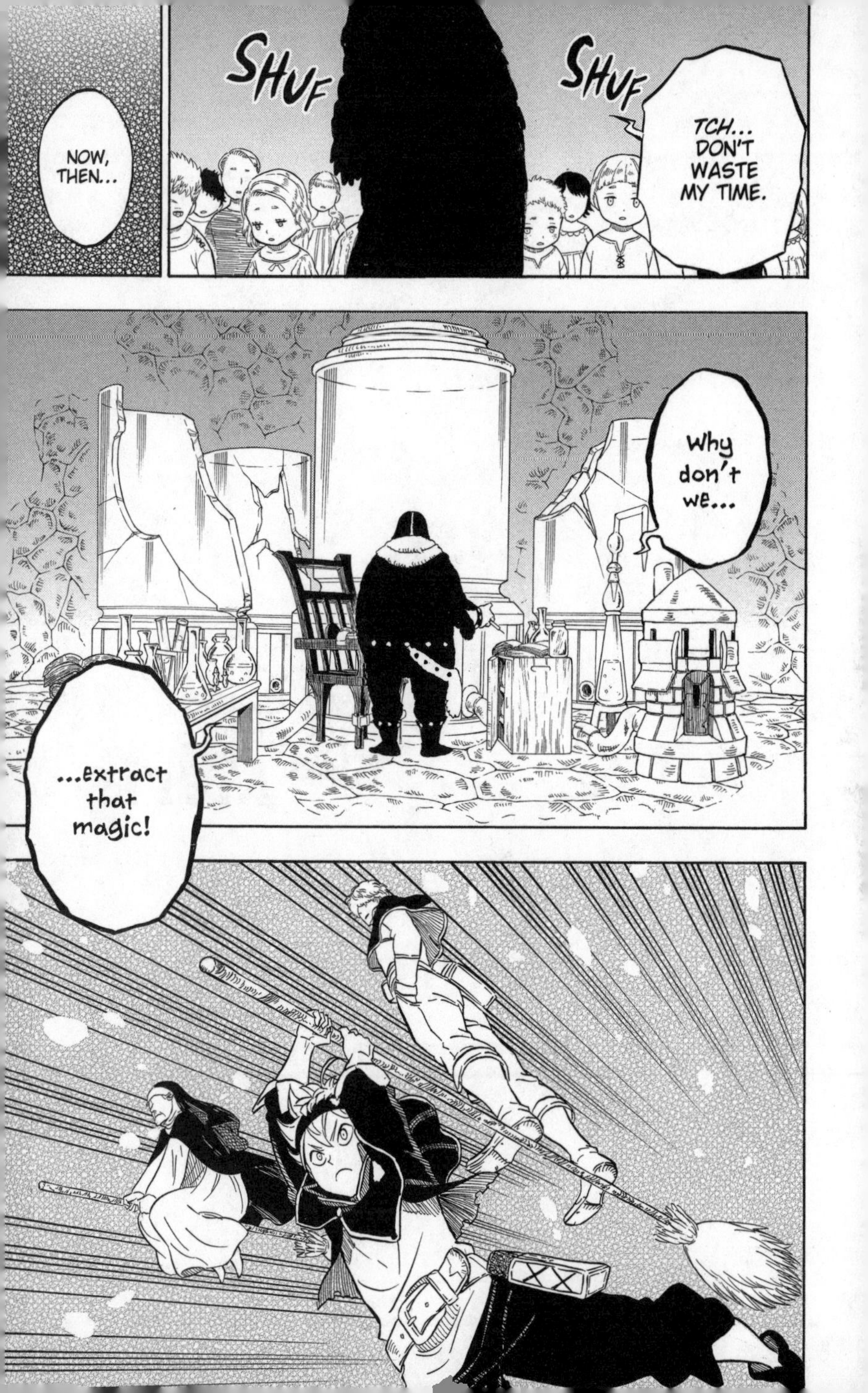
SHUF
TCH... DON'T WASTE MY TIME.
SHUF
NOW, THEN...
Why don't we...
...extract that magic!

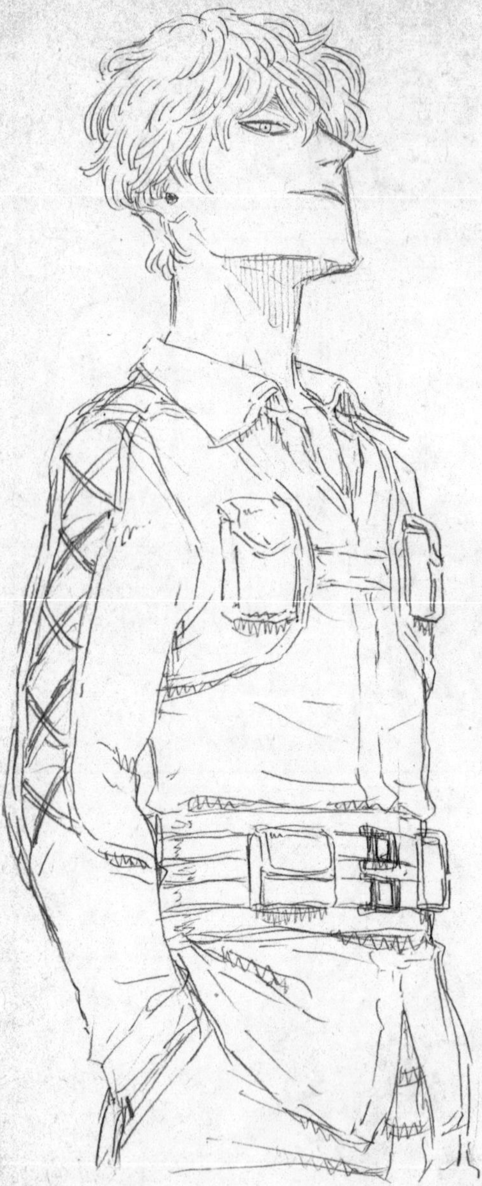

Gauche Adlai

Age: 19
Height: 181 cm
Birthday: June 27
Sign: Cancer
Blood Type: B
Likes: **Marie**

Character Profile

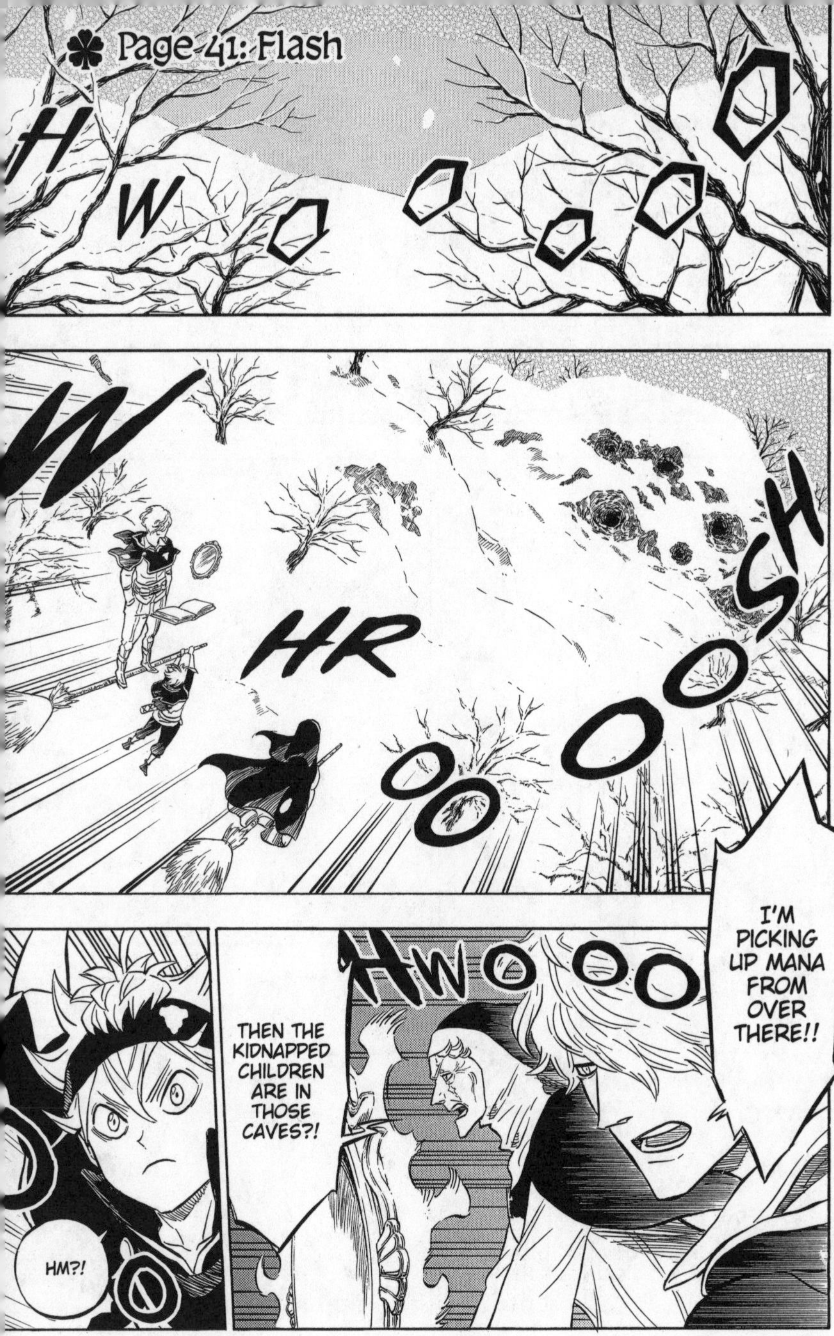
Page 41: Flash
HWOOOOOO
WHROOOOOSH
I'M PICKING UP MANA FROM OVER THERE!!
HWOOOO
THEN THE KIDNAPPED CHILDREN ARE IN THOSE CAVES?!
HM?!

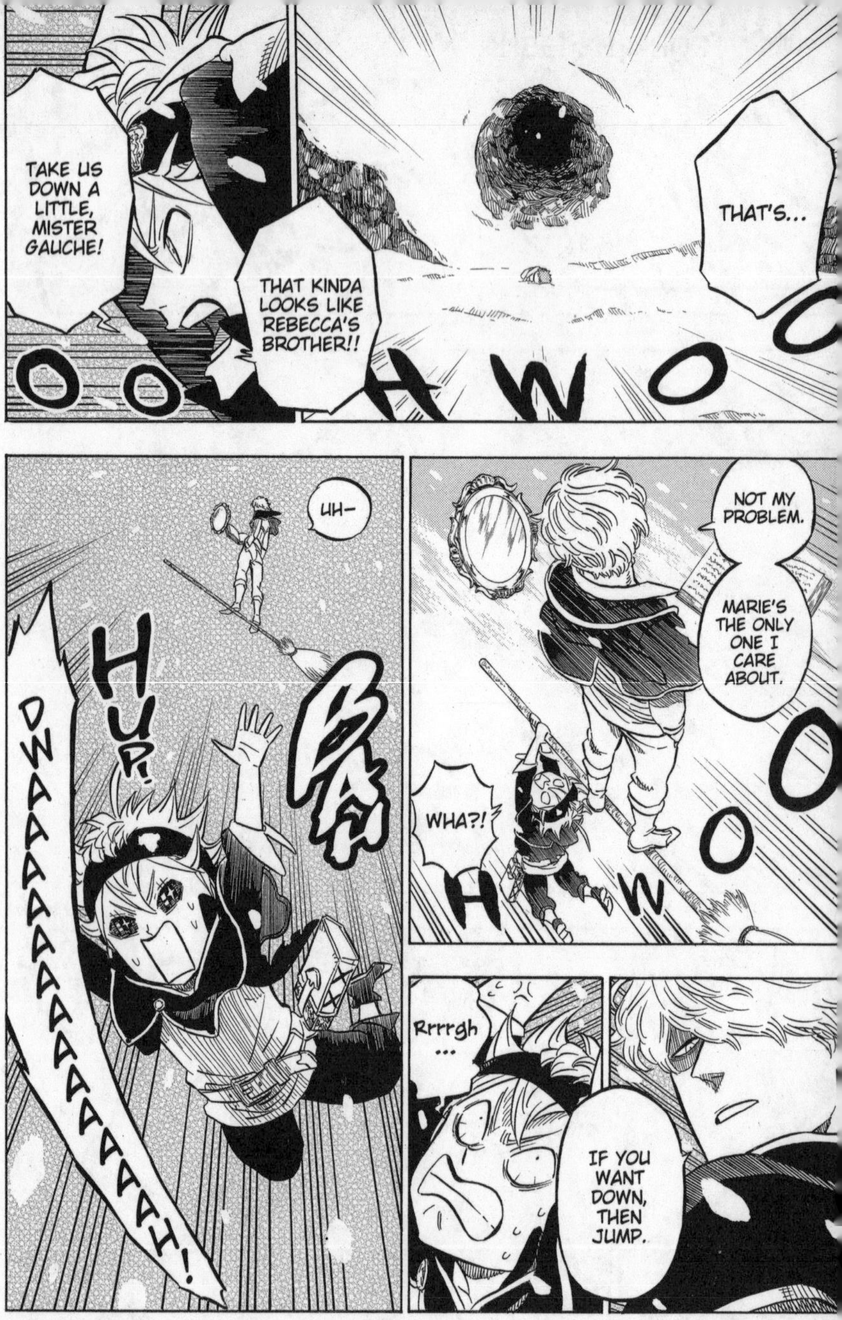
THAT'S...
THAT KINDA LOOKS LIKE REBECCA'S BROTHER!!
TAKE US DOWN A LITTLE, MISTER GAUCHE!
OOHWOOO
NOT MY PROBLEM.
MARIE'S THE ONLY ONE I CARE ABOUT.
WHA?!
HWOO
Rrrrgh...
IF YOU WANT DOWN, THEN JUMP.
UH-
HUP!
DWAAAAAAAAAAAAAAAH!

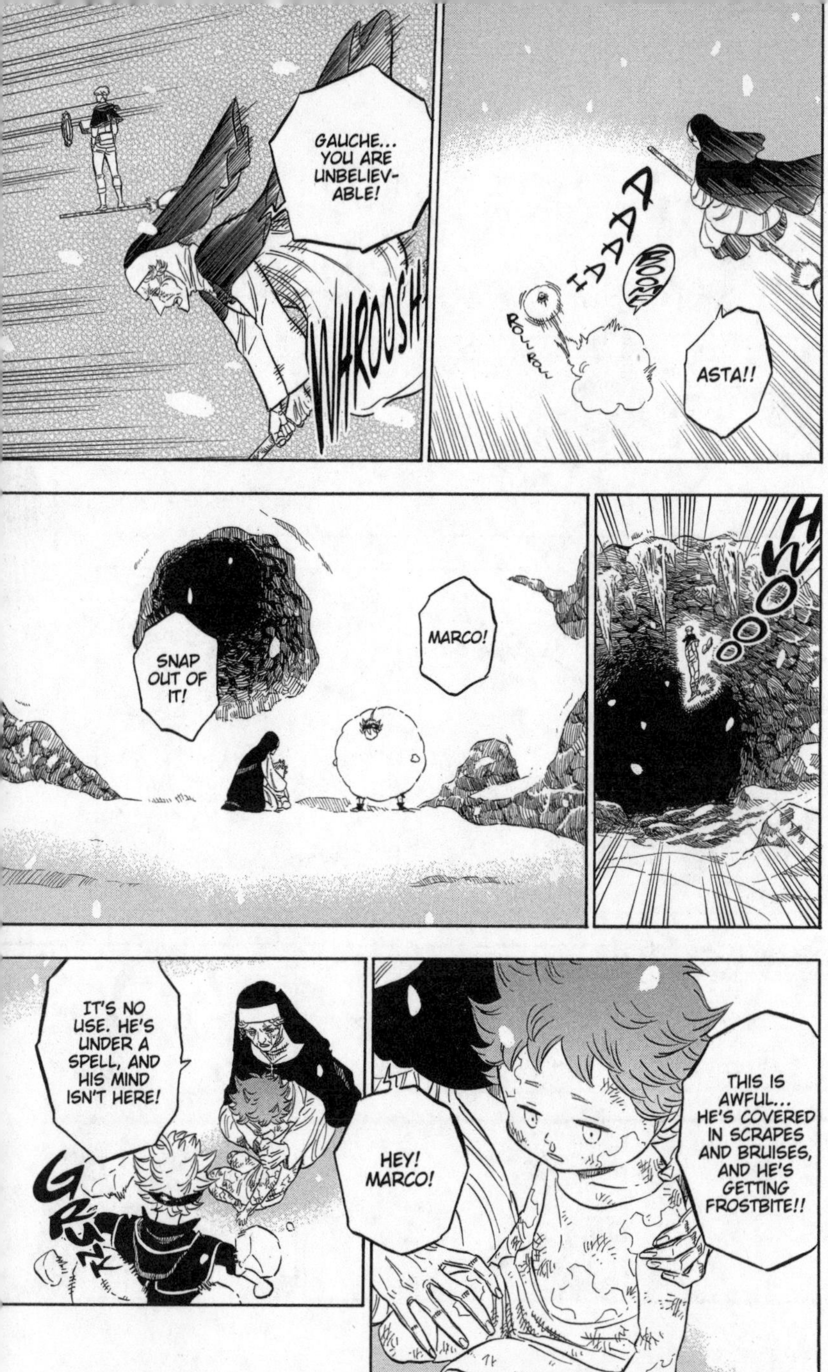

ROLL ROLL
ASTA!!
GAUCHE... YOU ARE UNBELIEV-ABLE!
WHROOSH
MARCO!
SNAP OUT OF IT!
THIS IS AWFUL... HE'S COVERED IN SCRAPES AND BRUISES, AND HE'S GETTING FROSTBITE!!
HEY! MARCO!
IT'S NO USE. HE'S UNDER A SPELL, AND HIS MIND ISN'T HERE!
GRUNK

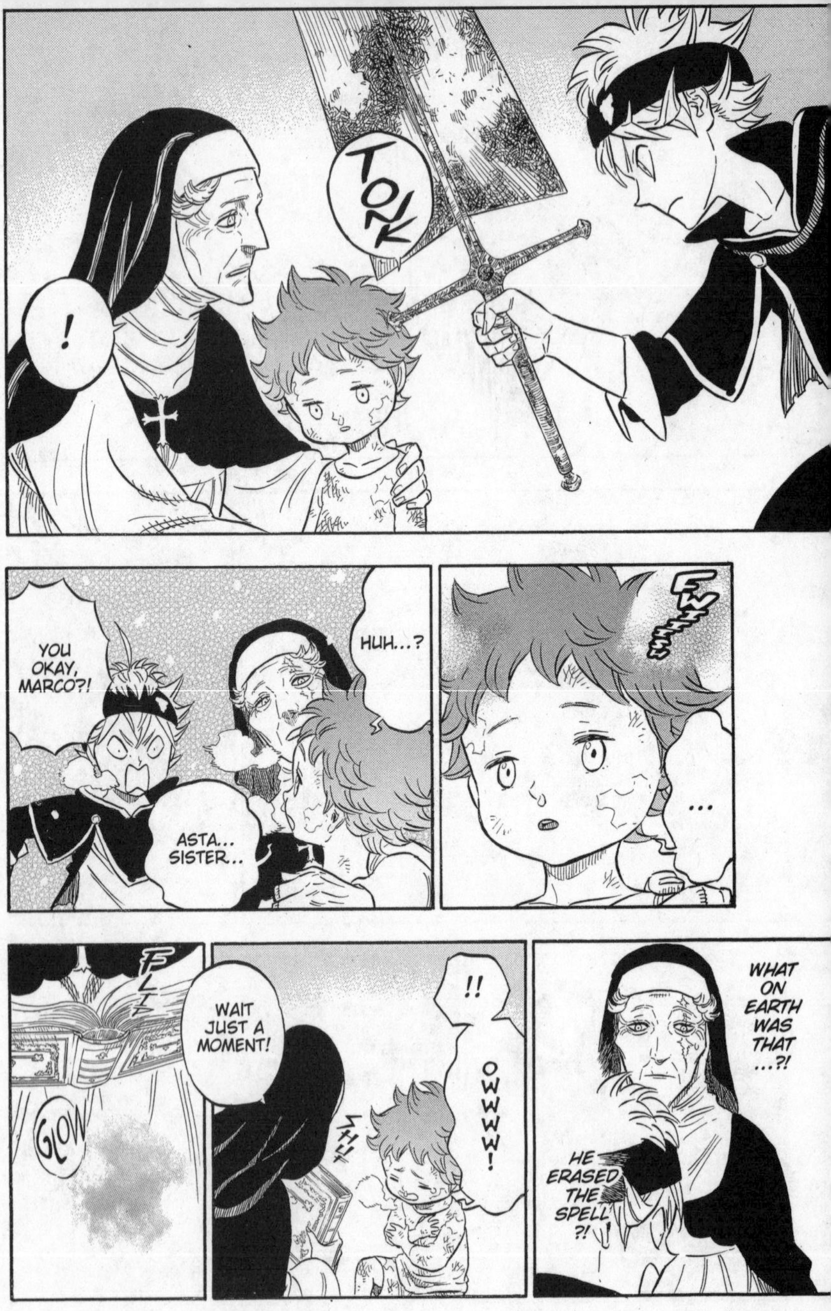
TONK
!
FWIIISH
...
HUH...?
YOU OKAY, MARCO?!
ASTA... SISTER...
WHAT ON EARTH WAS THAT...?!
HE ERASED THE SPELL?!
!!
OWWWW!
WAIT JUST A MOMENT!
SHUF
FLIP
GLOW

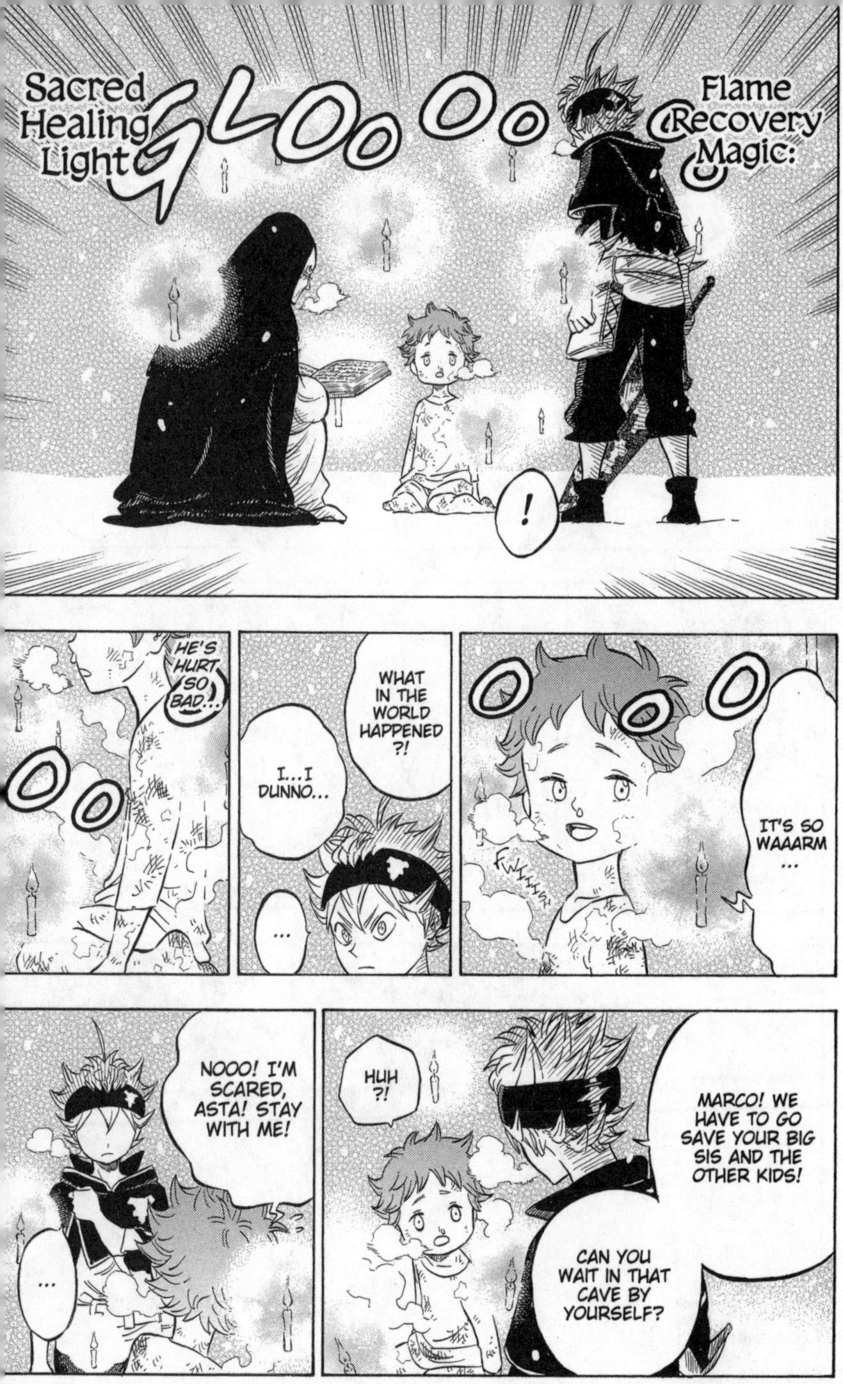
Flame Recovery Magic:
GLOOOOO
Sacred Healing Light
!
IT'S SO WAAARM ...
OOO
WHAT IN THE WORLD HAPPENED ?!
I...I DUNNO...
...
HE'S HURT SO BAD...
OO
MARCO! WE HAVE TO GO SAVE YOUR BIG SIS AND THE OTHER KIDS!
HUH ?!
CAN YOU WAIT IN THAT CAVE BY YOURSELF?
NOOO! I'M SCARED, ASTA! STAY WITH ME!
...

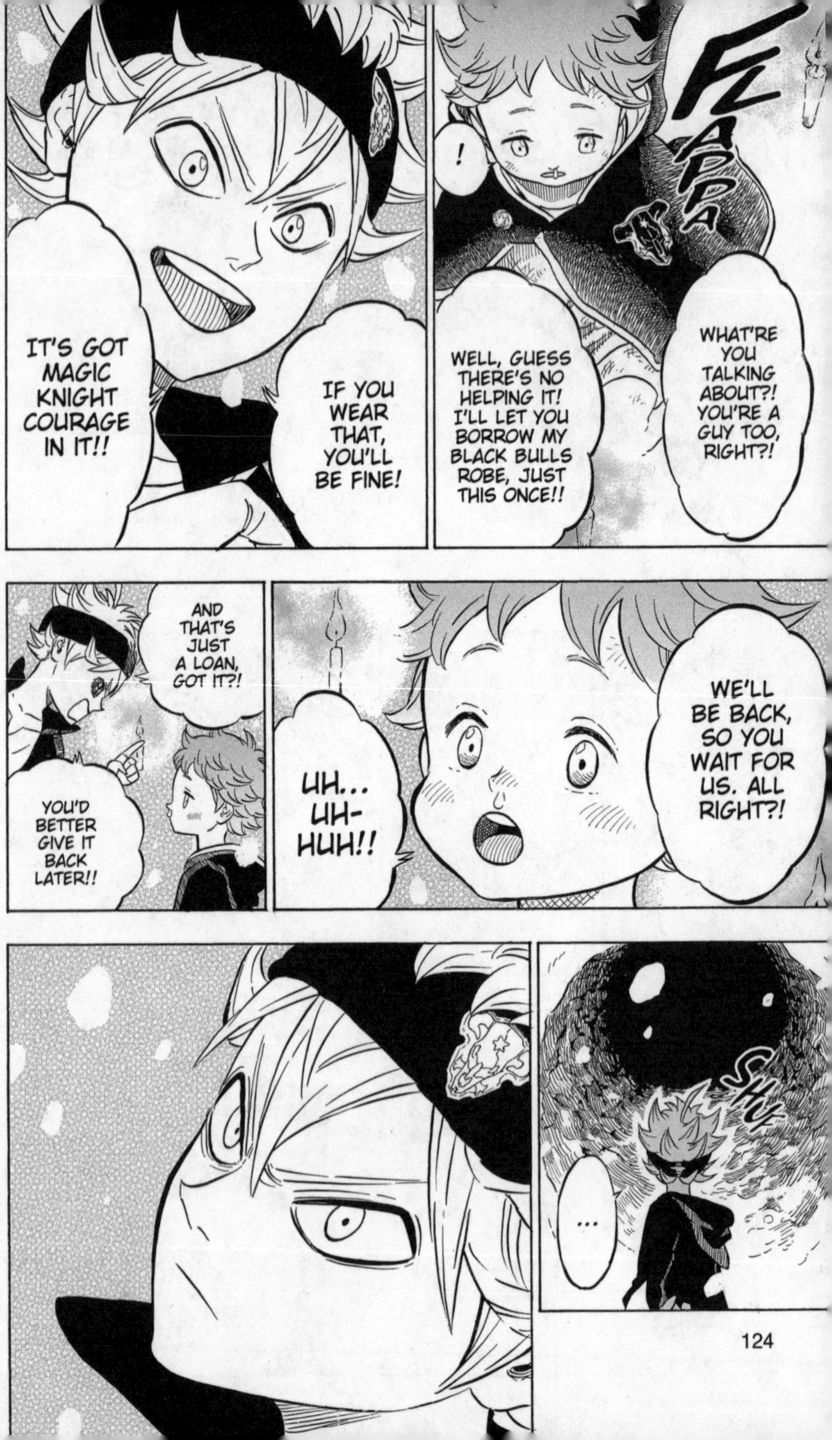
!
FLAPPA
WHAT'RE YOU TALKING ABOUT?! YOU'RE A GUY TOO, RIGHT?!
WELL, GUESS THERE'S NO HELPING IT! I'LL LET YOU BORROW MY BLACK BULLS ROBE, JUST THIS ONCE!!
IF YOU WEAR THAT, YOU'LL BE FINE!
IT'S GOT MAGIC KNIGHT COURAGE IN IT!!
WE'LL BE BACK, SO YOU WAIT FOR US. ALL RIGHT?!
UH... UH-HUH!!
AND THAT'S JUST A LOAN, GOT IT?!
YOU'D BETTER GIVE IT BACK LATER!!
SHU
...

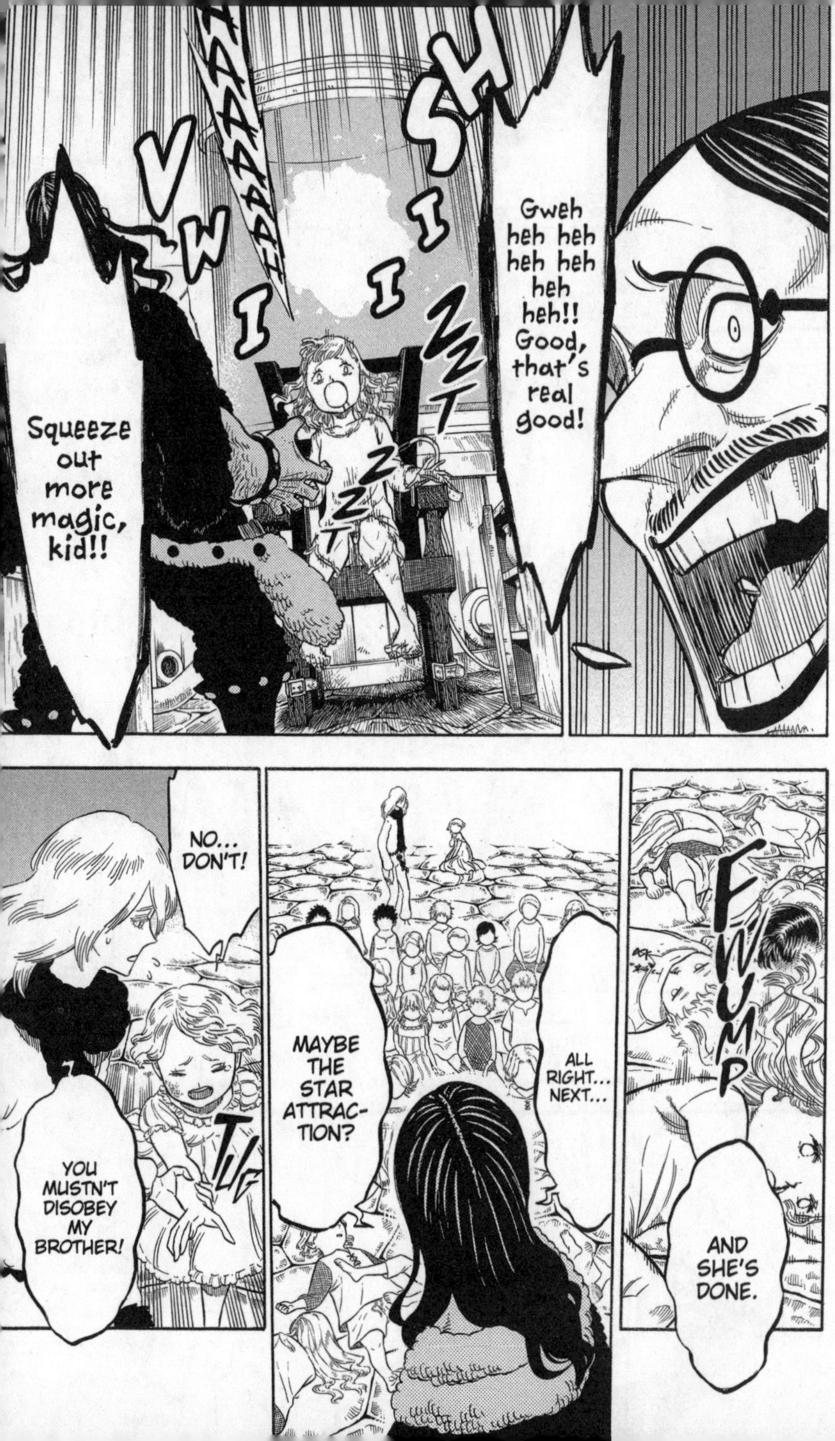
Gweh heh heh heh heh heh heh!! Good, that's real good!
Squeeze out more magic, kid!!
FWUMP
AND SHE'S DONE.
ALL RIGHT... NEXT...
MAYBE THE STAR ATTRACTION?
NO... DON'T!
YOU MUSTN'T DISOBEY MY BROTHER!

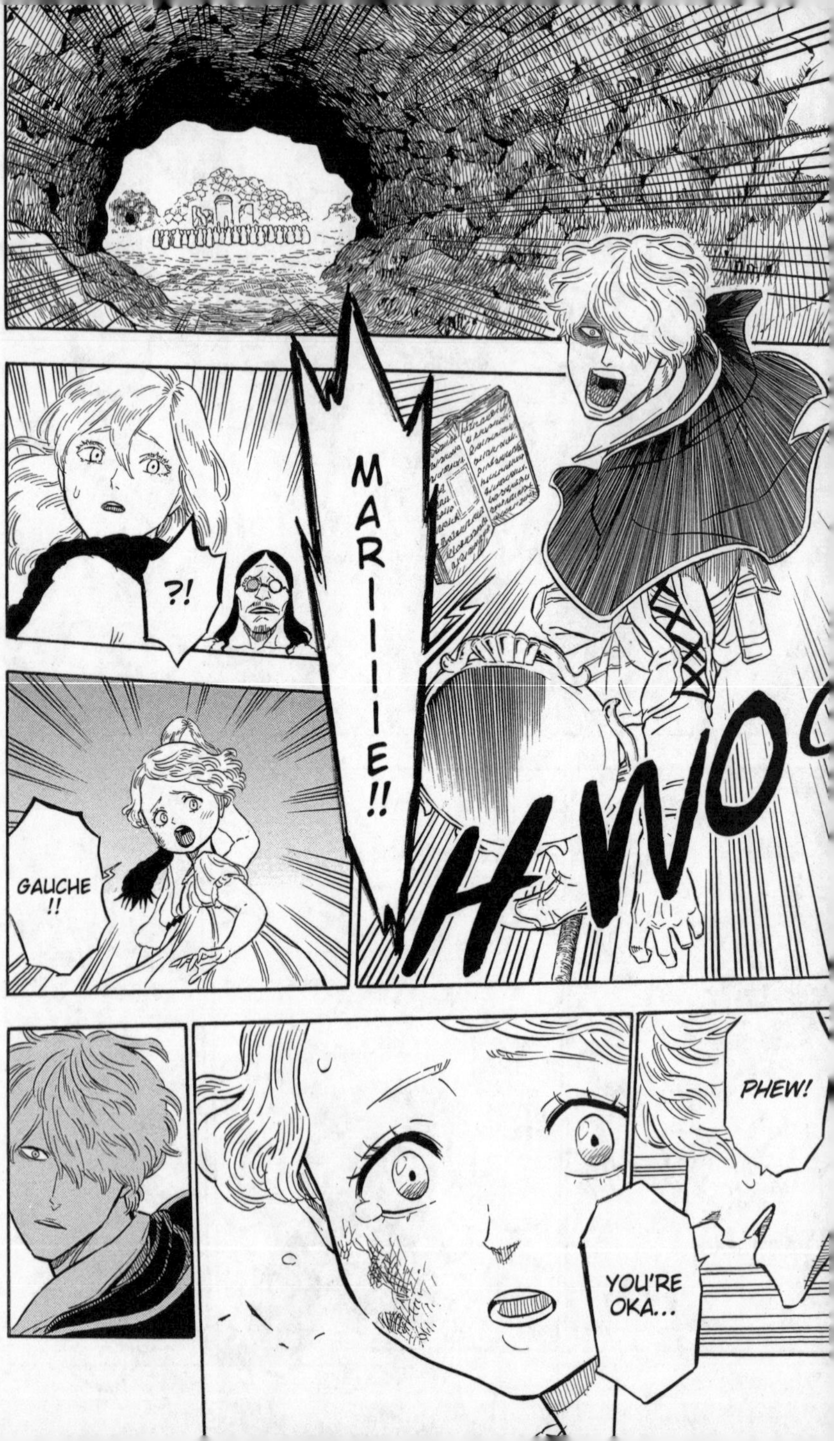
MARIIIIE!!
HWO
?!
GAUCHE !!
PHEW!
YOU'RE OKA...

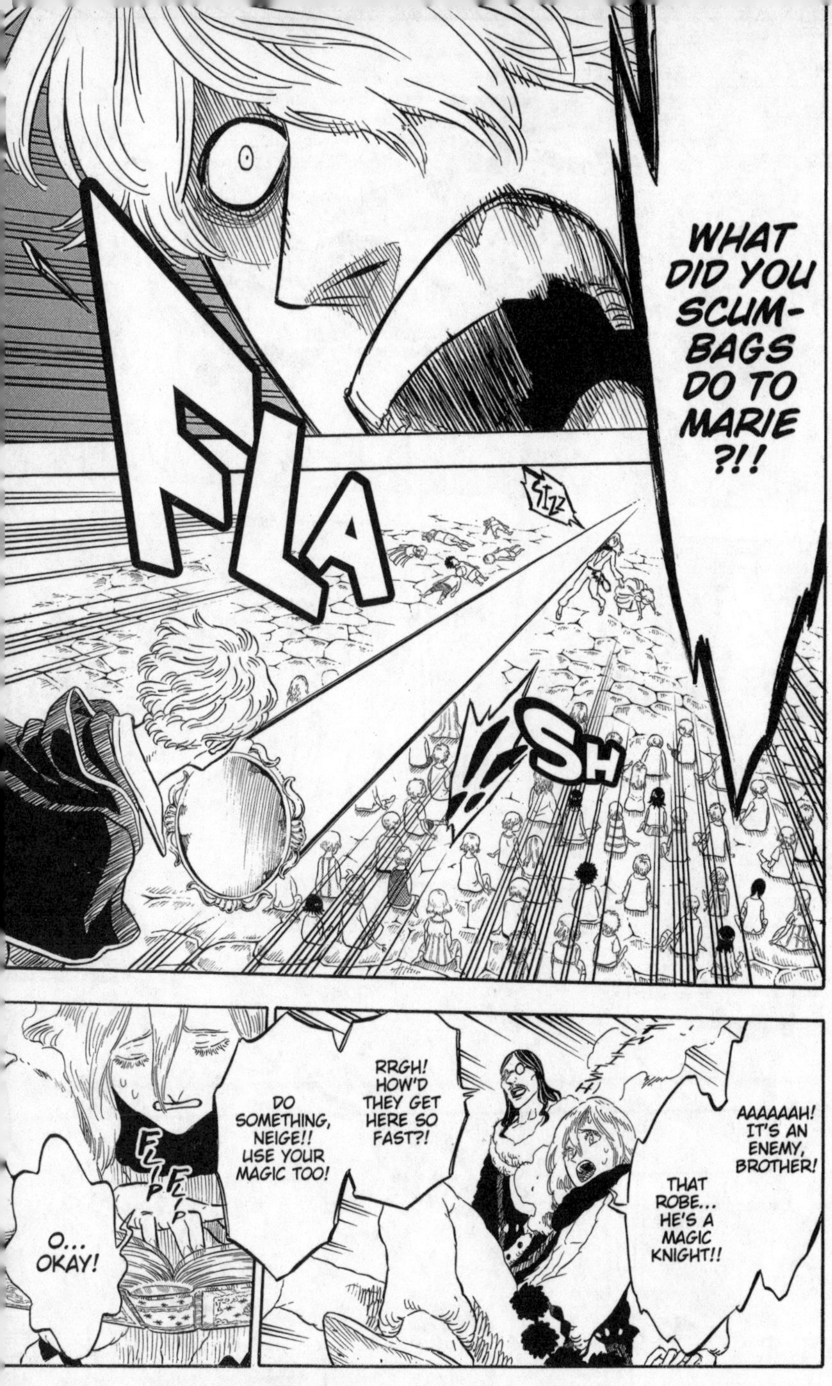
WHAT DID YOU SCUM-BAGS DO TO MARIE?!!
FLA
SIZZ
SH
AAAAAAH! IT'S AN ENEMY, BROTHER!
THAT ROBE... HE'S A MAGIC KNIGHT!!
RRGH! HOW'D THEY GET HERE SO FAST?!
DO SOMETHING, NEIGE!! USE YOUR MAGIC TOO!
FLIP FLIP
O... OKAY!

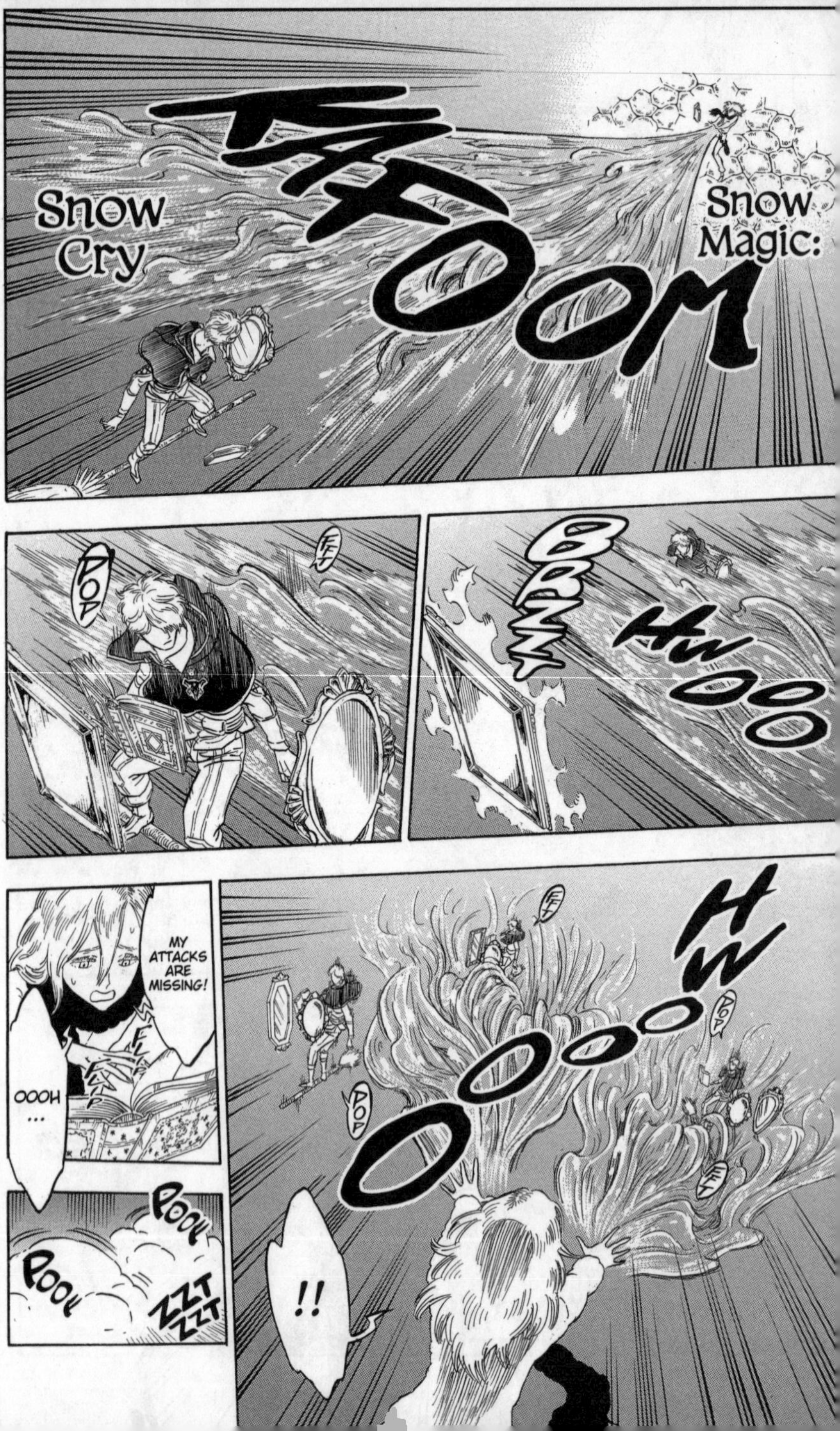
Snow Magic:
Snow Cry
FWOOM
BOOOM
HWOOO
FFT
POP
HWOOOOOO
FFT
POP
POP
FFT
!!
MY ATTACKS ARE MISSING!
FLIP
FLIP
OOOH ...
POOF
POOF
ZZZT ZZZT

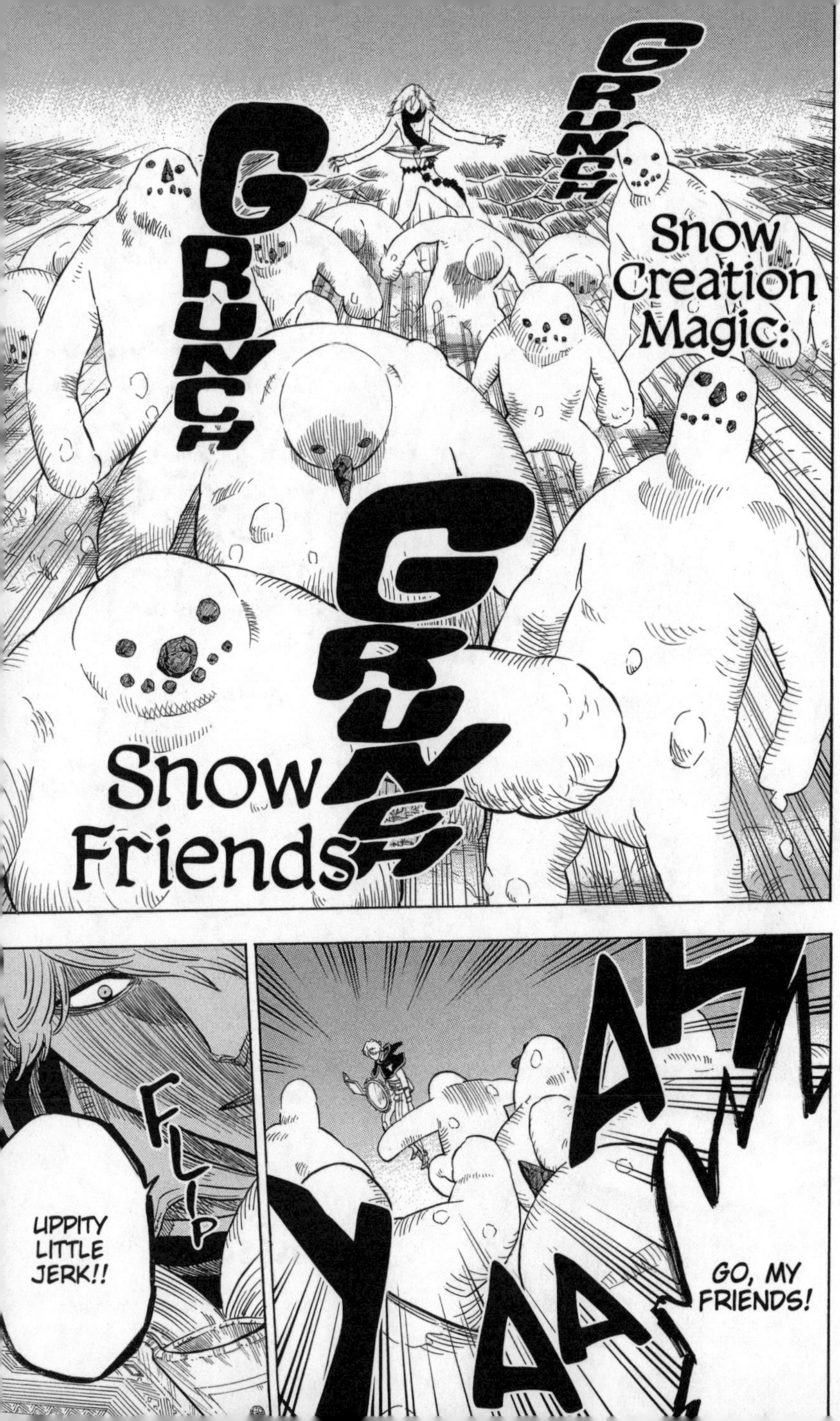
GRUNCH
Snow Creation Magic:
GRUNCH
GRUNCH
Snow Friends
GO, MY FRIENDS!
FLIP
UPPITY LITTLE JERK!!

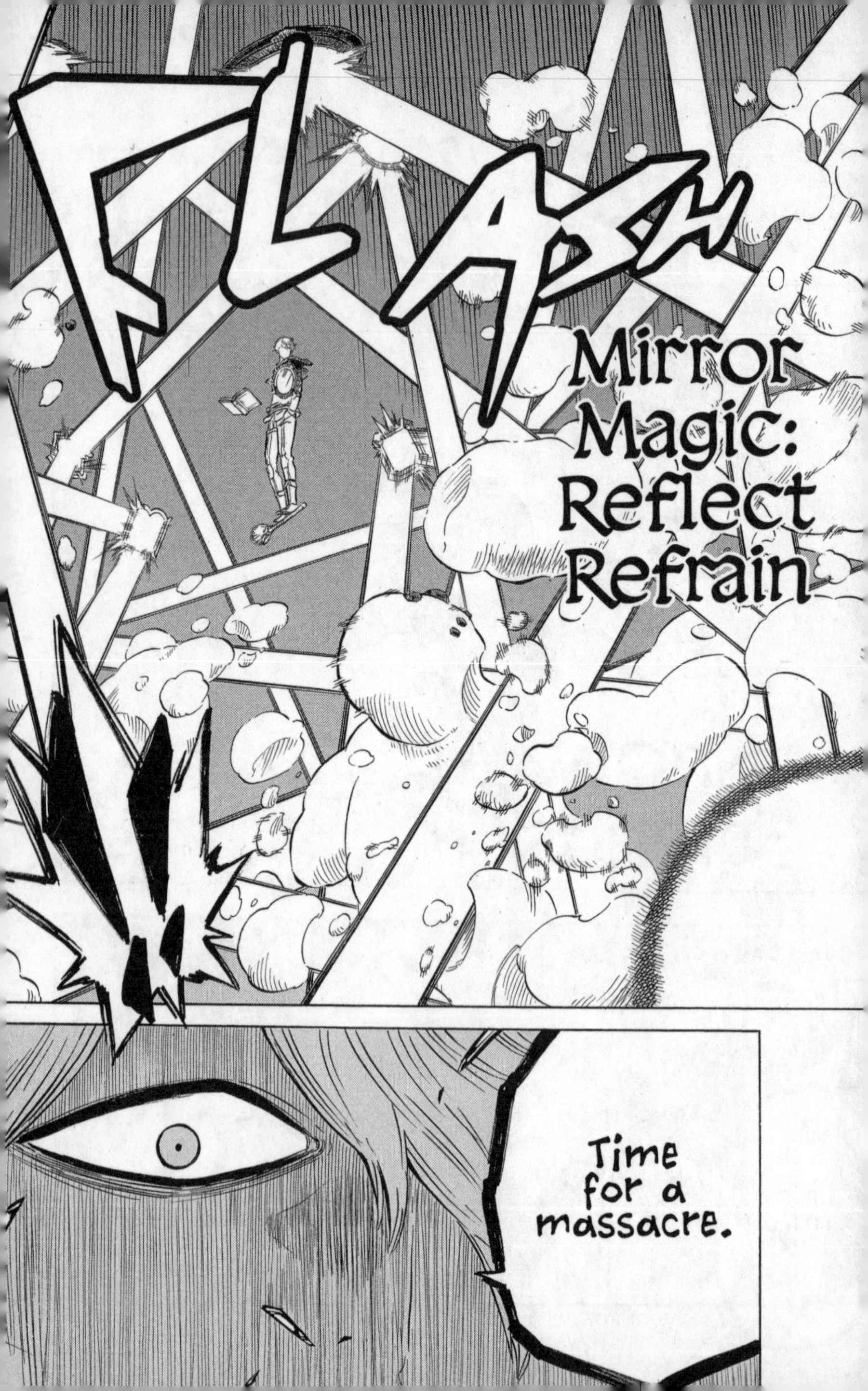
FLASH
Mirror Magic: Reflect Refrain
Time for a massacre.

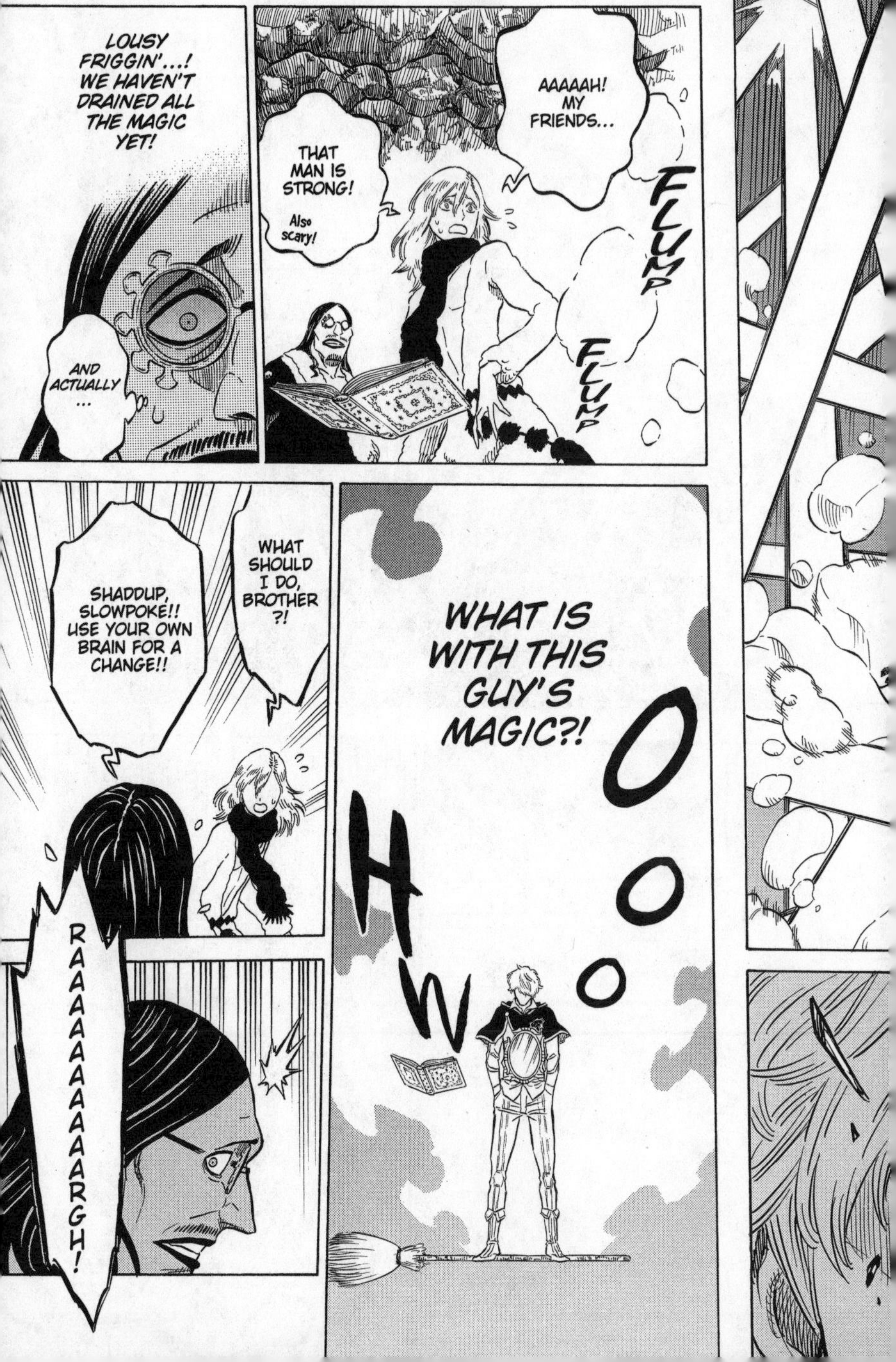
AAAAAH! MY FRIENDS...
THAT MAN IS STRONG!
Also scary!
FLUMP
FLUMP
LOUSY FRIGGIN'...! WE HAVEN'T DRAINED ALL THE MAGIC YET!
AND ACTUALLY ...
WHAT IS WITH THIS GUY'S MAGIC?!
WHOOO
WHAT SHOULD I DO, BROTHER?!
SHADDUP, SLOWPOKE!! USE YOUR OWN BRAIN FOR A CHANGE!!
RAAAAAAAAAAAAARGH!

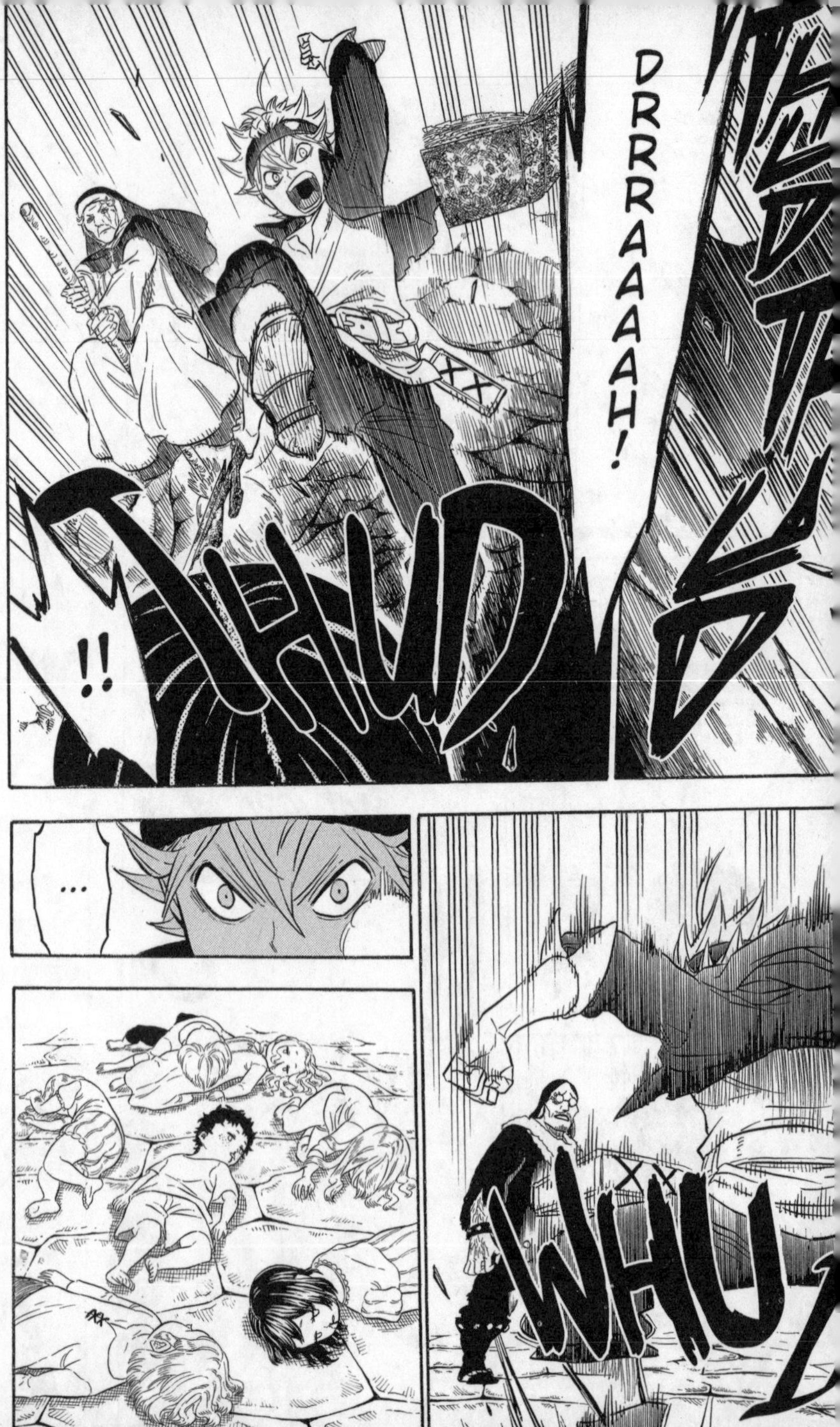
DRRRAAAAAH!
THUD
!!
...

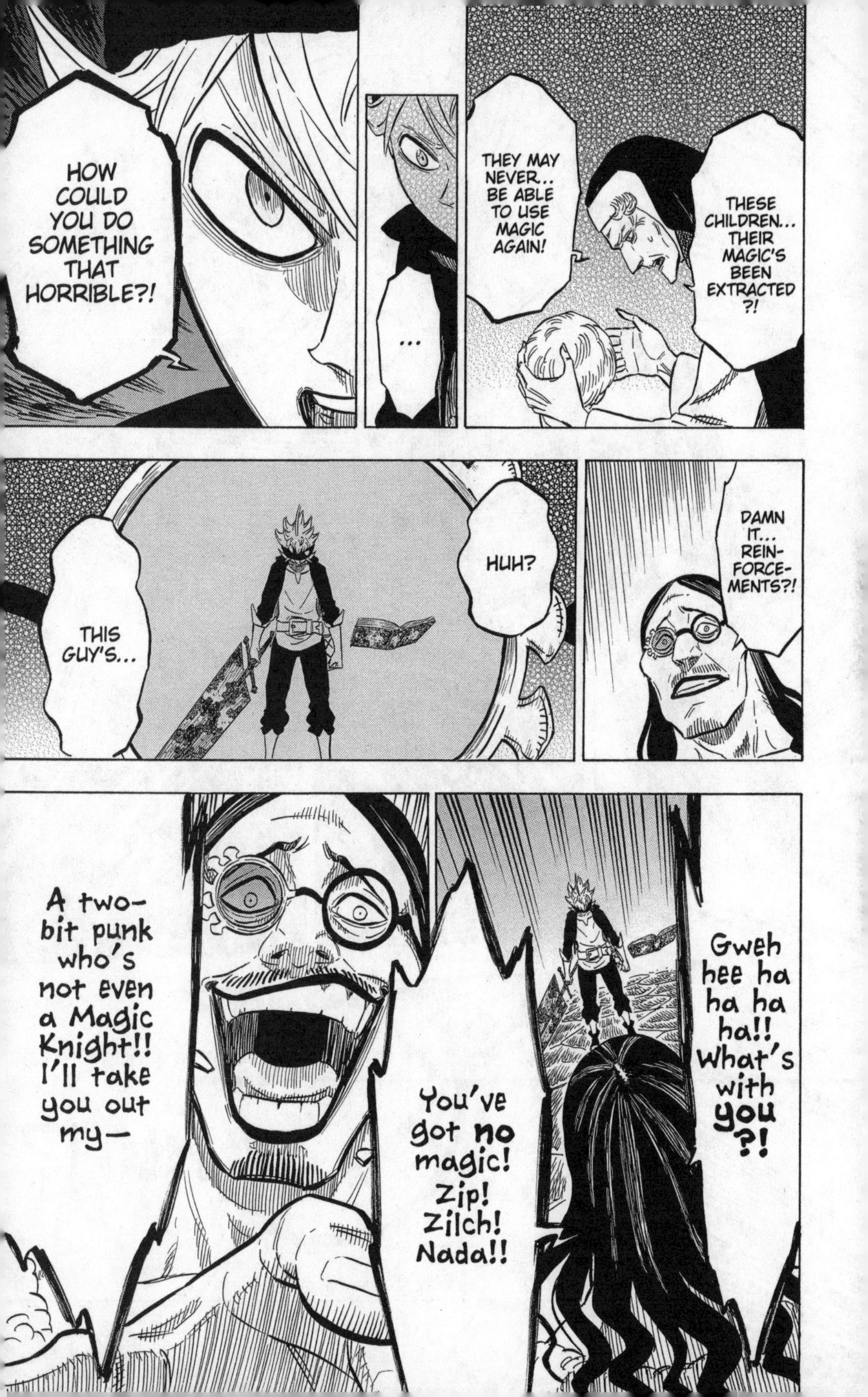
THESE CHILDREN... THEIR MAGIC'S BEEN EXTRACTED?!
THEY MAY NEVER... BE ABLE TO USE MAGIC AGAIN!
...
HOW COULD YOU DO SOMETHING THAT HORRIBLE?!
DAMN IT... REIN-FORCE-MENTS?!
HUH?
THIS GUY'S...
Gweh hee ha ha ha ha!! What's with you?!
You've got no magic! Zip! Zilch! Nada!!
A two-bit punk who's not even a Magic Knight!! I'll take you out my—

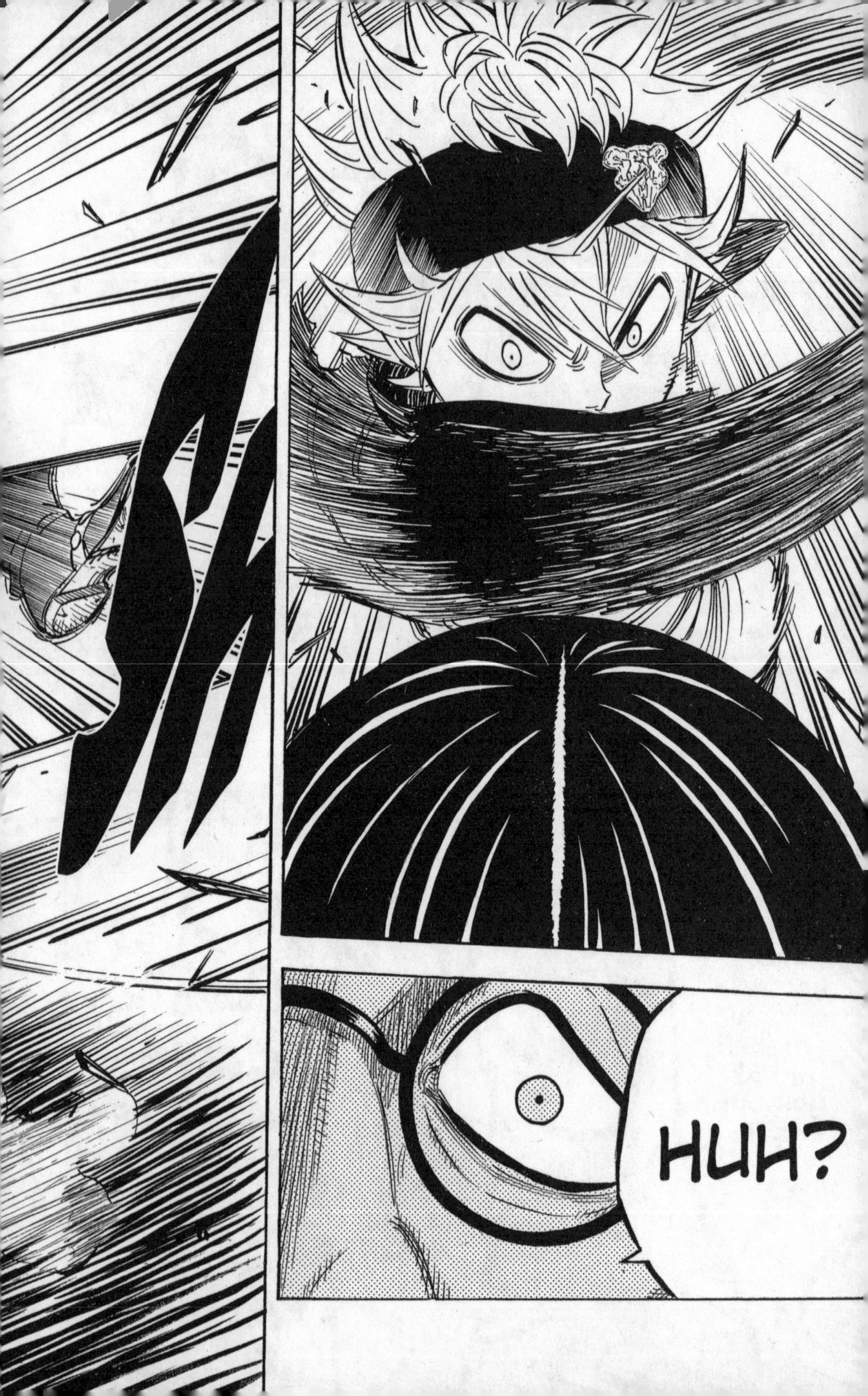
HUH?

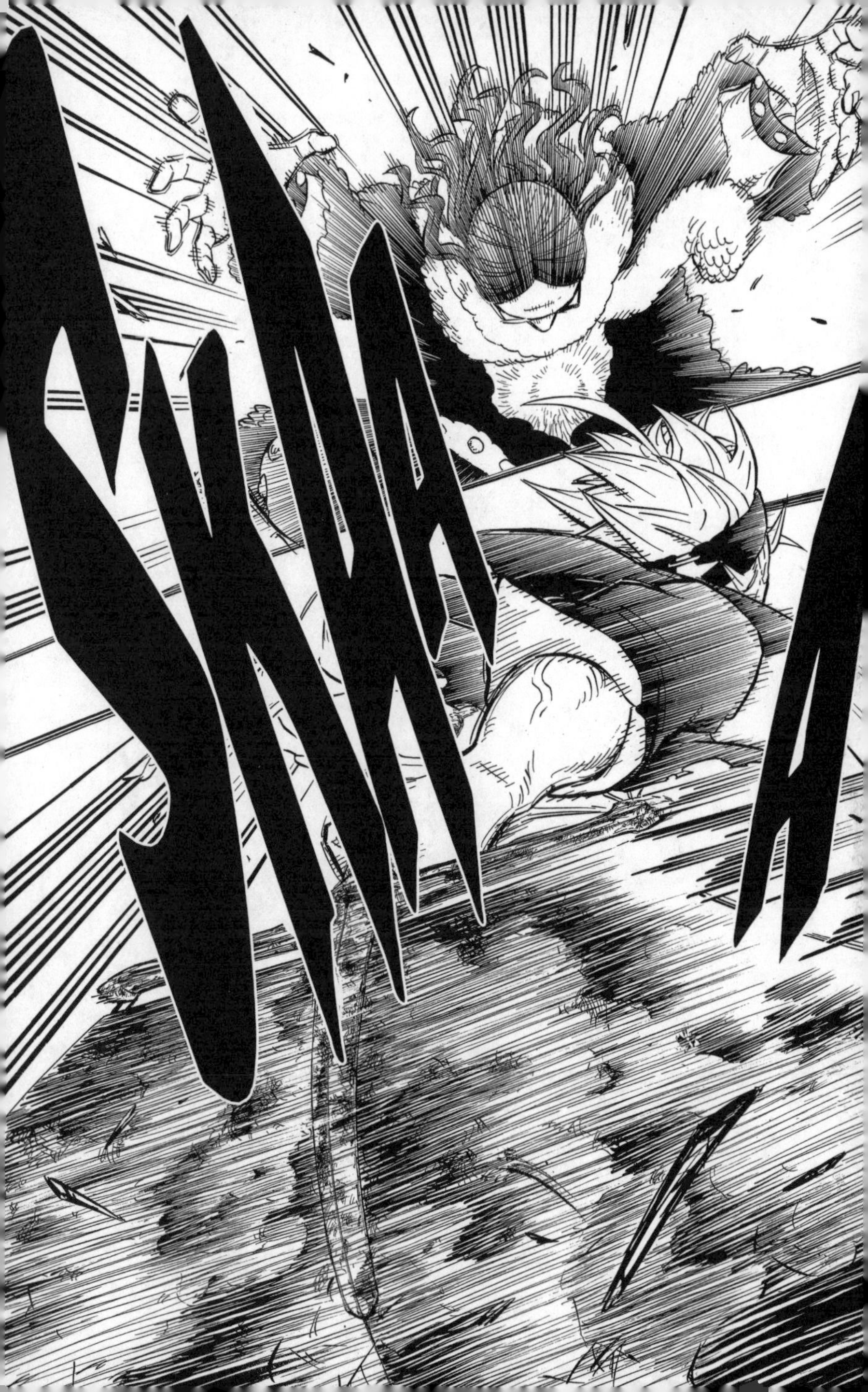
SHAA

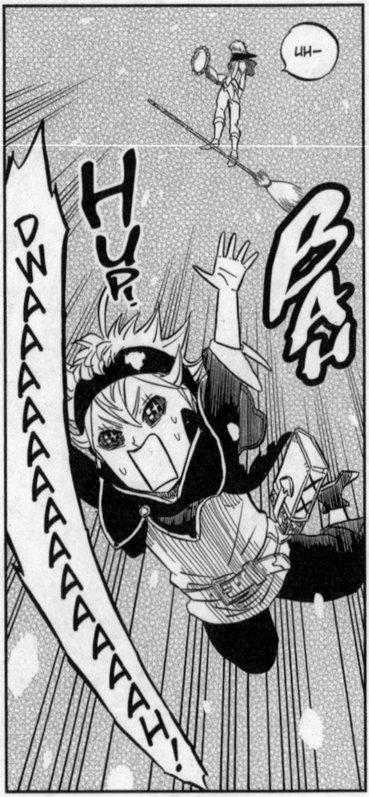
UH-
HUP!
DWAAAAAAAAAAAAAAAAH!

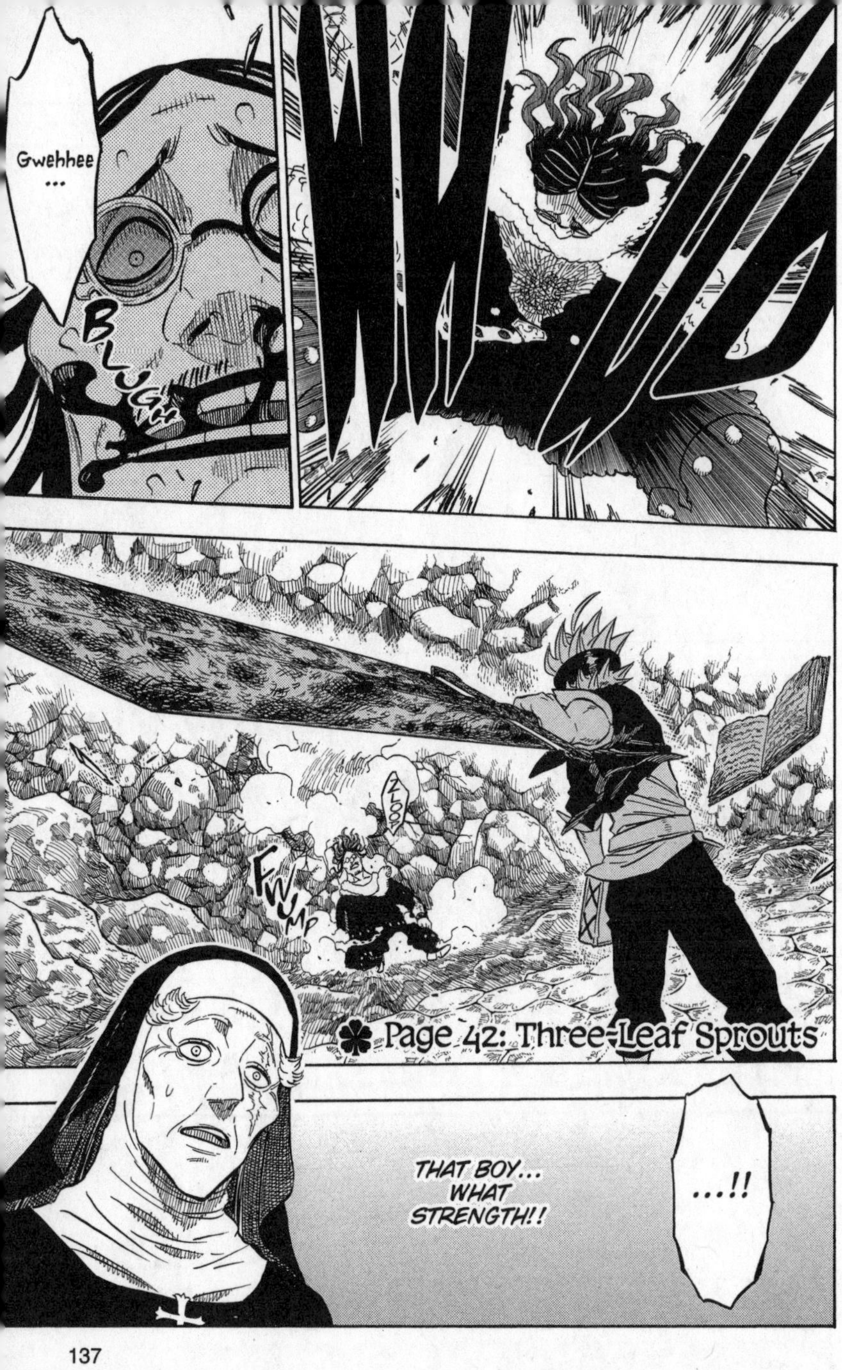
WHUD
Gwehhee...
BLUGH
ZLOOP
FWUMP
Page 42: Three-Leaf Sprouts
...!!
THAT BOY... WHAT STRENGTH!!

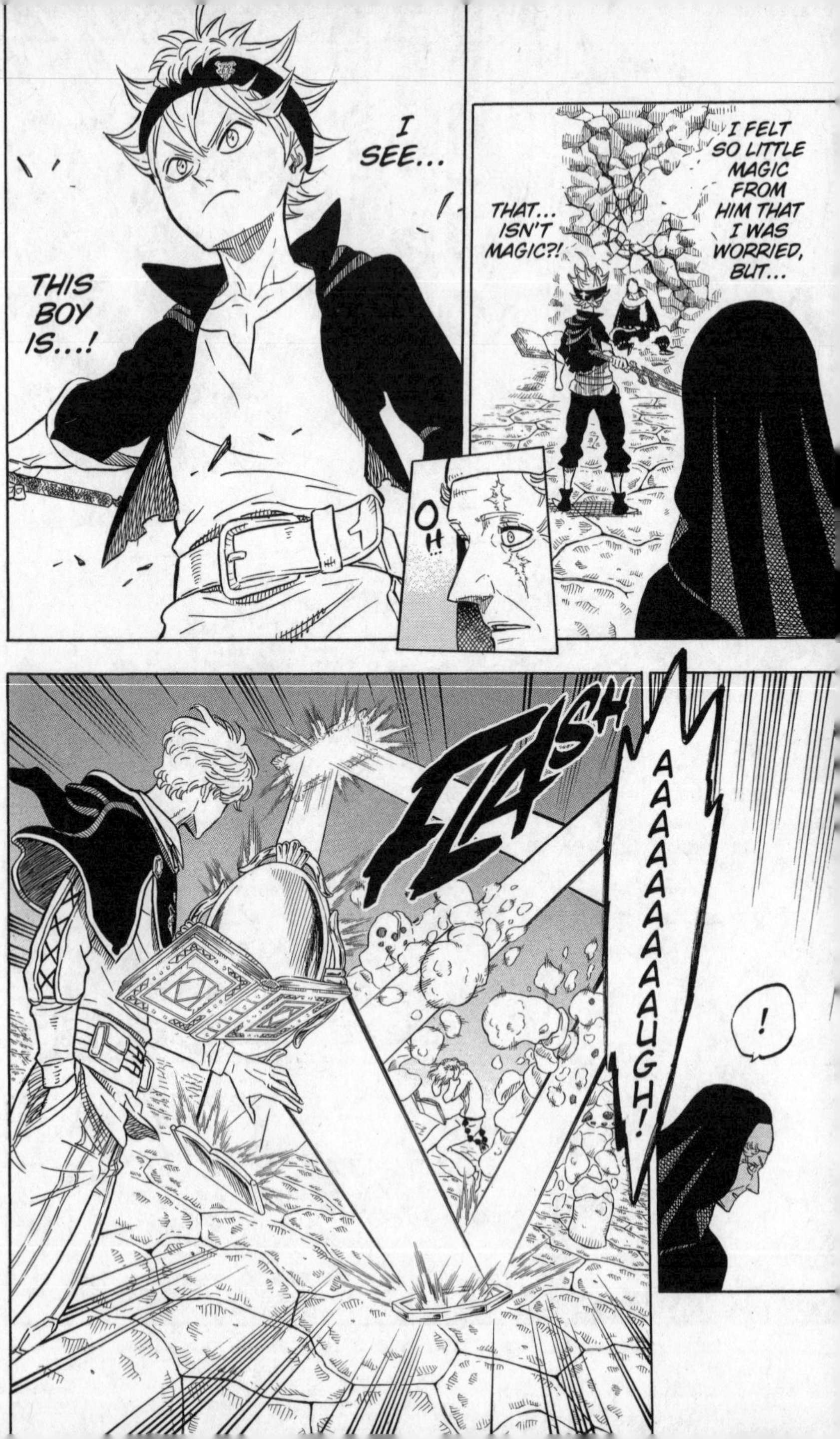
I FELT SO LITTLE MAGIC FROM HIM THAT I WAS WORRIED, BUT...
THAT... ISN'T MAGIC?!
OH...
I SEE...
THIS BOY IS...!
FLASH
AAAAAAAAAAAUGH!
!

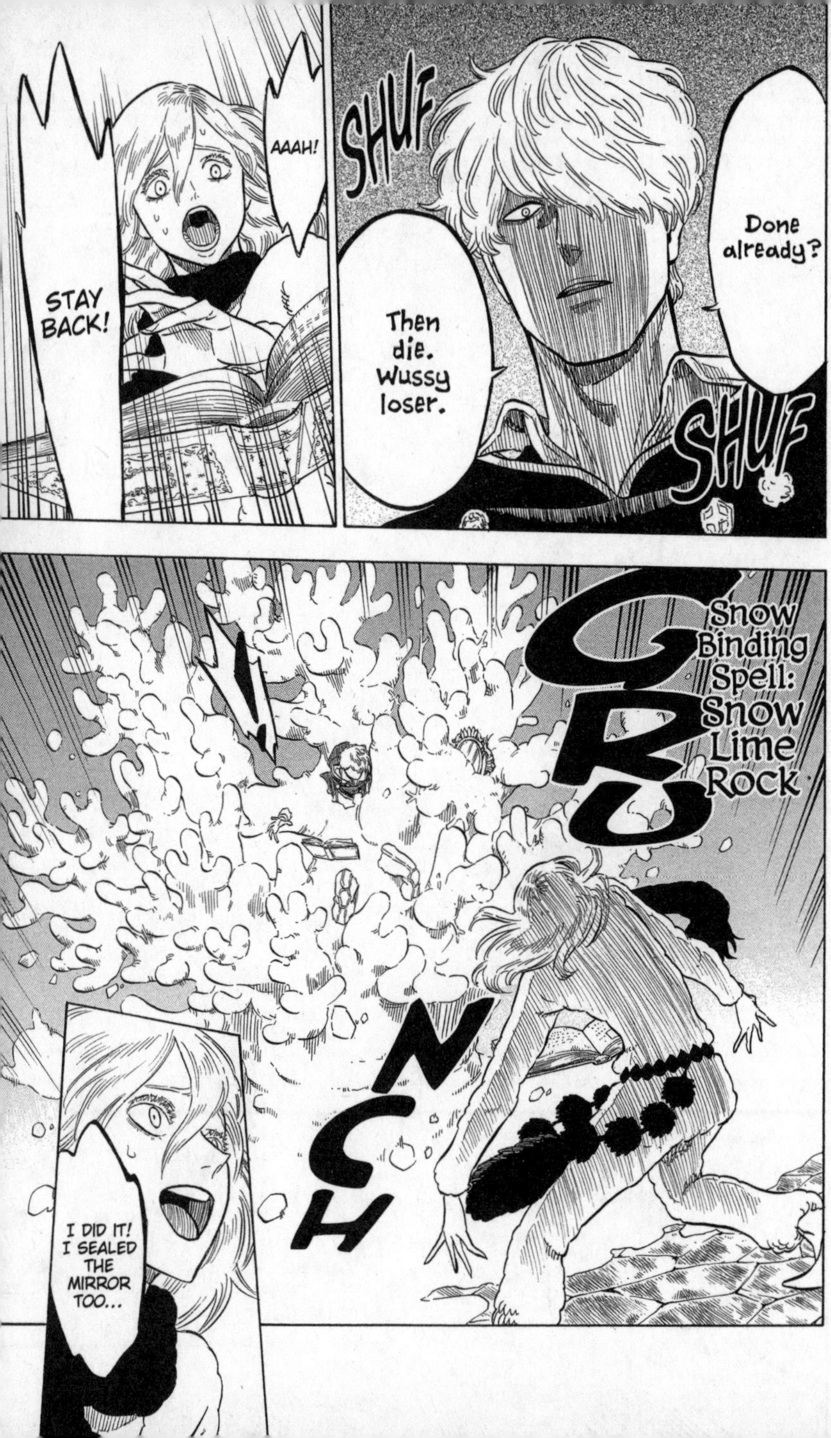
SHUF
Done already?
Then die. Wussy loser.
SHUF
AAAH!
STAY BACK!
Snow Binding Spell: Snow Lime Rock
GRUNCH
I DID IT! I SEALED THE MIRROR TOO...

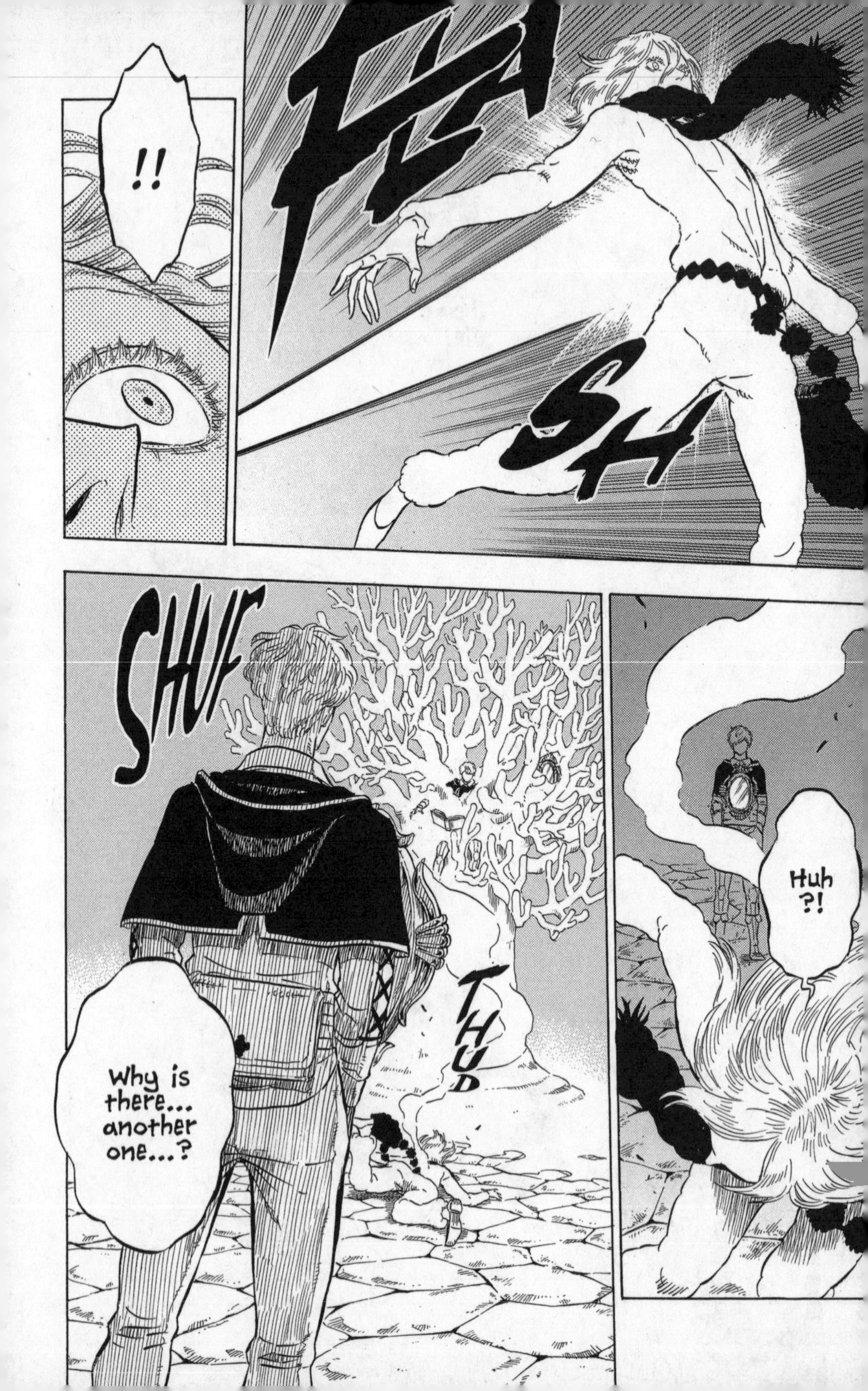
SH
!!
Huh ?!
SHUF
THUD
Why is there... another one...?

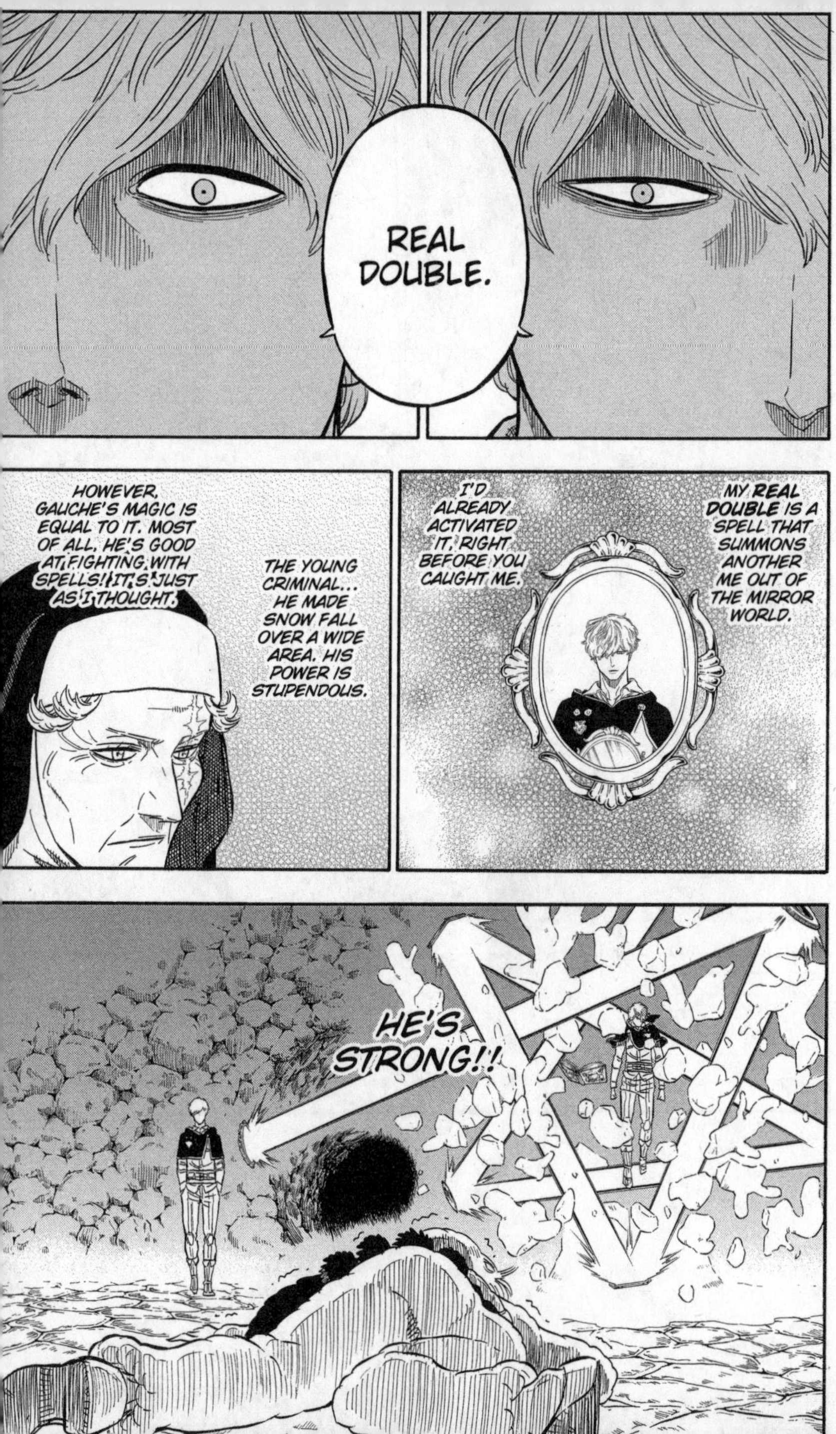
REAL DOUBLE.
MY REAL DOUBLE IS A SPELL THAT SUMMONS ANOTHER ME OUT OF THE MIRROR WORLD.
I'D ALREADY ACTIVATED IT, RIGHT BEFORE YOU CAUGHT ME.
THE YOUNG CRIMINAL... HE MADE SNOW FALL OVER A WIDE AREA. HIS POWER IS STUPENDOUS.
HOWEVER, GAUCHE'S MAGIC IS EQUAL TO IT. MOST OF ALL, HE'S GOOD AT FIGHTING WITH SPELLS!! IT'S JUST AS I THOUGHT.
HE'S STRONG!!

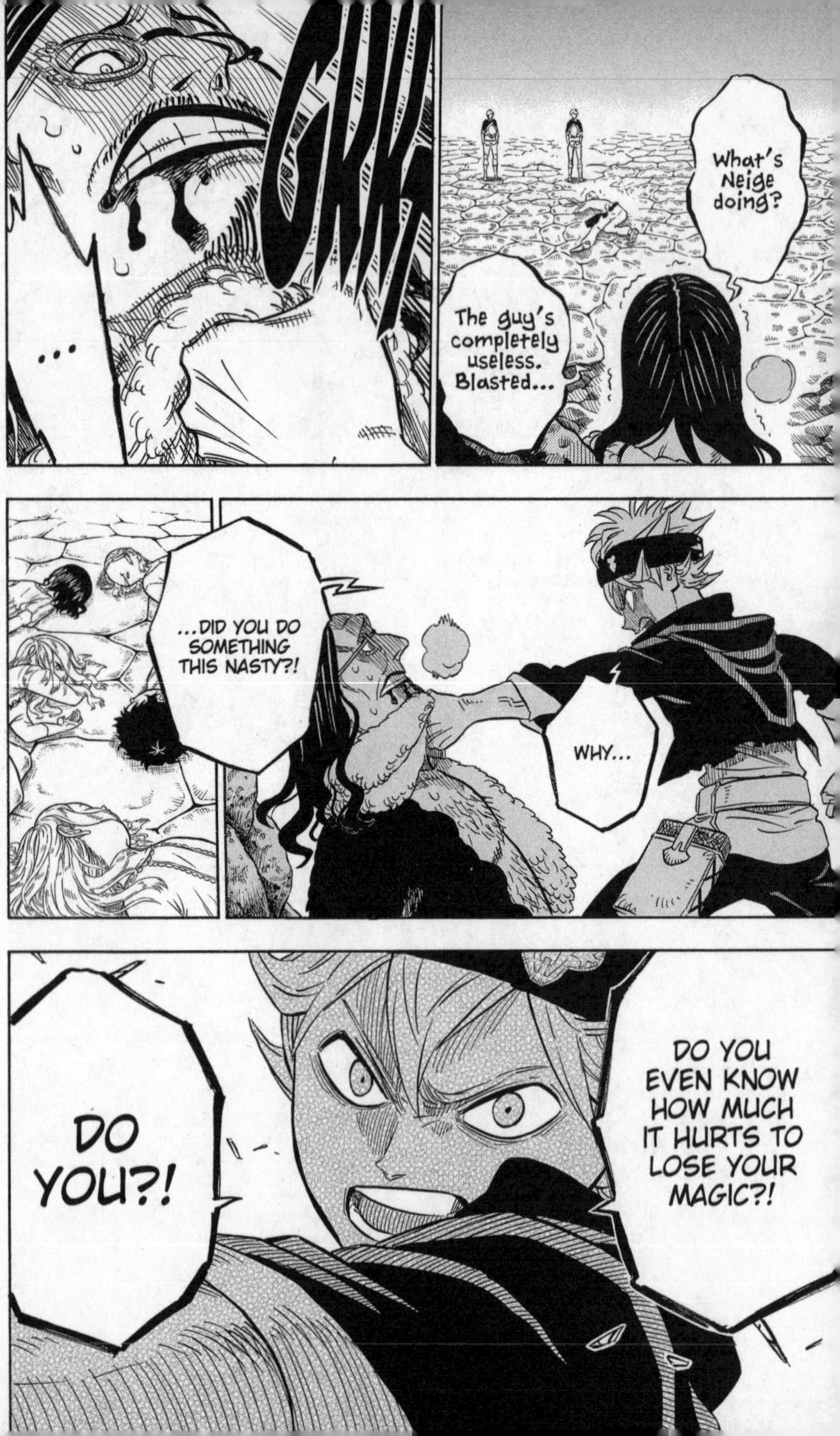
What's Neige doing?
The guy's completely useless. Blasted...
GHK
...
WHY...
...DID YOU DO SOMETHING THIS NASTY?!
DO YOU EVEN KNOW HOW MUCH IT HURTS TO LOSE YOUR MAGIC?!
DO YOU?!

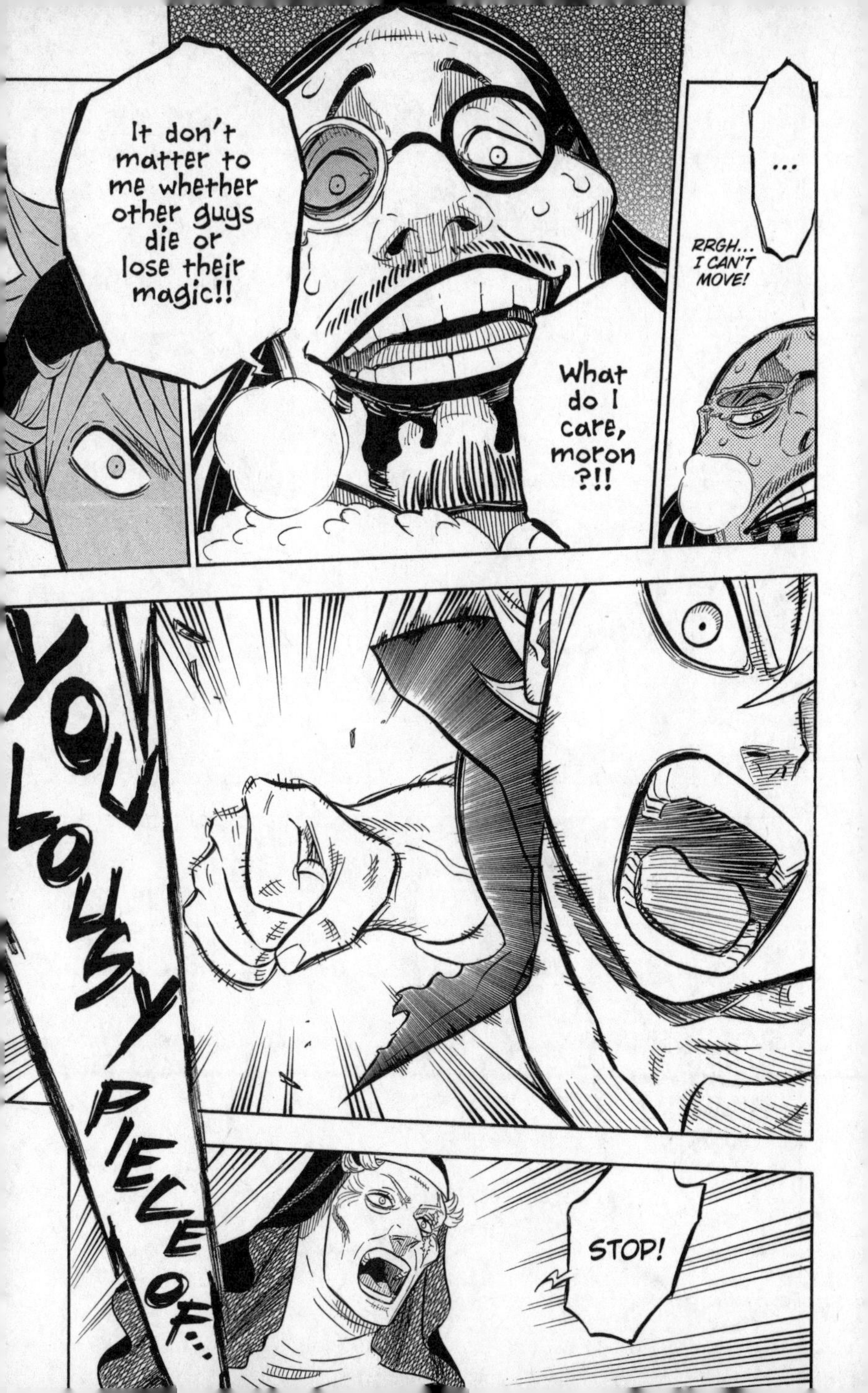
...
RRGH... I CAN'T MOVE!
It don't matter to me whether other guys die or lose their magic!!
What do I care, moron?!!
YOU LOUSY PIECE OF...
STOP!

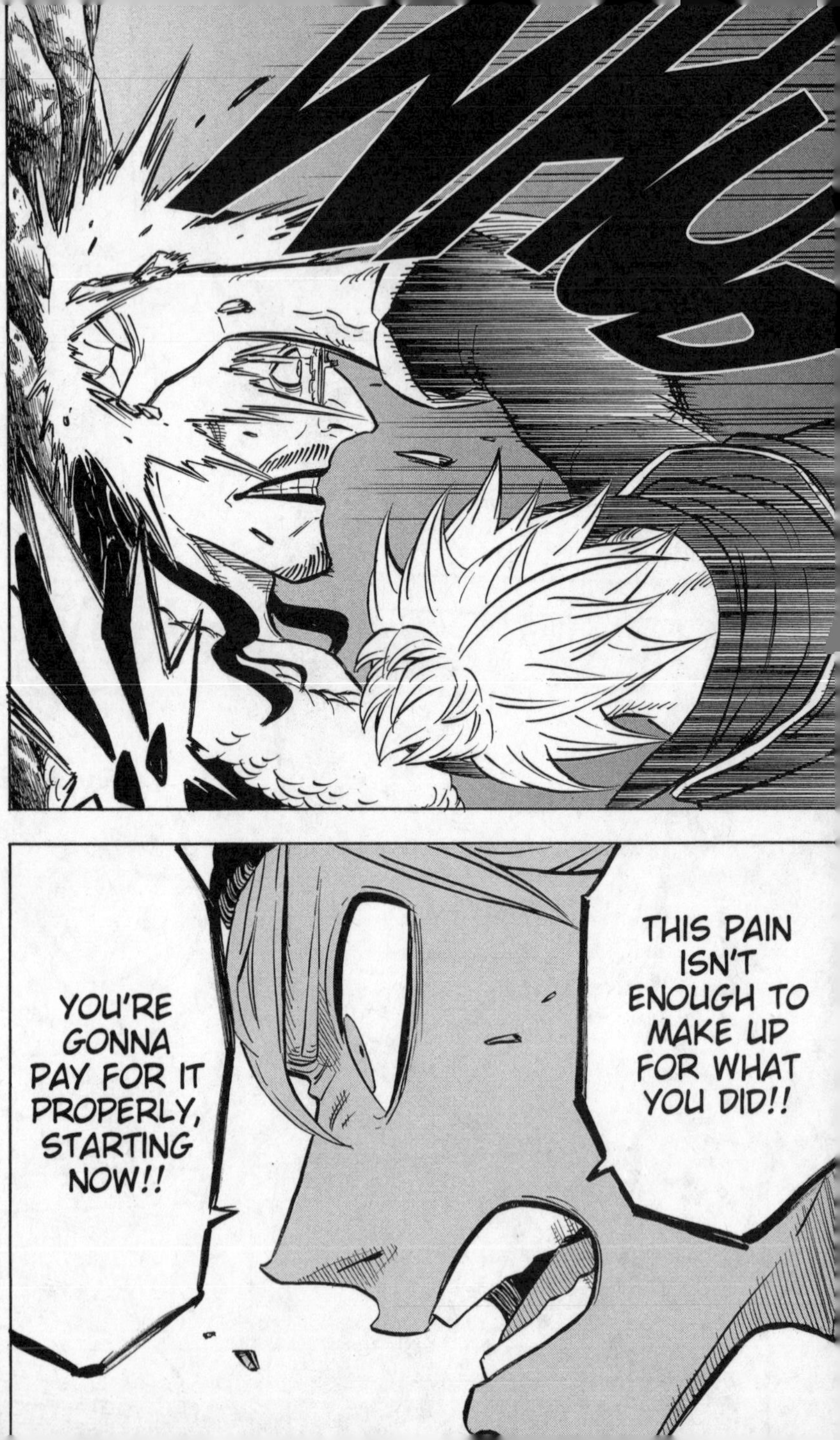
THIS PAIN ISN'T ENOUGH TO MAKE UP FOR WHAT YOU DID!!
YOU'RE GONNA PAY FOR IT PROPERLY, STARTING NOW!!

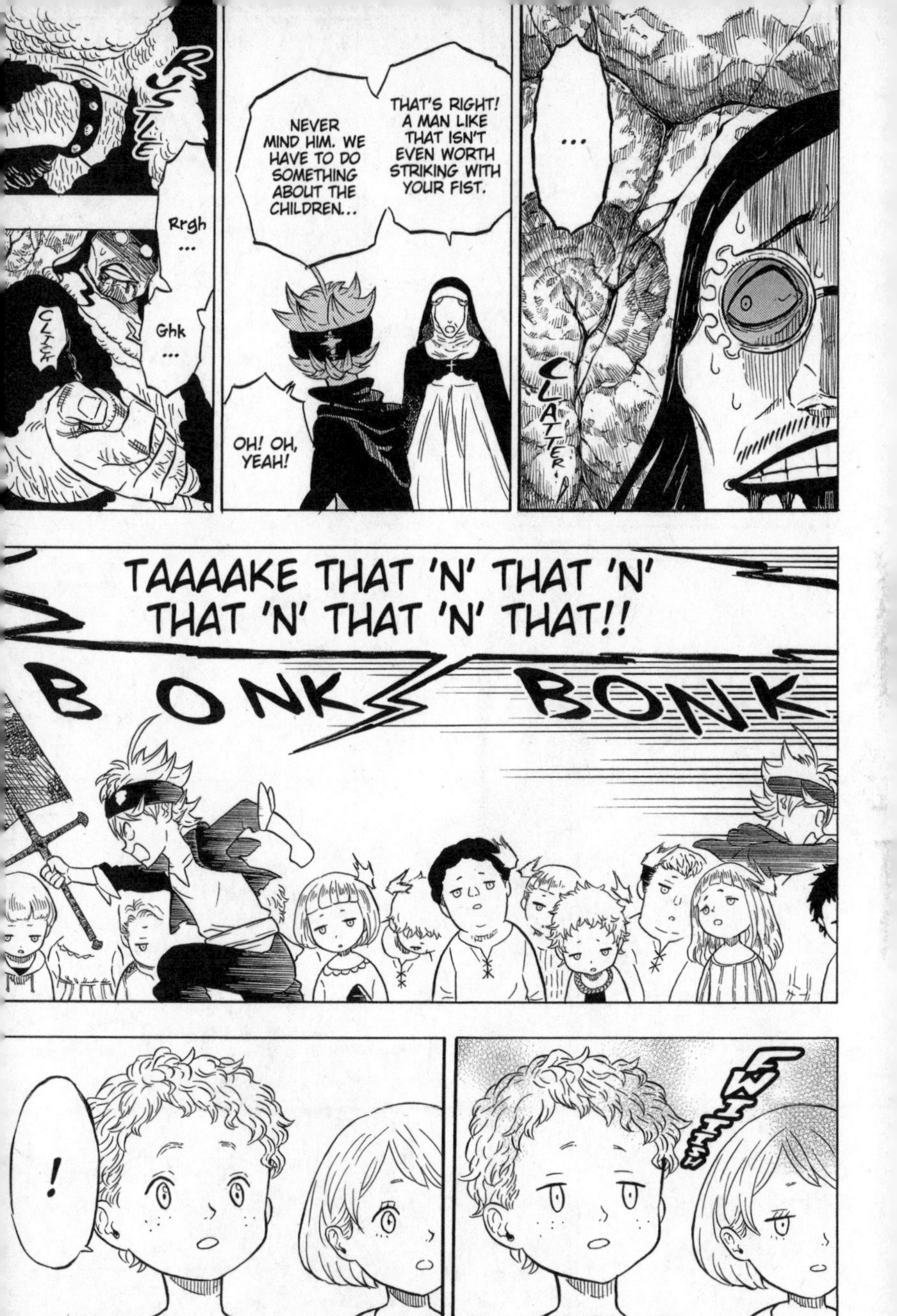
...
CLATTER!
THAT'S RIGHT! A MAN LIKE THAT ISN'T EVEN WORTH STRIKING WITH YOUR FIST.
NEVER MIND HIM. WE HAVE TO DO SOMETHING ABOUT THE CHILDREN...
OH! OH, YEAH!
RUSTLE
Rrgh ...
CLICK
Ghk ...
TAAAAKE THAT 'N' THAT 'N' THAT 'N' THAT 'N' THAT!!
BONK
BONK
TWITCH
!

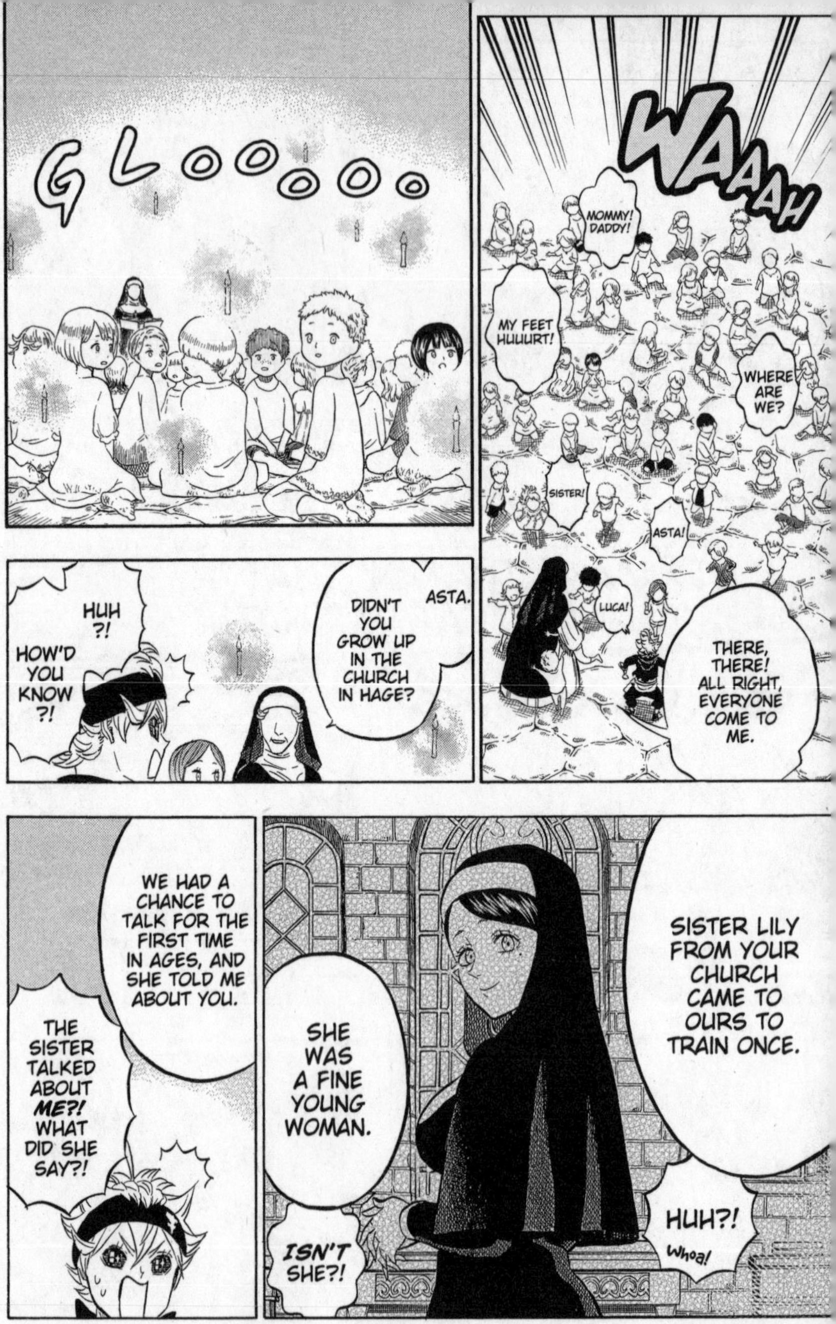
WAAAH
MOMMY! DADDY!
MY FEET HUUURT!
WHERE ARE WE?
SISTER!
ASTA!
LUCA!
THERE, THERE! ALL RIGHT, EVERYONE COME TO ME.
GLOOOOOO
ASTA.
DIDN'T YOU GROW UP IN THE CHURCH IN HAGE?
HUH?!
HOW'D YOU KNOW?!
SISTER LILY FROM YOUR CHURCH CAME TO OURS TO TRAIN ONCE.
SHE WAS A FINE YOUNG WOMAN.
ISN'T SHE?!
HUH?!
Whoa!
WE HAD A CHANCE TO TALK FOR THE FIRST TIME IN AGES, AND SHE TOLD ME ABOUT YOU.
THE SISTER TALKED ABOUT ME?! WHAT DID SHE SAY?!

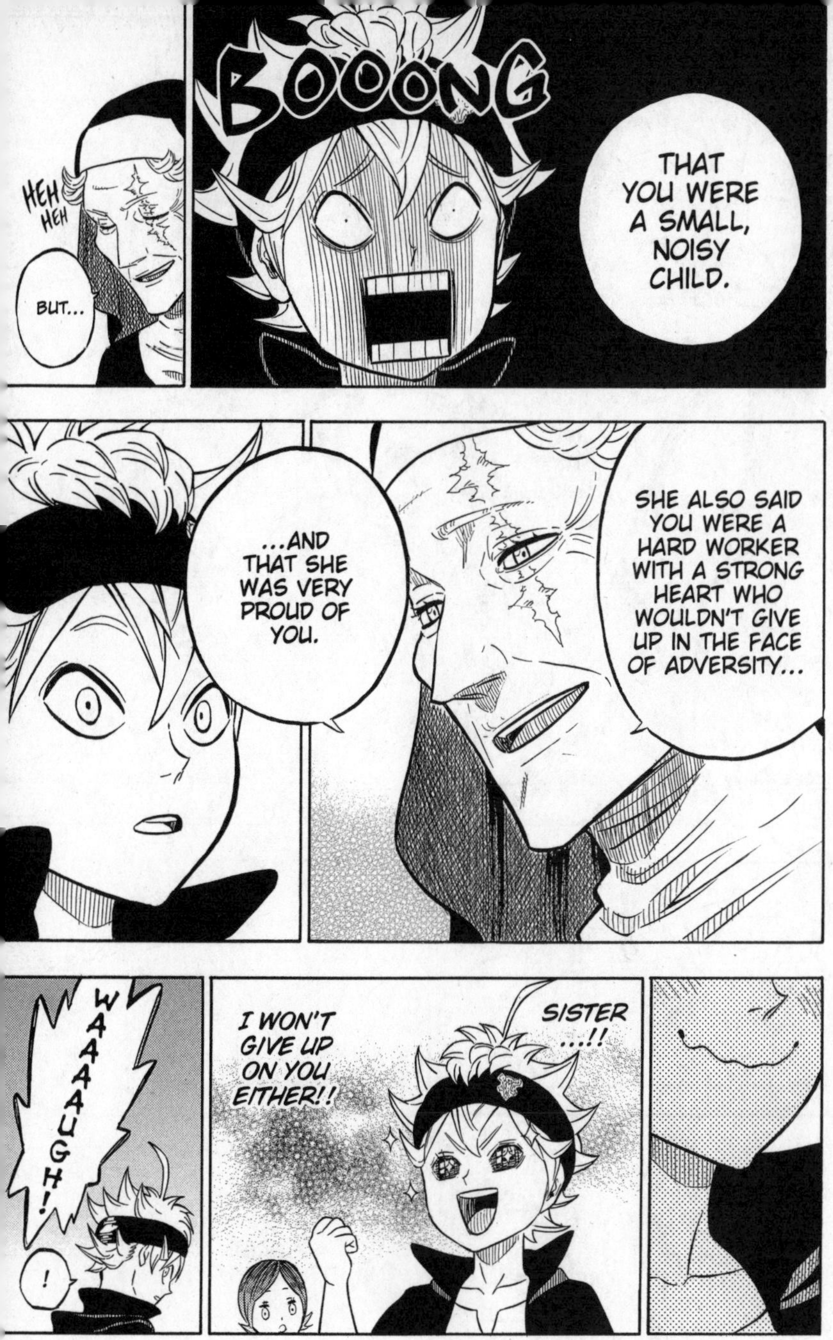
BOOONG
THAT YOU WERE A SMALL, NOISY CHILD.
HEH HEH
BUT...
SHE ALSO SAID YOU WERE A HARD WORKER WITH A STRONG HEART WHO WOULDN'T GIVE UP IN THE FACE OF ADVERSITY...
...AND THAT SHE WAS VERY PROUD OF YOU.
SISTER ...!!
I WON'T GIVE UP ON YOU EITHER!!
WAAAAAUGH!!
!

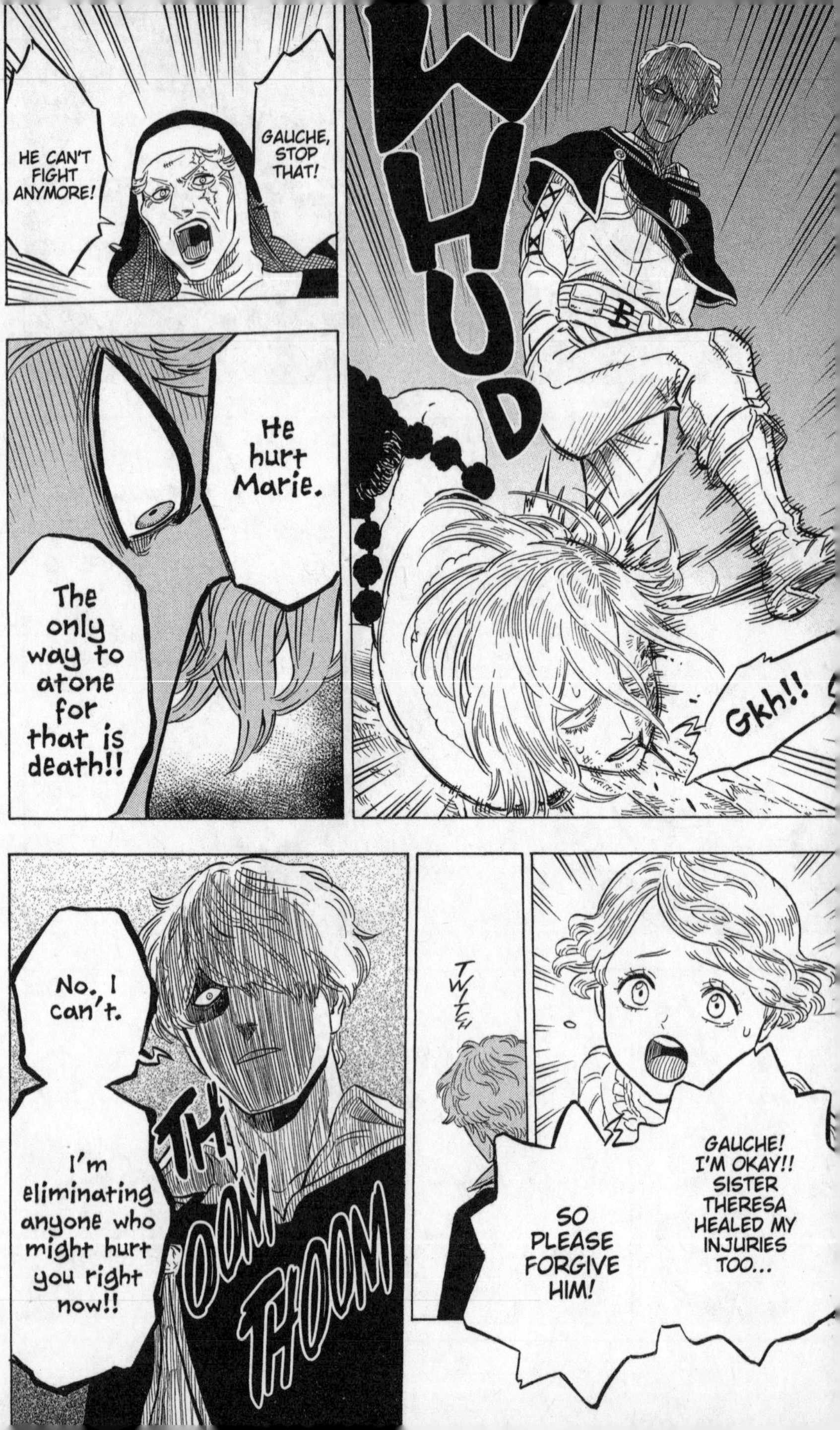
WHUD
Gkh!!
GAUCHE, STOP THAT!
HE CAN'T FIGHT ANYMORE!
He hurt Marie.
The only way to atone for that is death!!
TWITCH
GAUCHE! I'M OKAY!! SISTER THERESA HEALED MY INJURIES TOO...
SO PLEASE FORGIVE HIM!
No, I can't.
I'm eliminating anyone who might hurt you right now!!
THOOM THOOM

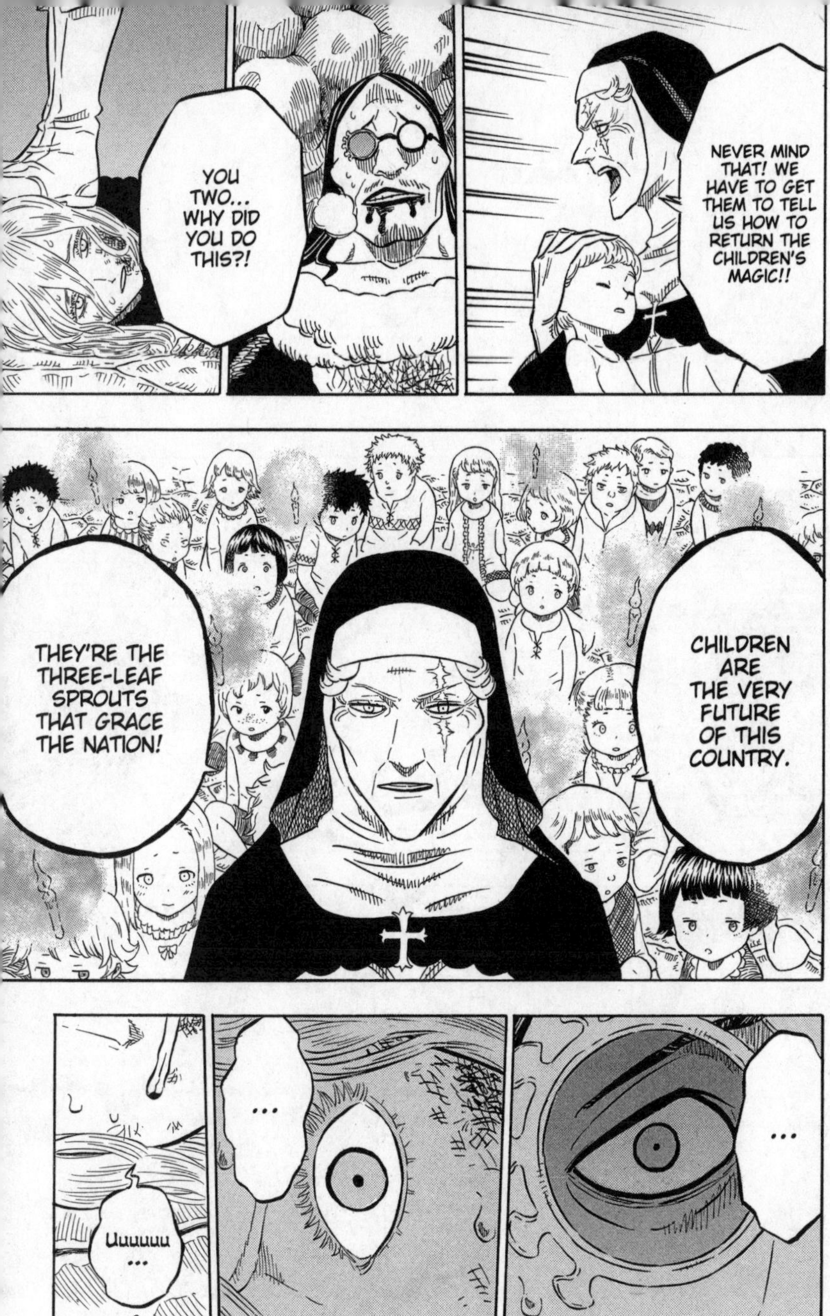
NEVER MIND THAT! WE HAVE TO GET THEM TO TELL US HOW TO RETURN THE CHILDREN'S MAGIC!!
YOU TWO... WHY DID YOU DO THIS?!
CHILDREN ARE THE VERY FUTURE OF THIS COUNTRY.
THEY'RE THE THREE-LEAF SPROUTS THAT GRACE THE NATION!
...
...
Uuuuuu...

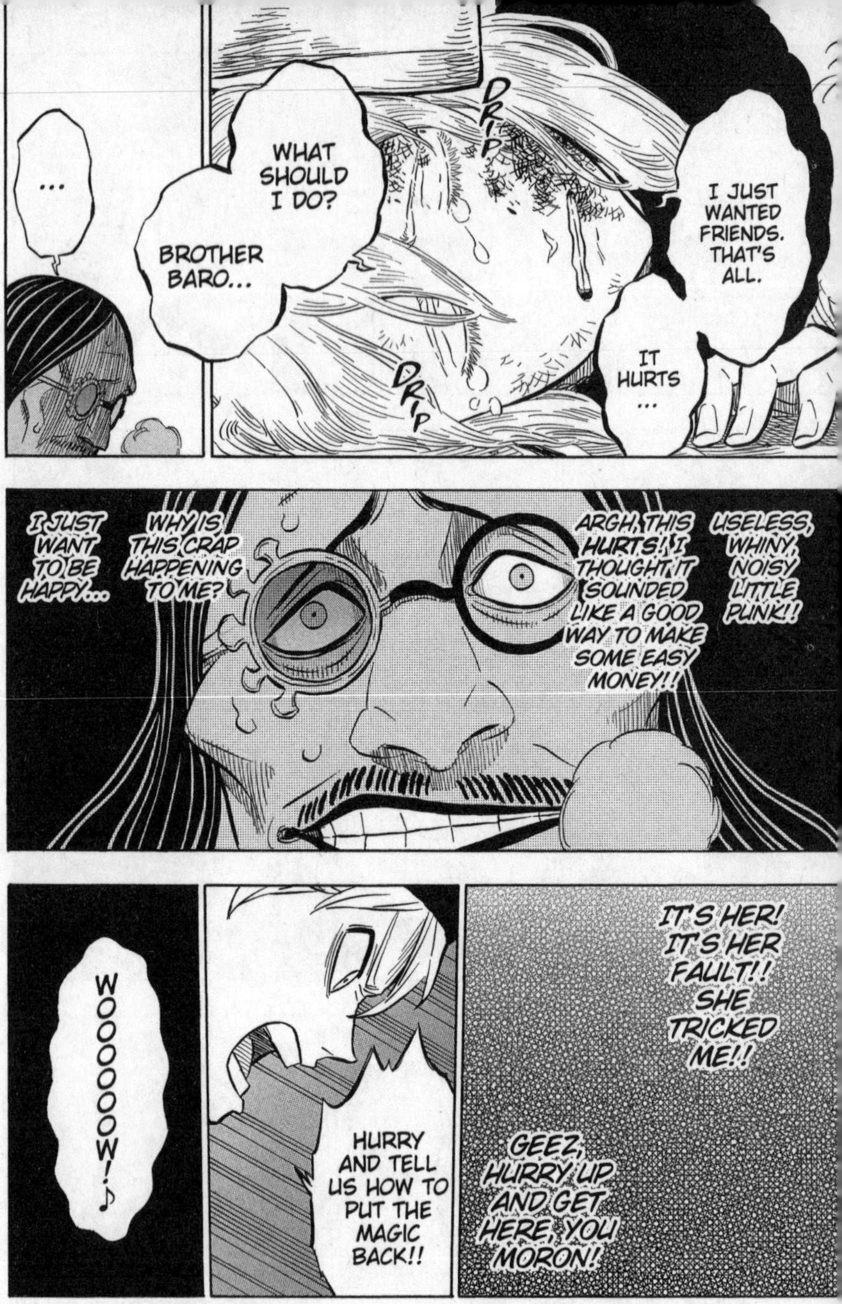
DRIP
I JUST WANTED FRIENDS. THAT'S ALL.
IT HURTS...
WHAT SHOULD I DO?
BROTHER BARO...
DRIP
...
USELESS, WHINY, NOISY LITTLE PUNK!!
ARGH, THIS HURTS! I THOUGHT IT SOUNDED LIKE A GOOD WAY TO MAKE SOME EASY MONEY!!
WHY IS THIS CRAP HAPPENING TO ME?
I JUST WANT TO BE HAPPY...
IT'S HER! IT'S HER FAULT!! SHE TRICKED ME!!
GEEZ, HURRY UP AND GET HERE, YOU MORON!
HURRY AND TELL US HOW TO PUT THE MAGIC BACK!!
WOOOOOOOW!♪

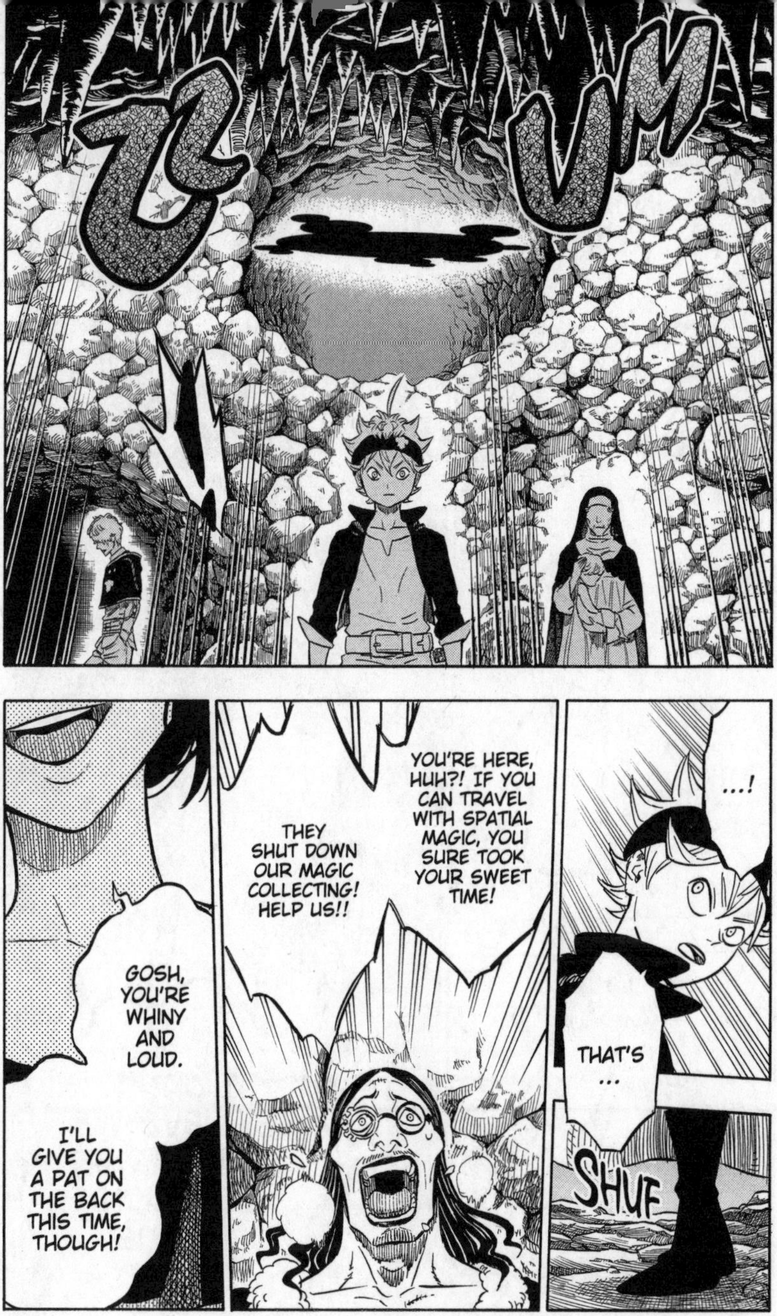
UM
...!
THAT'S ...
SHUF
YOU'RE HERE, HUH?! IF YOU CAN TRAVEL WITH SPATIAL MAGIC, YOU SURE TOOK YOUR SWEET TIME!
THEY SHUT DOWN OUR MAGIC COLLECTING! HELP US!!
GOSH, YOU'RE WHINY AND LOUD.
I'LL GIVE YOU A PAT ON THE BACK THIS TIME, THOUGH!

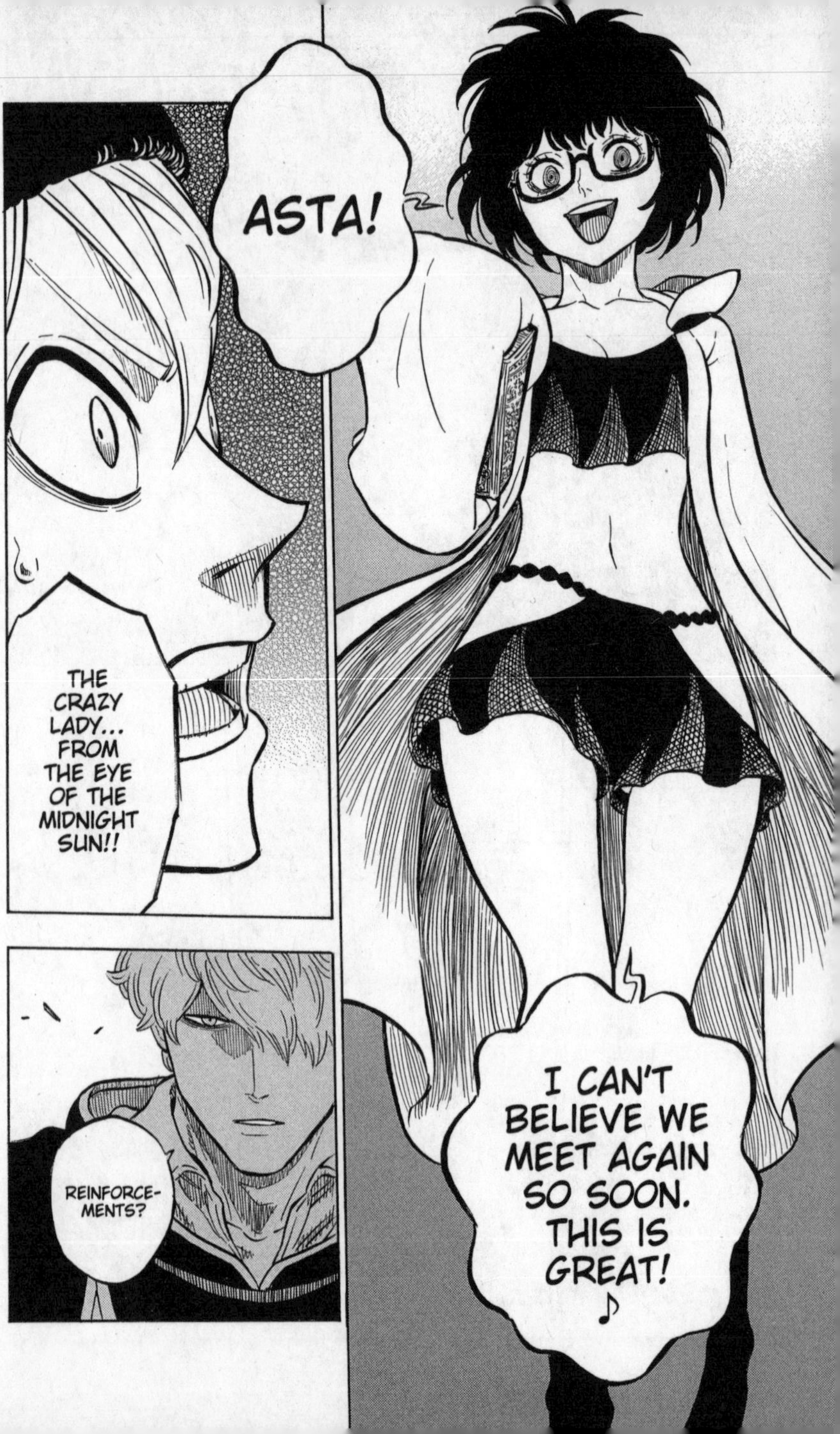
ASTA!
I CAN'T BELIEVE WE MEET AGAIN SO SOON. THIS IS GREAT! ♪
THE CRAZY LADY... FROM THE EYE OF THE MIDNIGHT SUN!!
REINFORCE-MENTS?

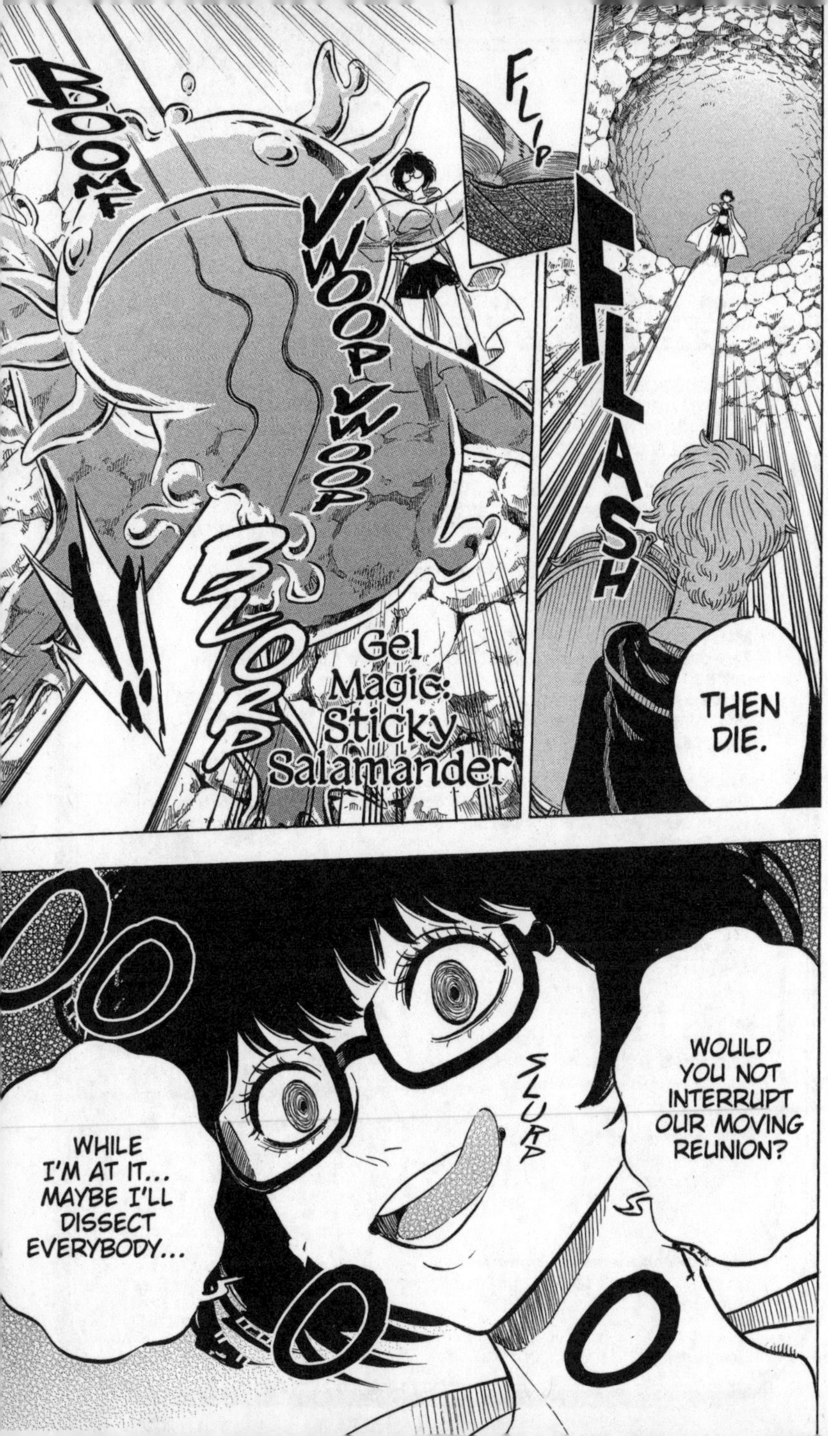
FLIP
FLASH
THEN DIE.
VWOOP VWOOP
BLORP
Gel Magic: Sticky Salamander
BOOMF
!!
WOULD YOU NOT INTERRUPT OUR MOVING REUNION?
SLURP
WHILE I'M AT IT... MAYBE I'LL DISSECT EVERYBODY...

Black Clover fan!
Special comment from Honoka Akimoto!

This is the sort of classic among classics that makes you think, "Now this is *Shonen Jump* manga!" (ノ`･∀･)ノ
It's packed with friendship, hard work and victory! *Jump* kids, if you don't read this one, you'll spend your whole life missing out.

When I see Asta barreling straight ahead and working hard at everything without cutting corners, it makes me want to do my best too. I wish I had a little brother like him. (｡−∀−｡)

And check out the relationship between the "hot-blooded failure" Asta and his friend, the "coolheaded genius" Yuno!!! After all, in the sort of manga where the hero's aiming for the top (Wizard King), you've just got to have a rival!

He has all sorts of other unique companions too.
My particular favorite is Charmy Pappitson.♥
She looks unreliable, but she's actually superstrong, and on top of that, she's cute! It's not fair!
I heard she's modeled on Tabata-sensei's wife, and now I'm really curious. (−▼−)

Most of all, the art is pretty.☆
The drawings in every single panel are practically fine art, instead of comics. \ (o°ω°o)ノ
Before now, I never cared about anything except the story of a manga, but after meeting *Black Clover*, I've started to pay attention to the art too.

Another great thing about it is all the amazing dialog that resonates with you! These are my personal top three:

Honoka Akimoto

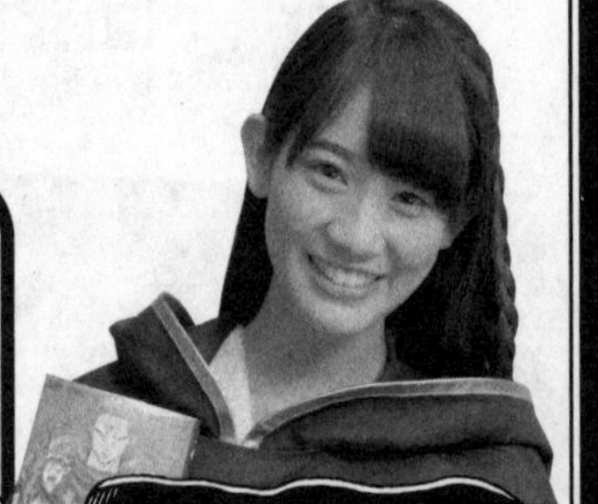

1. Asta
"Gravel may be gravel, but me? I'm gravel that shatters diamonds!!!!"

2. Charmy
"I don't care who they are~ Nobody touches my food!"

3. Noelle
"It's your fault for standing there. Who gave you permission to be there?"

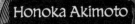

The center of the girls' high school idol singer group Team Shachihoko from Nagoya, affiliated with Section 3 of Stardust Promotion. Her image color is Nagoya Red. She's actually a huge *Black Clover* fan, and she sent us a special comment!

I really can't wait to find out what happens next. (^^)

I want to know how Noelle and Mimosa's loves are going to turn out too...♥

Page 43: Explosion of Malice

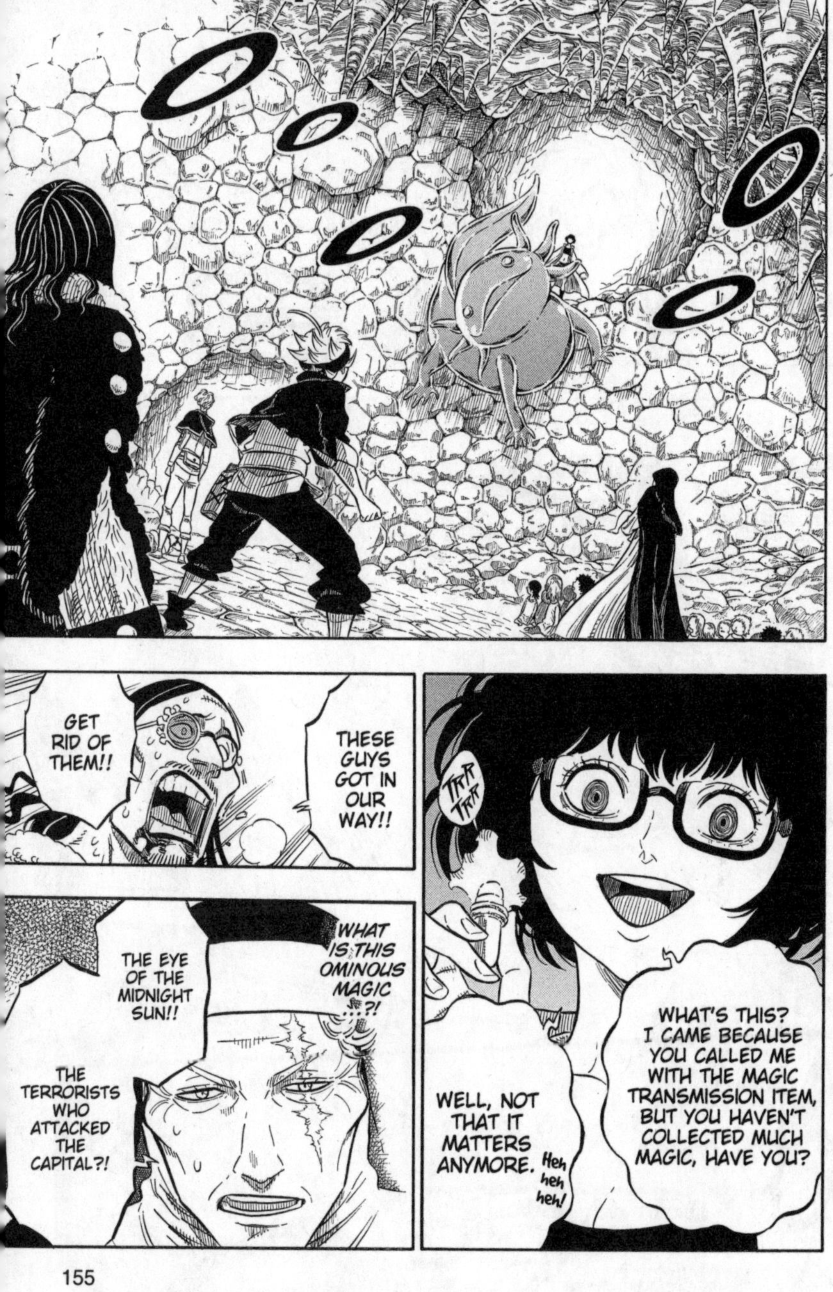
TRR TRR
WHAT'S THIS? I CAME BECAUSE YOU CALLED ME WITH THE MAGIC TRANSMISSION ITEM, BUT YOU HAVEN'T COLLECTED MUCH MAGIC, HAVE YOU?
WELL, NOT THAT IT MATTERS ANYMORE.
Heh heh heh!
THESE GUYS GOT IN OUR WAY!!
GET RID OF THEM!!
WHAT IS THIS OMINOUS MAGIC ...?!
THE EYE OF THE MIDNIGHT SUN!!
THE TERRORISTS WHO ATTACKED THE CAPITAL?!

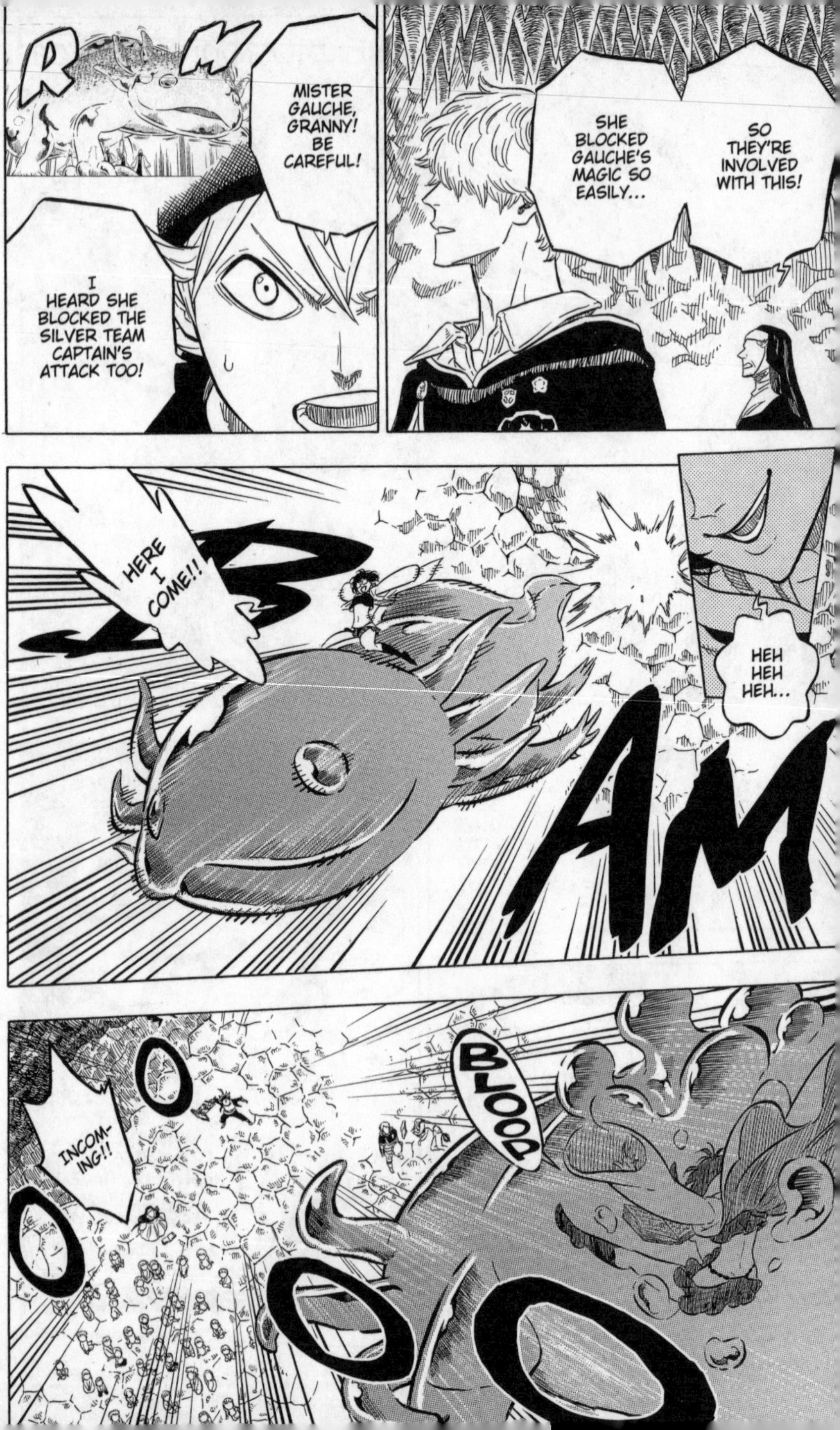
SO THEY'RE INVOLVED WITH THIS!
SHE BLOCKED GAUCHE'S MAGIC SO EASILY...
MISTER GAUCHE, GRANNY! BE CAREFUL!
I HEARD SHE BLOCKED THE SILVER TEAM CAPTAIN'S ATTACK TOO!
HEH HEH HEH...
HERE I COME!!
AM
BLOOP
INCOM-ING!!

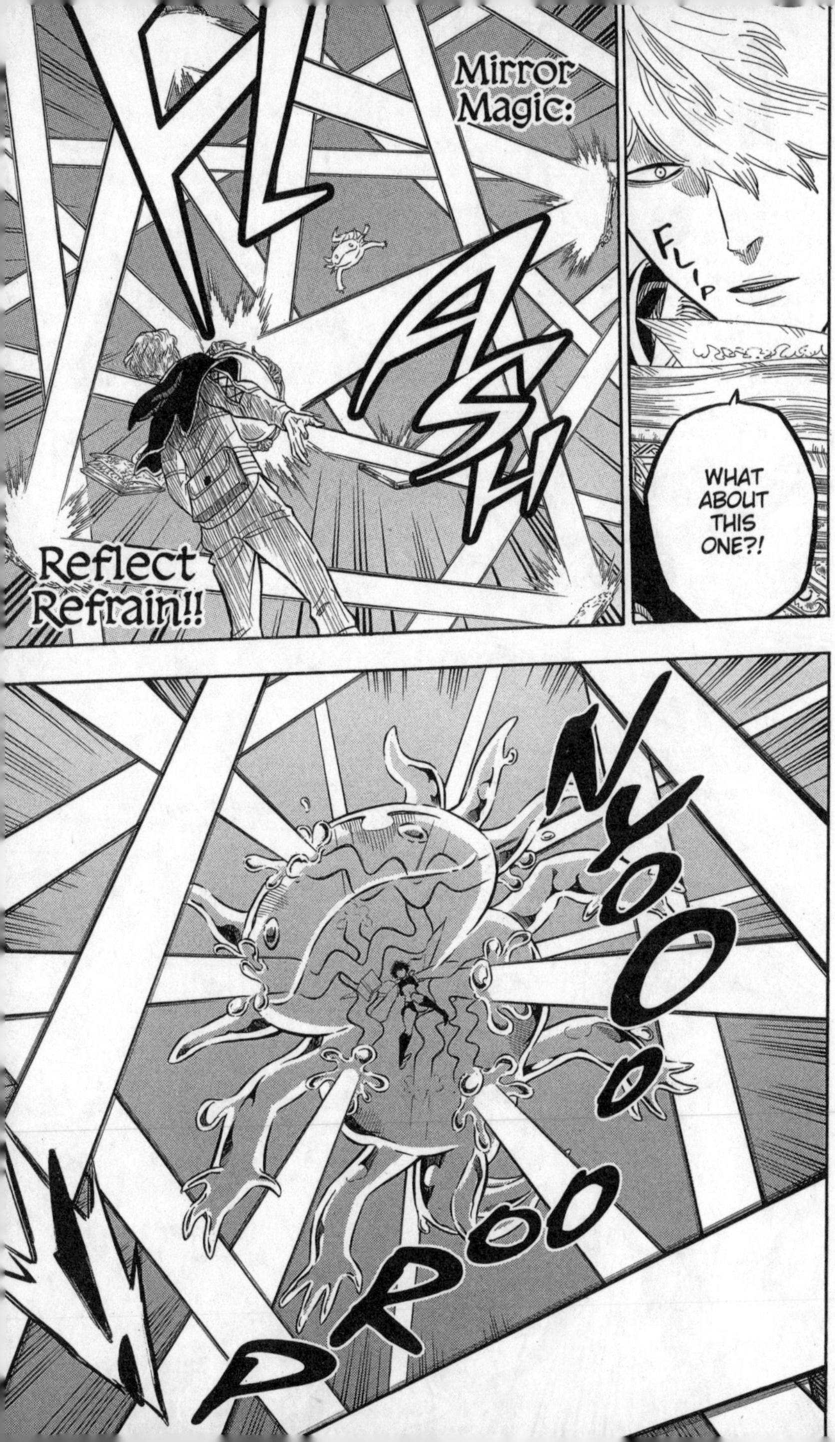
FLIP
WHAT ABOUT THIS ONE?!
Mirror Magic:
FLASH
Reflect Refrain!!

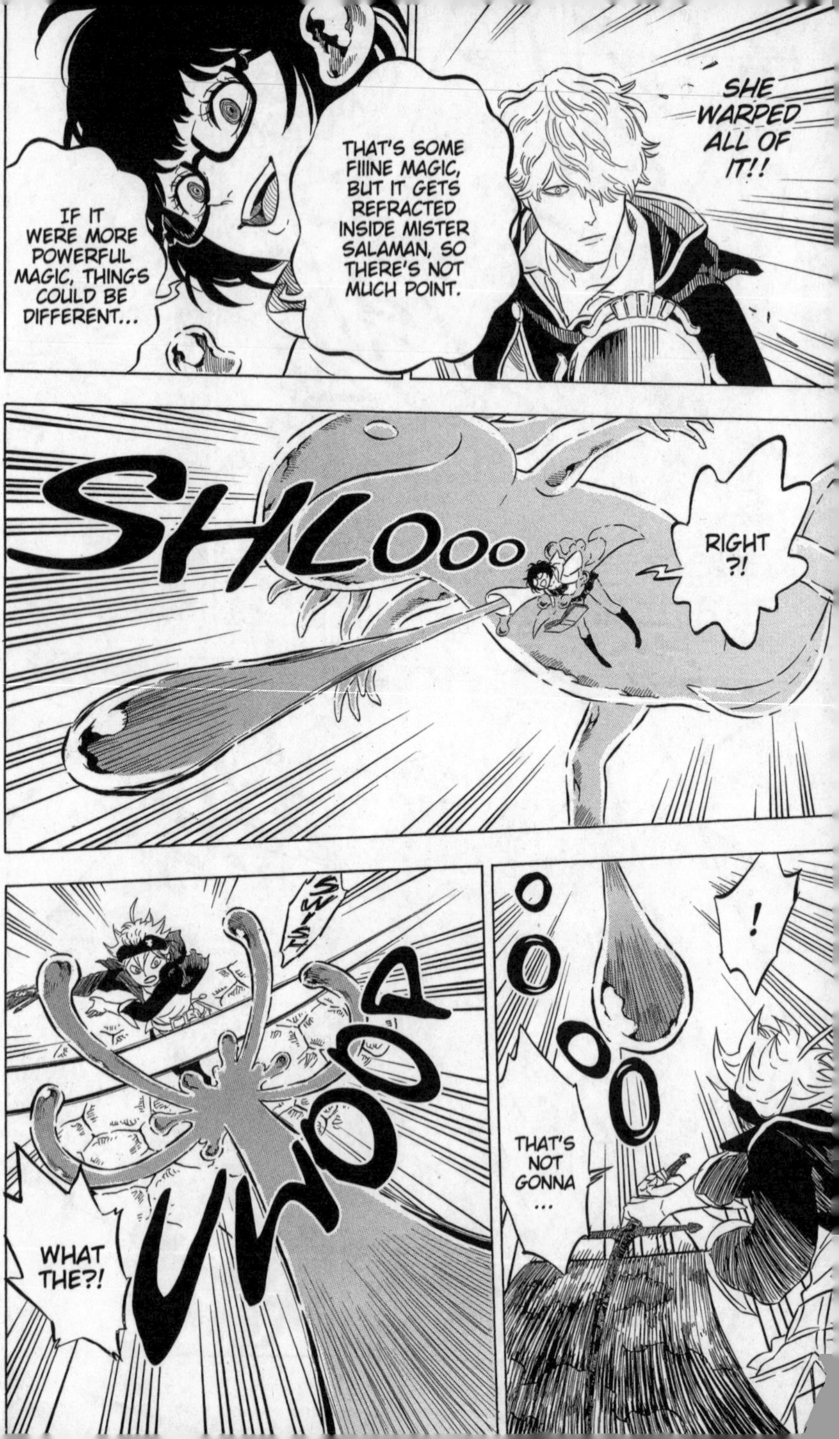
SHE WARPED ALL OF IT!!
THAT'S SOME FIIINE MAGIC, BUT IT GETS REFRACTED INSIDE MISTER SALAMAN, SO THERE'S NOT MUCH POINT.
IF IT WERE MORE POWERFUL MAGIC, THINGS COULD BE DIFFERENT...
SHLOOO
RIGHT?!
!
THAT'S NOT GONNA ...
WHOOOOOOOO
SWISH
WHAT THE?!

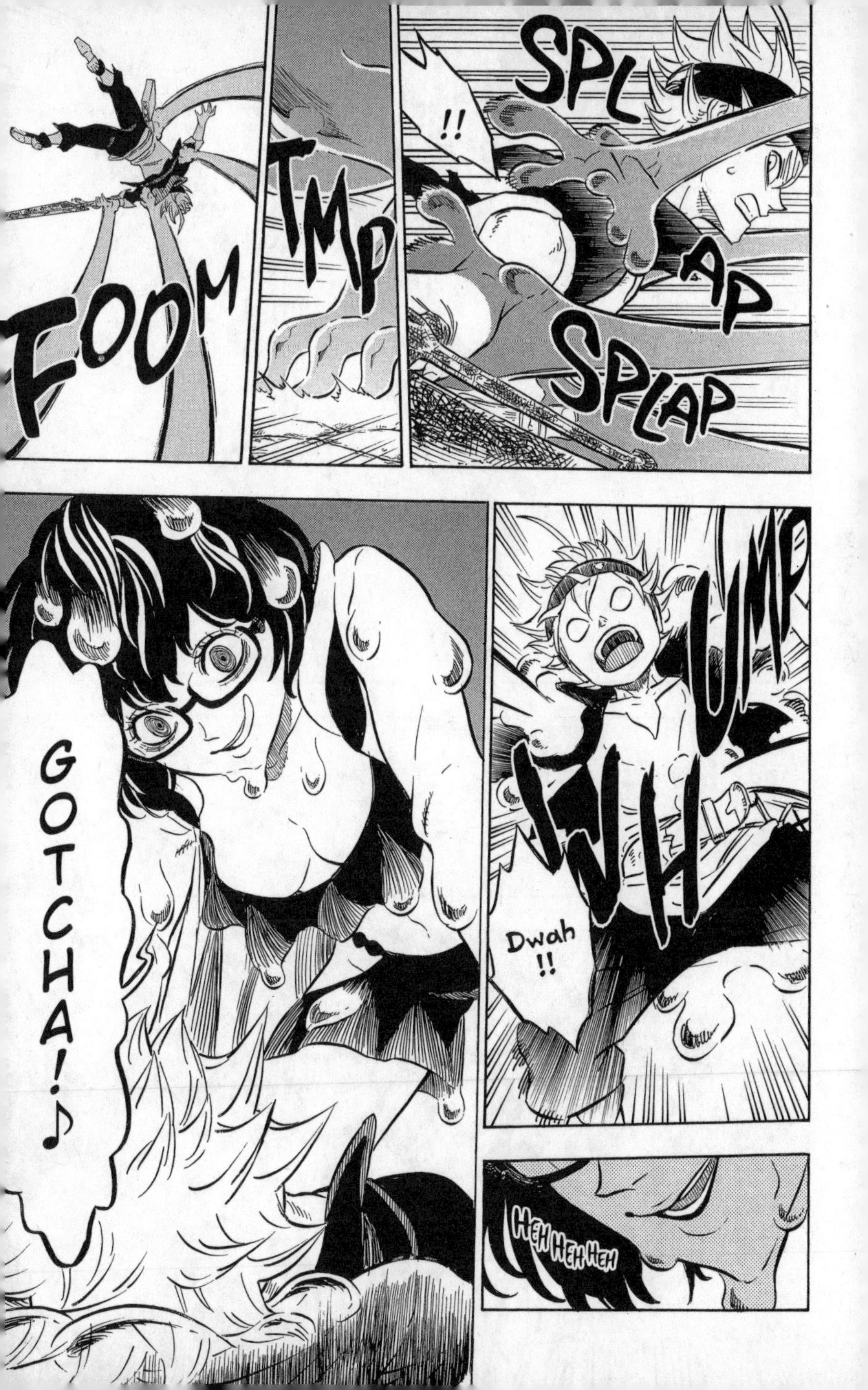
!!
SPLAP
SPLAP
TMP
FOOM
WHUMP
Dwah !!
HEH HEH HEH
GOTCHA!♪

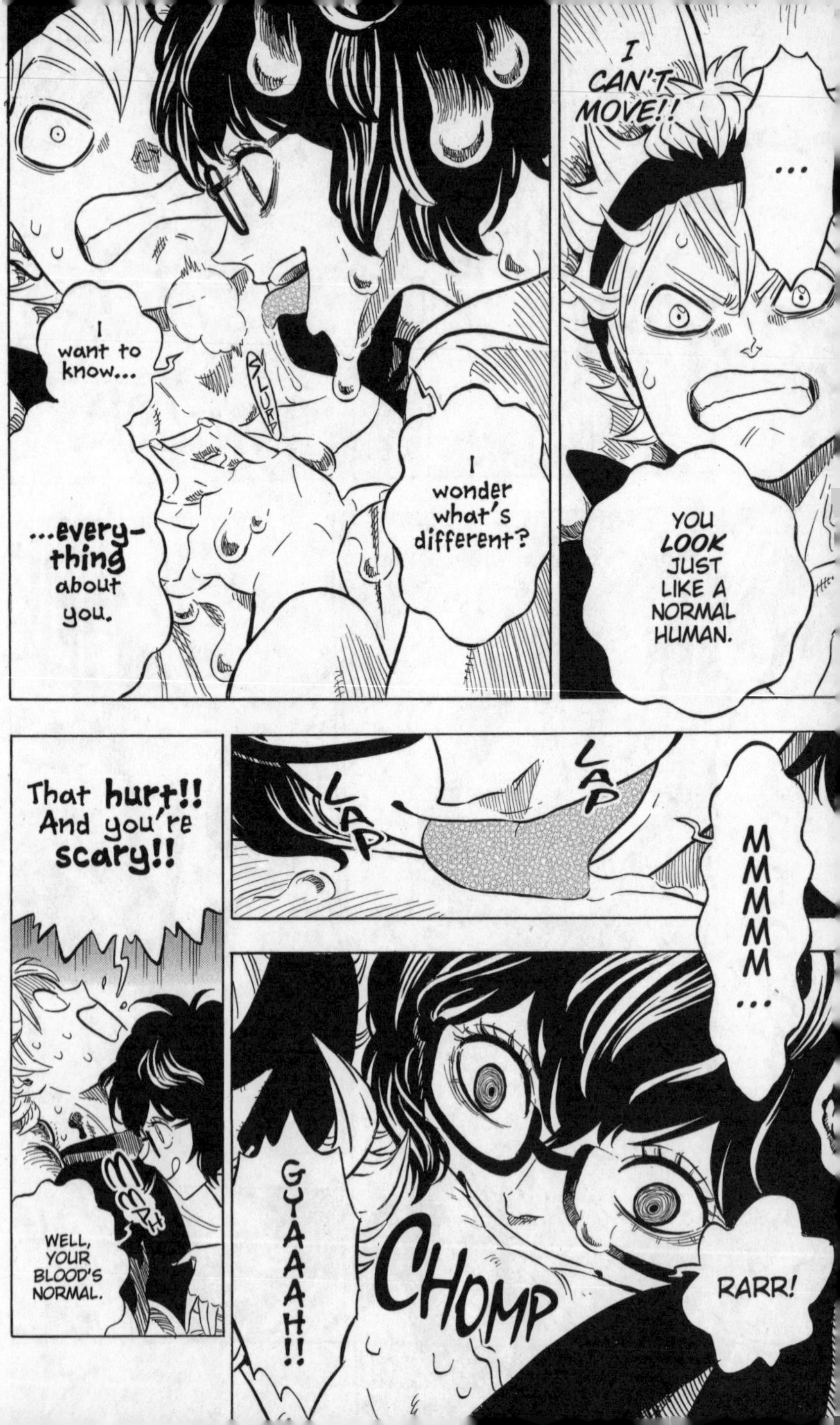
I CAN'T MOVE!!
...
YOU LOOK JUST LIKE A NORMAL HUMAN.
I wonder what's different?
SLURP
I want to know...
...everything about you.
LAP
LAP
MMMMM...
RARR!
CHOMP
GYAAAAH!!
That hurt!! And you're scary!!
MMPH
WELL, YOUR BLOOD'S NORMAL.

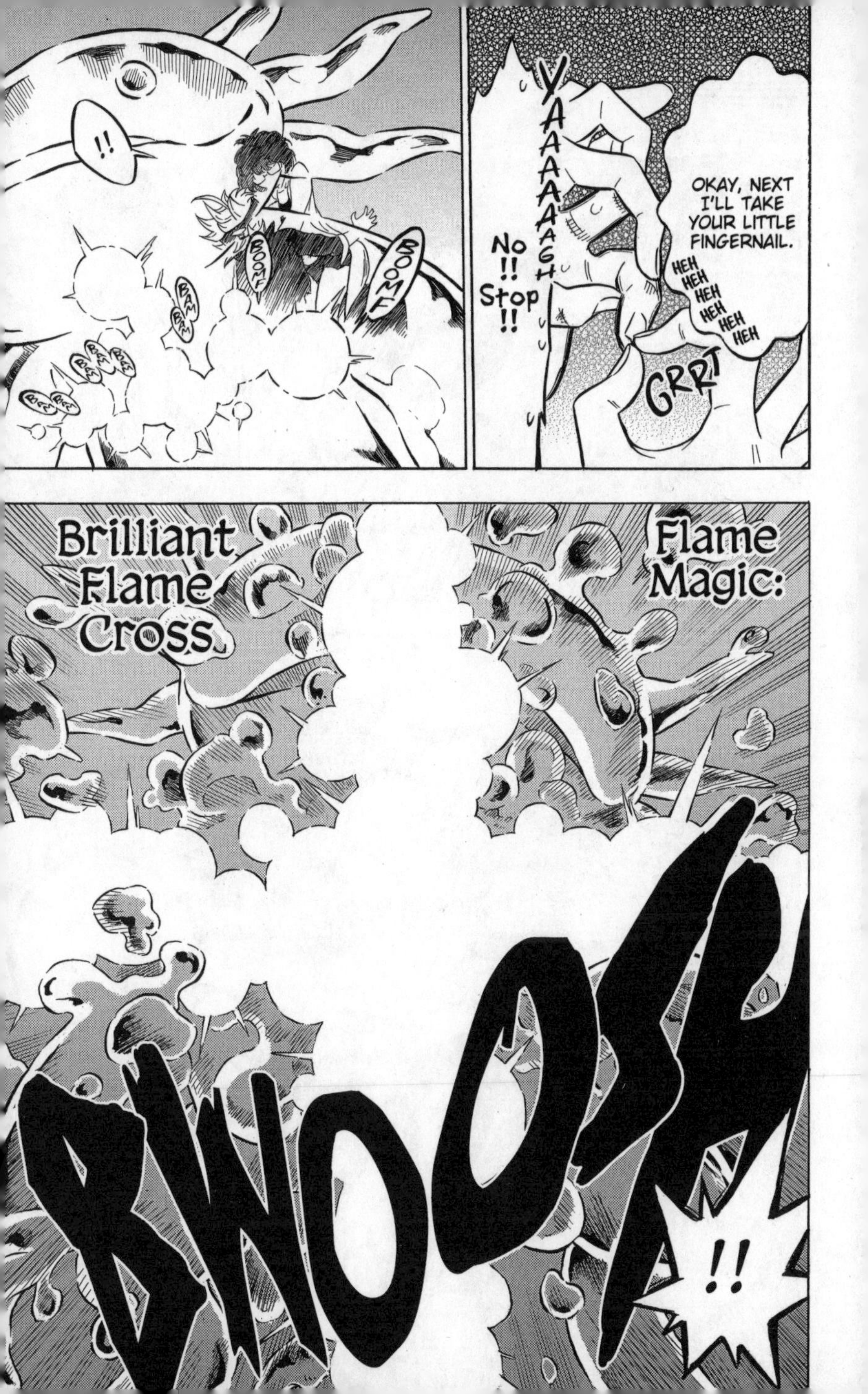
OKAY, NEXT I'LL TAKE YOUR LITTLE FINGERNAIL.
YAAAAAAAAGH
No!! Stop!!
HEH HEH HEH HEH HEH HEH
GRRT
!!
BOOMF
BOOMF
BAM BAM
Flame Magic:
Brilliant Flame Cross
BWOOSH
!!

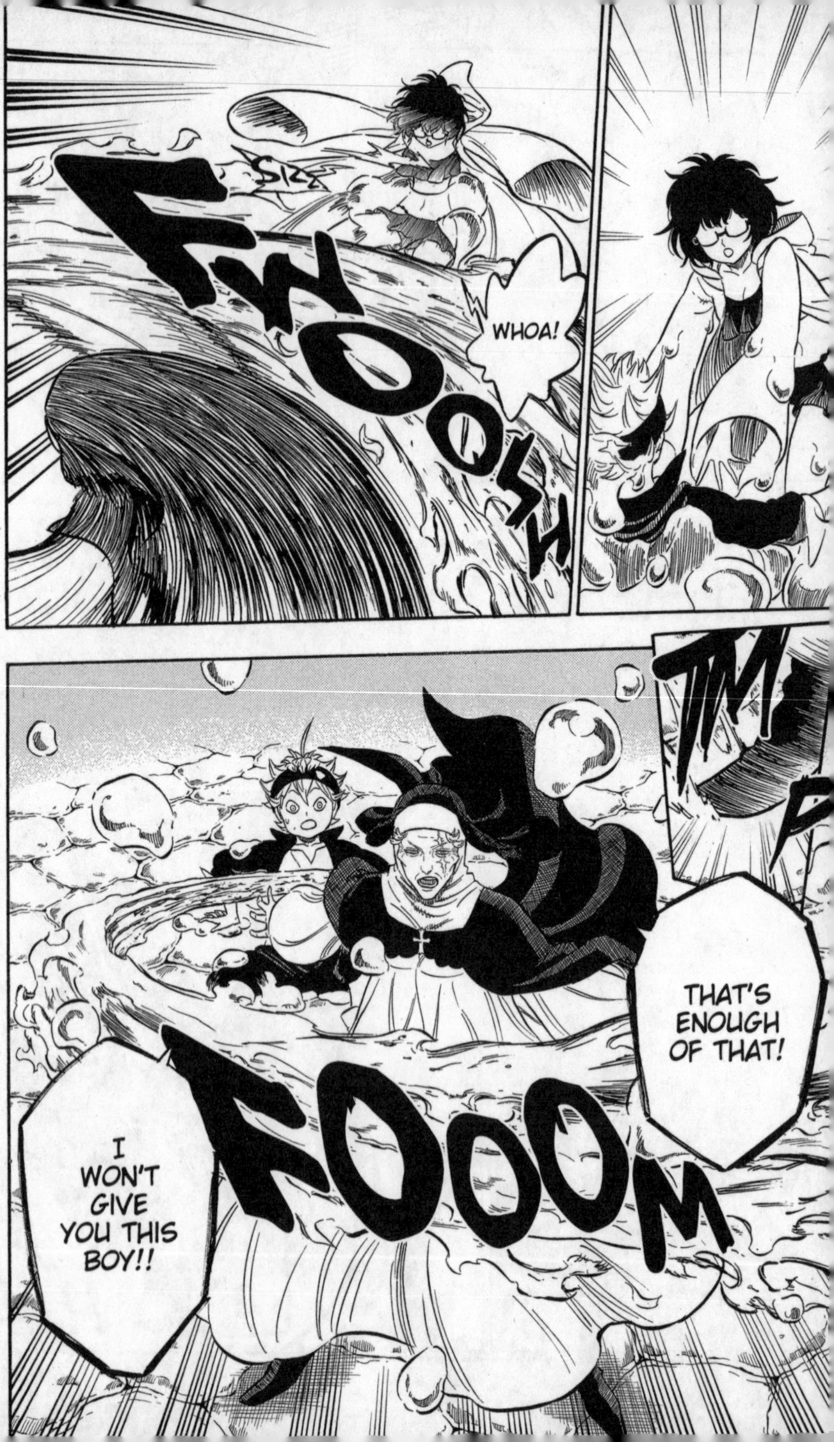
SIZZ
FWOOSH
WHOA!
THAT'S ENOUGH OF THAT!
FOOOM
I WON'T GIVE YOU THIS BOY!!

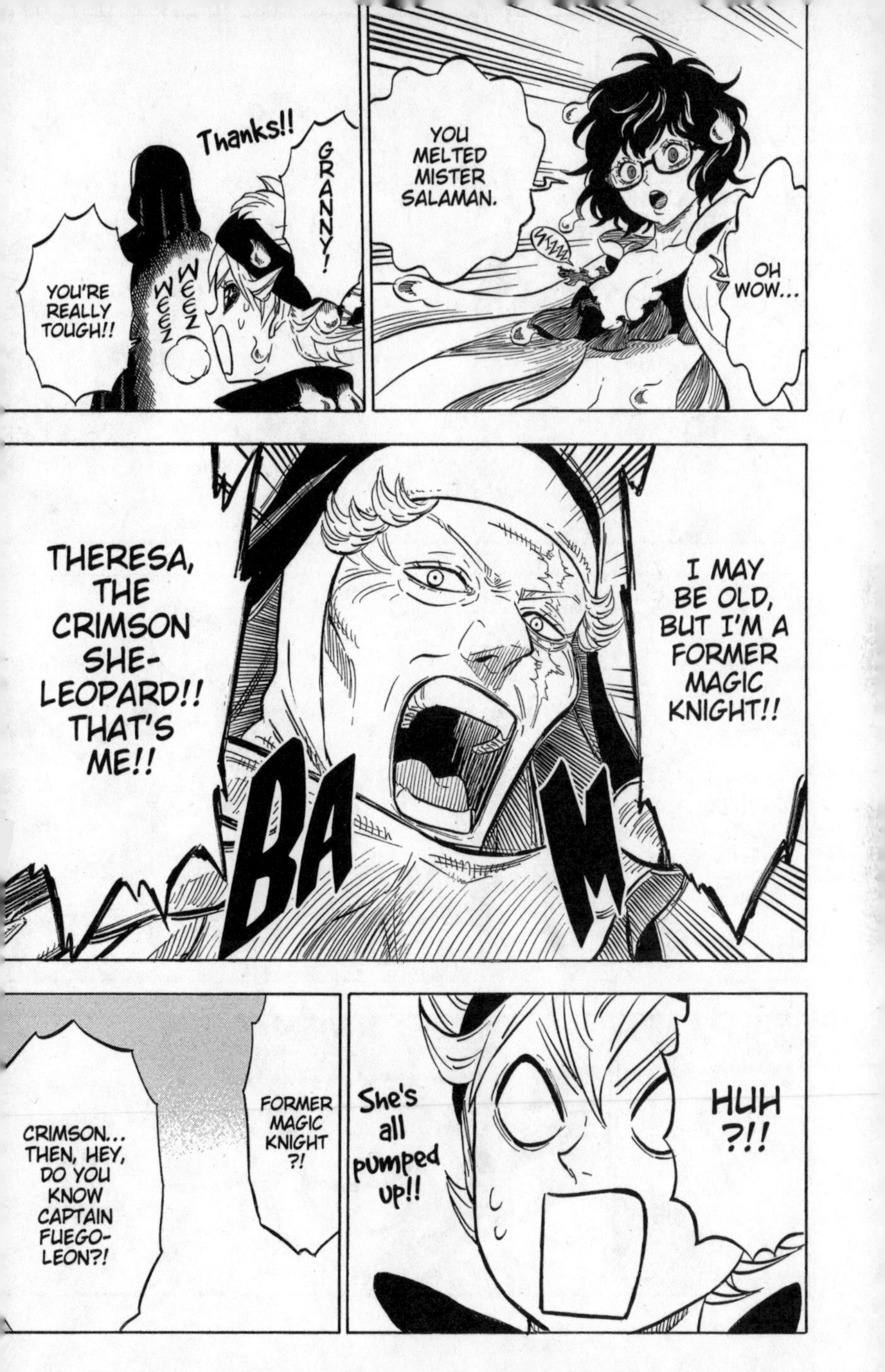
OH WOW...
YOU MELTED MISTER SALAMAN.
GRANNY!
Thanks!!
WEEZ WEEZ
YOU'RE REALLY TOUGH!!
I MAY BE OLD, BUT I'M A FORMER MAGIC KNIGHT!!
THERESA, THE CRIMSON SHE-LEOPARD!! THAT'S ME!!
BAM
HUH ?!!
She's all pumped up!!
FORMER MAGIC KNIGHT ?!
CRIMSON... THEN, HEY, DO YOU KNOW CAPTAIN FUEGO-LEON?!

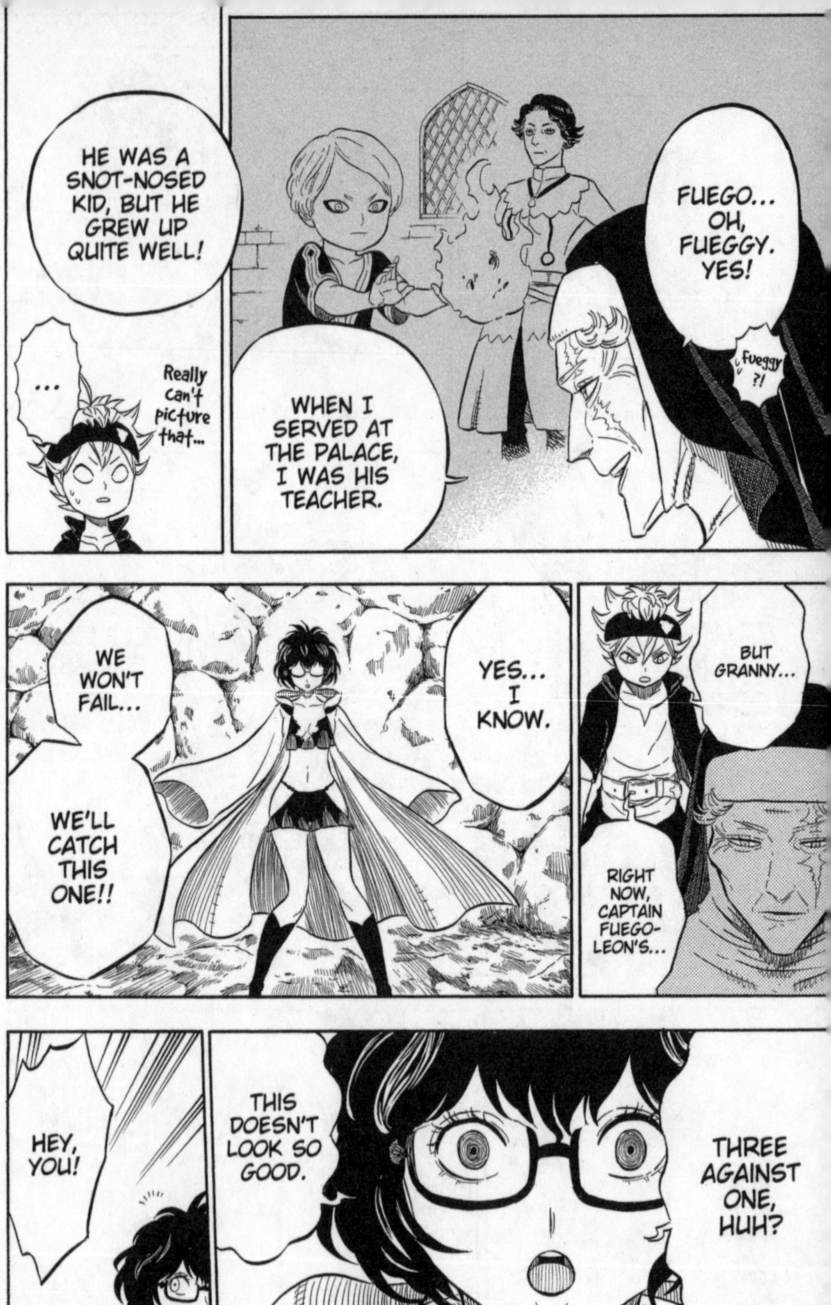
FUEGO... OH, FUEGGY. YES!
Fueggy ?!
WHEN I SERVED AT THE PALACE, I WAS HIS TEACHER.
HE WAS A SNOT-NOSED KID, BUT HE GREW UP QUITE WELL!
...
Really can't picture that...
BUT GRANNY...
RIGHT NOW, CAPTAIN FUEGO-LEON'S...
YES... I KNOW.
WE WON'T FAIL...
WE'LL CATCH THIS ONE!!
THREE AGAINST ONE, HUH?
THIS DOESN'T LOOK SO GOOD.
HEY, YOU!

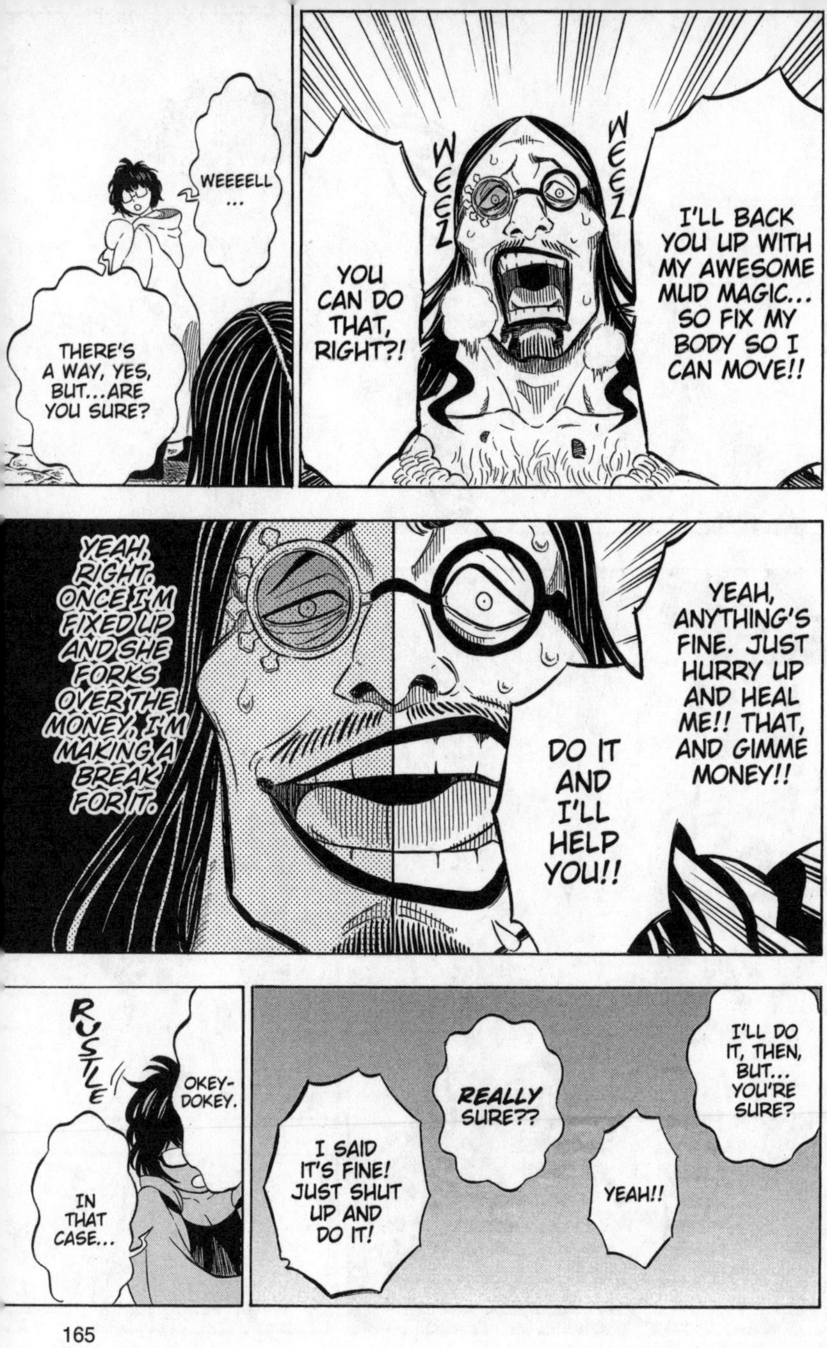
WEEZ
I'LL BACK YOU UP WITH MY AWESOME MUD MAGIC... SO FIX MY BODY SO I CAN MOVE!!
WEEZ
YOU CAN DO THAT, RIGHT?!
WEEEELL ...
THERE'S A WAY, YES, BUT...ARE YOU SURE?
YEAH, ANYTHING'S FINE. JUST HURRY UP AND HEAL ME!! THAT, AND GIMME MONEY!!
DO IT AND I'LL HELP YOU!!
YEAH. RIGHT. ONCE I'M FIXED UP AND SHE FORKS OVER THE MONEY, I'M MAKING A BREAK FOR IT.
I'LL DO IT, THEN, BUT... YOU'RE SURE?
REALLY SURE??
YEAH!!
I SAID IT'S FINE! JUST SHUT UP AND DO IT!
RUSTLE
OKEY-DOKEY.
IN THAT CASE...

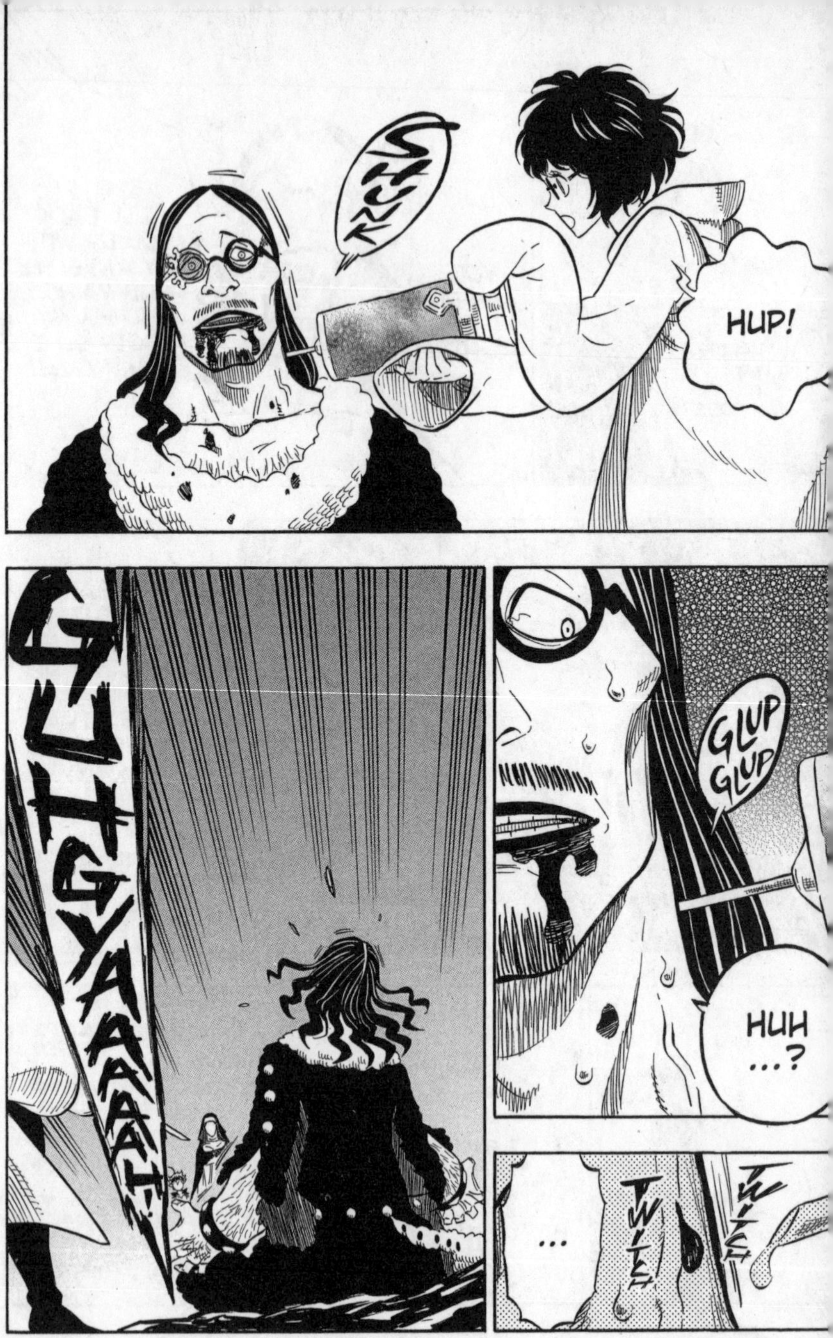
HUP!
SHUNK
GLUP GLUP
HUH ...?
TWITCH
TWITCH
...
GUGYAAAAAH!

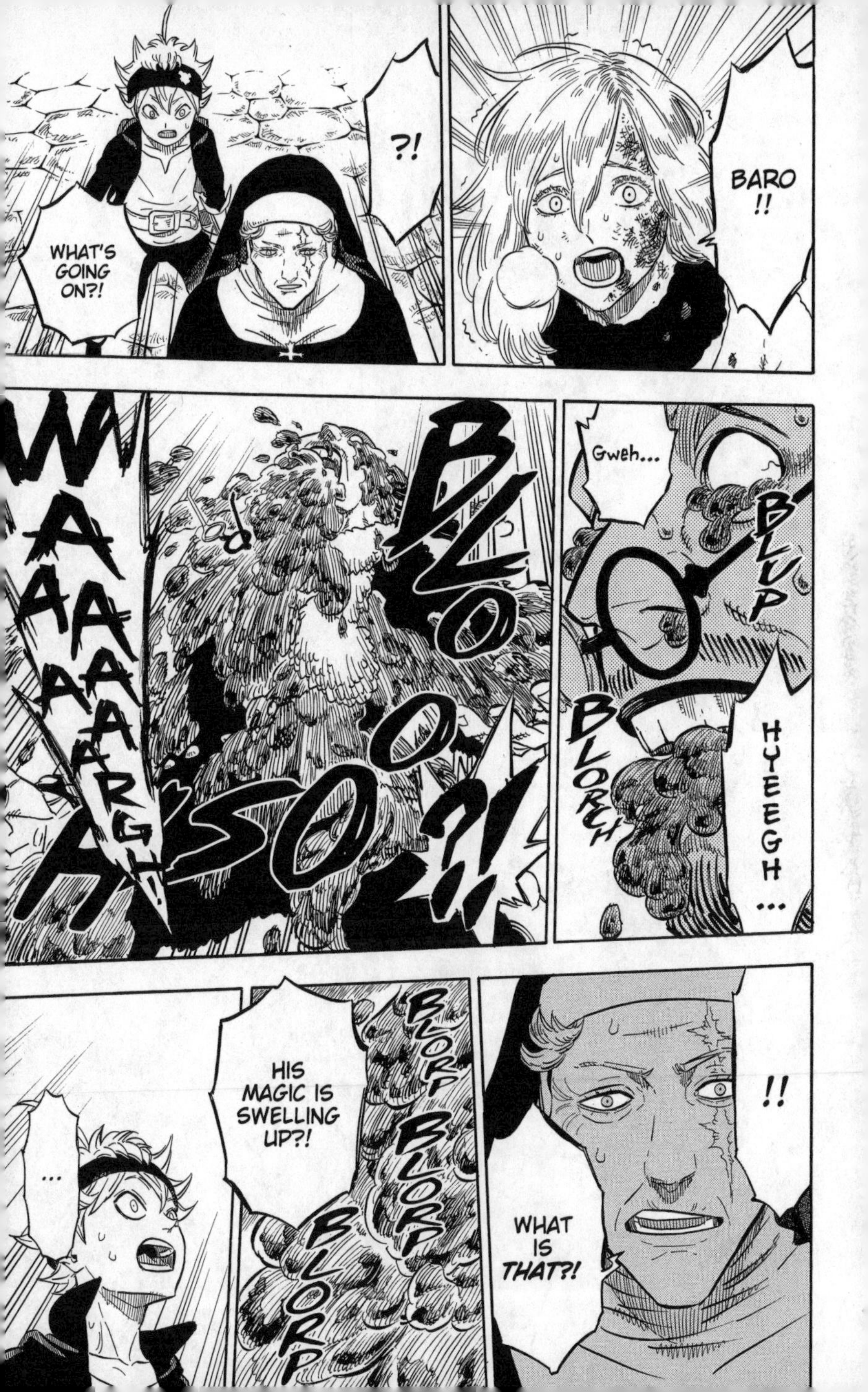
BARO !!
?!
WHAT'S GOING ON?!
Gweh...
BLUP
BLORCH
HYEEGH...
BLOOOSO?!!
WAAAAARGH!
!!
WHAT IS THAT?!
HIS MAGIC IS SWELLING UP?!
BLORP
BLORP
BLORP
...

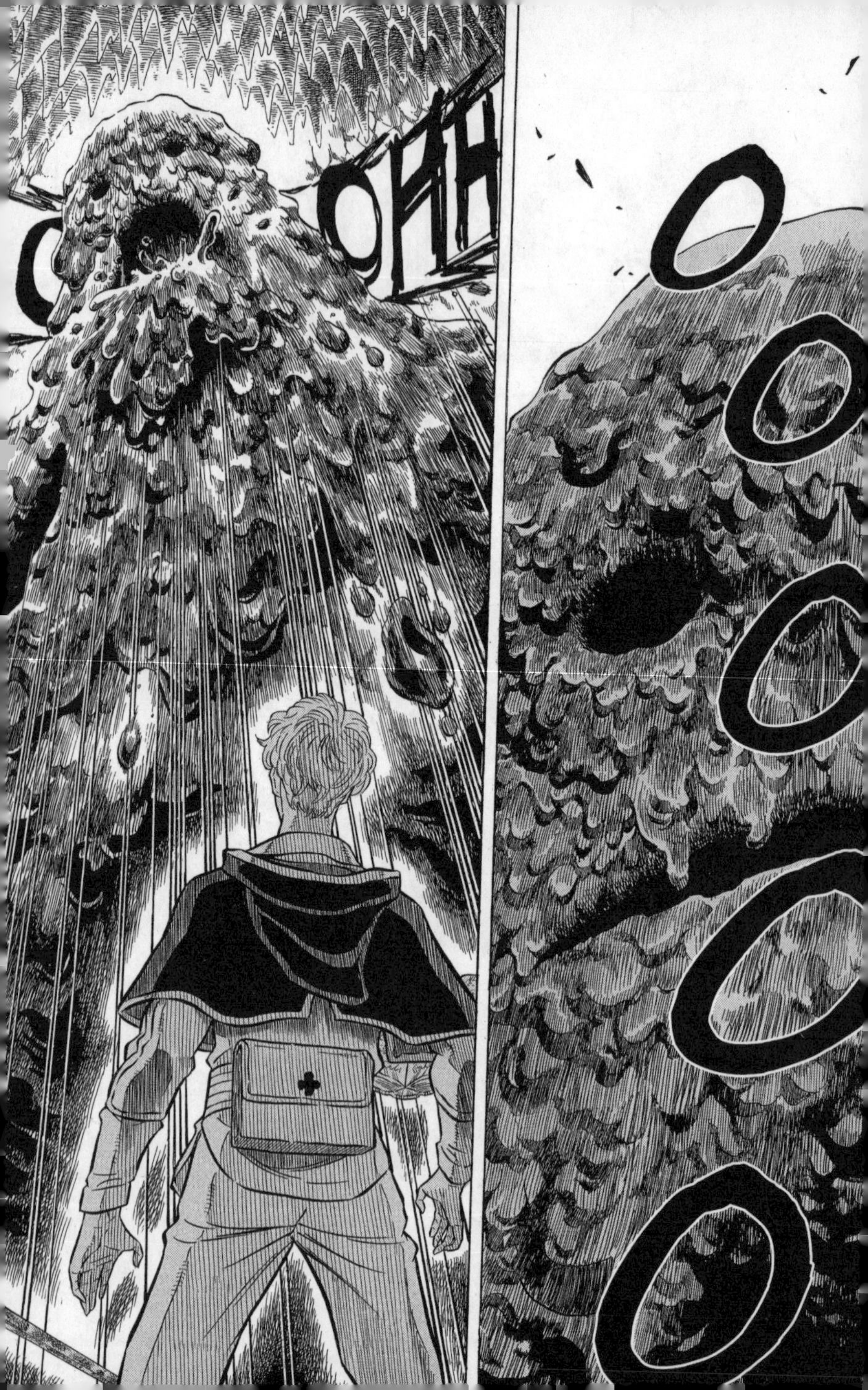
OOOOOO
COHH

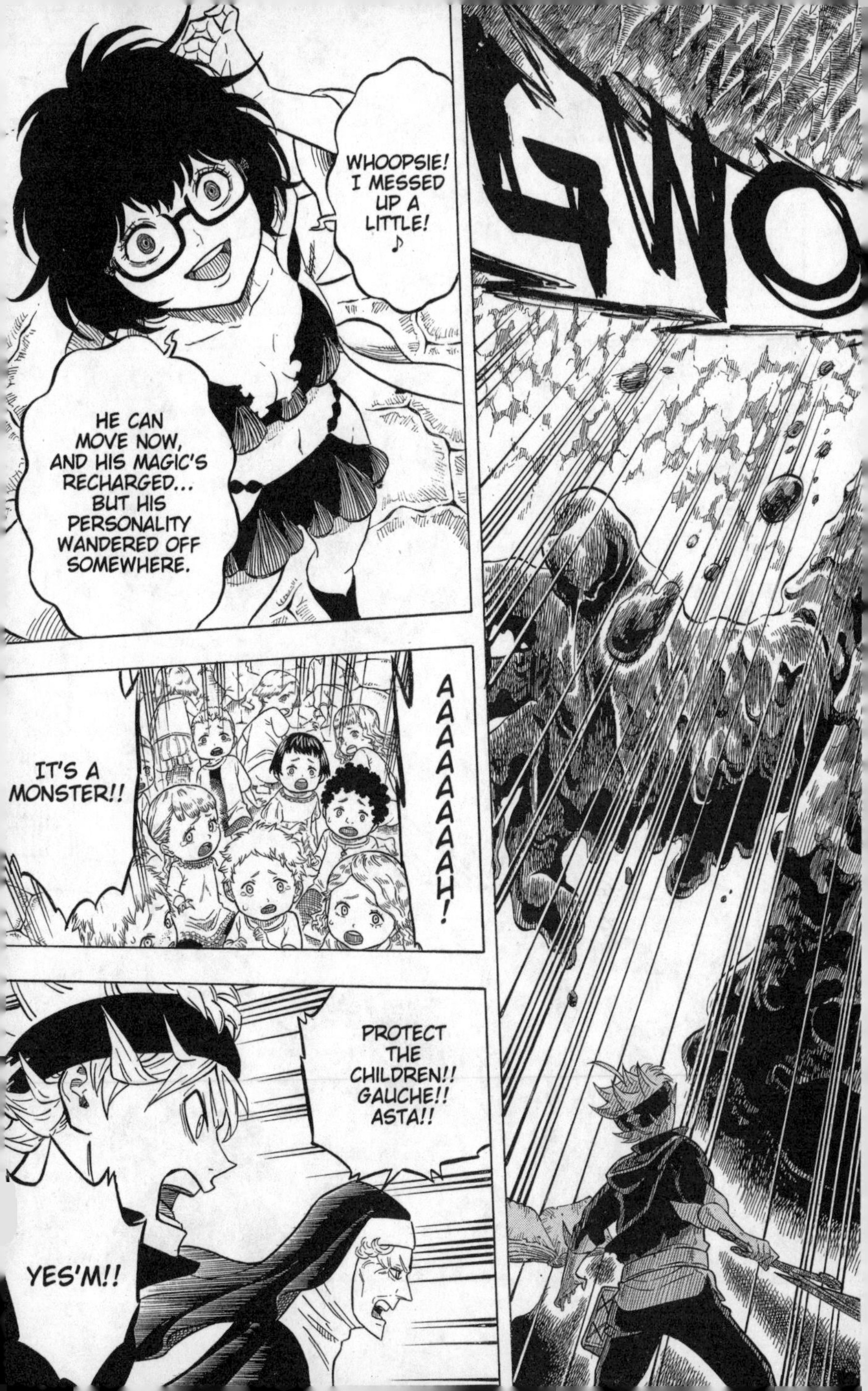
GWO
WHOOPSIE! I MESSED UP A LITTLE! ♪
HE CAN MOVE NOW, AND HIS MAGIC'S RECHARGED... BUT HIS PERSONALITY WANDERED OFF SOMEWHERE.
AAAAAAAAH!
IT'S A MONSTER!!
PROTECT THE CHILDREN!! GAUCHE!! ASTA!!
YES'M!!

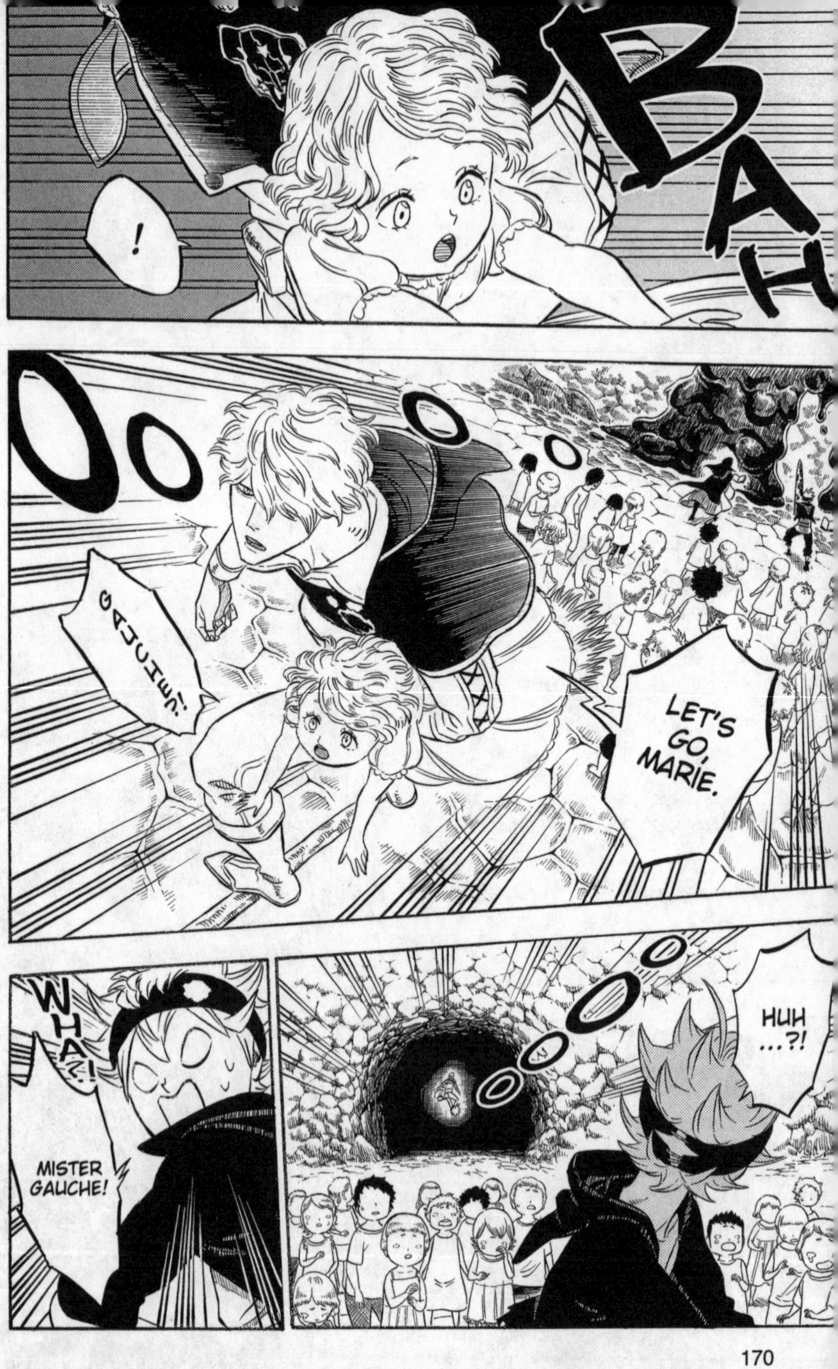
BAH
!
LET'S GO, MARIE.
GAUCHE?!
HUH ...?!
WHA?!
MISTER GAUCHE!

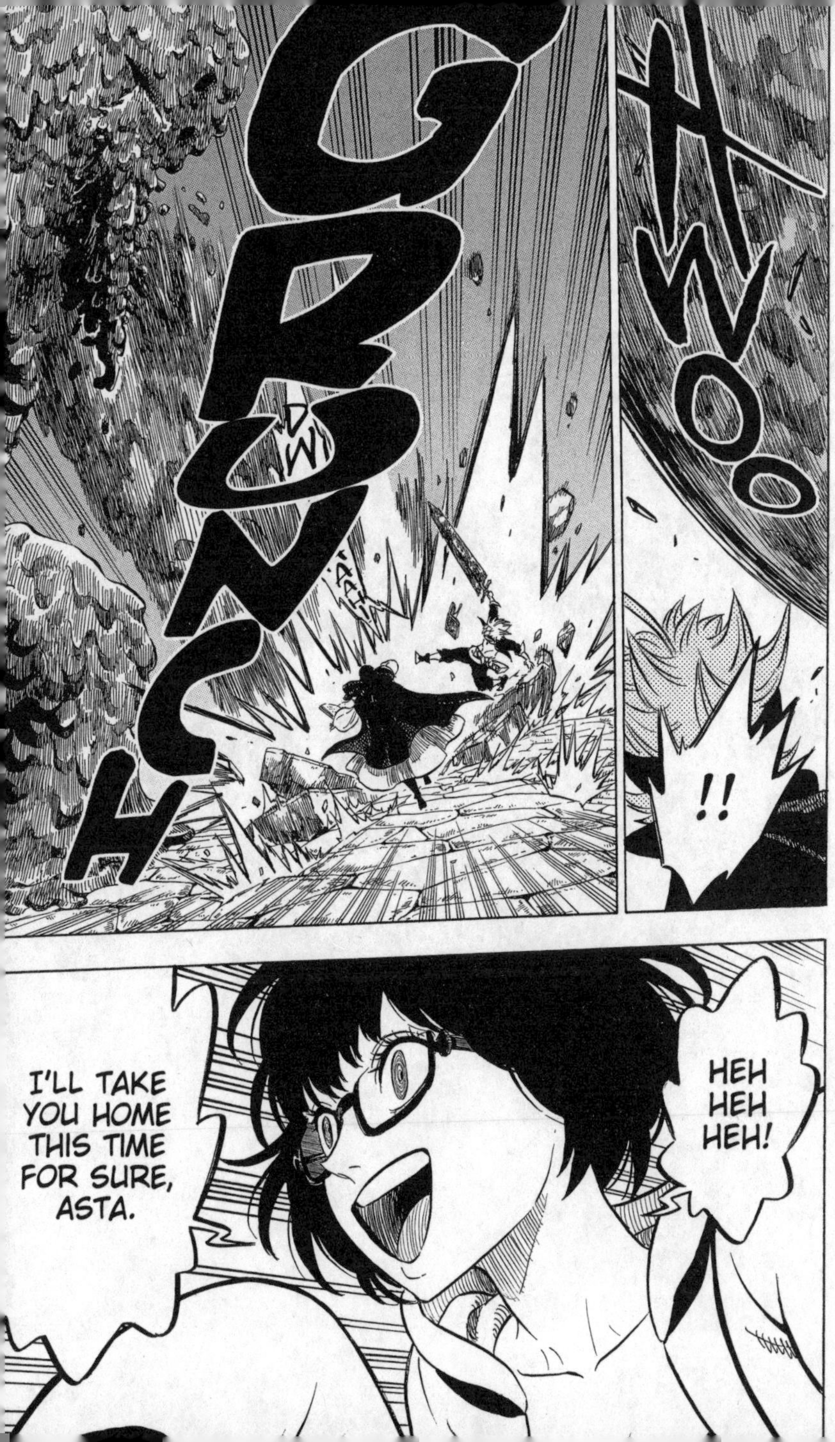
!!
HEH HEH HEH!
I'LL TAKE YOU HOME THIS TIME FOR SURE, ASTA.

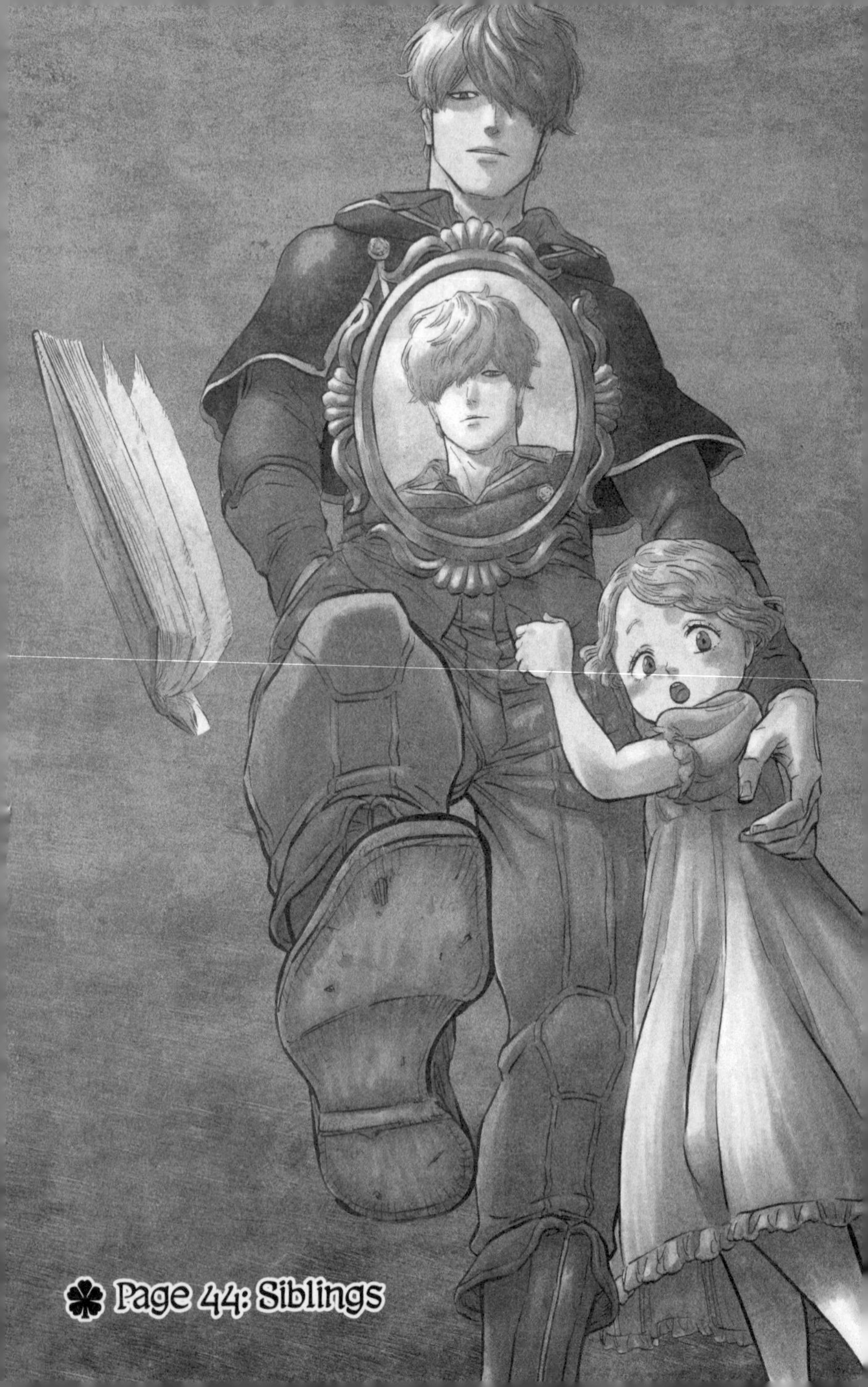

Page 44: Siblings

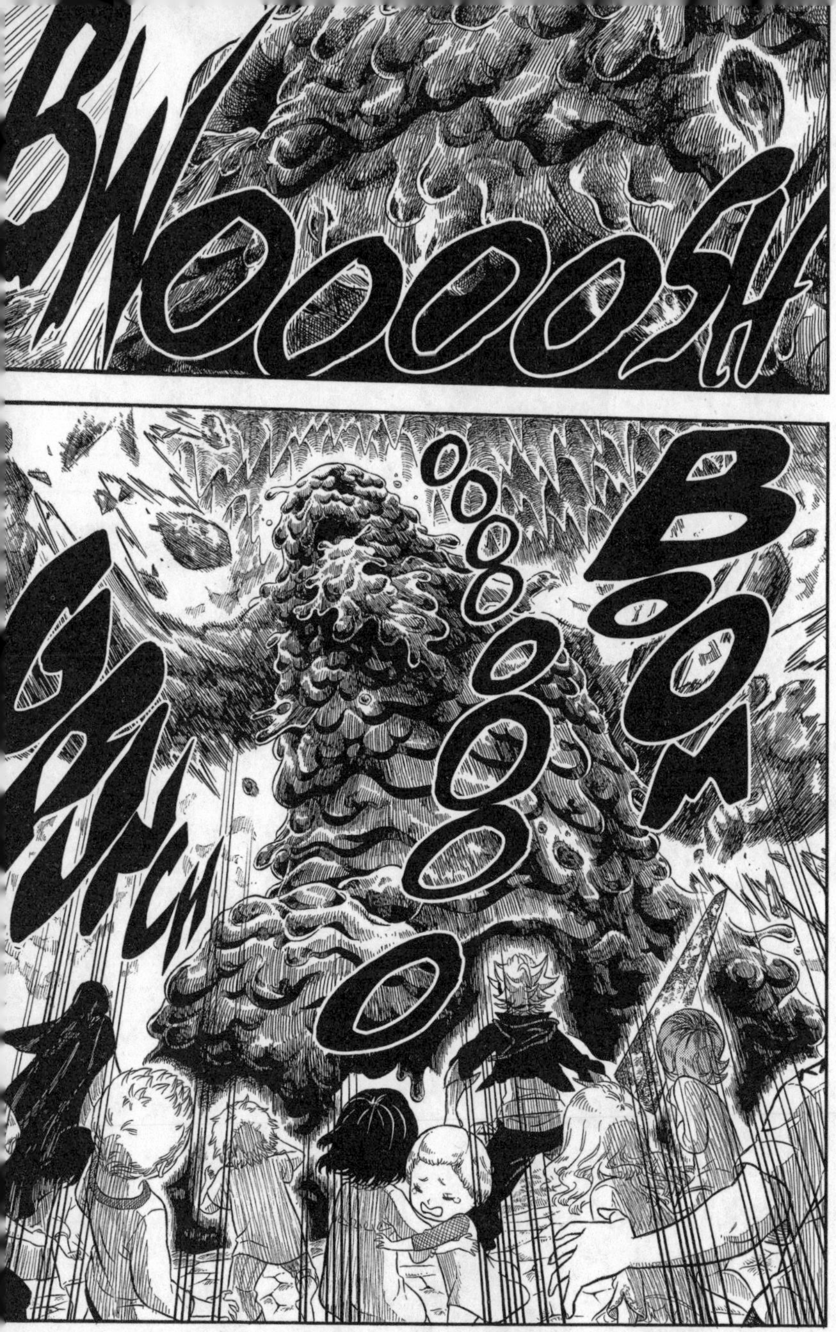
BWOOOOOSH

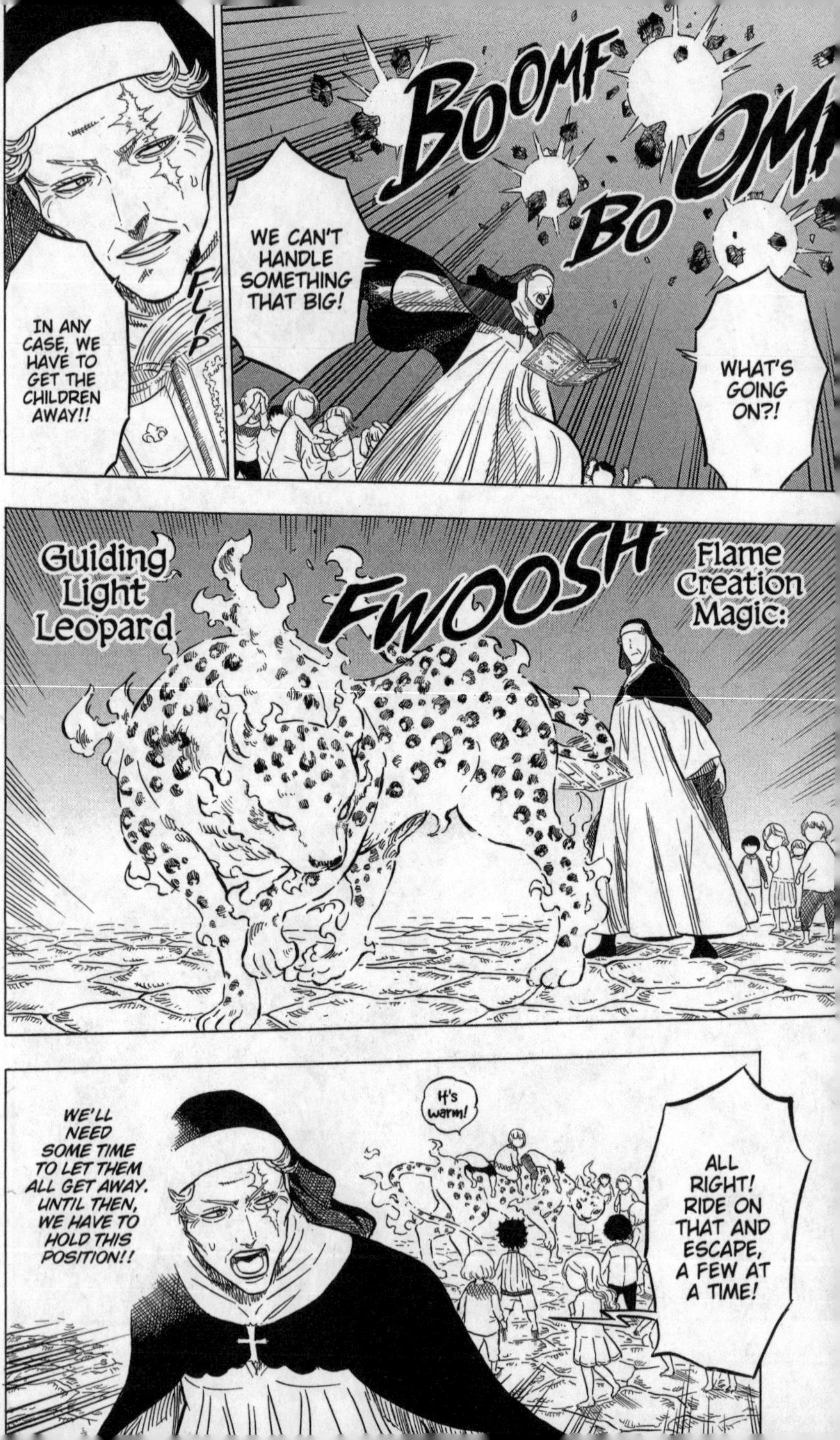
BOOMF
BOOM
WHAT'S GOING ON?!
WE CAN'T HANDLE SOMETHING THAT BIG!
FLIP
IN ANY CASE, WE HAVE TO GET THE CHILDREN AWAY!!
Flame Creation Magic:
FWOOSH
Guiding Light Leopard
ALL RIGHT! RIDE ON THAT AND ESCAPE, A FEW AT A TIME!
It's warm!
WE'LL NEED SOME TIME TO LET THEM ALL GET AWAY. UNTIL THEN, WE HAVE TO HOLD THIS POSITION!!

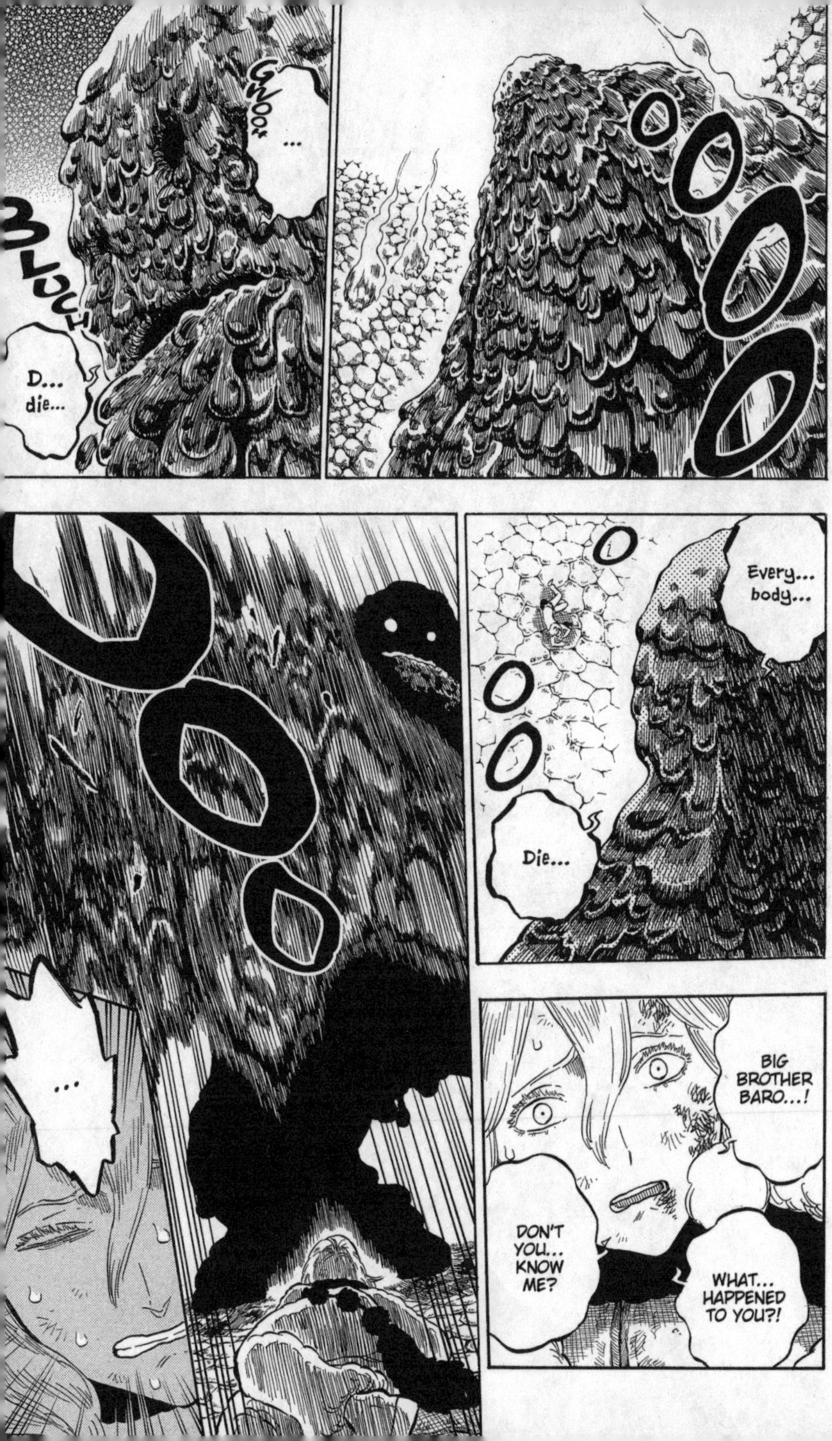
OOOO
GWOO
...
BLUCH
D... die...
Every... body...
OOO
Die...
BIG BROTHER BARO...!
WHAT... HAPPENED TO YOU?!
DON'T YOU... KNOW ME?
OOOO
...

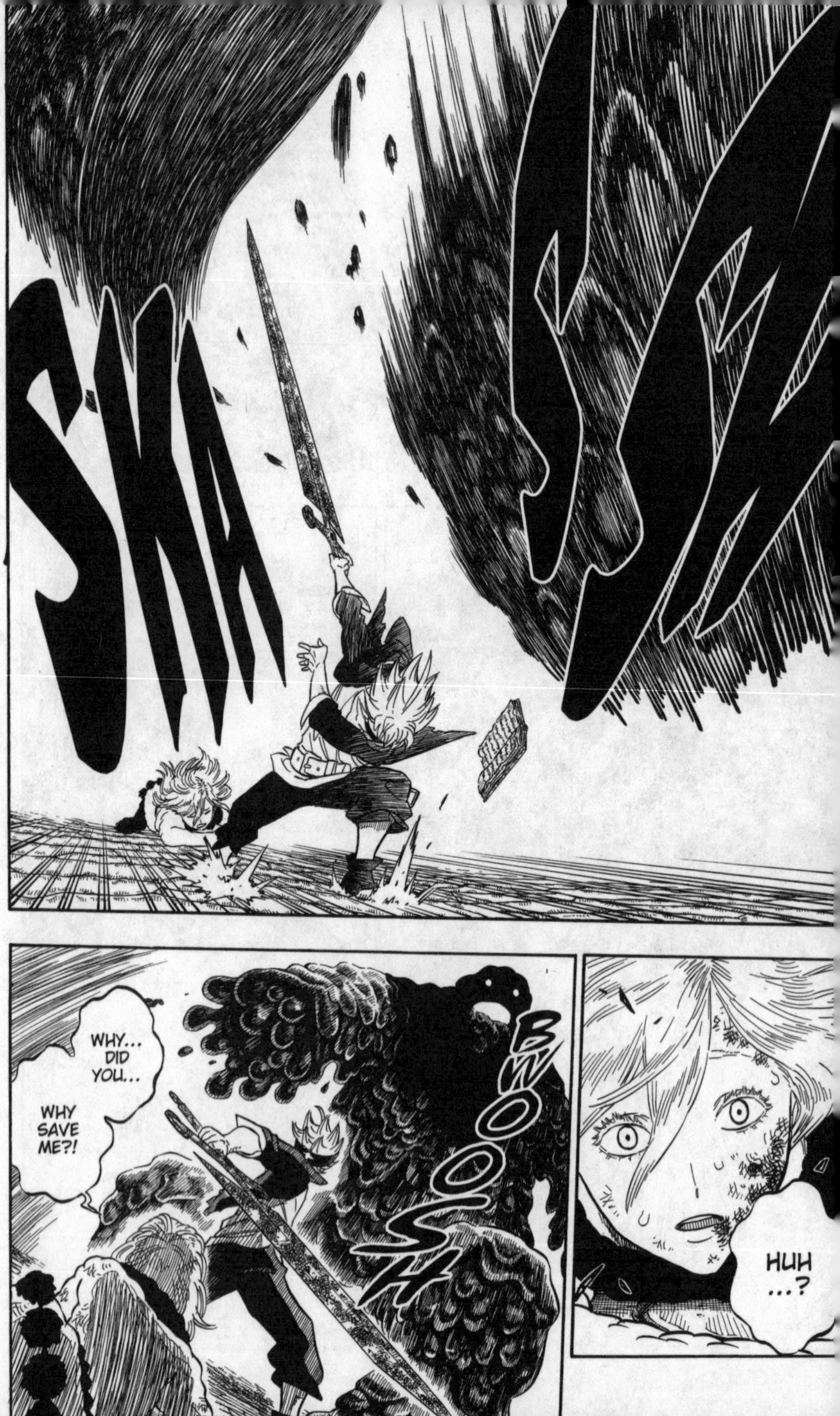
SHA
HUH ...?
WHY... DID YOU...
WHY SAVE ME?!
BWOOOOSH

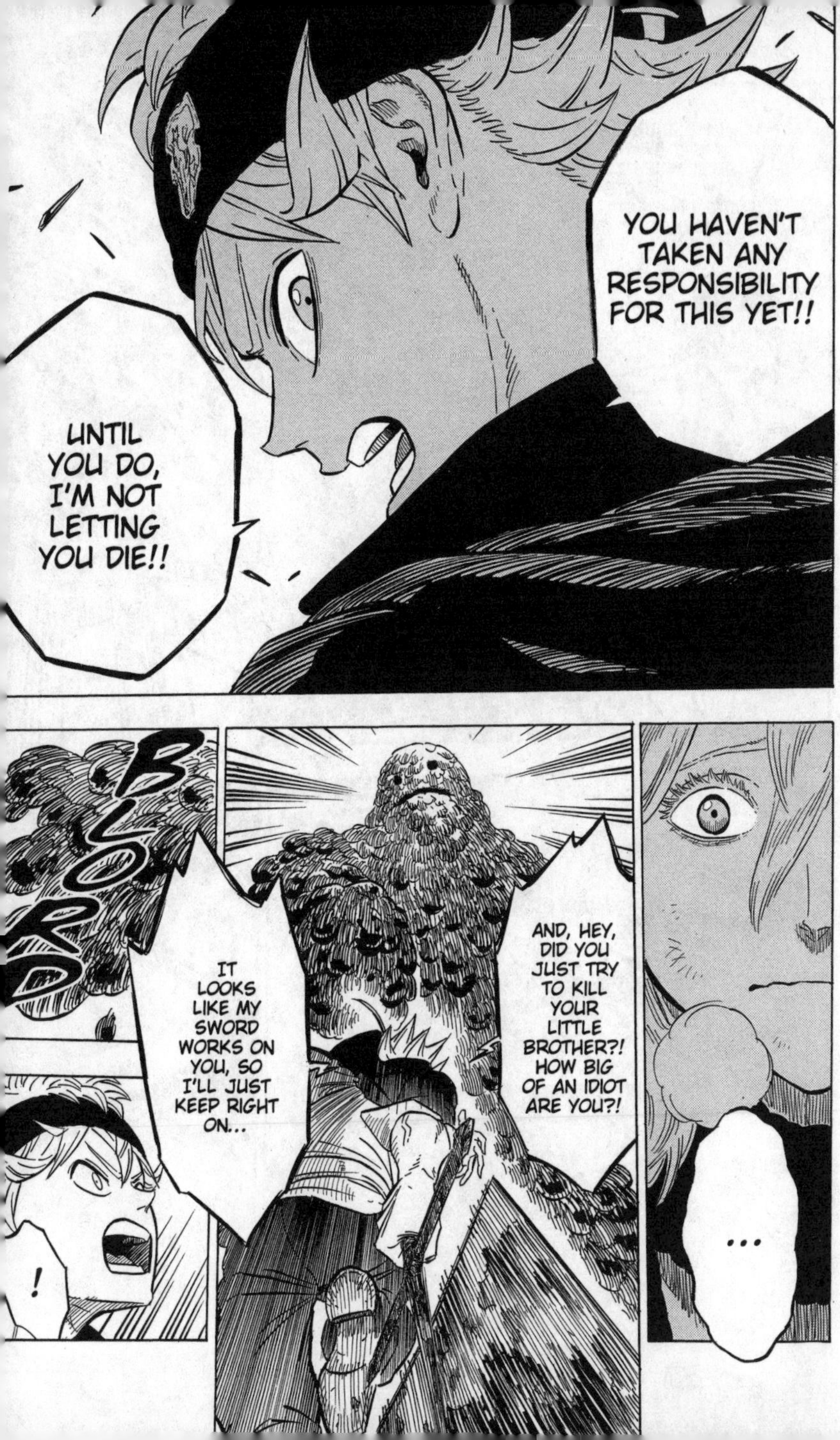
YOU HAVEN'T TAKEN ANY RESPONSIBILITY FOR THIS YET!!
UNTIL YOU DO, I'M NOT LETTING YOU DIE!!
...
AND, HEY, DID YOU JUST TRY TO KILL YOUR LITTLE BROTHER?! HOW BIG OF AN IDIOT ARE YOU?!
IT LOOKS LIKE MY SWORD WORKS ON YOU, SO I'LL JUST KEEP RIGHT ON...
BLORRD
!

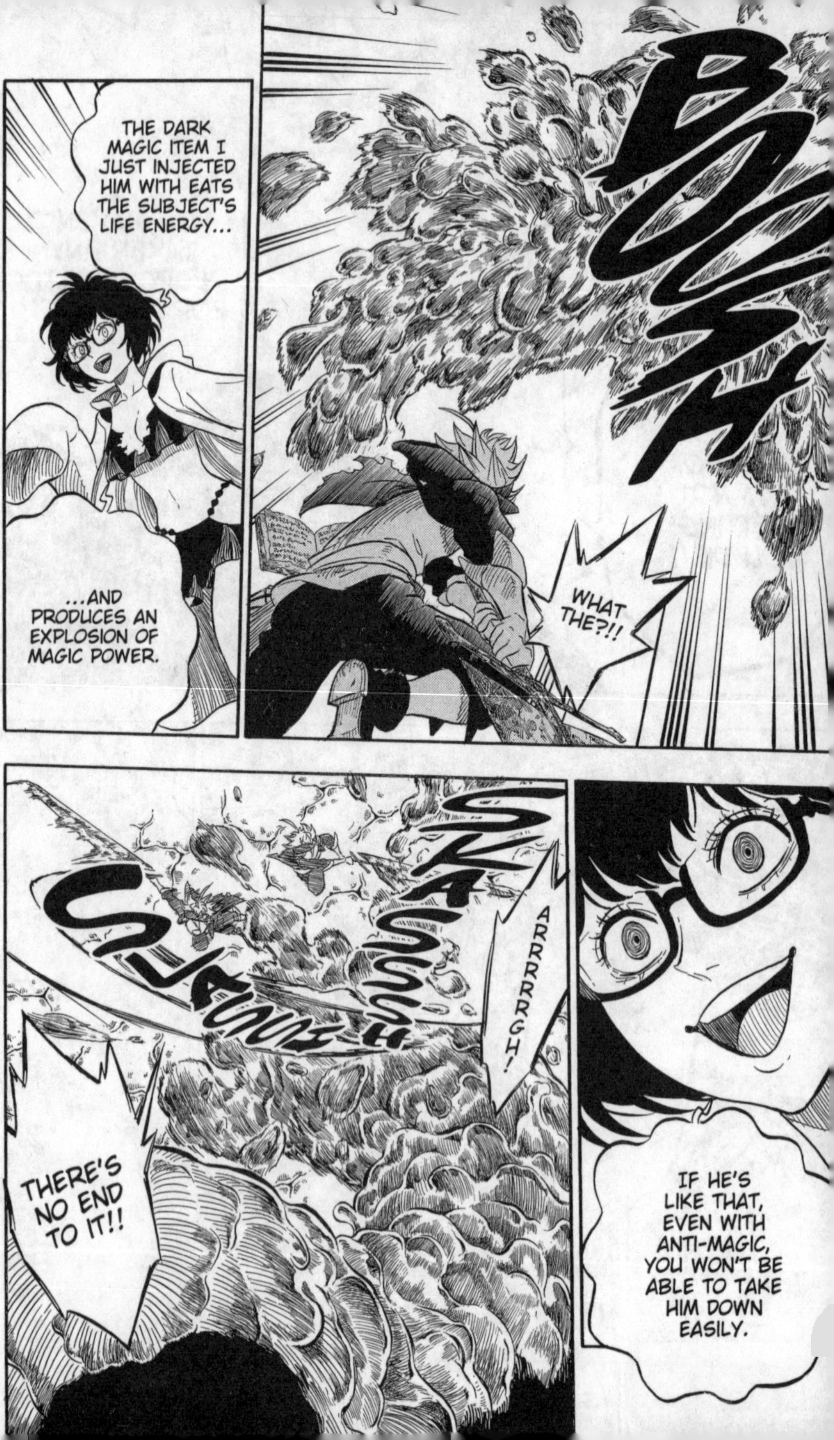
WHAT THE?!!
THE DARK MAGIC ITEM I JUST INJECTED HIM WITH EATS THE SUBJECT'S LIFE ENERGY...
...AND PRODUCES AN EXPLOSION OF MAGIC POWER.
IF HE'S LIKE THAT, EVEN WITH ANTI-MAGIC, YOU WON'T BE ABLE TO TAKE HIM DOWN EASILY.
ARRRRRGH!
THERE'S NO END TO IT!!

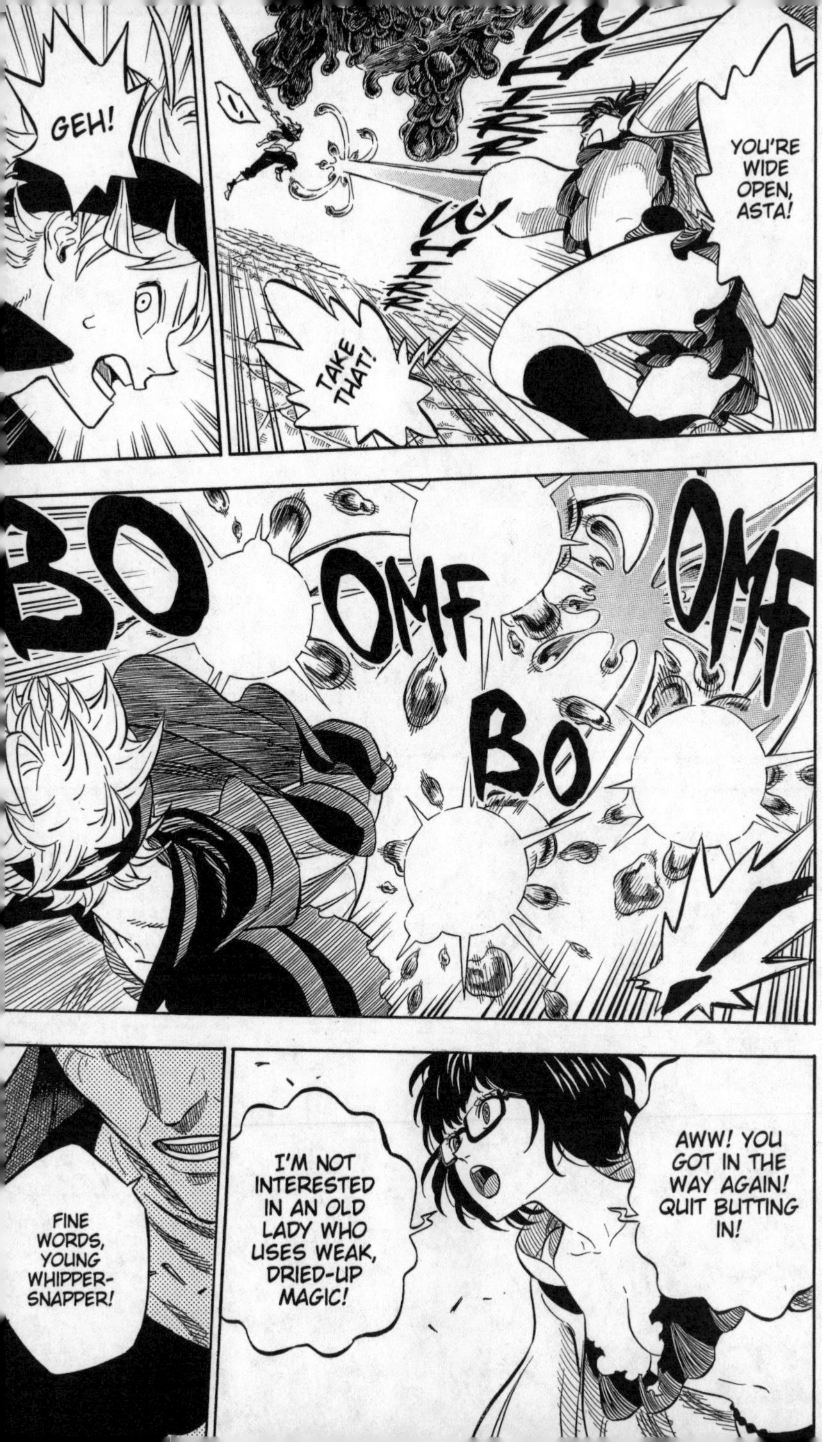
YOU'RE WIDE OPEN, ASTA!
WHIRR
WHIRR
!
TAKE THAT!
GEH!
OMF
BO
OMF
BO
AWW! YOU GOT IN THE WAY AGAIN! QUIT BUTTING IN!
I'M NOT INTERESTED IN AN OLD LADY WHO USES WEAK, DRIED-UP MAGIC!
FINE WORDS, YOUNG WHIPPER-SNAPPER!

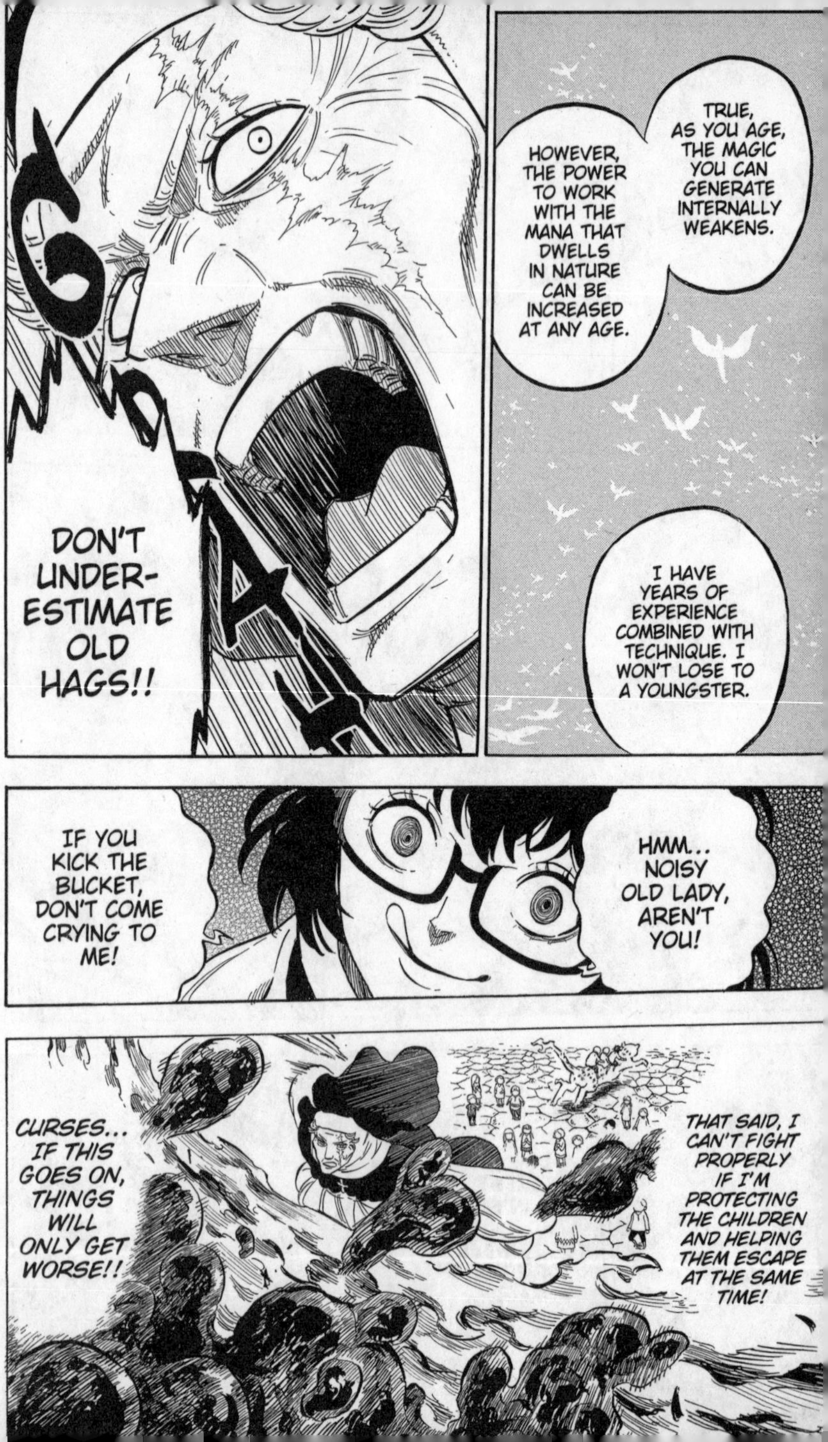
TRUE, AS YOU AGE, THE MAGIC YOU CAN GENERATE INTERNALLY WEAKENS.
HOWEVER, THE POWER TO WORK WITH THE MANA THAT DWELLS IN NATURE CAN BE INCREASED AT ANY AGE.
I HAVE YEARS OF EXPERIENCE COMBINED WITH TECHNIQUE. I WON'T LOSE TO A YOUNGSTER.
DON'T UNDER-ESTIMATE OLD HAGS!!
HMM... NOISY OLD LADY, AREN'T YOU!
IF YOU KICK THE BUCKET, DON'T COME CRYING TO ME!
THAT SAID, I CAN'T FIGHT PROPERLY IF I'M PROTECTING THE CHILDREN AND HELPING THEM ESCAPE AT THE SAME TIME!
CURSES... IF THIS GOES ON, THINGS WILL ONLY GET WORSE!!

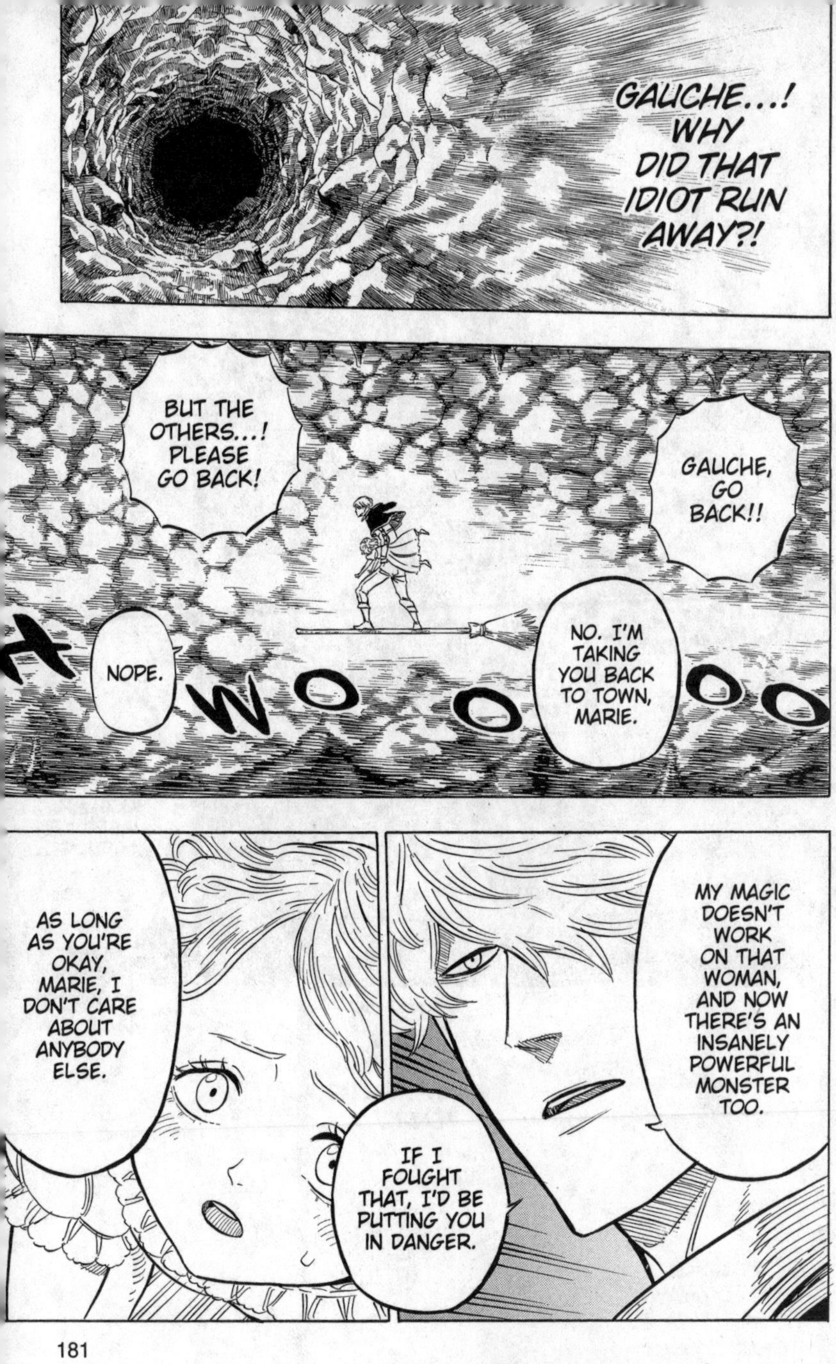
GAUCHE...! WHY DID THAT IDIOT RUN AWAY?!
GAUCHE, GO BACK!!
NO. I'M TAKING YOU BACK TO TOWN, MARIE.
BUT THE OTHERS...! PLEASE GO BACK!
NOPE.
HWOOOOO
MY MAGIC DOESN'T WORK ON THAT WOMAN, AND NOW THERE'S AN INSANELY POWERFUL MONSTER TOO.
IF I FOUGHT THAT, I'D BE PUTTING YOU IN DANGER.
AS LONG AS YOU'RE OKAY, MARIE, I DON'T CARE ABOUT ANYBODY ELSE.

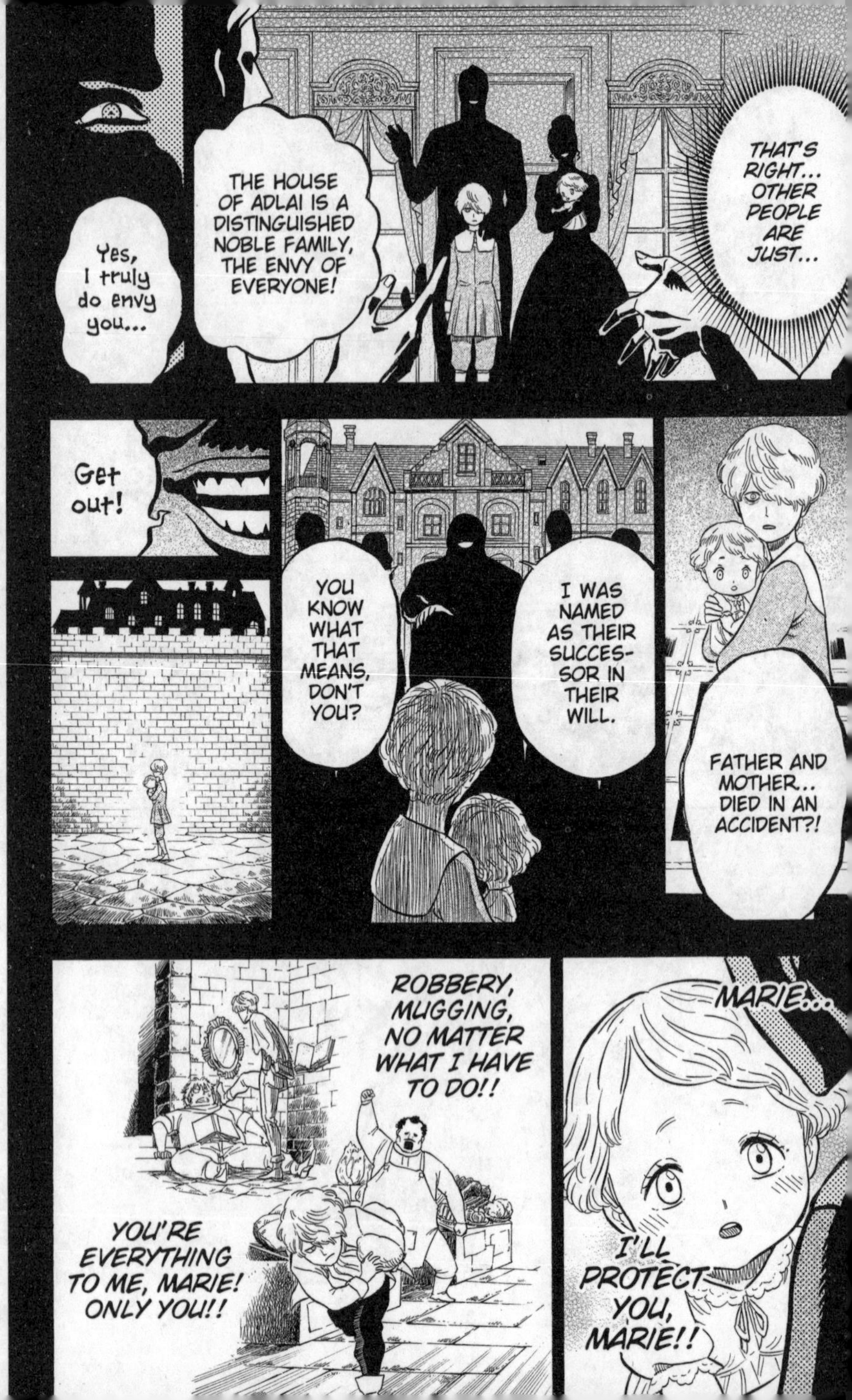
THAT'S RIGHT... OTHER PEOPLE ARE JUST...
THE HOUSE OF ADLAI IS A DISTINGUISHED NOBLE FAMILY, THE ENVY OF EVERYONE!
Yes, I truly do envy you...
FATHER AND MOTHER... DIED IN AN ACCIDENT?!
I WAS NAMED AS THEIR SUCCES-SOR IN THEIR WILL.
YOU KNOW WHAT THAT MEANS, DON'T YOU?
Get out!
MARIE...
I'LL PROTECT YOU, MARIE!!
ROBBERY, MUGGING, NO MATTER WHAT I HAVE TO DO!!
YOU'RE EVERYTHING TO ME, MARIE! ONLY YOU!!

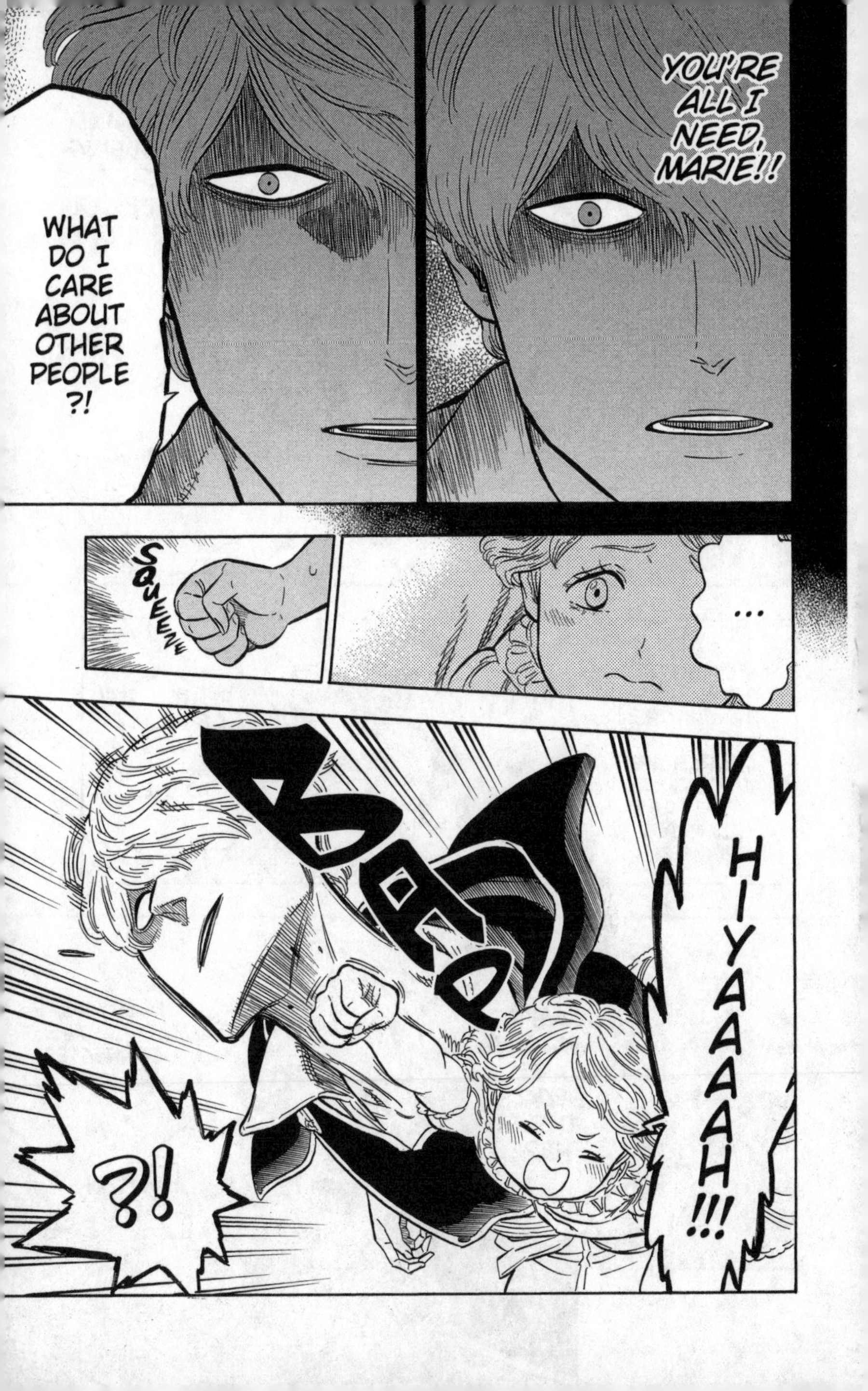
YOU'RE ALL I NEED, MARIE!!
WHAT DO I CARE ABOUT OTHER PEOPLE ?!
...
SQUEEZE
HIYAAAAAH!!!
BAM
?!

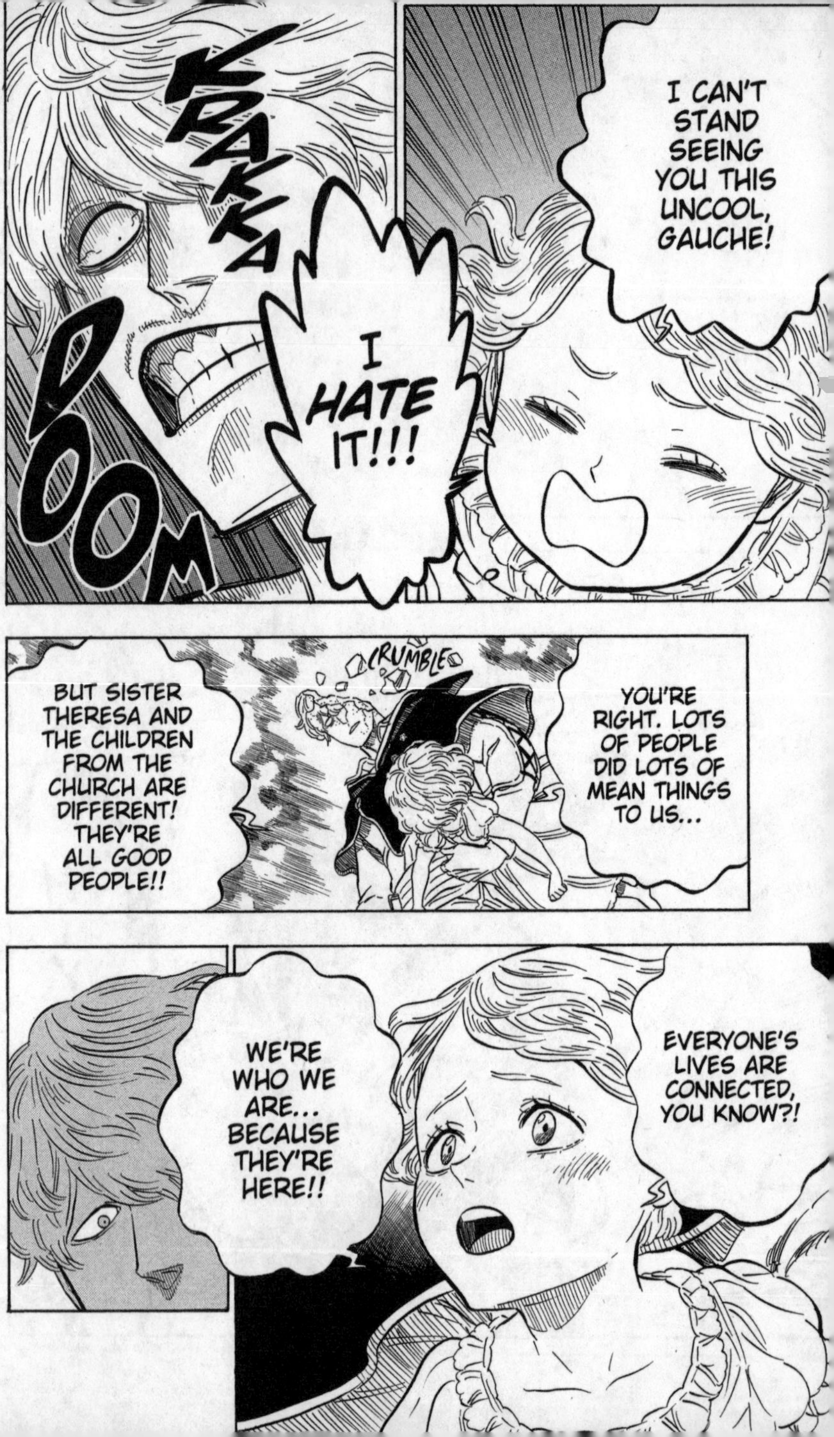
I CAN'T STAND SEEING YOU THIS UNCOOL, GAUCHE!
I HATE IT!!!
KRAKKA
DOOM
YOU'RE RIGHT. LOTS OF PEOPLE DID LOTS OF MEAN THINGS TO US...
CRUMBLE
BUT SISTER THERESA AND THE CHILDREN FROM THE CHURCH ARE DIFFERENT! THEY'RE ALL GOOD PEOPLE!!
EVERYONE'S LIVES ARE CONNECTED, YOU KNOW?!
WE'RE WHO WE ARE... BECAUSE THEY'RE HERE!!

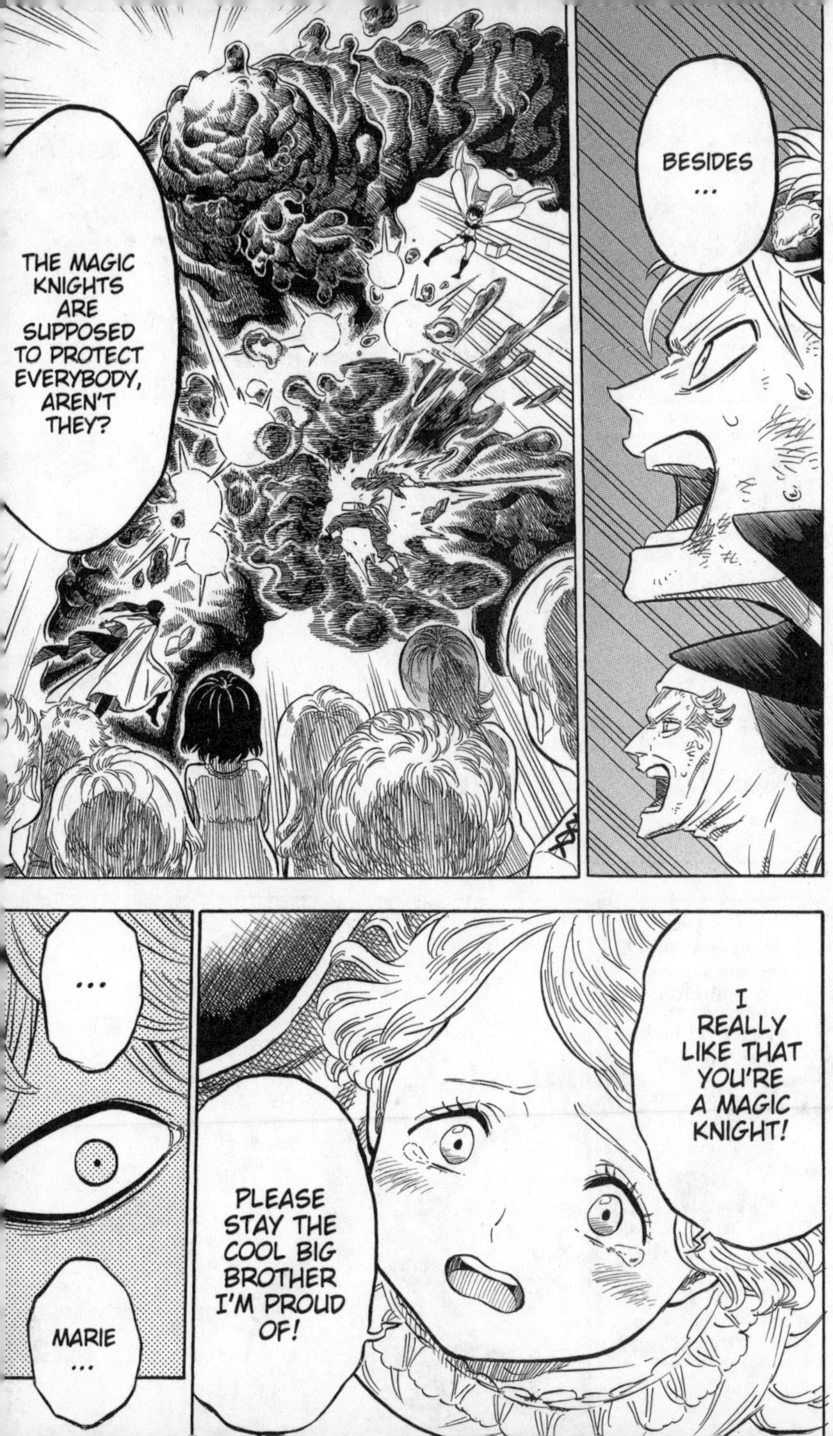
BESIDES...
THE MAGIC KNIGHTS ARE SUPPOSED TO PROTECT EVERYBODY, AREN'T THEY?
I REALLY LIKE THAT YOU'RE A MAGIC KNIGHT!
PLEASE STAY THE COOL BIG BROTHER I'M PROUD OF!
...
MARIE...

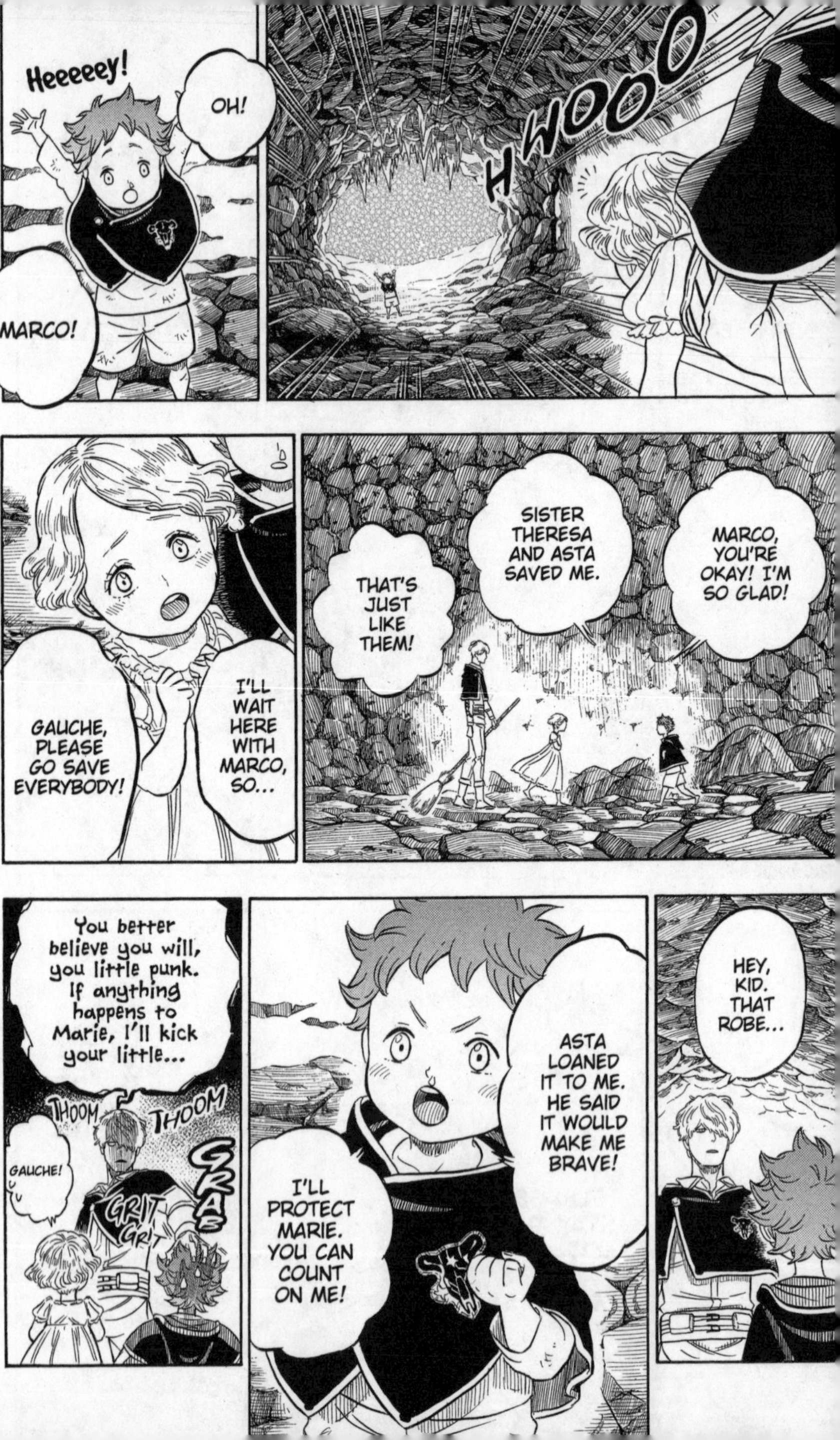
HWOOO
OH!
Heeeeey!
MARCO!
MARCO, YOU'RE OKAY! I'M SO GLAD!
SISTER THERESA AND ASTA SAVED ME.
THAT'S JUST LIKE THEM!
I'LL WAIT HERE WITH MARCO, SO...
GAUCHE, PLEASE GO SAVE EVERYBODY!
HEY, KID. THAT ROBE...
ASTA LOANED IT TO ME. HE SAID IT WOULD MAKE ME BRAVE!
I'LL PROTECT MARIE. YOU CAN COUNT ON ME!
You better believe you will, you little punk. If anything happens to Marie, I'll kick your little...
THOOM THOOM
GRAB
GAUCHE!
GRIT GRIT

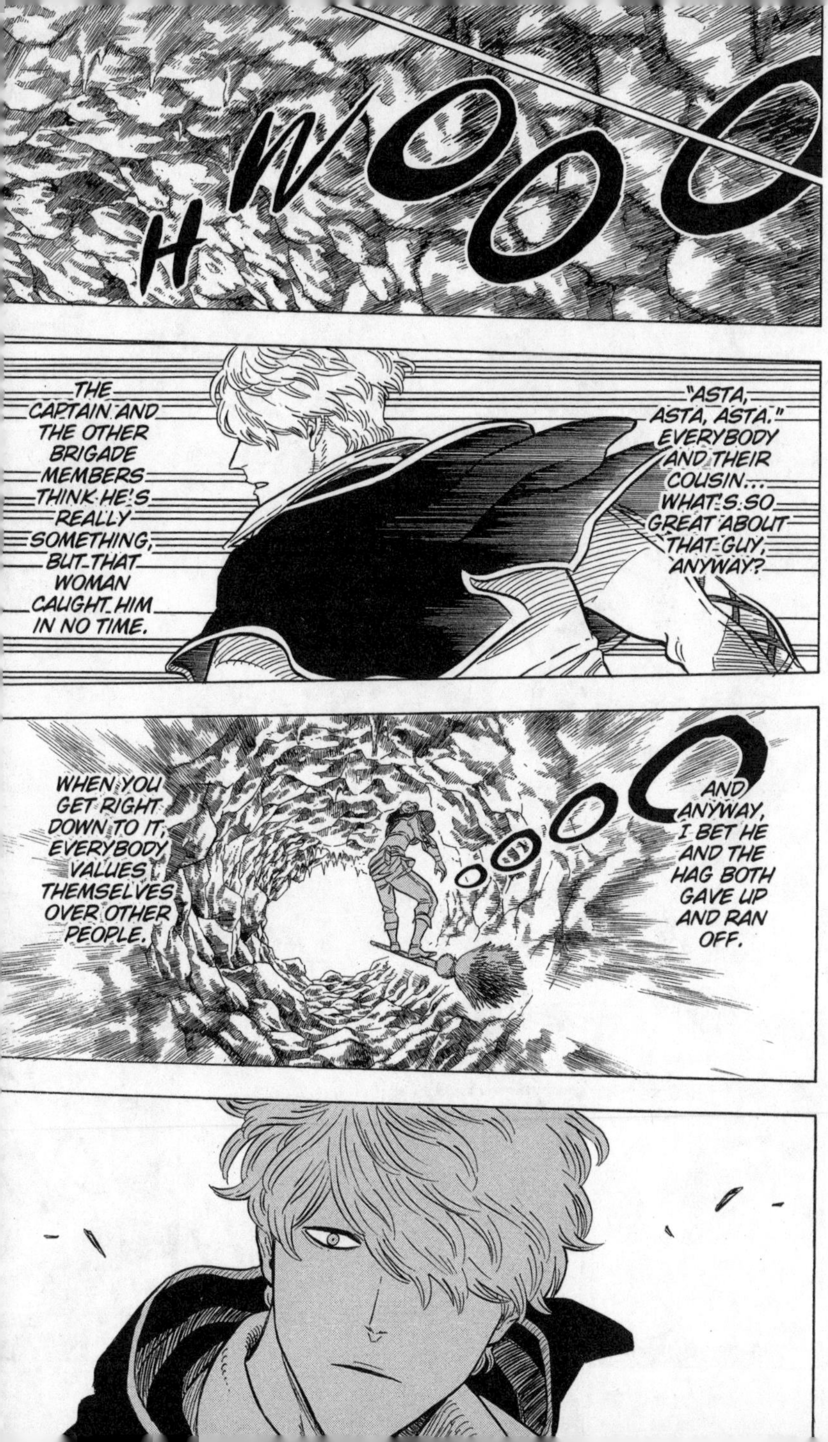
HWOOO
"ASTA, ASTA, ASTA." EVERYBODY AND THEIR COUSIN... WHAT'S SO GREAT ABOUT THAT GUY, ANYWAY?
THE CAPTAIN AND THE OTHER BRIGADE MEMBERS THINK HE'S REALLY SOMETHING, BUT THAT WOMAN CAUGHT HIM IN NO TIME.
AND ANYWAY, I BET HE AND THE HAG BOTH GAVE UP AND RAN OFF.
WHEN YOU GET RIGHT DOWN TO IT, EVERYBODY VALUES THEMSELVES OVER OTHER PEOPLE.

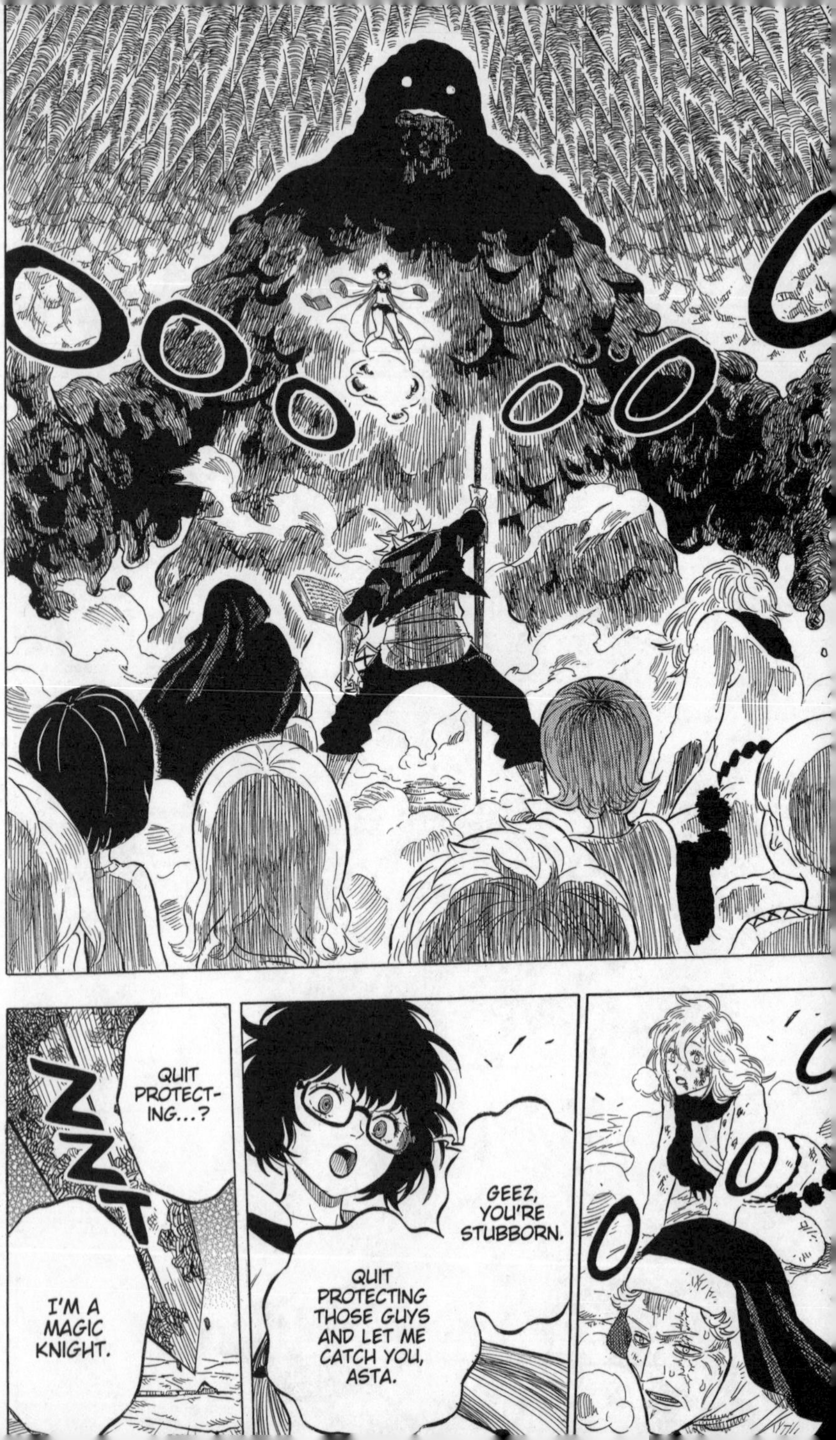
GEEZ, YOU'RE STUBBORN.
QUIT PROTECTING THOSE GUYS AND LET ME CATCH YOU, ASTA.
QUIT PROTECTING...?
ZZT
I'M A MAGIC KNIGHT.

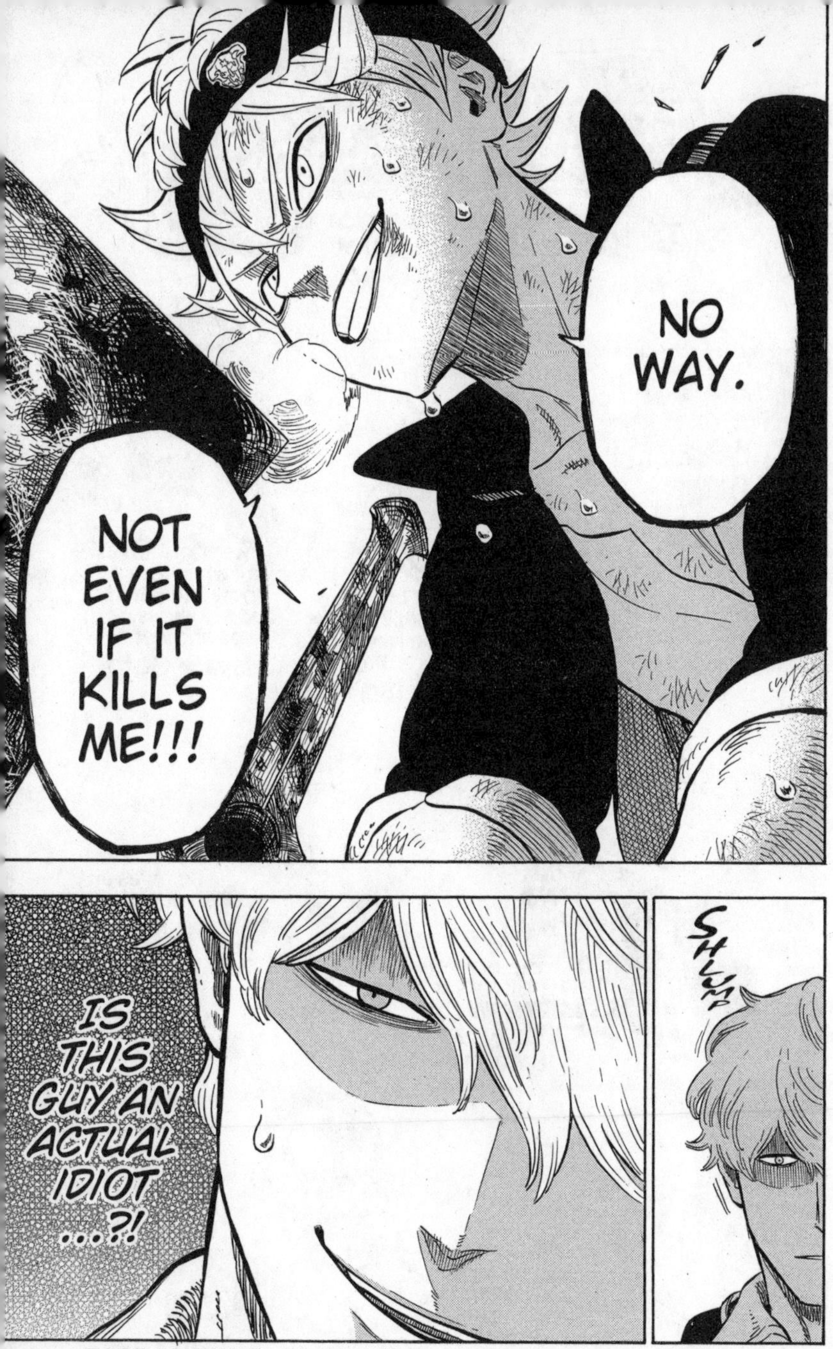
NO WAY.
NOT EVEN IF IT KILLS ME!!!
SHWMP
IS THIS GUY AN ACTUAL IDIOT ...?!

TO BE CONTINUED IN VOLUME 6!

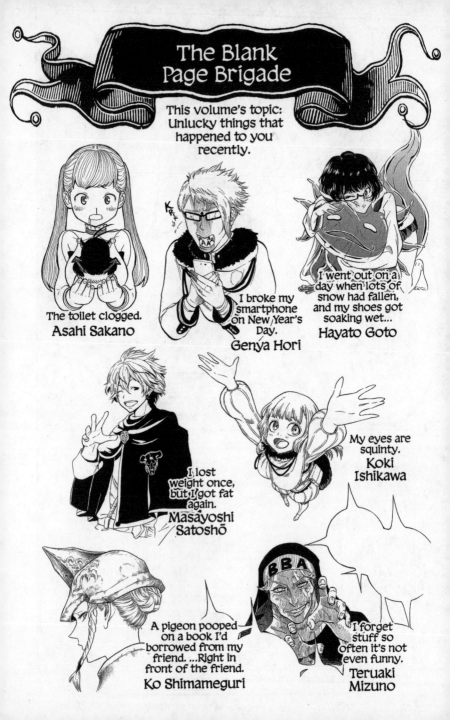

The Blank Page Brigade

This volume's topic: Unlucky things that happened to you recently.

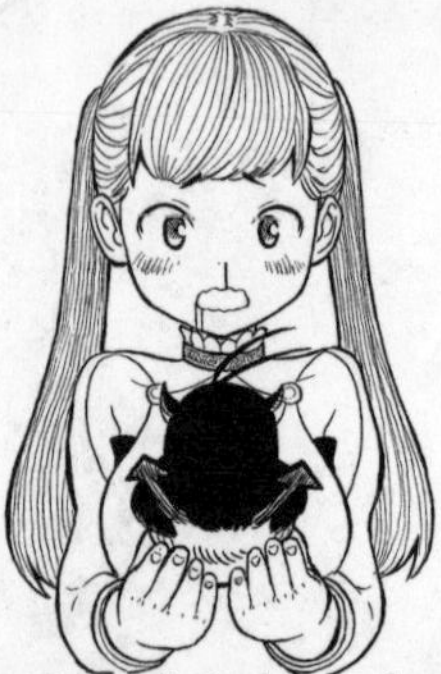

The toilet clogged.

Asahi Sakano

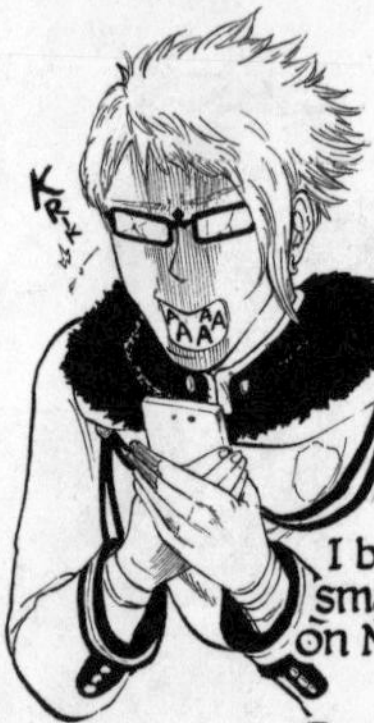
KRRK
AAAAA

I broke my smartphone on New Year's Day.

Genya Hori

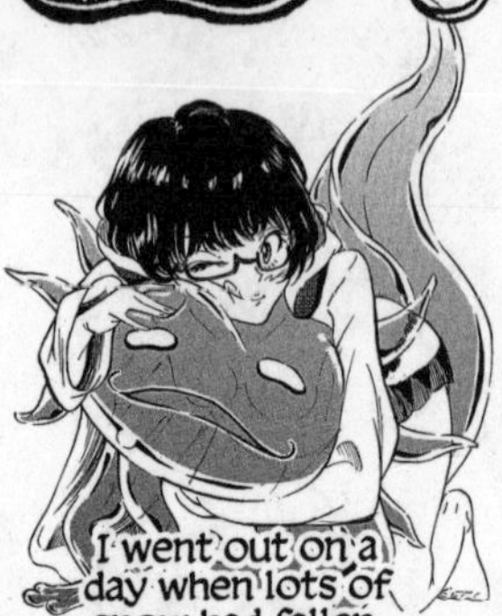

I went out on a day when lots of snow had fallen, and my shoes got soaking wet...

Hayato Goto

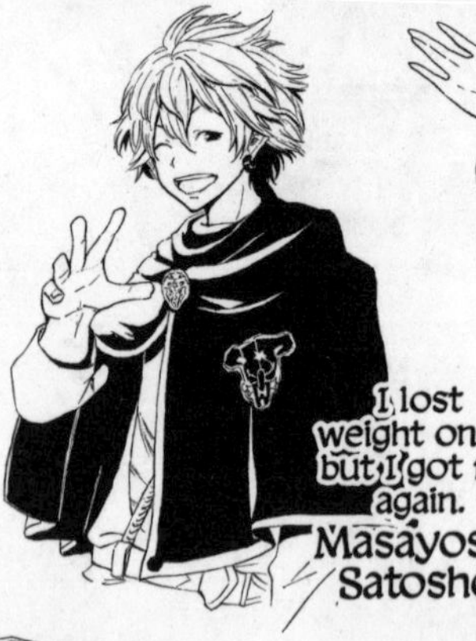

I lost weight once, but I got fat again.

Masayoshi Satoshō

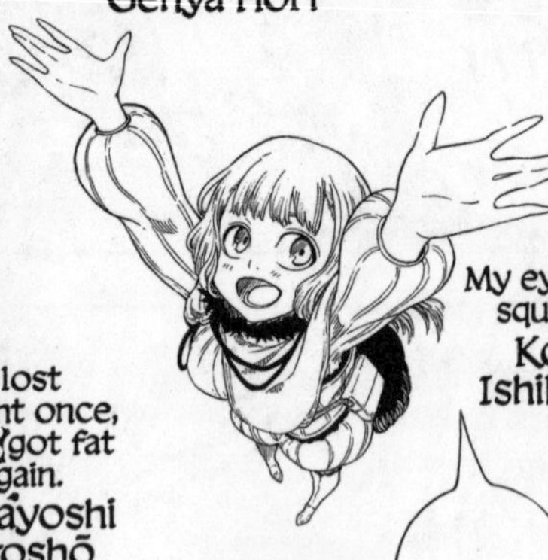

My eyes are squinty.

Koki Ishikawa

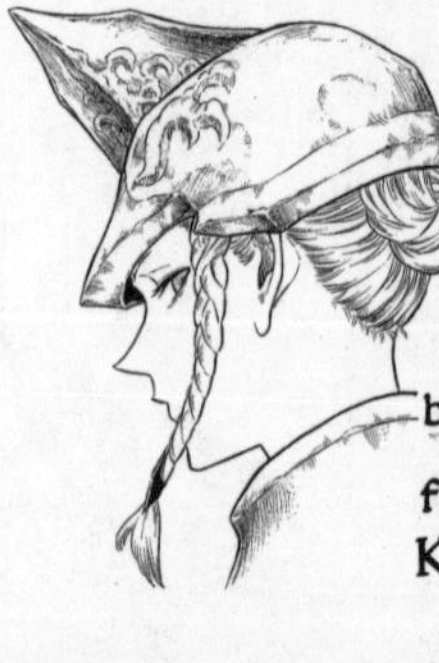

A pigeon pooped on a book I'd borrowed from my friend. ...Right in front of the friend.

Ko Shimameguri

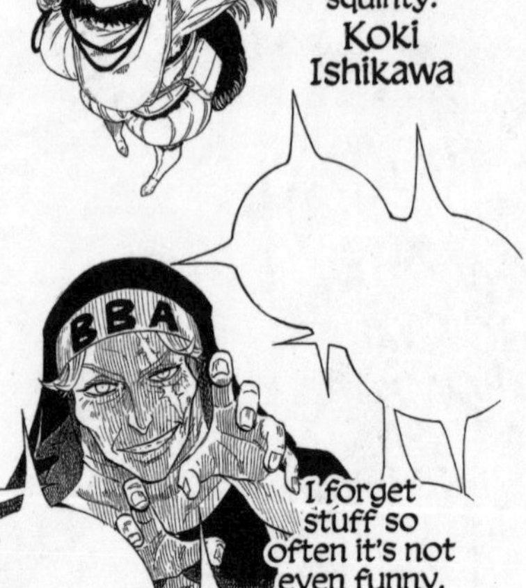
BBA

I forget stuff so often it's not even funny.

Teruaki Mizuno

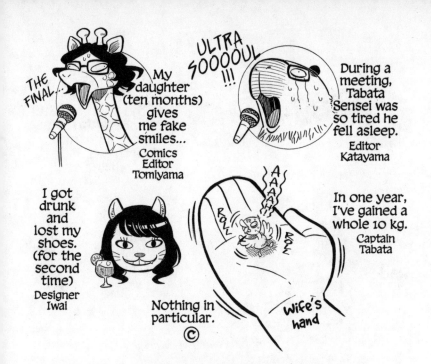

ULTRA SOOOOUL !!!
During a meeting, Tabata Sensei was so tired he fell asleep.
Editor Katayama
THE FINAL...
My daughter (ten months) gives me fake smiles...
Comics Editor Tomiyama
AAAAH!!
ROLL
ROLL
In one year, I've gained a whole 10 kg.
Captain Tabata
Wife's hand
I got drunk and lost my shoes. (for the second time)
Designer Iwai
Nothing in particular.
©

AFTERWORD

✽

This time, guess what?!
I got a comment from Honoka Akimoto, one of the members of the very happening idol singer group Team Shachihoko! (It's on Page 154.)
Thank you very much!

I also got a signed DVD and CD, and I'm letting the fantastic performances and singing boost my morale.

I couldn't be happier or more grateful that a person like that, someone who can cheer people up, is reading my manga! I'll keep doing my very best!
Raaaaaaah!!

Special Bonus Materials

Presenting early sketches of the Eye of the Midnight Sun members! And was there a phantom fourth girl at that mixer?!

Rades

Sally

The girls from
the mixer chapter.

Baro

Neige

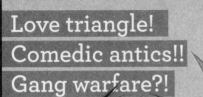

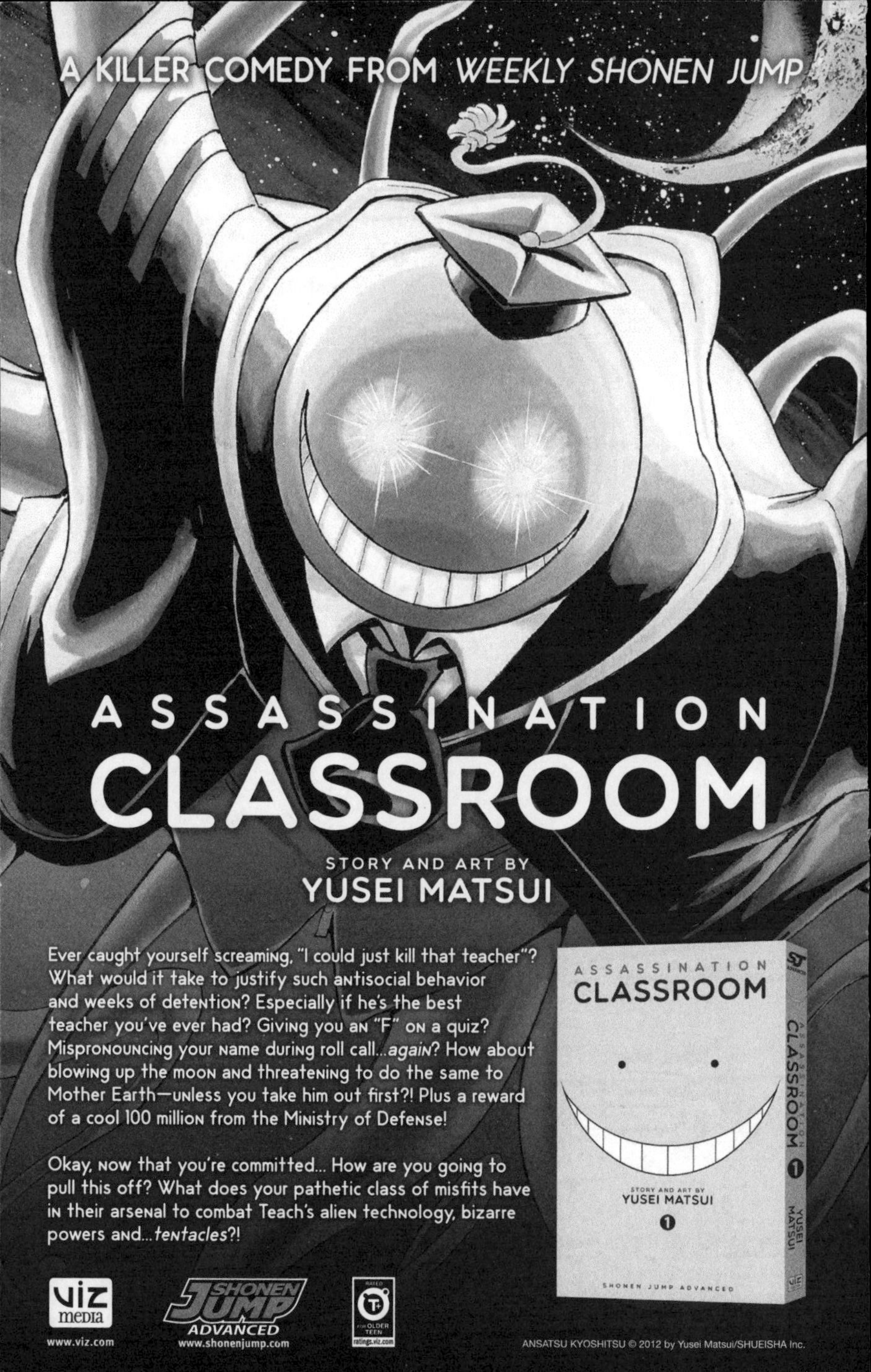
A KILLER COMEDY FROM *WEEKLY SHONEN JUMP*
ASSASSINATION
CLASSROOM
STORY AND ART BY
YUSEI MATSUI
Ever caught yourself screaming, "I could just kill that teacher"? What would it take to justify such antisocial behavior and weeks of detention? Especially if he's the best teacher you've ever had? Giving you an "F" on a quiz? Mispronouncing your name during roll call...*again*? How about blowing up the moon and threatening to do the same to Mother Earth—unless you take him out first?! Plus a reward of a cool 100 million from the Ministry of Defense!
Okay, now that you're committed... How are you going to pull this off? What does your pathetic class of misfits have in their arsenal to combat Teach's alien technology, bizarre powers and...*tentacles*?!
ASSASSINATION
CLASSROOM
STORY AND ART BY
YUSEI MATSUI
1
SHONEN JUMP ADVANCED
viz media
www.viz.com
SHONEN JUMP ADVANCED
www.shonenjump.com
RATED T+ FOR OLDER TEEN
ratings.viz.com
ANSATSU KYOSHITSU © 2012 by Yusei Matsui/SHUEISHA Inc.

Seraph of the End
VAMPIRE REIGN

STORY BY Takaya Kagami ART BY Yamato Yamamoto
STORYBOARDS BY Daisuke Furuya

Vampires reign— humans revolt!

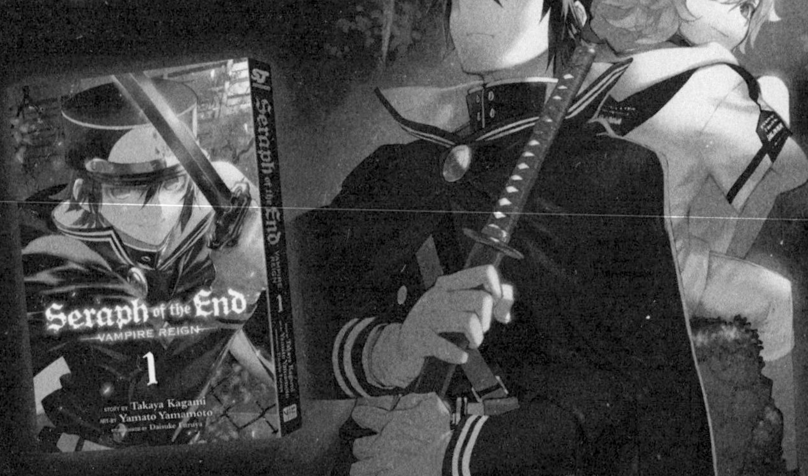

Seraph of the End
VAMPIRE REIGN
1
STORY BY Takaya Kagami
ART BY Yamato Yamamoto
Daisuke Furuya

Yuichiro's dream of killing every vampire is near-impossible, given that vampires are seven times stronger than humans, and the only way to kill them is by mastering Cursed Gear, advanced demon-possessed weaponry. Not to mention that humanity's most elite Vampire Extermination Unit, the Moon Demon Company, wants nothing to do with Yuichiro unless he can prove he's willing to work in a team—which is the last thing he wants!

THE LATEST CHAPTERS SERIALIZED IN WEEKLY SHONEN JUMP

RATED T+ FOR OLDER TEEN ratings.viz.com
SHONEN JUMP ADVANCED www.shonenjump.com
VIZ media www.viz.com

DEMON SLAYER
KIMETSU NO YAIBA

Story and Art by
KOYOHARU GOTOUGE

In Taisho-era Japan, kindhearted Tanjiro Kamado makes a living selling charcoal. But his peaceful life is shattered when a demon slaughters his entire family. His little sister Nezuko is the only survivor, but she has been transformed into a demon herself! Tanjiro sets out on a dangerous journey to find a way to return his sister to normal and destroy the demon who ruined his life.

Story and Art by
KOYOHARU GOTOUGE

NARUTO

Story and Art by
Masashi Kishimoto

Naruto is determined to become the greatest ninja ever!

Twelve years ago the Village Hidden in the Leaves was attacked by a fearsome threat. A nine-tailed fox spirit claimed the life of the village leader, the Hokage, and many others. Today, the village is at peace and a troublemaking kid named Naruto is struggling to graduate from Ninja Academy. His goal may be to become the next Hokage, but his true destiny will be much more complicated. The adventure begins now!

WORLD'S BEST SELLING MANGA!

www.shonenjump.com   www.viz.com

Stop

YOU'RE READING
THE WRONG WAY!

BLACK CLOVER

reads from right to left, starting
in the upper-right corner. Japanese
is read from right to left, meaning
that action, sound effects, and
word-balloon order are completely
reversed from English order.